JOYCE'S REVENGE

JOYCE'S REVENGE

History, Politics, and
Aesthetics in Ulysses

ANDREW GIBSON

OXFORD
UNIVERSITY PRESS

OXFORD
UNIVERSITY PRESS

Great Clarendon Street, Oxford OX2 6DP

Oxford University Press is a department of the University of Oxford.
It furthers the University's objective of excellence in research, scholarship,
and education by publishing worldwide in

Oxford New York

Auckland Bangkok Buenos Aires Cape Town Chennai
Dar es Salaam Delhi Hong Kong Istanbul Karachi Kolkata
Kuala Lumpur Madrid Melbourne Mexico City Mumbai Nairobi
São Paulo Shanghai Singapore Taipei Tokyo Toronto

with an associated company in Berlin

Oxford is a registered trade mark of Oxford University Press
in the UK and in certain other countries

Published in the United States
by Oxford University Press Inc., New York

© Andrew Gibson 2002

British Library Cataloguing in Publication Data
Data available

Library of Congress Cataloging in Publication Data
Data available

ISBN 0-19-818495-6

1 3 5 7 9 10 8 6 4 2

Typeset in Sabon
by J&L Composition Ltd, Filey, North Yorkshire
Printed in Great Britain
on acid free paper by
Biddles Ltd
Guildford and King's Lynn

To LEN, SALLY,
LUCY, *and* CHARLIE

Acknowledgements

I OWE A particular debt to those who read the final draft of this book, Vince Cheng, Ian Littlewood, Bernard McGinley, Steven Morrison, Len Platt, Fritz Senn, and that generous stalwart of the Utah Joyce list, John Smurthwaite. They read judiciously, with care and meticulous attention, and saved me from many occasions for embarrassment. Some of them are mentioned again below, for different reasons.

The book has taken me fifteen years to write, and, not being blessed with Joyce's prodigious memory, I shan't be able to name everyone who has contributed to its making. Nor shall I list all those articles, essays, reviews, lectures, and conference papers of my own on which I drew. Some of them will be found in my bibliography. I am most grateful to all those who have invited me to write or speak about *Ulysses* over the years, responded to what I produced, and granted me permission to reprint. They include Anne Fogarty, Josh Cohen, Angus Easson, Philip Martin, Timothy Martin, Roger Richardson, Christine van Boheemen, and Henry Woudhuysen. Many Joyce scholars gave me help or contributed, sometimes in conversation and more than they may have known. They include Derek Attridge, Brian Caraher, Greg Downing, Luke Gibbons, Michael Groden, Clive Hart, Suzette Henke, Declan Kiberd, Christine O'Neill, Patrick Parrinder, Ferenc Takács, George Watson, and Wolfgang Wicht. I am particularly grateful to Vince Cheng, who has for years been not only a support but an inspiration. Friends and colleagues listened, talked, offered advice and assistance in many different ways: thanks to Steve Connor, Thomas Docherty, Martin Dzelzainis, Diane Elam, Thomas Kabdebo, Jeremy Maule, Adam Roberts, Michael Slater, David Trotter, and Sue Wiseman. I am grateful to the Yeats scholars Warwick Gould and (in particular) Deirdre Toomey, who was extraordinarily generous with her knowledge and her time. I learnt a great deal from various research students who have worked on Joyce with me, particularly Francis Duggan, Steven Morrison, Debbie Peers, Chen Shu-I, and Mark Sutton, and owe a very large debt of gratitude to my Head of Department, Kiernan Ryan, for his invigorating and unfailing belief in my work. My thanks also go to three departmental secretaries, Daphne Pollen, Jane Cowell, and especially Jean Rayner, whose patience and good humour were very valuable to me in the closing stages. When I started the London University Seminar for Research into Joyce's *Ulysses* in 1986, I had no idea that it might still be flourishing in 2002. Many scholars and enthusiasts have joined (and left) us over the years, from London, elsewhere in the UK, and abroad. Most if not all of them have contributed to this book in one way or another. I am grateful to them for their ideas and perceptions and their support and encouragement; in particular, to Phil Baker, Joe Brooker, Finn Fordham, Clare Hutton, Caroline Hyland, Blanche Levenkind, Bernard McGinley, Katy Mullins, Joan Peake, Mike Peake, Derval Tubridy, and John Wyse Jackson. Above all, I owe heartfelt thanks to Robert Hampson and Katie Wales, who helped me set the seminar up and were for many years its most faithful members. The London Joyce group has long enjoyed a friendly and productive relationship with the Joyce group at the University of Leeds, and I am particularly grateful to three of its members, Alistair Stead, Pieter Bekker, and, above all, Richard Brown.

The biggest debts are the hardest to express. This book owes a very great deal to the helpfulness and seemingly untiring patience of librarians: in the University of London Library, the National Library of Ireland, the Newspaper Library at Colindale in London, and, above all, the Rare Books room of the British Library. Special thanks to Luca Crispi at the Poetry/Rare Books Collection, University of Buffalo. The London Joyce scholar Charles Peake was a model of exactitude. His conviction that, in principle, one ought to have one's own explanation for everything in *Ulysses* was important to me. Fritz Senn's learning, dedication, and acute sensitivity to Joyce's texts have always been exemplary. For many Joyce scholars, that goes without saying. I also want to thank him and his colleagues at the James Joyce Foundation in Zurich for their personal support over many years. My father has been much in my mind whilst writing this: I learnt most of what I know about 'an inherited tenacity of heterodox resistance' from him. But my biggest debt is to Len Platt. From the late eighties, when there was little to work with apart from scattered writings by Seamus Deane, we argued about Joyce and cultural politics, Joyce and England, Joyce and Anglo-Ireland, Joyce and Irish Ireland, and Joyce and nationalism in various South London pubs, but chiefly in the Commercial on Railton Road. I learnt an immense amount from Len. The traces of our arguments are everywhere in this book. I hope the arguments continue and are sustained and deepened by others over the coming decades.

Finally, my thanks to Jason Freeman, who first commissioned this book; to Sophie Goldsworthy and Matthew Hollis, who have faithfully seen it through to publication with Oxford University Press; and to Rowena Anketell, who copy-edited my text to the highest standards, and for whose many pains I was extremely grateful.

A.G.

London, 2002

Contents

Note on Text of *Ulysses*

All quotations are taken from *Ulysses*, ed. Hans Walter Gabler with Wolfhard Steppe and Claus Melchior, afterword by Michael Groden (New York and London: Garland Publishing, 1984, 1986), and are referred to by chapter and line number in the text.

Abbreviations

Works by James Joyce

CW   *The Critical Writings of James Joyce*, ed. Ellsworth Mason and Richard Ellmann (New York: Viking Press, 1959)

D   *Dubliners: An Annotated Edition*, ed. John Wyse Jackson and Bernard McGinley (London: Sinclair-Stevenson, 1993)

DD   'Daniel Defoe', ed. and trans. Joseph Prescott, *Buffalo Studies*, 1/1 (Dec. 1964), 3–27.

Letters *Letters of James Joyce*, vol. i, ed. Stuart Gilbert (London: Faber and Faber, 1957); vols. ii and iii, ed. Richard Ellmann (London: Faber and Faber, 1966)

P   *A Portrait of the Artist as a Young Man*, the definitive text corrected from the Dublin holograph by Chester G. Anderson and ed. Richard Ellmann (London: Jonathan Cape, 1968)

SH   James Joyce, *Stephen Hero*, ed. Theodore Spencer, rev. edn. with additional foreword by John J. Slocum and Herbert Cahoon (London: Jonathan Cape, 1956)

Other

CH	Robert H. Deming (ed.), *James Joyce: The Critical Heritage* (2 vols., London: Routledge & Kegan Paul, 1970)
DE	*The Daily Express (Dublin)*
FJ	*Freeman's Journal*
IT	*Irish Times*
L	*The Leader*
LON	*The Lady's Own Novelette*
LP	*Lady's Pictorial*
OED	*Oxford English Dictionary*
PN	*The Princess's Novelettes*
PW	*Pearson's Weekly*
T	*The Times*

Introduction

Écrasez l'infâme!

In 1935, John Eglinton published an account of Joyce in *Irish Literary Portraits*. It must have seemed to Joyce, wrote Eglinton, 'that he held English, his country's spiritual enemy, in the palm of his hand'. Alas, the English language 'found itself constrained by its new master to perform tasks to which it was unaccustomed in the service of pure literature. . . . Joyce rejoiced darkly in causing the language of Milton and Wordsworth to utter all but unimaginable filth and treason.'[1] Eglinton argued that *Ulysses* was an act of 'treason' fuelled by an 'ironic detachment from the whole of the English tradition.'[2] It was Joyce's 'Celtic revenge' on the colonial power.[3]

This study seeks to revive Eglinton's way of reading Joyce. But it will also revise, complicate, and transform his terms of reference. Joe Brooker has pointed out how far the early responses to Joyce's novel tended to be of two kinds.[4] Ezra Pound is representative of one and H. G. Wells of the other. Pound writes of Joyce as chiefly concerned to attain 'an international standard' in art and writing. Pound's Joyce is anti- and post-nationalist and intent on rising above his Irish origins into modern Europe 'as a contemporary of continental writers'.[5] But Wells saw Joyce quite differently. In Brooker's phrase, for Wells, Joyce is still deeply 'enmeshed in the national politics from which he has emerged'.[6] Both Joyce and his art are not only self-evidently Irish and Catholic, but also 'insurrectionary'.[7] Wells effectively identified the multifaceted outrageousness of *Ulysses* with a

---

[1] *Irish Literary Portraits* (London: Macmillan, 1935), 145–6.
[2] Ibid. 143–4. [3] Ibid. 146.
[4] See 'Reading in Transit: A Study of Joyce's Anglophone Reception' (Ph.D. thesis, University of London, 1999), 21–4.
[5] ' "Dubliners" and Mr. James Joyce', *Egoist*, 1/14 (15 July 1914), 267; repr. in *CH* i. 66–8, at 66. [6] 'Reading in Transit', 22.
[7] Quoted in Richard Ellmann, *James Joyce* (rev. edn.; Oxford: Oxford University Press, 1982), 608.

political and cultural offensive.[8] However, his was just one of the most prominent in a chorus of similar English and Anglo-Irish voices raised early in the 1920s.[9] These voices tended to say much the same things: Joyce's works might be 'powerful', but they were also shocking in their 'squalor', 'dirtiness', 'unpleasantness', 'coarseness', and 'astounding bad manners'.[10] This was not surprising: Joyce was Irish, and so was his subject matter.[11] Furthermore, Joyce had introduced the sordid and obscene elements in the novel with malign or seditious intent. They were part of his Irish assault on England and English culture. Shane Leslie describes *Ulysses*, for example, as 'an attempted Clerkenwell explosion in the well-guarded, well-built, classical prison of English literature'.[12] For Alfred Noyes, what he called the 'Joyce cult' was part of a contemporary depreciation of 'the value of some of the noblest pages in our literary history'.[13] For S. P. B. Mais, reading Joyce was 'like making an excursion into Bolshevist Russia'. Joyce's art was aimed at the very heart of the English tradition, and it would be necessary to put up a fight 'to preserve the noble qualities of balance, rhythm, harmony, and reverence for simple majesty that have been for three centuries the glory of our written tongue'.[14] '*Écrasez l'infâme!*', wrote Leslie.[15] If his was an extreme reaction, it was by no means altogether untypical.

---

[8] This didn't stop him from praising the novel very highly, and Joyce saw him as 'a very appreciative critic of my writings'. See Frank Budgen, *James Joyce and the Making of 'Ulysses'*, introd. Clive Hart (Oxford: Oxford University Press, 1972), 108.

[9] See also John Middleton Murry, review, *Nation & Athenaeum*, 31 (22 Apr. 1922), 124–5; Holbrook Jackson, 'Ulysses à la Joyce', *To-Day* (June 1922), 47–9; Sisley Huddleston, review, *Observer*, 6823 (5 Mar. 1922), 4; and Gilbert Seldes, review, *Nation*, 115/2982 (30 Aug. 1922), 211–12; repr. in *CH* i. 195–8, 198–200, 213–16, 235–9, respectively.

[10] See unsigned review, *Everyman* (23 Feb. 1917), 398; H. G. Wells, review, *Nation*, 20 (24 Feb. 1917), 710, 712; and unsigned review, *Literary World*, 83/1, 985 (1 March 1917), 43; repr. in *CH* i. 85, 86–8, 91–2, respectively.

[11] Valéry Larbaud identified the reaction of 'shock' itself as specifically 'English and Protestant'. See 'The *Ulysses* of James Joyce', *Criterion*, 1/1 (Oct. 1922), 94–103; trans. of 'James Joyce', *Nouvelle Revue Française*, 18 (Apr. 1922), 385–405; repr. in *CH* i. 252–62, esp. 257.

[12] '*Ulysses*', *Quarterly Review*, 238 (Oct. 1922), 219–14; repr. in *CH* i. 206-11, at 211.

[13] 'Rottenness in Literature', *Sunday Chronicle* (29 Oct. 1922), 2; repr. in *CH* i. 274–5, at 275.

[14] 'An Irish Revel: And Some Flappers', *Daily Express*, (25 Mar. 1922), n.p.; repr. in *CH* i. 191.

[15] 'Domini Canis' (Shane Leslie), *Dublin Review*, 171 (Sept. 1922), 112–19; repr. in *CH* i. 200–3, at 201. By the time he wrote his reviews of *Ulysses*, the Irish Leslie had converted to Catholicism and become a nationalist. But many of his attitudes remained those of a privileged, English-oriented member of an elite, landed gentry family.

A Foreign Power

In effect, Pound began the view of Joyce that, until very recently, has dominated the critical tradition. There has been no substantial, countervailing 'Wellsian' tradition in Joyce studies. The major departure from the 'Poundian' tradition has come only in recent years, and has been largely initiated by a number of gifted Irish scholars and critics (Deane, Kiberd, Gibbons, Nolan, and others) with some distinguished help from elsewhere (Cheng, Platt).[16] In some ways, however, a 'Wellsian' critic might have fleshed out his or her account of Joyce with little trouble. John Wyse Jackson and Peter Costello have comprehensively demonstrated, in very specific, historical, and biographical terms, how deep nationalism, Fenianism, sympathies with the Land League, anti-Healyism, pro-Boerism, and anticlericalism all ran in the Joyce family.[17] The Joyces were extremely proud of their family connections with Daniel O'Connell and Peter Paul McSwiney.[18] The Christmas dinner scene in the first chapter of Joyce's *Portrait of the Artist as a Young Man* famously reveals the agonies of a politically riven culture. But the political divisions emerge in the context of what is none the less a profound and shared antagonism towards the colonizer.

[16] See e.g. Seamus Deane, 'Joyce and Stephen: the Provincial Intellectual', and 'Joyce and Nationalism', in *Celtic Revivals: Essays in Modern Irish Literature 1880–1980* (London: Faber, 1985), 75–91 and 92–107 respectively; ' "Masked with Matthew Arnold's Face": Joyce and Liberalism', in Morris Beja et al. (eds.), *James Joyce: The Centennial Symposium* (Urbana, Ill.: University of Illinois Press, 1986), 9–21; and *Strange Country: Modernity and Nationhood in Irish Writing since 1790* (Oxford: Clarendon Press, 1997), 94–9; Declan Kiberd, 'The Vulgarity of Heroics: Joyce's *Ulysses*', in Suheil Badi Bushrui and Bernard Benstock (eds.), *James Joyce, An International Perspective: Centenary Essays in Honour of the Late Sir Desmond Cochrane*, foreword by Richard Ellmann (Gerrards Cross: Colin Smythe, 1982), 156–69; 'Introduction', *Ulysses* (London: Penguin, 1992), pp. ix–lxxx; and *Inventing Ireland: The Literature of the Modern Nation* (London: Vintage, 1996), *passim*, esp. 327–55; Richard Kearney, *Transitions: Narratives in Modern Irish Culture* (Manchester: Manchester University Press, 1988), 31–47; G. J. Watson, 'The Politics of *Ulysses*', in Robert D. Newman and Weldon Thornton (eds.), *Joyce's 'Ulysses': The Larger Perspective* (Newark, Del.: University of Delaware Press, 1987), 39–59; Luke Gibbons, *Transformations in Irish Culture* (Cork: Cork University Press, 1996), 134–47, 149–63; Emer Nolan, *James Joyce and Nationalism* (London: Routledge, 1995); Vincent J. Cheng, *Joyce, Race and Empire* (Cambridge: Cambridge University Press, 1995); and Len Platt, *Joyce and the Anglo-Irish: A Study of Joyce and the Literary Revival* (Amsterdam and Atlanta, Ga.: Rodopi, 1998).

[17] *John Stanislaus Joyce: The Voluminous Life and Genius of James Joyce's Father* (London: Fourth Estate, 1997), *passim*.   [18] Ibid. 20–1, 27.

As such, however, *Portrait* merely documents a small, domestic instance of the pervasive hostility to England within Irish political and cultural nationalism from the late nineteenth century to the Free State and beyond. This hostility was not a simple phenomenon. It had different strains, some with a longer history than others. It was crucial to the formation of the young James Joyce. R. F. Foster has written a powerful account of its dominant strain as what he calls Irish 'Anglophobia'.[19] The Irish Ireland movement and the work of D. P. Moran, for example, were 'Anglophobic' in Foster's sense.[20] There was a part of Joyce that was sufficiently 'Anglophobic' to describe the English as a 'reptile people'[21] and English literature as 'pompous and hypocritical' (*CW*, 212). This Joyce informed Claud Sykes that 'an Irish safety pin is more important than an English epic',[22] and claimed that 'it is my revolt against the English conventions, literary and otherwise, that is the main source of my talent. I don't write in English'.[23] Padraic and Mary Colum thought Joyce was fundamentally hostile to the 'English-speaking civilization'.[24] But Joyce's antagonism towards England and English culture characteristically took far subtler, more arrogantly insouciant, and much more cunning forms than—say—Moran's. I shall briefly mention two: the antagonism of the Parnellite, and the antagonism of the ironist or trickster.

Joyce's devotion to Parnell is very well documented; less so, the fact that it was a devotion to a particular mythology with particular features. This mythology was most notably formulated in R. Barry O'Brien's *The Life of Charles Stewart Parnell*. O'Brien's classic account was 'in great demand' in late nineteenth- and early twentieth-

---

[19] See *Modern Ireland 1600–1972* (London: Penguin, 1989), chs. 18–23, *passim*, esp. 447–50, 453–4, 471–2, 506, 508, 516–19.

[20] For some account of Moran in relation to Joyce, see my ' "Strangers in my House, Bad Manners to Them!": England in "Circe" ', in Andrew Gibson (ed.), *Reading Joyce's 'Circe'* (European Joyce Studies, 3; Amsterdam and Atlanta, Ga.: Rodopi, 1994), 179–221, esp. 186–7. I suggest that, whilst Joyce can obviously not be 'assimilated to Irish Ireland', he shares but also deepens and transforms certain of its 'attitudes to Irish culture'. For a learned and powerfully critical account of Moran, see Deirdre Toomey, 'Moran's Collar: Yeats and Irish Ireland', *Yeats Annual*, 12 (1996), 45–86.

[21] Jackson with Costello, *John Stanislaus Joyce*, 226.

[22] Ellmann, *James Joyce*, 423.

[23] Arthur Power, *The Joyce We Knew*, ed. Ulick Connor (Cork: The Mercier Press, 1967), 107.

[24] *Our Friend James Joyce* (London: Gollancz, 1959), 44.

century Dublin.[25] Joyce had it in his collection in Trieste,[26] and there are echoes of it in *Portrait, Ulysses*, 'The Shade of Parnell' (*CW*, 223–8), and elsewhere in the critical writings. O'Brien particularly insists on Parnell's 'aversion to England'. He also argues that that 'aversion' was at the root of Parnell's political strategies and his personal tactics.[27] In O'Brien's account of them, Parnell's tactics— silence, cunning, the pose of calculated indifference that so impressed Gladstone—frequently resemble the tactics adopted or recommended by Stephen Dedalus and the young James Joyce.[28] But Joyce's Parnellism was much more than just a set of tactics. The emphasis on the refusal to serve, on the annihilation of the ruler within, on the 'forging' or 'reawakening' of an Irish conscience: Stephen Dedalus shares all of them with the mythic Parnell.[29] These concerns were central to Parnell's political practice. They made him an immensely subtle and skilful harasser of English interests, an expert in provocation, in 'rubbing the English up', as Joseph Biggar put it.[30] Parnell was determined to 'shock English sentiment', to 'show a bold spirit of resistance to English law and English custom'.[31] In Sir Charles Dilke's phrase, he set his face intently against 'English modes of thought'.[32] For Dilke, this was so much the case that 'dealing with him was like dealing with a foreign Power'.[33]

Of course, the Parnell myth did not give the whole picture: it ignored the Parnell who defended the Empire, for example, the Parnell at ease with the idea of dominion status for Ireland. But the myth was pervasive. Joyce's work partly represents a continuation in

---

[25] See Letter to Lady Gregory, 13 Nov. 1898, in Yeats, *Collected Letters*, ii. 1896–1900, ed. Warwick Gould et al. (Oxford: Clarendon Press, 1997), 299–300 n. 1. According to the editors, Yeats's image of Parnell 'was largely formed by O'Brien's book'.

[26] See the source for all my references to Joyce's Trieste library, Michael Gillespie, *James Joyce's Trieste Library: A Catalogue of Materials at the Harry Ransom Research Centre, University of Texas at Austin*, ed. with the assistance of Erik Bradford Stocker (Austin: The Centre, 1986).

[27] *The Life of Charles Stewart Parnell*, pref. by John E. Redmond MP (London: Thomas Nelson & Sons, 1910), 47.

[28] See e.g. ibid. 89, 335, 408, 557. According to O'Brien, it was partly Parnell's capacity for silence that won the respect of the Fenians (ibid. 110).

[29] I have wilfully conflated Joyce's phrases from Joyce's essay on Mangan, 'Ireland, Island of Saints and Sages' and the end of *Portrait* with Parnell's claim that he had united 'the discordant elements of our race' (O'Brien, 502; cf. *Parnell*, 516, 519). At the end of *Portrait*, Stephen is clearly using the word 'race' with a very similar meaning to Parnell's (*P*, 257).

[30] Quoted in O'Brien, *Parnell*, 68.

[31] Ibid. 81. O'Brien is quoting the view of Fenians.   [32] Quoted ibid. 177.

[33] Quoted ibid.

the cultural sphere of the mythic Parnell's political project. Wells and Eglinton were responding to it as such. For Joyce, perhaps the greatest virtue of the mythic Parnell was his indomitability. This set him strikingly apart from the great line of the Irish 'court jesters to the English' that ran from Goldsmith—or rather, as Joyce surely knew, from an original who effectively did function as a jester to the English king, the great Earl of Kildare at the court of Henry VII—to Wilde (CW, 102).[34] According to Joyce, the court jester inherited 'a soul that yields up all its hate to a caress' (CW, 72). By contrast, Parnell was 'inexorable'.[35] But the Parnell myth also helped to make Joyce sly.[36] W. B. Yeats described Joyce as having 'a cruel playful mind like a great soft tiger cat'.[37] It is a complex, exact, inspired judgement. It is also a tribute to Joyce as heir to the legacy of the mythic Parnell.

Joyce's artistic and political cunning, however, also had other, less glamorous, more demotic, cultural sources. Whilst he no doubt did not need to borrow from it directly, one significant example of the culture in question would be a particular collection of Irish wit that he had in his library in Trieste, H. P. Kelly's *Irish Bulls and Puns*.[38] Collections of Irish bulls had been in existence for a century or more. The most famous, of course, was Richard and Maria Edgeworth's *Book of Irish Bulls*. The staple item in such books was a supposedly characteristic and comical Irish self-contradiction or lapse in rational consistency, what Sydney Smith called 'an apparent congruity, and real incongruity, of ideas'.[39] However, Kelly's book is unique among such collections. It contains plenty of bulls of the kind referred to by Smith. But it mixes them with bulls that function combatively, as retaliation or defiance. In particular, Kelly's Irish jokers frequently score little victories over powerful or high-ranking Englishmen or Anglo-Irishmen: a duke,[40] a military officer,[41] the landed gentry,[42] even 'the King of England' himself.[43] They make the

---

[34] For the Great Earl's ability to make Henry laugh, see Brian Fitzgerald, *The Geraldines: An Experiment in Irish Government 1169–1601* (London: Staples Press, 1951), 148.   [35] O'Brien, *Parnell*, 117.

[36] In parliament, e.g., the obstructionist Parnell was frequently devious, impeding legislation while pretending to improve it (ibid. 89).

[37] Letter to Olivia Shakespear (8 March 1922), in *CH* i. 284.

[38] *Irish Bulls and Puns* (London: Skeffington & Son, 1919).

[39] *Works* (4 vols., London: Longman, 1839), i. 66–7; quoted in Christopher Ricks, *Beckett's Dying Words* (Oxford: Oxford University Press, 1993), 191.

[40] *Irish Bulls and Puns*, 22–3.   [41] Ibid. 30–1.   [42] Ibid. 86–8.

[43] Ibid. 28.

bull into a triumph, a means of turning the tables on the (colonial) victor, and particularly on his sense of rectitude. In more ways than one, they momentarily reverse the logic of conquest.

In Kelly's presentation of them, bulls in general are wily. They both seduce and subvert. They seem to pay a tribute to power, but also outsmart it. Joyce frequently did the same. Take for instance the lecture on Defoe that he gave at the Università Popolare Triestina in 1912. Joyce clearly appreciated and learnt from Defoe's work, but also saw Defoe as having a symbolic significance.[44] The lecture praises the English novelist quite handsomely. Joyce solemnly claims that, in Defoe, the 'truly national [English] spirit' begins to emerge (*DD*, 7). As the lecture proceeds, however, this tribute becomes distinctly double-edged. The national spirit is partly embodied in Defoe's complete lack of poetry. Worse still, in Crusoe, Defoe created the very type of the Englishman:

The whole Anglo-Saxon spirit is in Crusoe: the manly independence; the unconscious cruelty; the persistence; the slow yet efficient intelligence; the sexual apathy; the practical, well-balanced religiousness; the calculating taciturnity. Whoever rereads this simple, moving book in the light of subsequent history cannot help but fall under its *prophetic* spell. (*DD*, 24–5; italics mine)

Less descriptive, note, than prophetic: the 'prophecy' in question is of course a prophecy of Empire. But Joyce is not merely ironically dismissive of the 'Anglo-Saxon spirit'. He even rewrites the history of English literature:

during the centuries which followed the French conquest, [English literature] was at school, and its masters were Boccaccio, Dante, Tasso, and Messer Lodovico. Chaucer's *Canterbury Tales* are a version of the *Decameron* or of the *Novellino*; Milton's *Paradise Lost* is a Puritan transcript of the *Divine Comedy*. Shakespeare, with his Titianesque palette, his flow of language, his epileptic passionateness, and his creative fury, is an Italianate Englishman. . . . (*DD*, 7)

In Joyce's account of matters, with Defoe—in effect, with the Battle of the Boyne, the Glorious Revolution, and the final triumph of the Protestant spirit in England—a richly European literature deriving from Catholic sources shrinks to mere Englishness. This, then, is

---

[44] Joyce partly saw Defoe as, to some extent, he saw himself, as the poet of a nation's emergence into modernity. See *DD*, 5, 23.

Joyce's version of 'the great tradition': an etiolated literature that runs from Defoe to Kipling and whose character is inseparable from a will to domination, however admirable some of its individual representatives may be. The mixture of ironical homage to and radical negation of English power in the lecture bears a family resemblance to the same mixture in some of Kelly's bulls.

An Hysterical Nationalism

Joyce was using the Defoe lecture to quarrel with what Stefan Collini has called 'the Whig interpretation of English literature'.[45] This line of thought was increasingly dominant in the late nineteenth and early twentieth centuries. It insisted on the continuity of English writing. Skeat wrote, for example, of the 'unbroken succession of authors from the reign of Alfred to that of Victoria'.[46] The 'Whig interpretation' made grandiose claims for the 'enduring spirit' of English literature.[47] By contrast, Joyce insists on historical discontinuity and violent rupture. In effect, he stresses the importance of a historically specific mode of thought. The emphasis on historical specificity is evident everywhere in his work, and asks the scholar to respond accordingly. Accordingly, I would stress that the England that features most largely in Joyce's work up to *Finnegans Wake* is the particular England that dates from his birth to the completion of *Ulysses*, 1882–1921.

Recent English cultural historians have increasingly identified more or less the same period, 1880–1920, as witnessing a particular mutation in English culture. Scholars and critics have had a lot to say about *Ulysses* as a novel written in a time of nationalisms, particularly Irish nationalism. There has been little or no discussion, however, of Joyce in relation to contemporary English nationalism. This is not surprising. As Collini points out, the English were supposed not to have been nationalistic.[48] In fact, however, the cultural histori-

[45] See *Public Moralists: Political Thought and Intellectual Life in Britain 1850–1930* (Oxford: Clarendon Press, 1991), 342–73.

[46] *Questions for Examination in English Literature: With an Introduction on the Study of English* (Cambridge, 1873), p. xii; quoted in Collini, *Public Moralists*, 359. On Joyce and Skeat, see Gregory M. Downing, 'Skeat and Joyce: A Garner of Words', *Dictionaries*, 18 (1997), 33–65.   [47] Collini, *Public Moralists*, 359.

[48] Ibid. 346.

ans—Baldick, Collini, and others—have increasingly presented the period of Joyce's life up to the completion of *Ulysses* as witnessing a developing, English, cultural nationalism and a specific, concerted construction of 'Englishness'. As Philip Dodd puts matters, in the years 1880–1920, both English political culture and English cultural institutions are preoccupied by the question of the 'English spirit'.[49] The reasons for this were clearly complex. Brian Doyle suggests that it reflected a perceived need for greater social stability and cohesion and an enhanced sense of social purpose. The Empire was no longer appreciably expanding. International competition was growing more intense. There was therefore widespread anxiety about whether English economic supremacy could be sustained. Many felt that the nation was under threat from ' "democratic" and popular economic and cultural processes'.[50] Powerful figures argued that the need to maintain a vast overseas empire and to ensure secure government at home demanded a renewal of leadership. They expected cultural institutions to respond to this demand, for such institutions were the guardians of the national character.

The response came partly from within existing bodies. But new ones were also created in reaction to the 'crisis'. On the one hand, for example, the period sees the emergence of a by now well-documented imperial, educational, and commercial programme for 'national efficiency'.[51] From the 1890s onwards, the programme drew in 'prominent figures from the worlds of politics, business and "letters" '.[52] The group in question linked the issue of national renewal and national morale precisely to the question of culture. On the other hand, the same period sees the emergence of a range of new institutions. These include the National Vigilance Association, the English Historical Review (1886), the National Trust (1895), the National Portrait Gallery (1896), the National Gallery of Modern Art (1897), the *Dictionary of National Biography* (1885–1900), a national Board of Education (1899), the British Academy (1903), the Historical Association (1906), the National Extension Movement, and the National Council of Adult Schools Association.

---

[49] 'Englishness and the National Culture', in Robert Colls and Philip Dodd, (eds.), *Englishness: Politics and Culture 1880–1920* (London: Croom Helm, 1986), 1–28, at 1.

[50] *English and Englishness* (London and New York: Routledge, 1989), 13.

[51] See e.g. G. R. Searle, *The Quest for National Efficiency: A Study in British Politics and Political Thought 1899–1914* (London: Ashfield, 1990).

[52] Doyle, *English and Englishness*, 30.

Between 1880 and 1920, English cultural nationalism had a significant impact on many different spheres of English and Irish cultural
life. Take literature, for example: Collini suggests that it is this period
that first sees the appearance of the 'symbolic and emotionally
charged selection of writing known as "English literature" '. This
'selection of writing' played a central role in the new politics of culture, becoming 'a crucial vehicle for establishing and negotiating a
sense of national identity . . . in increasingly official form'.[53] From
the 1880s onwards, it became a central symbolic expression of what
Benedict Anderson calls the 'imagined community'.[54] Men and
women of letters were increasingly concerned to define the English
literary heritage and to construct the genealogy specifically of
English literature. They also sought to disseminate the tradition they
constructed, not least in schools: the early publications of the
English Association, for example, show how far it was concerned
that children throughout the British Isles should be properly exposed
to the 'national literature'. The years 1880–1920 saw not only the
foundation of the English Association (1906) and the National
Home Reading Association, the appearance of the *New* (later
Oxford) *English Dictionary* and the *Cambridge History of English
Literature* (1907–16) and the formal establishment of a school of
English language and literature at both Oxford and Cambridge, but
also Macmillan's *Literature Primers* and *English Men of Letters*
series, soon to be followed by Longman's *English Worthies*, Scott's
Great Writers, Hodder's *Literary Lives*, and Cassell's *National
Library*.[55] Such series substantially promoted 'the Whig interpretation of literature'. 'For the English people', wrote Edith Morley,
'their own literature is the open sesame to all that is best in themselves and their history, the record of their achievements in the
past'.[56] The apotheosis of such thought—though also, as it hap-
pened, with Richards, Empson, Leavis, and professionalism round
the corner, its end point—was the *Newbolt Report: The Teaching of
English in England*. It evoked the continuity of English literature as

[53] *Public Moralists*, 347.
[54] *Imagined Communities: Reflections on the Origins and Spread of Nationalism*
(London: Verso, 1991).
[55] The *English Men of Letters* series was the chief of these. See John Gross, *The Rise
and Fall of the Man of Letters* (Harmondsworth: Penguin, 1973), 122–3.
[56] 'Literature as a Humane Study', in *The Teaching of Literature in Schools, English
Association Pamphlet*, 43 (May 1919), 33–4, at 33.

embodying (to quote from it) 'the deepest and most serious characteristics of the [English] race'.[57] It was published in 1921, as Joyce was
finishing *Ulysses*.

English cultural nationalism in general and the 'Whig interpretation of literature' in particular were not merely intended for home
consumption. They also had a global circulation. According to Chris
Baldick, one of the principal motivating factors 'behind the movement for English studies' at the turn of the century was colonialism.[58]
From the India Act in 1853, there was a growing emphasis on 'officially encouraging the study of English literature for the good of the
empire'.[59] In Gauri Viswanathan's terms, English not only came into
its own in an age of colonialism. It also took on 'the imperial mission
of educating and civilizing colonial subjects'.[60] In principle, both at
home and abroad, the process was one of homogenization. The cultural historians argue that the nationalization of English culture was
partly fuelled by an aspiration to erase conflict or difference that
stemmed from Matthew Arnold. According to Collini, nationalization involved 'the softening of many of the political and religious
divisions that had marked the first half of the [nineteenth] century'.[61]
Dodd suggests that the 'differences' most in question were those that
had appeared to marginalize particular ethnic and social groups, like
the Irish.[62] Certainly, from an Irish point of view, the new English
nationalism was likely to seem both alien and profoundly suspect.
For it projected a specious unity where union was neither possible
nor desirable.

The signs of English cultural nationalism were pervasively evident
in turn-of-the-century Ireland: in school and university syllabuses,
libraries and bookshops, newspapers and magazines, advertising,
commercial and popular culture. In 1904, for example, the year in
which *Ulysses* is set, 'national efficiency' and various questions

[57] Quoted in R. W. Chambers, *The Teaching of English in the Universities of England*,
English Association Pamphlet, 53 (July 1922), 9. Cf. Esther Quantrill's fascinating account
of the influence during the period of J. R. Green's *Short History of the English People*
(1874). See Esther Maeve Quantrill, 'Anthological Politics: Poetry and British Culture
1860–1914' (Ph.D. thesis, University of Texas at Austin, 1995), 119–37.

[58] *The Social Mission of English Criticism 1848–1932* (Oxford: Clarendon Press, 1987),
72. The India Act opened up the most lucrative and prestigious posts in the Empire to com-
petitive examination.   [59] Ibid. 20.

[60] *Masks of Conquest: Literary Study and British Rule in India* (London: Faber, 1990), 2.

[61] *Public Moralists*, 347. For the specific sense of 'nationalization', here, see ibid. 316.
Cf. Baldick on Arnold and literary criticism, *Social Mission*, 22.

[62] 'Englishness and National Culture', 1.

associated with it (like the supposed 'physical deterioration' of the nation) were live issues in both the serious and the popular English and Irish press. Joyce could hardly not be aware of the ideological formations in question. He encountered them repeatedly in the books he read as a reviewer in Dublin in the first years of the century. Alfred Ainger's book on Crabbe, for example, which Joyce reviewed in 1903, was in the *English Men of Letters* series.[63] At the back, it displayed the lists of the companion series *English Men of Action* and *Twelve English Statesmen*. More revealingly, at the back of James Anstie's *Colloquies of Common People*—which Joyce reviewed in the same year, along with Clive Phillips-Wolley's *Songs of an English Esau*—he would have found both titles advertised in Smith, Elder and Co.'s new list. The dominant tone of the latter was set by Conan Doyle's *The Great Boer War*, Sidney Lee's biography of *Queen Victoria*, and titles like *Nelson and his Captains* and *Wellington's Lieutenants*. The particular targets of Joyce's satire in the two reviews—Phillips-Wolley's fulsome, servile patriotism and the absurdity of what the well-connected Anstie means by 'common people'—are linked to this context.[64] Joyce repeatedly confronted the same ideological formation in his books in Trieste. He had a range of books from the kind of series just listed, including *Heinemann's Favourite Classics*, *Cassell's National Library*, and the *English Men of Letters*. He was well aware of the implications of such series, as is clear, for instance, from his references to the *English Men of Letters* at the beginning of his review of Walter Jerrold's *George Meredith* (CW, 88) and to the *English and Foreign Philosophical Library* at the beginning of his review of J. Lewis MacIntyre's *Giordano Bruno* (CW, 132). He owned various books from the *Nelson Library of Notable Books*, including a copy of Sidney Lee's *Great Englishmen of the Sixteenth Century*, which had a list of titles at the back that mixed Lee's book in promiscuously with *From the Cape to Cairo*, *With Kitchener to Khartum*, *The Making of a Frontier*, and *Life of General Gordon*. So, too, Joyce's *Selections from Tennyson*, for example, had an introduction and notes with a distinctly patriotic flavour, and a list of *English Classics for Indian*

---

[63] *Crabbe* (London: Macmillan, 1903).

[64] See Clive Phillipps-Wolley, *Songs of an English Esau* (London: Smith, Elder and Co., 1902); James Anstie, *Colloquies of Common People* (London: Smith, Elder and Co., 1902); and CW, 96, 97.

Students at the back.[65] Equally, it is striking (though hardly surprising) to find how many of the key names in the cultural historians' discussions of the literary nationalism of the period also turn up in Joyce's library in Trieste in one role or another: Saintsbury, Raleigh, Skeat, Lee, Herford, Dover Wilson, John Morley, Stopford Brooke.

Dedalus's Labyrinth

The argument of this book goes as follows: in *Ulysses*, Joyce works towards a liberation from the colonial power and its culture. He also takes his revenge on them. There is a will to freedom in *Ulysses*, and a will to justice, but also a recognition that the two do not necessarily coincide. Joyce's revenge gets much of its form from the novel's concern with Irish culture as shaped and determined by English cultural nationalism 1880–1920 (and by certain Anglo-Irish variants of that nationalism). In the first three chapters of *Ulysses*, through Stephen Dedalus, Joyce establishes resistance to England as a central theme. He makes this theme both general and historically extremely specific, not least, through Stephen's antagonism towards a particular Englishman, a 'gay betrayer' (1. 405), and an Ulsterman. Stephen is concerned with both liberation and revenge. But he is also a limited vehicle for them. For antagonism traps him in particular structures of thought and feeling: melancholy, sullen hatred, spiritual violence, a Manganesque despair of soul, the intimate complicity born of polar opposition. After the first three chapters, Joyce thus turns to Bloom instead. As a Jew whose family has not been long in Ireland, Bloom is not caught in the same traps as Stephen. He is thus an extremely effective weapon against colonial discursive and ideological formations. Joyce locates him solidly in the Dublin Catholic community, a community with whose politics Bloom is broadly sympathetic. But he also makes Bloom radically different to that community. Bloom's perspective on the colonizer's culture is therefore a doubly alienated one. This is very much the case where racism is at stake. For Joyce recognizes that both Bloom's position as a Jew and the kind of anti-Semitism he encounters are particular to colonial Irish culture, which bore the scars of its own deep-rooted 'racial distinctions', to quote

---

[65] *Selections from Tennyson*, ed. F. J. Rowe and W. T. Webb, with intro. and notes (London: Macmillan, 1889).

the liberal, Anglo-Irish, Protestant aristocrat Lord Dunraven, writing in 1904.[66]

Bloom is thus a more useful instrument than Stephen. Having allocated Bloom his collection of roles, however, Joyce leaves him to perform his own distinctive functions, and sets other processes in motion. He does this chiefly through the famous styles in the later chapters of the novel, where extremely particular historical, political, and aesthetic issues are inseparable from one another. The styles are thus the major concern of this book. As Fritz Senn has compellingly shown over many years, Joyce's aesthetic practices in *Ulysses* are not only very complex but highly specific, and require a highly specific description.[67] Their historical and cultural specificity—the extent to which they are engagements with particular English and Anglo-Irish discourses, and, above all, with the discourses of English cultural nationalism 1880–1920—has gone more or less unnoted. Stylistically, almost every chapter of *Ulysses* from the ninth onwards operates as a resistance to, a corruption or, to go back to Eglinton's terms, a seditious reworking of such discourses. It is here that, whilst both the social and, as we shall see, the discursive material of *Ulysses* belongs so largely to the period around 1904, Joyce the author most emphatically declares his distance from that period. Thus 'Scylla and Charybdis', 'Nausicaa', and 'Oxen of the Sun' engage with literary and sub-literary manifestations of English cultural nationalism (Victorian and Edwardian bardolatry, the Victorian and Edwardian anthology, the discourses of 'national fitness', and the so-called 'domestic ideology' as evident in women's magazines). 'Sirens' and 'Cyclops' are responses to late nineteenth-century, Anglo-Irish, revivalist musical and historiographical discourses. For Joyce, such discourses claimed to reinstate a historical Irish culture whilst actually appropriating it for the colonizer and conflating it with Englishness. Much of *Ulysses* resists the historical, English insistence on 'standard English' and its impact on Ireland,

[66] *FJ* (Mon. 4 Jan. 1904), 5.

[67] See 'Nausicaa', in *Joyce's Dislocutions: Essays on Reading as Translation*, ed. John Paul Riquelme (Baltimore and London: Johns Hopkins University Press, 1984), 160–87; ' "All Kinds of Words Changing Colour": Lexical Clashes in "Eumaeus" ', and 'Eumaean Titbits: As Someone Somewhere Says', in *Inductive Scrutinies: Focus on Joyce*, ed. Christine O'Neill (Dublin: Lilliput, 1997), 156–75 and 176–96; ' "Circe" as Harking Back in Provective Arrangement', in Gibson (ed.), *Joyce's 'Circe'*, 63–92; ' "Ithaca": Portrait of the Chapter as a Long List', in Andrew Gibson (ed.), *Joyce's 'Ithaca'* (European Joyce Studies, 6; Amsterdam and Atlanta, Ga.: Rodopi, 1996), 31–76; and many others.

particularly between 1880 and 1920. But 'Eumaeus' in particular is a chapter wholly composed of violations of the relevant 'standards' or rules. Many other English discourses are important for *Ulysses*: the discourses of late nineteenth-century English and Anglo-Irish political economy in 'Oxen', for example, or 'imperial science' in 'Ithaca'. 'Circe' 'carnivalizes' a number of such discourses as speech forms, in an exposure and transformation of the colonized character of the Dublin unconscious. Finally, in 'Penelope', Joyce pits Molly Bloom against an openly colonial and masculinist Victorian and Edwardian discourse which articulated imperial, British values in relation to what it took to be the central, symbolic significance of Gibraltar. Francis Duggan has noted Joyce's wariness in *Stephen Hero* of what he called the 'mimic warfare' of Irish nationalists (*SH*, 39). Duggan suggests that Joyce seeks to replace 'mimic warfare'—which includes not only obvious examples like Irish games and sports, but also political oratory—with a mode of 'aesthetic warfare'.[68] In *Ulysses* as a whole, the famously pacifist Joyce is partly concerned to translate a ferocious political struggle into the literary arena, thereby releasing it from its most debilitating features, notably passionate violence. Here if anywhere, Joyce's revenge is liberating rather than disabling. The styles in *Ulysses* are examples of this. They are wicked practices upon the colonizer's culture. But this does not mean that they have simple implications. In fact, the reverse is the case, as will be clear throughout this book: they also repeatedly function as delicate, ironical negotiations between a range of political positions that Joyce found unacceptable as wholes. Such an emphasis hardly seems to square with the clear, structural opposition with which I began: Joyce versus England. But the seeming seamlessness of any argument about Joyce needs to be unpicked at many seams. In fact, a reading of *Ulysses* as Joyce's revenge on the colonizer will work only if made so subtle as to seem almost self-contradictory. The late nineteenth and early twentieth centuries saw a growing movement for de-Anglicization in Ireland. Sinn Féin, the Gaelic League, the Gaelic Athletic Association, Douglas Hyde, Maud Gonne, Arthur Griffith, Moran, and many others espoused it.[69] Joyce partly shared the

---

[68] ' "Phrases of the Platform": Irish Political Oratory 1782–1922 in the Work of James Joyce' (Ph.D. thesis, University of London, in preparation).

[69] See Douglas Hyde, 'The Necessity for De-Anglicizing Ireland', in Sir Charles Gavan Duffy et al., *The Revival of Irish Literature* (London: T. Fisher Unwin, 1894), 115–61; and D P. Moran, *The Philosophy of Irish Ireland* (Dublin: James Duffy & Co., 1905). On Maud

passions that drove the movement. But he was not himself a de-Anglicizer. The history of Ireland had been 'lodged in the room of the infinite possibilities' it had 'ousted', to quote from *Ulysses* (2. 50–1). That history was 'not to be thought away' (2. 49). Joyce was very well aware of how far English nationalism had left its mark on Irish expressions of opposition to it, including those of the de-Anglicizers. In the very act of combating English cultural nationalism, its Irish opponents were in danger of producing another version of it.

So, too, it would be absurd to pit Joyce against a nationalistic construction of English literature without recognizing his ties to various aspects of English literature itself. English literature self-evidently helped form Joyce's very rebellion against 'the English conventions', via Blake and Shelley, for example. The same irony haunts Joyce's reverence for Parnell. For Parnell was Anglo-Irish and came from a class to whose interests, in many ways, Joyce was fiercely opposed, as Len Platt has comprehensively shown.[70] In A. M. Sullivan's phrase, Parnell even made a political virtue of having 'not a bit of the Celt about him'.[71] Of course, it is possible to exaggerate such ironies. The critical insistence on Joyce's debts to England, for example, owes much to the Anglophile Richard Ellmann who, as Empson was quick to point out and as Bernard McGinley has recently re-emphasized, was notably out of sympathy with the political turbulence of the early years of the twentieth century.[72] But the ironies are pervasively evident in *Ulysses*. They are apparent in Joyce's presentation of Irish culture at innumerable turns.

They also haunt accounts of Joyce's work, including mine. I draw *Ulysses* back into an English orbit, thereby re-establishing a connection which I argue myself that Joyce was partly intent on breaking.

Gonne, Inghinidhe na hÉireann, and de-Anglicization, see Margaret Ward, *Unmanageable Revolutionaries: Women and Irish Nationalism* (London: Pluto, 1983), 51. On Griffith, Sinn Féin, and de-Anglicization, see F. S. L. Lyons, *Culture and Anarchy in Ireland 1890–1939* (Oxford: Clarendon Press, 1979), 58.

[70] See *Joyce and the Anglo-Irish*, *passim*.

[71] Sullivan asserted that Parnell's success was due to the fact that he was himself 'a regular Englishman'. Quoted in O'Brien, *Parnell*, 228.

[72] See William Empson, 'Joyce's Intentions', *Using Biography* (1970: London: Chatto & Windus, 1984), 203–16, esp. 206–7. Empson also links Joyce and Wells, but in terms of their similarities (ibid. 213). Of course, the similarities were partly what helped Wells to understand Joyce. See also Bernard McGinley, *Joyce's Lives: Uses and Abuses of the Biografiend* (London: University of North London Press, 1996), 20.

Joyce's own contributions to early views of *Ulysses* clearly helped foster the 'Poundian' reading, not the 'Wellsian' one. That the traditional account of Joyce as a deracinated, international modernist has
fulfilled his intentions seems undeniable. Thus when Valente writes
about Joyce and justice or Osteen about Joyce and economics from a
theoretically abstracted rather than an informed, historically and
culturally focused perspective, both might seem to be more faithful
to Joyce than I am.[73] But to say only that is to neglect the ironic imperatives which continually drive Joyce back into the very structures
from which he seeks to free himself. The important thing is to grasp
Ulysses as governed by a paradoxical movement in which the drive to
liberation and the drive to revenge have a quite extraordinary momentum and yet always seem to be entrammelled. Joyce is well aware
of this problem, and explores it in many different ways in *Ulysses*.
Stephen Dedalus asserts that 'in here it is I must kill the priest and the
king' (15. 4436–7). As a whole, *Ulysses* at once sustains and ironizes
that assertion. The will to freedom and the will to justice which
power the novel also turn on each other and turn back incessantly on
themselves. In this respect, like the colonial culture from which it
emerges, Joyce's novel is founded on contradiction, or an 'incongruity of ideas', to return to Smith's phrase. In other words, *Ulysses*
functions like a gigantic version of the bull. More precisely, to quote
from it, it is 'an Irish bull in an English chinashop' (14. 581). The effects of an Irish bull in a china shop presumably depend on the kind
of bull it is. It can be very destructive. But it can also turn out to be a
harmless source of merriment, even seeming to rebound on its per-
petrator. Joyce's Irish bull establishes an extremely intricate balance
between these two kinds of effect.

Joyce's revenge is therefore *sui generis*. The point becomes clearer
with reference to the theme of *ressentiment*. Duffy has underlined
this, and it is surely a key theme for current Joyce criticism.[74] Joyce
had a deep understanding of and deeply identified with Irish *ressentiment*. But he also had deep misgivings about it and worked to overcome it or leave it behind. The reasons for his misgivings were
complex. But he particularly recognized how far *ressentiment* meant

[73] Joseph Valente, *James Joyce and the Problem of Justice: Negotiating Sexual and Colonial Difference* (Cambridge: Cambridge University Press, 1995); and Mark Osteen, *The
Economy of 'Ulysses': Making Both Ends Meet* (New York: Syracuse University Press, 1995).

[74] Enda Duffy, *The Subaltern 'Ulysses'* (Minneapolis: University of Minnesota Press,
1994).

continuing in servitude and degradation. He repeatedly demonstrates that those of his characters who are caught up in *ressentiment* are also still in thrall, subordinate to power in the very intensity of their reaction to it. Joyce made exactly this point about the nationalist poet and co-founder of Sinn Féin, William Rooney: Rooney's is 'a weary and foolish spirit . . . blaspheming against tyrants'. There is not one poem in his collection which has 'the quality of being *separate and whole*' (*CW*, 86–7; my italics). At a number of different levels, *ressentiment* obstructs the very will to independence it helps fuel. Critics have long seen that freedom from *ressentiment* is extremely important in *Ulysses*. When commentators working within the humanist tradition asserted that Joyce used Bloom to criticize and offset Stephen's moral limitations, they were effectively noting Bloom's importance as a weapon against *ressentiment*.[75] Postcolonial critics have tended to focus more on the political context. Thus Duffy argues, for example, that, 'by the close of the third episode', *Ulysses* supplants *ressentiment* with what 'is at the least a blueprint for the condition of a heterogeneous national community'.[76] According to Duffy, Joyce then develops this 'blueprint' throughout the novel. Both sets of critics agree, however, that the novel swiftly leaps clear of Stephen's bitter terms of reference. But this is not exactly the case. Joyce establishes the importance of *ressentiment* at the outset of his novel. He then spends the rest of the novel working on it. The work in question is not only protracted and extremely complicated, but uncompleted and uncompletable. There are at least three self-evident and pre-eminent 'Joycean virtues': historical specificity; work; and the clear-eyed recognition of difficulty or entanglement. If anything is written all over Joyce's oeuvre, it is the refusal in principle of the 'quick fix', whether artistic, political, intellectual, or ethical. It is in this respect, above all, that he resembles the great post-war French theorists—Derrida, Foucault, Lacan—with whom his name has so often been been linked. Joyce's work draws its readers into a labour which knows no end. As such, it resembles what Joyce himself shows to be the unremitting and unendingly ironical work of liberation.

[75] See e.g. Richard Kain, *Fabulous Voyager: James Joyce's 'Ulysses'* (Chicago: University of Chicago Press, 1947), 210–12; S. L. Goldberg, *The Classical Temper: A Study of James Joyce's 'Ulysses'* (London: Chatto and Windus, 1961), 116–18; and Charles Peake, *James Joyce: The Citizen and the Artist* (London: Edward Arnold, 1977), 113.
[76] *Subaltern 'Ulysses'*, 27–8.

To adapt a phrase that Steven Connor uses in another context, in the case of *Ulysses*, 'we should [therefore] attempt the difficult feat' of thinking *ressentiment* and the transformation and even transcendence of *ressentiment* together.[77] Ron Bush has recently argued that it is time to try to bridge the gap between Bloom-centred and Stephen-centred interpretations of *Ulysses*, that is, between the dominant tradition, with its emphasis on a European or international Joyce, and more recent work that locates him firmly in an Irish and/or colonial context.[78] I agree. But the question of exactly *how* to follow Bush's injunction is crucial, and anything but simple. The condition of *Ulysses* is not freedom. *Ulysses* is not a postcolonial novel. It is rather concerned with an extraordinarily arduous struggle towards a freedom that its author knows is at best partial or equivocal. Joyce began *Ulysses* in 1915 and 'announced that it was complete' on 29 October 1921.[79] But if 1921 sees the completion of *Ulysses* and the publication of the Newbolt Report, it is also the year of the Anglo-Irish Treaty. Joyce announces that *Ulysses* is complete nearly four months after the IRA and the British Army declare truce, eighteen days after the opening of the Anglo-Irish conference and just over five weeks before the signing of the Treaty itself. So Derek Attridge and Marjorie Howes are precise: *Ulysses* is in fact a 'semicolonial' novel, a novel of the last years of colonial rule in Ireland.[80] It is therefore also a novel that moves towards conciliation and reconciliation, if intermittently and rather contradictorily.[81] After all, on the realist level, perhaps the main theme of *Ulysses*—about which I shall have comparatively little to say as such—is (the difficulty of) accepting the invader's entry into a supposedly hallowed preserve. Not surprisingly, the movement in question is particularly marked in 'Penelope', which Joyce said was about *détente*, or 'the end of all resistance'.[82]

But to let the final emphasis fall decisively on reconciliation would be misleading. There are many other ways of managing political and cultural contradictions in *Ulysses*. The most important one, without

---

[77] *Theory and Cultural Value* (Oxford: Blackwell, 1992), 1.

[78] Review of Platt, *Joyce and the Anglo-Irish* and Marilyn Reizbaum, *James Joyce's Judaic Other*, *Textual Practice*, 14/2 (Summer 2000), 396–400.

[79] Ellmann, *James Joyce*, 519.

[80] *Semicolonial Joyce* (Cambridge: Cambridge University Press, 2000).

[81] For a relevant and illuminating discussion of reconciliation as 'a key term for Irish art and politics', see Seamus Deane, 'General Introduction', in Seamus Deane with Andrew Carpenter and Jonathan Williams, *Field Day Anthology of Irish Writing* (3 vols., Derry: Field Day Publications, 1991), vol. i, pp. xv–xvi, xxvi.   [82] Ellmann, *James Joyce*, 712.

a doubt, is laughter. Great gusts of laughter sweep unstoppably through *Ulysses* itself, creating innumerable little comic turbulences along the way, large and small, simple and complex. This laughter is too gargantuan and too sustained to be put down merely to 'a good sense of humour' or identified as a psychological survival mechanism. In a sense, it rather constitutes or *is* Joyce's political and cultural project. Joyce's laughter negotiates rifts and divisions that are historical, cultural, and inward at once. At one point in 'Scylla', Stephen delivers an emphatic judgement on Shakespeare which he immediately admits to be based partly on plays he has not read. Having shot himself in the foot—having turned his judgement into a bull—he laughs 'to free his mind from his mind's bondage' (9. 1016). The freedom achieved by means of a bull is an ambivalent freedom. Bulls can be a little like Pyrrhic victories (which also interested Joyce). Furthermore, the act of freeing oneself through laughter must be repeated indefinitely. All the same, at this point in the novel, Stephen begins to learn a lesson the effects of which are evident everywhere in *Ulysses*. It is a lesson in resisting, accepting, and transcending history at one and the same time. It is an artistic lesson, a political and an ethical one, and a lesson in negotiation between the claims of freedom and those of justice.

CHAPTER ONE

Patiens Ingemiscit:
Stephen Dedalus, Ireland, and History

The Seas' Ruler and 'Constructive Unionism'

The critical view of the 'Telemachiad' has recently changed quite markedly and radically. The (broadly humanist) tradition of Joyce criticism from Kain onwards interpreted Stephen Dedalus's early progress in particular ways. On the one hand, to adopt Charles Peake's terms, the 'Telemachiad' saw the emergence of Stephen the artist figure, to be followed by citizen Bloom.[1] As in the *Odyssey*, in *Ulysses*, son preceded (spiritual) father with whom he would establish a (more or less ironically treated) connection in later chapters. The organization and structural parallels of the first six chapters carefully contrasted the two characters. The contrasts were seldom thought to tell in Stephen's favour. He was narcissistic, selfish, or, at least, self-absorbed: 'All his thought derives from himself, returns to himself', wrote Hugh Kenner.[2] This line of argument was rather like Ellmann's case with regard to Joyce: Stephen was self-absorbed as Joyce had been absorbed in himself and his art. Stephen was sterile, sexually immature, cut off from the ordinary world in which Bloom was so immersed. He was also self-dramatizing, willingly and even contemptuously choosing exile. According to Bernard Benstock, he actually *insisted* on being dispossessed.[3] But his brooding melancholia was merely the alienation that precedes maturity, the

---

[1] *James Joyce: The Citizen and the Artist* (London: Edward Arnold, 1977), *passim*.

[2] *Ulysses* (London: George Allen and Unwin, 1982), 58.

[3] 'Telemachus', in Clive Hart and David Hayman (eds.), *James Joyce's 'Ulysses'* (Berkeley and Los Angeles: University of California Press, 1974), 1–16, esp. 12.

psychological consequence of unfulfilment.[4] The young man needed a woman. The artist needed contact with the ordinary world of Bloom. Joyce's attitude to Stephen was one of moral hauteur. When he told Budgen that he had not 'let [Stephen] off lightly',[5] he was assumed to be declaring his critical and moralistic distance from his character, rather than asserting the stark fidelity of his portrait of a bleak, inward struggle.

The advent of theory in Joyce studies broke decisively with this Leavisite consensus. By and large, theory had interests and concerns other than the plight of Stephen Dedalus. But it paved the way for new ways of understanding him. Thus the recent post-theoretical interest in a 'postcolonial Joyce' and in Irish history and politics in Joyce studies has given us a very different Stephen to that constructed by the humanists. Deane, Cheng, and Platt in particular have described Stephen's predicament as that of an aspiring, colonial intellectual and artist whose project—and whose problem—is precisely independence. For Seamus Deane, Stephen is a proud self-modeller, 'a Napoleon of art'. He has an un-English passion for the intellectual life which derives from his and his country's Catholicism. He is the first true intellectual in 'the provincial tradition' of the English novel, and is the basis on which Joyce thrusts a 'parodied form of the English novel' into Europe.[6] Vincent Cheng's Stephen is a Stephen ineluctably aware of his own subject status and the subject status of what he calls 'my people' (3. 305, 14. 375), with whom he substantially identifies, albeit with reservations. This 'people' is represented in the milkwoman in 'Telemachus', 'a figure for an Ireland' exploited by the colonizer (Haines) and 'his shoneen collaborator' (Mulligan).[7] For Cheng, the 'Telemachiad' is a powerful anatomy and exposure of English cultural hegemony in Ireland. For Len Platt, Joyce and Stephen are principally concerned with the very condition that Benstock took Stephen to be self-consciously acting out: dispossession. Stephen is the Irish artist who speaks with 'the voice of Esau'

    [4] For a more recent version of this line of argument, see Mark Morrison, 'Stephen Dedalus and the Ghost of the Mother', *Modern Fiction Studies* 39/2 (Summer 1993), 345–68.
    [5] Frank Budgen, *James Joyce and the Making of 'Ulysses'*, introd. Clive Hart (Oxford: Oxford University Press, 1972), 52. The context suggests the 'naturalistic' rather than the 'moralistic' interpretation.
    [6] 'Joyce and Stephen: The Provincial Intellectual', in *Celtic Revivals* (London: Faber, 1985), 75–91, at 82, 80, 79.
    [7] *Joyce, Race and Empire* (Cambridge: Cambridge University Press, 1995), 156–7.

because his birthright has fallen into the hands of the 'usurper' (9. 981, 1. 744).[8] To take Benstock's point of view is to collude in Stephen's dispossession as effected, above all, by the Anglo-Irish, by Unionism, revivalism, and West-Britonism. Deane, Cheng, and Platt have all rethought the logic to Stephen's 'vastation of soul', a phrase Joyce used of Mangan (CW, 80). It is determined by chronic historical, political, economic, and cultural deprivations, and is hardly to be resolved by a bit of sex and street life.

In fact, from the very start of the 'Telemachiad', Joyce pits Stephen against the English presence in Ireland. This is the structure most crucial to the first three chapters of *Ulysses*, and it is decisive for the novel as a whole. The England in question is historically extremely specific. Within what I have designated as the period of English cultural nationalism, the years most significant for the 'Telemachiad' are those of what became known as 'the Unionist government', the Salisbury and Balfour cabinets, 1895–1905.[9] As I shall show by focusing on a few specific issues, the English presence and its consequences are principally embodied in three figures in the first two chapters, Haines, Mulligan, and Deasy. All three characters require of Stephen an acquiescence that, with a more or less mute *non serviam*, he refuses to give. In resisting the others' overtures, Stephen resists English patronage, English blandishments, English influences, English advice. Most importantly, he resists the kind of politic compromise with England that is represented in Mulligan. At the same time, in 'Nestor', he begins to develop a line of thought within which lies the germ of a political aesthetic. This line of thought is most evident in 'Proteus'. But Stephen is unable to elaborate it beyond a certain point. Joyce is careful to trace the limit in question and to indicate the reasons for it. In both political and aesthetic terms, the logic of this limit is what leads, on the one hand, to the introduction of Bloom and, on the other, to the formal, stylistic, and linguistic practices in the later chapters of *Ulysses*.[10]

---

[8] See Len Platt, *Joyce and the Anglo-Irish: A Study of James Joyce and the Irish Literary Revival* (Amsterdam and Atlanta. Ga.: Rodopi, 1998), 49–59.

[9] Thomas E. Hachey, *Britain and Irish Separatism: From the Fenians to the Irish Free State, 1867–1922* (Chicago: Rand McNally, 1977), 34.

[10] My own emphasis is thus on Stephen's struggles, and therefore on the 'Telemachiad' as dynamic in itself, and part of a larger dynamic process. By contrast, like many others, Cheng and Platt tend to read it as anatomy, and therefore treat it as static.

Haines, of course, is the most important English character in the novel. It is no accident that *Ulysses* should begin with an edgy, bickering tension between two young Irishmen which focuses to such an extent on the problem of the Englishman in their midst. As Cheng points out,[11] Stephen asks what Joyce clearly means to be the pertinent, significant question—'How long is Haines going to stay in this tower?' (1. 49)—pointedly also declaring that 'if he stays on here I am off' (1. 62–3). The antagonism Stephen expresses, here—the antagonism with which *Ulysses* begins, the antagonism Stephen feels towards Haines, and towards Mulligan for his willingness to pander to the Englishman—is the novel's starting point. At the same time, the antagonism in question is not exactly simple, not least because Haines himself is a somewhat contradictory figure. Joyce places him in a contradictory position relative to Ireland, and this partly reflects the contradictory attitudes to Ireland evident in English politics and culture during the ten years of 'the Unionist government'.

The end of the Gladstone government in 1895 spelt finis for any hopes for Home Rule. The advent of a Conservative-Unionist government might have seemed ominous for Ireland. When Arthur Balfour had been chief secretary for Ireland between 1887 and 1891, for example, he had enforced the Crimes Act sufficiently vigorously for the Irish to dub him 'Bloody Balfour'.[12] Yet Salisbury's chief secretary for Ireland, Balfour's brother Gerald, soon spoke of the need 'to kill Home Rule with kindness'.[13] The Salisbury and Balfour governments were closely associated with such a policy. To some extent, they effectively maintained Liberal policies in Ireland (or, better, 'refurbished' them, to adopt the term Joyce uses for such tergiversations; CW, 199). But in a less nervous, post-Parnellite political climate, this bred a 'constructive Unionism' which seemed positively enabling to liberal Anglo-Irishmen like Horace Plunkett.[14] The 'Unionist government'—as it became known—pursued a policy that, in principle, mixed coercion and conciliation but, in practice, was more reformist than not and led to some progressive legislation,

---

[11] *Joyce, Race and Empire*, 152.   [12] Hachey, *Britain and Irish Separatism*, 35.
[13] In 1895. See Andrew Gailey, *Ireland and the Death of Kindness: The Experience of Constructive Unionism 1890–1905*, Studies in Irish History (Cork: Cork University Press, 1987), 25–6.
[14] On the origins and character of 'constructive Unionism', see ibid. 3–6, 63–8 and *passim*. See also John France, 'Salisbury and the Unionist Alliance', in Lord Blake and Hugh Cecil (eds.), *Salisbury: The Man and his Policies* (London: Macmillan, 1987), 219–51, esp. 237–40; and R.F. Foster, *Modern Ireland 1600–1972* (London: Penguin, 1989), 425–6.

particularly the Local Government Act (1898) and Wyndham's Land
Act (1903). Such legislation was decisive in transferring power from
the landlord class and the Anglo-Irish to Irish Catholics. But in
Foster's phrase, the legislators were chiefly concerned with 'the idea
of 'simultaneity' and 'equalization' between England and Ireland',
rather than any acceptance of their irreconcilable differences.[15] The
new legislation was actually accompanied by a 'treacly rhetoric of a
"union of hearts" ' contemptuously dismissed by the likes of the old
Fenian John O'Leary.[16] Prime Minister Balfour even wrote of the
need for a colonial policy conducted with 'sympathetic imagination'.[17] But of course, in the last few years of the nineteenth and the
opening years of the twentieth century, far from exhibiting any notable 'kindness', in its larger dimension, British colonial policy was
distinguished by a new militarism and aggressive imperialism, a drive
to expand the Empire, both geographically and economically. This
was the consequence of the fears for British economic supremacy
that I discussed in my introduction. It soon focused, above all, on
South Africa and the Boer War (1899–1902). In mobilizing against
the latter, Irish (nationalist) opinion adopted a hostile attitude towards the new imperialism.[18] But it also implicitly declared that it
had not forgotten the coercive force that lay behind conciliatory appearances. Nationalist pro-Boerism was effectively a defiant repudi-
ation of 'constructive Unionism'. In any case, according to Gailey, in
the end, 'constructive Unionism' itself was really a 'rhetorical myth'
primarily intended for a British electorate.[19]

Of course, Haines's characteristics cannot be systematically
matched with the principal features of 'constructive Unionism'. But
the general outlines of a correspondence are clearly evident. Haines's
sentimental doublethink is English and of its time. On the one hand,
he functions as Joyce's (parodic) representative of the contemporary
English conscience with regard to Ireland ('We feel in England that we
have treated you rather unfairly', 1. 648). A sardonic Stephen partly
sees him as such: 'Speaking to me. They wash and tub and scrub.

[15] *Modern Ireland*, 425.
[16] The full phrase quoted is Foster's, *Modern Ireland*, 423. He is referring to the period
preceding that of 'the Unionist government'. But the concept of the 'union of hearts' was
still current in the later 1890s, as is clear from O'Leary's *Recollections of Fenians and
Fenianism* (2 vols., London: Downey and Co., 1897), esp. the footnotes, which are late
additions. See e.g. i. 9; ii. 25, 39, 141 n. 2, 201.
[17] 'Mr. Balfour on the Opposition' (13 May 1896), 10.
[18] See Foster, *Modern Ireland*, 433.   [19] *Ireland and the Death of Kindness*, 310–11.

Agenbite of inwit. Conscience. Yet here's a spot' (1. 481–2). Like the progressive legislation of the period, some of what Haines says implies a view of Ireland as virtually a separate nation with a separate national identity, as though power were no longer in the colonizer's hands (e.g. 1. 469–70, 647–8, 666–8). So, too, Haines articulates his own (rather wooden) version of Conservative-Unionist 'kindness' (as at 1. 488–9, 647–9). He even does his stiff, inhibited best to be 'treacly' ('I intend to make a collection of your sayings if you will let me', 1. 480). Joyce and Stephen, however, emphatically identify him as another version of the figure of the 'conqueror' (1.405). In a telling little vignette (1. 573–6), Joyce even pointedly casts him in the posture of 'the seas' ruler'. For a moment, Haines seems emblematic of the new British militarism. In spite of his efforts at self-exculpation, for Joyce and Stephen he remains the English colonial intruder (according to Mulligan, the heir to money made from colonial exploitation, 1. 156–7). His anxiety specifically about 'German jews' (1. 667) appears to conflate the English concern over the threat of 'pan-Germanism' that was growing from 1903 with contemporary English anxieties about Jewish immigration, about which more in Chapter 2. More generally, Haines's paranoid fear of the threat posed by foreigners to imperial British power, his very sense of a 'national problem' in England to which he has his own particular solution (1. 667–8) relate him to some of the dominant anxieties within English cultural nationalism. Joyce pointedly gives him South African connections, as though to stress that an apparent sympathy with the oppressed in one corner of the Empire does not preclude collusion in their oppression in another. But in any case, even superficially, Haines's actual faculty of 'sympathetic imagination' is as limited as Balfour's. He markedly fails to understand Irish difference. His most revealing moment comes in 'Wandering Rocks', when he displays a seigneurial wariness of being 'imposed on' by a servant (10. 1094–5).

Stephen exhibits a precise understanding of Hainesian (and 'constructive Unionist') doublethink, and refuses to be cajoled by either. Platt rightly emphasizes the fact that the model for Haines, Dermot Chenevix Trench, was actually of an old Anglo-Irish family.[20] But this merely adds to the significance of Joyce's decision to make him English.[21] Joyce turns Trench into an Englishman, not just because it

---

[20] *Joyce and Anglo-Irish*, 56.
[21] The 'decision', however, partly underlines what was already the case: the Trenches

makes him fit more neatly into 'a classically nationalist' formula,[22] but to initiate a (deliberately provocative) conflation of England and Anglo-Ireland that will run insistently through *Ulysses*. In effect, contrary to many of his Anglo-Irish contemporaries' insistence on their supposed Irishness, from the start of the novel, Joyce implies that the Anglo-Irish are 'forever English in Ireland'.[23] Haines's sentimental Celticism, his interest in the Irish language and in Irish folklore all associate him with Anglo-Irish revivalism. But Joyce also uses Haines to situate revivalism in relation to an English ideological formation that was particularly evident in this specific phase of the history of the colonial power. Together with Stephen, he ruthlessly lays bare the contradictions in the culture of 'constructive Unionism'. He exposes the ideology, structures of power and historical determinations that lay behind 'kind', progressive, English façades in the period of 'the Unionist government'.[24] Stephen may sound frankly rude, but that is because Haines repeatedly fudges or ducks the crucial issues. In 'Nestor', Deasy calls Stephen a 'fenian' (2. 272). If the word is to some extent appropriate, this is true, not least, of Stephen's resistance to Haines. To use some of his own adjectives: Joyce associated Stephen's kind of 'ironic' and 'intransigent' resistance to England with Fenianism.[25] Stephen's uncompromising attitude is close, for example, to O'Leary's scathing rejections of English Hibernophilia and English liberal condescension.[26]

In contrast to Haines's sentimentalism, Stephen insists on the stark brutality of the colonial relation, as, for example, in his recollection of May Dedalus's death (1. 273–9). In 1904, Joyce wrote to Nora of his mother: 'When I looked on her face as she lay in the coffin—a face grey and wasted with cancer—I understood that I was looking on the face of a victim and I cursed the system which made

were part of the English establishment. Dermot's grandfather Richard, who had been dean of Westminster and archbishop of Dublin, was buried with 'the mighty dead' in Westminster Abbey. See Thomas Richard Frederick Cooke-Trench, *A Memoir of the Trench Family* (London: Spottiswoode and Co, 1897), 125.

[22] Platt, *Joyce and Anglo-Irish*, 56.

[23] Declan Kiberd, 'Oscar Wilde: The Resurgence of Lying', in Peter Raby (ed.), *The Cambridge Companion to Oscar Wilde* (Cambridge: Cambridge University Press, 1997), 276–94, at 279.

[24] Cf. Joyce's view of Liberalism along with Vaticanism as the 'most powerful weapons the English can use against the Irish', CW, 195.

[25] See 'Fenianism', CW, 187–92, at 188–9. Joyce emphasizes the sturdiness of Fenian resistance, the fact that it is not just 'one of the usual flashes of Celtic temperament'.

[26] See e.g. O'Leary, *Fenians and Fenianism*, i. 77–8, 255.

her a victim' (*Letters* ii, 48). Stephen curses in similar fashion. The cruel horror of the deathbed scene is compounded by the cruel, ironic inappropriateness of the dying woman's demand of him. Stephen recalls the scene with the grave respect that is his mother's due. But he also continues both to resist her appeal and, at the same time, to accuse the dominant powers. Hence the brief explosion of the 'rage of Caliban' (1. 143)—'Ghoul! Chewer of corpses!' (1. 278)—in which he resorts to the established trope of the colonizer as vampire.[27] This should prepare us for his message to Mulligan: '*The sentimentalist is he who would enjoy without incurring the immense debtorship for a thing done*' (9. 550–1). In effect, Stephen is telling Mulligan why he won't buy Haines a drink. Haines is the sentimentalist who would enjoy 'Irishness' without accepting the burden of the immense historical debt owed by the English to Ireland (on which Joyce insisted, elsewhere).[28] As is well known, the quotation is from Meredith's *The Ordeal of Richard Feverel*. Meredith himself is important, here. He was neither a Conservative nor a supporter of 'the Unionist government'. But nor was he a fan of Gladstone's. He was rather an 'evolutionary radical', a dissident or radical liberal.[29] Like his father before him, who imagined he had 'sprung from grand Celtic ancestors', Meredith had 'Celtic sympathies'.[30] From the late 1860s, he was politically pro-Irish, a critic of coercion and landlordism who called for the English to govern more humanely in Ireland. From 1886, he was also a committed advocate of Home Rule. But, for Meredith, Home Rule was conceivable only within the context of the Union, of which he was an equally passionate defender. Thus *Diana of the Crossways* (1885) argues the case for better English government in Ireland. But whilst it makes the appropriate 'concession to the Celt', to quote the title of a pro-Home Rule piece

[27] On the vampire trope, see Mark Sutton, ' "All Livia's Daughtersons": Death and the Dead in the Prose Fiction of James Joyce' (Ph.D. thesis, University of London, 1997), 132. In the passage from 'Telemachus', it is not clear whether Stephen is momentarily digressing from his main theme to curse the colonial power, or using a metaphor referring to one of Ireland's two 'imperial masters' (1. 643–4) to arraign the other. Either way, the ambiguity allows Joyce to implicate both of them.   [28] See e.g. CW, 195.
[29] The terms is J. S. Stone's. See his *George Meredith's Politics, as seen in his Life, Friendships and Works* (Port Credit: P. F. Meany, 1986).
[30] 'Introduction', George Meredith, *The Ordeal of Richard Feverel: A History of Father and Son*, ed. with introd. and notes by Edward Mendelson (London: Penguin, 1998), xiii. All page refs. are to this edn. unless otherwise stated. Stone emphasizes Meredith's 'Celtic sympathies'. See *Meredith's Politics, passim*.

that Meredith published in the *Fortnightly Review* in 1886, it is also a Unionist text, ending with a meaningful union of England and Ireland as represented in Diana's marriage to a trustworthy, dominant male, the English Redworth. Even in his last work, the unfinished *Celt and Saxon* (1910), whilst he is clearly beginning to wonder whether the English and Irish may not be politically and culturally incompatible, Meredith nonetheless continues to assume the importance of continuing with the Union.

To Irishmen like Redmond and Dillon, Meredith's kind of position on Ireland was simply 'out of touch with the Irish scene'.[31] Joyce was undoubtedly aware of Meredith's interest in and, in outline, at least, his position on Ireland.[32] He also surely recognized that, for all Meredith's opposition to Conservative policies, his insistence on the Union on the one hand and on kindness on the other made him sound close in attitude to 'the Unionist government'. There is even a sense in which, though it antedates 'constructive Unionism' by ten years, *Diana of the Crossways* argues something resembling the 'constructive Unionist' cause. Indeed, after his own fashion, Meredith was also a 'constructive Unionist'. If there are analogies between Haines's approach to Ireland and that of 'the Unionist government', there are similar analogies between Haines and Meredith. The deliberation with which Haines attends to Stephen's reference to the 'imperial British state', for example, detaching 'from his underlip some fibres of tobacco' (1. 643, 645–6), is clearly related to a political climate in which 'the Unionist government' was trying to respond more 'thoughtfully' to the Irish situation and liberals like Meredith were arguing the importance of listening more carefully 'to Irish complaints'.[33] Joyce retorts to Haines, Meredith, and the political culture they represent by having Stephen turn Meredith's own words against him, wilfully twisting their meaning as he does so. In *The Ordeal of Richard Feverel*, the sentence Stephen (more or less) quotes is from the Pilgrim's Scrip, a book of aphorisms compiled by Richard's father, Sir Austin.[34] Sir Austin was based on Meredith's own father, and

---

[31] The phrase is Stone's, *Meredith's Politics*, 129. He makes this observation of Meredith's friend John Morley, whose views on Ireland were very similar to Meredith's.

[32] R. Barry O'Brien refers to Meredith's interest in Irish politics, e.g. See *The Life of Charles Stewart Parnell*, pref. by John E. Redmond MP (London: Thomas Nelson & Sons, 1910), 404.

[33] On the extent to which *Celt and Saxon* produces such an argument, e.g. see Stone, *Meredith's Politics*, 155.

[34] In the edition of *The Ordeal of Richard Feverel* that Joyce used, the exact wording is:

is like him in waxing sentimental about the Celtic 'tinge' he sees in the family's 'habits and mental cast'.[35] Interestingly, the Feverels are of Cambro-Norman descent, like the original invaders who came to Ireland from English shores. Ironically, given his aphorism, Sir Austin is also a sentimentalist in being incapable of passionate and particularly sexual commitment.[36] He is chronically and, in the end, disastrously abstracted from real emotions and needs: disastrously, because Richard has been 'pollarded' by Sir Austin's 'despotic' rationalism, in Meredith's phrase,[37] and this is what leads to the final tragedy. Joyce's inspired strategy is to take Meredith's irony and make it rebound on him and Haines together and on their sentimental Celticism in particular. Through Meredith and Haines, however, the irony strikes deeper, at contemporary English attitudes to and policies in Ireland. In effect, it strikes at 'constructive Unionism'.

Court Jester to the English

In a sense, Haines might be thought of as representing the cultural, even the psychological features of the 'constructive Unionist' project of 'equalization'. As 'Telemachus' effectively and repeatedly insists, this project was fraudulent. For it was founded on a categorical inequality that was simply assumed not to be negotiable. The significance of Mulligan is well captured in his intermittent resort to English public-school locutions ('in a funk', 1. 59; 'give him a ragging', 1. 163; 'You'll look spiffing', 1. 118; 'beastly', 1. 210). He represents the tradition of the 'court jester to the English' which Joyce saw as acquiescing in, even hoping to benefit from, inequality, the subordination of Ireland.[38] Mulligan thinks that acquiescence means power ('Why don't you play them as I do?', 1. 506). Stephen knows that it spells continuing disempowerment. Throughout the whole of 'Telemachus', Mulligan struggles to wheedle, coax, tease,

---

' "Sentimentalists," says the PILGRIM'S SCRIP, "are they who seek to enjoy, without incurring the Immense Debtorship for a thing done" ' (George Meredith, *The Ordeal of Richard Feverel: A History of Father and Son* [2 vols., Leipzig: Bernhard Tauchnitz, 1875], vol. 1, 262).

[35] *Ordeal of Richard Feverel*, 118.

[36] This is very much the point to the use of the aphorism in the immediate context, a fact of which Joyce was surely aware.   [37] *Ordeal of Richard Feverel*, 233.

[38] See Joyce's discussion of the aspect of this 'tradition' that appears to have been most important to him in 'Oscar Wilde: The Poet of "Salome" ', *CW*, 201–5, at 202.

taunt, and bully Stephen into a servile complicity with England. If Stephen refuses to surrender, it is because he takes 'not serving' to be the very condition of his integrity. Mulligan is clever, and his stratagems are varied; after all, his own sense of cultural identity is also at stake. But whether the gambit is playful (as in his suggestion of a trip to Athens, 1. 43); unctuous (as in his ascription of 'the real Oxford manner' to Stephen, 1. 54); speciously intimate (as in his reference to a joint project for Ireland, 1. 157–8; or his suggestion of an Oxford-style revenge on the Oxford man, 1. 162–4); sage ('Look at the sea. What does it care about offences?', 1. 231); matily self-deprecating (1. 235–6), cynical (1. 505–7), peremptory (1. 485), or coercive (1. 721, 724), again and again, the struggle is enacted on the same terrain. It is a struggle between two classes, political cultures, and ways of thinking both the past and the future of Irish culture, and the question of the relationship to England is at the centre of it.

One particular example will demonstrate just how deep this goes. When Mulligan denies any wish to offend the memory of Stephen's mother, Stephen replies:

—I am not thinking of the offence to my mother.
—Of what then? Buck Mulligan asked.
—Of the offence to me, Stephen answered.
    Buck Mulligan swung round on his heel.
—O, an impossible person! he exclaimed. (1. 218–22)

Critics have most frequently read this exchange as another instance of Stephen's juvenile narcissism. But in fact, Stephen is deliberately persisting in the struggle I have just described. Intermittently throughout *Ulysses*, he insists on the (political) importance of the use of Irish terms and frames of reference as opposed to English ones. Thus Richard Burke is 'tanist of his sept' (3. 247), Russell an 'ollav holyeyed' (9. 30), and so on. This insistence is not 'nativist'. But it implicitly calls for the expression, imagination, recognition, and articulation of Irish difference. Historically, of course, one principal site for the preservation of Irish difference had been Brehon law. In what Foster calls its 'intuitive, archaic' subtlety, Brehon law 'imposed a powerful obstacle to the spread of English law' and 'sustained an underground existence even in post-Elizabethan times'.[39] Stephen conflicts with Mulligan, here, not just because the latter is trivial, but

---

[39] *Modern Ireland*, 26.

because, in contradistinction to the West-Briton's flabby, unspecific sense of principle, Stephen's own stems quite precisely from Brehon law. Kinship—like honour and respect—is crucial, as is loyalty to the *fine* or family.[40] In certain cases, members of the *fine* must 'enter into suretiship for each other'.[41] Certain kinds of insult are 'regarded with the utmost seriousness' and must not be ignored, particularly after death.[42] As opposed to the *macc té* or dependent son, the *macc sóerléicthe* or son who has arrived at independence has precise responsibilities to his kin.[43] Most importantly of all, 'a crime against a woman is normally regarded as a crime against her guardian (husband, father, son, head of kin)'.[44] When Stephen's claims that Mulligan's 'offence' is against him as well as his mother, these principles converge. If Stephen is 'impossible', it is because he conflates his grief with an awareness of a different kind of loss. He refuses to accept the kind of cultural amnesia, the wholesale obliteration of an alternative, Irish mode of judgement that, implicitly, Mulligan is urging upon him.

Ulster Will Fight

The refusal may seem somewhat studied, at this particular moment, at least. But the will to open up another logic—to broach or sustain or radically to deepen an Irish dispute with England—is characteristic of Stephen in *Ulysses*. It is evident in 'Scylla', 'Oxen', and 'Circe'. In 'Nestor', it takes the form of resistance to Ulster Unionism as the latter had developed from 1886 and, in particular, from 1892. The self-image of the Anglo-Irish during the period was by no means necessarily that of a class bound to be 'forever English in Ireland'. By contrast, the Ulster Unionists were becoming proudly, assertively 'English'. For that matter, many Englishmen and women of the period saw Ulster as 'distinct [from the rest of Ireland] as a centre of natural Englishism and loyalty', in Matthew Arnold's

[40] For details, see Lawrence Ginnell, *The Brehon Laws: A Legal Handbook* (London: T. Fisher Unwin, 1894), 102–6.   [41] Ibid. 106.
[42] Fergus Kelly, *A Guide to Early Irish Law*, Early Irish Law Series, vol. iii (Dublin: Dublin Institute for Advanced Studies, 1988), 137–8. Whilst Kelly writes largely of 'satire' (and occasionally of 'verbal assaults') he makes it clear that the Brehon definition of 'satire' was very different to the modern one, and included much that the modern mind would think of as insult. See e.g. ibid. 337. Mulligan falls within the category of the *cáinte* or *rindile*, the 'purveyor of illegal satire' (ibid. 49).   [43] Ibid. 69.   [44] Ibid. 79.

phrase.[45] When Stephen ironically recites the Ulster battle-cry to himself ('*For Ulster will fight | And Ulster will be right*', 2. 397–8), he is recalling its significance not only for militant Ulster Protestants, but within the discourses of contemporary English nationalism. If Randolph Churchill was apparently the origin of the phrase, it was also associated with Balfour.[46] The conception of Ulster as a centre of 'Englishism' became common both in England and in Ulster itself during the land war of 1879–82. The English and Unionist tendency 'to emphasize the "English" identity of Ulster Protestants' then grew 'as their importance to the anti-Home Rule case was recognized'.[47] The Home Rule initiative of 1885–6 and the crisis that ensued 'united almost the entire [Ulster] Protestant population behind its banner' and 'solidified the confrontational nature of Ulster politics'.[48] The Ulster Convention of 1892 took place as the threat of another Home Rule bill loomed large, and symbolized the determination of the Protestant Ascendancy 'to retain its place in Ulster'.[49] The Convention was decisive. The ensuing period saw 'the emergence of an integrated party machine'.[50] This culminated in the formation in 1905 of the Ulster Unionist Council. What was at stake, in the Ulster Unionist and often the English view of matters, was loyalty; the loyalty *to* England of what English and Unionist discourses constructed as a stubbornly English element *within* Ireland.

The loyalist question is very much at stake in 'Nestor'. If, as Gibbon suggests, the Ulster Convention saw the birth of a new being, the 'Ulsterman',[51] then Deasy is that phenomenon. Throughout his interview with Stephen, he is energized by a new, historically specific consciousness of who he is and what he represents that would not have been available to him before the 1890s. So, too, the gulf between

[45] Quoted in James Loughlin, *Ulster Unionism and British National Identity since 1885* (London and New York: Pinter, 1995), 24.

[46] See Don Gifford with Robert J. Seidman, '*Ulysses' Annotated: Notes for James Joyce's 'Ulysses'* (rev. edn., Berkeley and Los Angeles: University of California Press, 1988), 40; and Jason Tomes, *Balfour and Foreign Policy: The International Thought of a Conservative Statesman* (Cambridge: Cambridge University Press, 1997), 78.

[47] Loughlin, *Ulster Unionism*, 23. The assertion of the Englishness as opposed to the Britishness of Ulster Protestants may sound a little odd today. But Loughlin points out with reference to the period 1886–1910 that 'the terms "British" and "English" [were] virtually interchangeable' (ibid. 27).

[48] Peter Gibbon, *The Origins of Ulster Unionism: Popular Protestant Politics and Ideology in Nineteenth-Century Ireland* (Manchester: Manchester University Press, 1975), 1; and Foster, *Modern Ireland*, 420.   [49] Foster, *Modern Ireland*, 420.

[50] See Gibbon, *Ulster Unionism*, 112–42.   [51] Ibid. 136.

Deasy's boisterousness and Stephen's melancholy reflects the difference in the political fortunes of their respective cultures under the
Balfour government. Deasy's commitment to England is historically
distinctive in being ideological as much as it is passionate. In this
respect, it is informed by what Loughlin describes as the dominant
Ulster Unionist discourses on national identity in the period
1886–1910. These discourses insisted that 'the characteristics that
made Britain great' were also those that characterized 'the "hard-
headed" Ulster Protestant'.[52] In his brief appearance in *Ulysses*,
Deasy lays more or less explicit claim to most of these virtues as described by Loughlin:[53] pragmatism (2. 262–3), shrewdness (2. 236–7),
enterprise (2. 338–42), industry (2. 419–21), efficiency (2. 331),
common sense (2. 294–5), economic prudence (2. 230), knowledge
(2. 238), resolution (2. 395–6), organization (2. 191–2), and manly
vigour (2. 424–5). He claims them in contrast to what the discourses
in question defined as Celtic characteristics, many of which lie
behind or are explicit in Deasy's treatment of Stephen or his view
of the Romanist Irish in general: fecklessness (2. 229–30), lawless-
ness (2. 278–9), improvidence (2. 262), treachery (2. 271–2), fancy
(2. 242–3), feminine softness (2. 392–3), lack of application
(2. 401–2), volubility (2. 419–20), ignorance (2. 272), and general
backwardness (2. 376). Deasy is by no means altogether unkind to
Stephen. As we'll see in a moment, that's important. But he is
unrelentingly patronizing, not least, because his conception of
Stephen is thoroughly infected by the stereotype in question, and he
automatically treats the young man in accordance with it.

   Joyce and Stephen respond by strategically inverting various of the
insistences in the discourses I've just mentioned. Stephen's oppressed,
laconic manner, for example, is precisely not the volubility that Deasy
appears to expect. Stephen's attitude to money is casual partly because, for him, money is not an inert abstraction, but 'symbols soiled
with greed and misery' (2. 227–8). Stephen is not ignorant where
Deasy is knowledgeable, but 'a learner' (2. 403) where Deasy is a dog-
matist for whom there can usually 'be no two opinions on the matter'
(2. 322–3). It would not be hard to multiply examples. To this project,
however—a strenuous effort to put a discourse into reverse—Joyce
adds another, the radical interrogation of a historical narrative bound
up with the discourse in question. Deasy's interest in and close

[52] Loughlin, *Ulster Unionism*, 27.   [53] Ibid. 22–8.

connections with business (2. 324–44, 415–18) are important, here. The Ulster Convention of 1892 was dominated by businessmen, by 'essentially respectable citizens'.[54] The politics of the new Unionism which ensued 'was largely the politics of a vigorous class of entrepreneurs'.[55] In some ways, their views were actually 'moderate and constitutional'.[56] As such, they should be clearly distinguished from those of the hard men—Carson, Craig—who came to the fore from 1912, still more from, say, Ian Paisley. They by no means represented the whole of contemporary, Ulster Unionist culture: we will catch glimpses of other aspects of it in Chapter 2. Indeed, Gailey points out that 'constructive Unionism' itself continually divided Ulster Unionists during the period.[57] Nonetheless, Deasy is an Ulster Unionist with 'constructive Unionist' leanings. His politics are clearly those of a comparatively enlightened, 'respectable citizen': that is why critics have not always found him particularly dislikeable. Loughlin argues that Ulster Unionist discourses on national identity 1886–1910 were not without contradictions, 'with race, class and national distinctions often ambiguously and confusedly employed'.[58] Confusions of this kind are perceptible in Deasy's admission that he has 'rebel blood' in him (2.278), for example, and his argument that the Orange lodges anticipated O'Connell's agitation for repeal (2. 270–1). His position is not as confident, as coherent, or as free from the taint of 'Celtic irrationalism' as part of him appears to assume, witness his uncertainty about Stephen's 'old wisdom' (2. 376). He is not ferociously sectarian. Up to a point, for all his dogmatism, he can therefore be surprisingly flexible.

But this is not to suggest that Joyce lets Ulster Unionism off the hook. To the contrary: he suggests that a comparatively 'moderate' Unionism is not incompatible with an impulse to bigotry. He pointedly has Deasy produce his most vigorous expression of his anti-Semitism at the end of 'Nestor', thus decisively undermining any sense of a fundamental *disposition* to moderation that his character may have previously conveyed. Deasy's anti-Semitism erodes any claim to the 'superior civilization' of 'Englishism' that he might appear implicitly to be making. This is important: the claim was central to Ulster Unionist discourses of the period and their construction

[54] D. George Boyce, 'Ulster Unionism: Great Britain and Ireland, 1885–1921', Patrick J. Roche and Brian Barton (eds.), *The Northern Ireland Question: Nationalism, Unionism and Partition* (Aldershot: Ashgate, 1999), 30–46, at 40.

[55] Gibbon, *Ulster Unionism*, 138.   [56] Boyce, *Ulster Unionism*, 40.

[57] *Ireland*, 319. Cf. 229–31.   [58] *Ulster Unionism*, 27.

of the North–South relationship. It was a claim that stemmed from Macaulay's patriotic *History of England* (1848–61). Macaulay's *History* and its moral fable of the English nation were enormously significant for Ulster Unionism, for Macaulay combined lavish praise of Ulster Protestants with an insistence on the differences between the civilized 'Englishry' and the 'aboriginal' people in Ireland.[59] The insistence became 'common currency' in the Victorian era.[60] It was crucial to the mythology of respectable Ulster Unionism, which was much concerned to raise to 'a civilized expression' what it worried were the 'elemental fears and drives', the disquieting proclivities of the unreconstructed Ulsterman.[61] In other words, it wanted to sublimate and thus forget about them. Joyce has Stephen swiftly destroy this pretension, and the will to historical amnesia on which it was predicated:

Glorious, pious and immortal memory. The lodge of Diamond in Armagh the splendid behung with corpses of papishes. Hoarse, masked and armed, the planters' covenant. The black north and true blue bible. Croppies lie down. (2. 273–6)

Stephen evokes the Protestant pogroms of the 1790s. These were carried out by a nascent Orange Order whose system of lodges eventually provided the new Unionism with 'the ready-made framework for effective organization'.[62] Stephen repudiates a narrative that turns the 'Englishry's' invasion of Ireland into a process bringing civilization to the barbarians. He insists, instead, on the barbarities for which the 'Englishry' themselves were responsible. He also insists that their current claims to 'civilization' cannot be separated from a history of outrage.

Fettered and Branded

But if Stephen continues to resist the colonizer and his influence, he also increasingly struggles to think past that opposition and the

---

[59] Thomas Babington Macaulay, *The History of England from the Accession of James II*, ed. T. F. Henderson (London and New York: George Routledge, 1907), 42; quoted in Louglin, *Ulster Unionism*, 24–5.   [60] Loughlin, *Ulster Unionism*, 24.

[61] Gibbon, *Ulster Unionism*, 135

[62] Ronald MacNeill, *Ulster's Stand for Union* (London: John Murray, 1922), 30; quoted in Gibbon, *Ulster Unionism*, 121.

history that produced it, or think it otherwise. This struggle is not always obvious, because he so often thinks analogically and even allegorically. But it is nonetheless increasingly important and forms much of the substance of 'Proteus'. Thus a double movement dominates the 'Telemachiad' as a whole. This movement subsequently extends into the rest of *Ulysses*, with many different shifts and oscillations. On the one hand, in 'Proteus', Stephen poignantly recalls his visit to Fenian Kevin Egan (3. 216–64). Francis Duggan refers to what Stephen calls 'the first of my explosives' in *Stephen Hero* (*SH*, 86), suggesting that, in 'Proteus', Stephen is absorbing the spirit of the dynamitard in order to translate it into an explosive art.[63] This is partly an index of what is to follow, in Joyce's novel. But Stephen is also still caught up in inherited antagonisms. On the other hand, 'Proteus' is very much concerned with the question of thinking change. Stephen is interested in the thought and perception of 'modality' (3. 1–9), reversibility (3. 187–90), motion or the protean character of the world (3. 332–63). He is equally concerned with the question of 'ineluctability' or givenness (as at the beginning of the chapter, 3. 10–28). Here again, two of the most prominent contending forces in Stephen's psychomachia are English and Irish. Though disguised for the most part, the figures most crucial to his inner debate at the beginning of 'Proteus', particularly at 1. 4–6, are Berkeley the Irish idealist and Johnson the English conservative, materialist, and sceptic. Stephen's reference to Aristotle becoming 'aware' of 'bodies' by 'knocking his sconce against them' (3. 5–6) is a wryly Irish, Catholicized version of the famous kick at the stone by which Johnson 'refuted' Berkeley.[64] Once again, as with Deasy, Stephen is struggling with a pragmatic common sense that leaves no scope for thinking the possible.

This is why he meditates on the historical actualities that, like colons or planters, have been 'lodged in the room of the infinite possibilities they have ousted' (2. 50–1). The 'Telemachiad' is haunted by the long perspectives of futility opened up by Irish history. For Stephen, history is a 'nightmare' (2. 377) partly because, in the case of his country, it seems so sheerly intractable. Like the deaths of Pyrrhus and Caesar, it is 'not to be thought away' (2. 49). The admission, here,

---

[63] See ' "Phrases of the Platform": Irish Political Oratory 1782–1922 in the Work of James Joyce' (Ph.D. thesis, University of London, in preparation).

[64] Fritz Senn points out to me that it is Bloom who actually 'knocks his sconce', in 'Ithaca' (17. 1274).

is bleakly Johnsonian: this is the moment at which Stephen is closest to intellectual capitulation. Not surprisingly, he has just been thinking about the capitulators who 'chose the smooth caress' because 'for them history was a tale like any other too often heard' (2. 45–7). Yet shortly afterwards, in a moment of 'candescent' tranquillity, he concludes from Aristotle that history must in fact 'be a movement . . . an actuality of the possible *as possible*' (3. 67; my italics). A historical actuality (the colonial history of Ireland, for example) was one possibility among others (like the free development of Irish society through history). These other possibilities cannot be granted the same status as an actuality. But that does not mean that they were without value, nor does it render them null and void. They are still available *to thought* (and therefore to art). Possibility is not merely the negative where actuality is the positive term. This is the liberating recognition on which Stephen builds, in 'Proteus'. As we'll see, its repercussions for *Ulysses* as a whole go far beyond that chapter.

The trouble for Stephen is that, however persuasive such reflections may seem, they are abstract. They present themselves in a different mode to the nightmare of history. Stephen is endowed with a power of historical imagination that is precise, exquisite, and cast in a language of the most extraordinary beauty. But it is also compulsive. He is not so much given to imagining the history of his country as he is 'a changeling' (3. 307–8) tumultuously beset by it. The account of Sandymount Strand gives one of the most simple and vivid evocations of this: 'The grainy sand had gone from under his feet. His boots trod again a damp crackling mast, razorshells, squeaking pebbles, that on the unnumbered pebbles beats, wood sieved by the shipworm, lost Armada' (3. 147–9). The traces of history are strewn among the 'unnumbered pebbles', cannot be forgotten within them. This quality of redolence—the tendency of any given detail to appear redolent of historical situations and historical concerns—is pervasive in the 'Telemachiad'. The sensibility in question is Irish-centred, even if the context is not: thus a memory of early morning Paris, for example, which features affluent, gold-toothed 'beauties' and 'curled *conquistadores*' (3. 209–15), is clearly heavily overdetermined by Irish colonial politics (particularly when we recall Stephen's consciousness of the difference between Mulligan's gold teeth and his own rotten ones).[65] The 'strandentwining cable' always

---

[65] Cf. Margot Norris, *Joyce's Web: The Social Unravelling of Modernism* (Austin: University of Texas Press, 1992), 200.

binds present to past (3. 37). Stephen's sense of walking gingerly over surfaces beneath which lie troubling depths (3. 150–2) is thus a figure for the 'Telemachiad' as a whole. '*Diebus ac noctibus iniurias patiens ingemiscit*': 'by day and by night it groans', suffering injuries, wrongs, 'offences' (3. 466). Stephen's quotation as he contemplates the sea is from St Ambrose's *Commentary on Romans*, an aptly named source.[66] As Joyce was surely aware, Stephen might be speaking of himself—or Ireland.

For Stephen, the 'ineluctable' truth is the fact that 'the cords of all link back' (3. 37). He is part of a community profoundly rooted in history: 'Their blood is in me, their lusts my waves' (3. 306–7). As at the end of *Portrait*, he feels he must represent his 'people'. Whether recalling Egan, Richie Goulding, or, above all, his mother, or trying to help Sargent avoid being 'trampled' by what Stephen pointedly calls 'the race of the world' (2. 141), Stephen's condition is actually one of painful belonging rather than alienation. This is a predicament for him, because it ceaselessly draws him backwards, into old hostilities, rages, frustrations, despairs. It leaves him still enslaved, 'fettered' and 'branded' (2. 50) in his very opposition to the powers that, from the sixteenth century, had been responsible for the transportation of Irishmen and women.[67] It prevents him from sustaining his theoretical commitment to possibility and orienting himself towards the future, his own and the community's. He may instruct himself to 'come out of' the past and his melancholy together (3. 106). Nonetheless, Joyce was emphatic: whatever his intellectual achievements in 'Proteus', Stephen 'has a shape that can't be changed'.[68] Significantly, the last image in the 'Telemachiad' is of him 'rere

---

[66] It would be interesting to know whether St Ambrose did not have some currency in nationalist circles at the time. James Connolly and Maud Gonne quote him, e.g. as a writer concerned with the sufferings of the poor. See Maud Gonne, 'The Rights to Life and the Rights of Property', *The Workers' Republic* (Aug. 1898), 7. Deirdre Toomey tells me that the article (originally a pamphlet) was in fact co-written with Connolly.

[67] For a depressing example of the historical experience to which Stephen's metaphors obviously allude, see Con Costeßπllo, *Botany Bay: The Story of the Convicts Transported from Ireland to Australia 1791–1852* (Cork and Dublin: Mercier, 1987). The 'convicts', of course, were not just common criminals, but included, in succession, United Irishmen, Defenders, Whiteboys, Young Irelanders, and Fenians. For the 'brisk traffic in Irish' transported to America and the West Indies in the 1650s, including supernumerary vagrants, see T. C. Barnard, *Cromwellian Ireland: English Government and Reform in Ireland 1649–1660*, Oxford Historical Monographs (Oxford: Oxford University Press, 2000), 44, 74.

[68] Richard Ellmann, *James Joyce* (revised edn., Oxford: Oxford University Press, 1982), 459. He is quoting from Frank Budgen, *James Joyce*, 107.

regardant', watching an English ship 'silently moving' up the Liffey (3. 503–5).

In the 'Telemachiad', then, Joyce articulates Stephen's 'nightmare' and sketches in a mode of resistance in theoretical or philosophical terms. The rest of *Ulysses* serves as a massive elaboration on that original act of resistance. Gregory Castle argues that Stephen knows that he cannot hope to destroy the reality of the historical world or even to create an alternative to it. He rather inaugurates a critique of the historical nightmare which 'serves as a kind of object lesson' and is conducted in the name of 'ousted possibilities'.[69] The emphasis on 'ousted possibilities' is important: but much more is at stake than mere 'critique', at least, in *Ulysses* as a whole. David Lloyd rather suggests that Joyce wanted to resist a selective, homogenizing use of the past in narratives of progress. He refuses to capitulate to historicism of this kind. Instead, he continually opens 'the historical narrative to undeveloped possibilities', thus refusing 'the reductive logic of domination'.[70] This 'refusal' is surely evident throughout *Ulysses*. The novel repeatedly questions a dominant cultural form on the basis of an undeveloped possibility, or uses the second to distort or corrupt the first. Thus Bloom represents an 'undeveloped possibility' within an Irish culture devastated by its colonial history. From 'Scylla and Charybdis' to 'Ithaca', on the other hand, Joyce takes as an 'actuality' a colonial (English or Anglo-Irish) discourse, and then rewrites it in terms of 'undeveloped possibilities', or 'overwrites' it with them. Indeed, what distinguishes *Ulysses* from the world in which it is located is in large part the extent to which it recasts that actual historical world and a historical set of discourses in terms of such possibilities. It is here that, categorically, *Ulysses* is neither a novel of 1904 nor one penned in Dublin. Finally, however, Lloyd only presents one side of the story. If *Ulysses* partly engages in a liberating struggle with a 'reductive logic', it also cannot escape that logic. The traces of the latter are everywhere in the novel. Joyce pointedly has Stephen tell Mulligan to 'let [Haines] stay' (1. 177). He makes no unequivocal claim to transcend history: hence the fact that *Ulysses* is also an act of

---

[69] 'Ousted Possibilities: Critical Histories in James Joyce's *Ulysses*', *Twentieth-Century Literature*, 39/3 (Fall 1993), 306–28, at 310. See also his ' "I Am Almosting It": History, Nature and the Will to Power in "Proteus" ', *James Joyce Quarterly*, 29/2 (Winter, 1992), 281–96.

[70] *Anomalous States: Irish Writing and the Post-Colonial Moment* (Dublin: Lilliput, 1993), 10.

gleeful 'Celtic revenge'. Like Stephen, it is continually thrust back into the historical world it struggles with. As a whole, the novel thus sustains but also reworks and transforms the 'double movement' of the 'Telemachiad'. It is both an act of resistance, and one that keeps in mind a condition of freedom beyond resistance. Perhaps the most important difference between Stephen and the Joyce of *Ulysses* is that Joyce does not polarize the actual and the possible, theory and sensibility, freedom and servitude, as Stephen tends to. There is no question of one or the other. Joyce rather commits himself to *work*, a work which will loosen if not break the fetters of 'actuality'. It is thus—as a massively protracted labour to ease off the shackles of a devastating history—that I shall be reading the rest of *Ulysses*.

CHAPTER TWO

Only a Foreigner Would Do: Leopold Bloom, Ireland, and Jews

'What about the Jews?'

Critical accounts of the Jewish theme in *Ulysses* have often not been sufficiently historically specific. Alternatively, they have been so in one way but not another: precise about Jews and anti-Semitism in the modern Europe in which Joyce composed his novel, much less exact about the same subjects in the Ireland in which Joyce grew up, the Ireland of *Ulysses*. Neil Davison and, above all, Dermot Keogh have recently started to redress the balance.[1] But even Keogh's reading of *Ulysses* veers away from the implications of the historical material he provides. Neither scholar can break with a well-established structure which counterposes Bloom as a supposedly more or less representative European Jew to the emergence of a generalized, modern anti-Semitism. As far as the Jewish theme is concerned, it would seem that Joyce can only be either a paradigm of liberal tolerance and decency and a defender of humanist principle against dark forces of reaction, or a humanist in principle but given to lapses, for historical and cultural reasons. At this juncture, no other reading seems possible.

The problem with the critical tradition is its reluctance to think Jews and Irish together. Thus Marilyn Reizbaum's recent *James Joyce's Judaic Other* casts a Bloom- and Europe-centred reading of the novel precisely against one centred on Stephen and Ireland.[2] Yet when the citizen asks Bloom what his nation is, in 'Cyclops', Bloom

---

[1] Davison, *James Joyce, 'Ulysses' and the Construction of Jewish Identity: Culture, Biography and 'the Jew' in Modernist Europe* (Cambridge: Cambridge University Press, 1996); and Keogh, *Jews in Twentieth-Century Ireland* (Cork: Cork University Press, 1998).

[2] See *James Joyce's Judaic Other* (Stanford: Stanford University Press, 1999).

replies 'Ireland . . . I was born here. Ireland' (12. 1431). The repetition is emphatic and, on one level, the fact is simple but crucial: Bloom is an Irishman, and Joyce intended him to stand as both Jew and Irishman at once. To think this double identity, however, between 1882, the year of Joyce's birth, and 1922, the year in which *Ulysses* was published, is to think an extremely specific phenomenon. Critics have addressed the question of the historical and cultural specificity of the Irish Jew in Ireland only in relation to the abstract structure just described. But this limits any formulation of the Irish-Jewish relation, for the structure in question tends to cast Bloom as modern European Jew in opposition to a benighted Ireland. More often than not, Bloom becomes a gauge of the unregenerate backwardness of the Dublin Catholic community. Indeed, Joyce's profound sympathy with Jews has frequently been linked to a tendency to denigrate his own people, for whom the critic him- or herself sometimes has at best a limited feeling (the case with Davison, for instance). What Joyce took to be the analogy between two traumatic histories was crucial to his interest in Jews. But his critics have often tended to treat the Jewish catastrophe with due respect, whilst hearing an emphasis on the Irish historical catastrophe as merely nationalist griping or sentimental self-indulgence. In effect, at the heart of what it understands to be Joyce's philo-Semitic humanism, criticism has repeatedly placed an extraordinary indifference to the long history of suffering and injustice about which he knew most. In this respect, *Ulysses* has been read as a post-Holocaust rather than as a post-Famine novel.

Without questioning or diminishing Joyce's stature as an opponent of anti-Semitism, I would argue for quite a radical departure from the critical tradition. This does not mean that I want to dismiss the more established emphases. Instead, I want to position them differently, to take them less for granted, to place them in a complex Irish historical context, and thus to see them as outcomes of an arduous, winding, difficult process of thought. The most significant and arresting features of Joyce's treatment of his Jewish theme are historically particular to late nineteenth- and early twentieth-century Ireland. His Jew is a historically specific Irishman. The anti-Semitism with which he deals is a historically and culturally specific anti-Semitism. Most importantly of all: in *Ulysses*, both Jew and anti-Semitism exist in a culture that is European but also colonial, that is, in a culture to which a politics of race is historically endemic and where it is pervasive in social relations. The position of Jewish people and the emergence and persistence of anti-Semitism within such a culture ask to be thought quite differently. So, too, do literary and political responses to Jews and resistances to anti-Semitism, like Joyce's in *Ulysses*.

In late nineteenth- and early twentieth-century Ireland, Jewish issues always insert themselves into an already existing politics. They form part of that politics and cannot properly be separated from it. In dealing with Jews and the Jewish theme, *Ulysses* necessarily also engages with the politics in question. It is therefore a much more complicated and sophisticated—or, better, more cunning—response to the situation of Irish Jews than has so far been recognized. The complex political formation at issue here can be addressed in various ways. My chief example—the Limerick pogrom—is familiar, but nonetheless representative. Its relevance to *Ulysses* has long been noted.[3] Both Davison and Keogh have recently reminded us of it in fresh contexts. The pogrom was a significant outbreak of Irish anti-Semitism historically close to the date at which the novel is set. There would seem to be no explicit mention of it in *Ulysses*. But certain references in the novel show that Joyce was well aware of it and had read about it in newspapers. Indeed, the instances of anti-Semitism which punctuate Bloom's day have a precise, historical character. Many of the characters in *Ulysses* reveal a heightened awareness of Bloom's Jewishness. This is partly the result, not only of the events in Limerick, but of the coverage of those events in the Irish and, to a lesser extent, the English press. Indeed, as we'll see later, such an awareness is also the consequence of a particular kind of concern about Jews that was widespread at the time in England and Ireland.

The disturbances in Limerick started in mid-January 1904, and then rumbled on for quite a long time afterwards. So did the press coverage. Arthur Griffith's *United Irishman*, for example, was still pursuing the issue energetically—and arguing with pro-Jewish nationalists—through April and May.[4] *Ulysses* responds to the Limerick pogrom, the climate that was its aftermath, and other kinds of manifestation of anti-Semitism in early twentieth-century Ireland. But Joyce was not directly concerned with a pure, unmedi-

---

[3] See Marvin Magalaner, 'The Anti-Semitic Limerick Incidents in Joyce's Bloomsday', *PMLA* 68 (1953), 1219–23.

[4] For further evidence of anti-Semitic disturbances and the effects of the Limerick pogrom on Irish culture until more or less the date when *Ulysses* is set, see *DE* (Sat. 4 June 1904), 5; *FJ* (Wed. 27 Apr. 1904), 6; and *L* (Sat. 30 Apr. 1904), 148–50.

ated manifestation of racial hatred. Insofar as he knew of the
pogrom, he knew of it precisely through the newspapers, as involving
questions of representation and discourse. Furthermore, terms like
'bigotry', 'tolerance' and 'intolerance' that were in circulation in discussions of Limerick were already contested and the site of a political and ideological struggle. The Limerick pogrom often made the
news (quite literally) alongside two other Irish issues, the University
question and the question of the Handbook of the Catholic Association. The three issues tended to get mixed up in Irish and English
newspapers and in people's minds. In the first instance, during this
period, the question of a separate university for Irish Catholics had
re-emerged. Amidst expectations that the Balfour government would
at long last deliver, January saw numerous meetings throughout
Ireland in support of a Catholic university. But it also saw growing
Unionist resistance to what, speaking to an Orange demonstration in
Belfast, the government minister Lord Londonderry called this 'ret-
rograde movement'.[5] For Catholics—and indeed many enlightened,
liberal Protestants—the establishment of a separate university was
simply a question of equality and right.[6] It meant redressing a historical injustice and bringing an end to the 'racial distinctions' in education with which, as I noted earlier, Lord Dunraven claimed the walls
of Trinity College were 'saturated'.[7] In the terms of the *Freeman's
Journal*, any refusal to establish a Catholic university would be an
anachronistic perpetuation of a colonial politics, a 'continuance in
the twentieth century of the spirit and principles of the Penal code of
the eighteenth'.[8] On the other hand, Unionists declared that the case
for a Catholic university was rooted in an illiberal sectarianism. This
argument barely concealed Protestants' anxieties at the erosion of
their cultural power. In certain quarters, at least, there also lurked
within it a consciousness of race and class. The Unionist *Daily
Express* in Dublin, for example, repeatedly argued that a Catholic
university would mean 'an absolute lowering of the educational standard'.[9] J. P. Mahaffy later expressed a similar contempt with reference to the University question, describing Joyce himself as 'a living
argument in favour of my contention that it was a mistake to establish a separate university for the aborigines of this island—for the

[5] *FJ* (Sat. 23 Jan. 1904), 6.
[6] See e.g. the editorial in *FJ* (Fri. 15 Jan. 1904), 4; and *FJ* (Wed. 27 Jan. 1904), 5.
[7] See *FJ* (Mon. 4 Jan. 1904), 5.   [8] Editorial, *FJ* (Thurs. 14 Jan. 1904), 4.
[9] *DE* (Thurs. 7 Jan. 1904), 4.

corner-boys who spit in the Liffey'.[10] By early February, Unionist pressure had led to a statement in the Commons from George Wyndham, the Chief Secretary for Ireland. The Tory government, he announced, would take no steps to legislate for a Catholic university in the current parliament.[11]

The Catholic Association of Ireland had been formed in 1902 for the promotion of Catholic interests. In R.F. Foster's terms, it was out to 'destroy' Protestant influence.[12] In Catholic terms, it was intent on disputing the long history of the 'monopolies and privileges', the 'unjust and overwhelming prerogatives of ascendency'.[13] Its handbook had appeared late in 1903, to Protestant alarm, in that it struck a newly belligerent note. On the one hand, Catholics claimed that the sole aim and object of the Association was to give them the means to defend themselves against at least certain Protestant elements, 'to protect Roman Catholics from the bigotry and intolerance of the other side'.[14] Protestants retorted that the Association was itself a vehicle for bigotry. This accusation is fired back once again at Protestants by Catholics, not least in the nationalist press. The crucial point, here, is that, in this respect, a manifestation of Catholic anti-Semitism was a gift to the ideological cause of Unionism. Thus in Protestant accounts, the alleged bigotry of the Catholic Association was repeatedly linked with the Limerick Catholic 'attacks on and the persecution of the Jews'.[15] *The Times* in London made the same connection, associating Catholic anti-Semitism with nationalist anti-Englishness.[16] Catholics had claimed that the British and Unionist attitude to the University question was a form of persistence in 'a cruel persecution'.[17] But Protestants, Unionists, and their press claimed that Limerick offered ample evidence of the *Catholic* will to persecute.[18] This latter had simply been 'peculiarly vindictive in the case of the Hebrews'.[19] With the University question, Limerick, and

---

[10] From Gerald Griffin, *The Wild Geese: Pen Portaits of Irish Exiles* (1938); quoted in Richard Ellmann, *James Joyce* (rev. edn., Oxford: Oxford University Press, 1982), 58.

[11] See *FJ* (Sat. 6 Feb. 1904), 6.

[12] *Modern Ireland 1600–1972* (London: Penguin, 1989), 453.

[13] The phrase is the Revd Dr Hogan of Maynooth's. See *DE* (Fri. 24 June 1904), 5.

[14] Revd John Manning, quoted in *IT* (Mon. 18 Jan. 1904), 4.

[15] *IT* (Sat. 23 Jan. 1904), 9.   [16] *T* (Tues. 19 Jan. 1904), 4. Cf. 7.

[17] Bishop O'Dwyer of Limerick, quoted in *FJ* (Tues.16 Feb. 1904), 6.

[18] The Protestant Irish Mission to the Jews e.g. expressed its solidarity with the Limerick Jews, and hoped that they would be 'properly protected by the Government against persecution'. *IT* (Thurs. 21 Jan. 1904), 7.

[19] Mr R. Lindsay Crawford, quoted in *IT* (Sat. 23 Jan. 1904), 9.

Irish anti-Semitism all in mind, Bishop O'Dwyer of Limerick asserted that Catholic Irish shortcomings were the result of 'a defec-
tive, if not vicious education'.[20] But for many Protestants, in the
words of James Stanley Monck, any claim made for the tolerance of
'the Roman Catholic proletariat' could from now on be summarily
disposed of 'by asking the very simple question: "What about the
Jews?" '. Belfast was allegedly a stronghold 'of Protestant bigotry
and intolerance'. But its Protestants had willingly appointed a Jew as
their mayor.[21]

This was not the only way in which Unionist Ireland and (less frequently) England used the case of the Limerick Jews. If only the inhabitants of Limerick had been 'as hardworking as the Jews',
lamented one of the prosecuting lawyers at the trial of some of those
responsible for the offences, 'Limerick would be a great deal more
prosperous'.[22] The 'industrious, honest and law-abiding Jew'[23]
swiftly became the implicit countertype of the slothful, feckless, deceitful, unruly and, indeed, sometimes still savage Irish Catholic
worker or peasant. To a correspondent in the *Daily Express*, for example, Irish anti-Semitism made it seem hardly surprising that 'some
English people think the Irish but little removed from barbarism'.[24]
Jewish cleverness, too, became the countertype of Irish stupidity, as
when E. H. Lewis Crosby, head of the Church of Ireland Mission,
suggested that the ease with which the Limerick Jews had outwitted
them demonstrated how 'very foolish or ignorant' a set of people
'Father Creagh's flock' were.[25] More generally, Unionists asserted
that the Limerick Catholics had displayed a characteristic Irish 'in-
flammability', that their anti-Semitism showed how medieval they
still were (as opposed to England, where anti-Semitic violence had
supposedly died out in the Middle Ages).[26] What is remarkable is
how far a Protestant, Unionist, and to some extent English rhetoric
identifies the Jewish with the English and Protestant cause, especially

[20] Quoted in *FJ* (Tues. 16 Feb. 1904), 6.
[21] Quoted in *IT* (Thurs. 28 Jan. 1904), 6. Similarly, in opposing the Catholic Association, the Protestant Defence Association cast itself as representing the 'civil and religious
liberty' and 'sacred principles of mental freedom' guaranteed by being British. See *IT* (23
Jan. 1904), 9. In June, the Lord-Lieutenant was urging the Irish to respect the principles of
decency and tolerance, claiming the wisdom of an 'outsider'. See *DE* (Sat. 4 June 1904), 5.
[22] Quoted in *FJ* (Sat. 23 Jan. 1904), 6.   [23] Ibid.
[24] Letter from 'Galatea', *DE* (Thurs. 14 Jan. 1904), 6.
[25] Quoted in *IT* (Sat. 23 Jan. 1904), 5.   [26] See *DE* (Tues. 19 Jan. 1904), 4.

in opposing the Catholic Irish.[27] Lewis Crosby argued that, historically but to their own detriment, it had been Catholic countries that had banished Jews. Over the centuries, Protestant countries had welcomed Jews and benefited from their talents, business acumen, energy, and thrift.[28] Protestants even asserted that, like the Irish Jews, they themselves were now vulnerable to Catholic persecution. Like the Jews, they depended on—and must have—British justice and fair play, the protection of the British government; in other words, the Union. In a strange twist of affairs—especially given the tradition of nationalist use of the Irish-Jewish analogy, of which more shortly— 'To your tents, O Israel' even becomes a Protestant battle-cry.[29]

House of Bondage

The most significant contexts for the political discourses concerning the Jews in early twentieth-century Ireland are perceptible here. This formation—exemplified in but not confined to responses to the Limerick pogrom—is the dominant discursive formation with regard to Irish Jews in 1904. It should be clear from the start that Joyce's attitude to the Jews in Ireland must be sharply distinguished from the tradition of modern, Anglo-Saxon, liberal tolerance. Joyce had a very precise sense of how far that tradition could be specious; how far, in Ireland, especially in Unionist hands, it could be betrayed in being placed at the service of political calculations. Readily resorted to in certain cases (like the Limerick Jews), it was also categorically left out of account in the case of other Irishmen. The problem that then arises is a familiar one which Joyce confronts repeatedly: how to broach difficult questions for those Stephen addresses as 'his people' (14. 367–400) without disavowing what is also a fundamental identification with them. As far as the Jewish theme is concerned, in *Ulysses* as a whole, Joyce evolves a range of complex and subtle practices. In doing so, he seeks to repudiate and counter the Scylla of Irish Catholic anti-Semitism without identifying with the Charybdis of an 'enlightened' English and Anglo-Irish tolerance.

---

[27] See e.g. the account of Wyndham's speech to parliament on continuing disturbances in Limerick as reported in *FJ* (Wed. 27 Apr. 1904), 6.

[28] *IT* (Thurs. 28 Jan. 1904), 8.

[29] See *FJ* (Sat. 23 Jan. 1904), 6. The quotation is from 1 Kings 12: 16. Use of the phrase can be found elsewhere, e.g. in Fabian literature of the period.

For in this context, the latter is inseparable from a demonization of Irish Catholicism per se. As both Davison and Keogh have pointed out, Catholic and nationalist anti-Semitism was not confined to Creagh and his Limerick flock. According to Keogh, it had begun in the 1880s, with the sudden influx of Jewish immigrants fleeing Russian pogroms, the result being a rapid expansion of the Jewish population in the larger Irish towns and cities.[30] This produced anti-Semitic poster campaigns and letters to the press.[31] The most decisive instances of nationalist anti-Semitism before Limerick, however, came from Arthur Griffith in the *United Irishman* from 1899 and, a little later, D. P. Moran and other contributors to *The Leader*. During this period, for the first time, significant voices in Catholic and nationalist Ireland were raised in numbers against Jews in general and Irish Jewry in particular.

The newness of this phenomenon is very important for an understanding of the Jewish theme in *Ulysses*. Keogh argues convincingly that in Ireland, unlike other European countries, although the theological, liturgical, and intellectual foundation for anti-Semitism were certainly present, Catholicism was 'not characterized by a hostility to the Jews'.[32] The reasons for this are not altogether proud ones: as a colonized people, the Catholic Irish were preoccupied with their antagonism towards the colonizer. But throughout the nineteenth century, there had nonetheless been an honourable tradition of Catholic *and* Protestant nationalist identification of the Irish with the Jewish people. It ran from Tone to Parnell through O'Connell. There was of course a tradition of allegorization of the Irish as the Jewish people awaiting their redeemer or, more commonly, their Moses to deliver them from captivity. But the identification of Irish and Jews was more than an abstraction or a biblical trope. It also involved an insistence on the resemblances between Irish and Jewish histories: oppression, persecution, victimization, immiseration, demonization, disempowerment, diaspora. At times, it was a political matter: O'Connell allied himself with English Jews on questions of religious emancipation.[33] Indeed, the nationalist identification with the Jews was to some extent reciprocated: in the earlier nineteenth century, Jews had often felt a common bond with Irish Catholics

[30] *Jews in Ireland*, 2.   [31] Ibid. 19.   [32] Ibid. 26.

[33] However, O'Connell's hostility to Disraeli as a Conservative leader and prime minister fiercely opposed to Irish emancipation also led him to identify Disraeli's conduct on the Irish issue with his being Jewish. See Davison, *Joyce, 'Ulysses' and Jewish Identity*, 30–1.

precisely because of the extent to which areas of public life were closed to both races on religious grounds.[34] Jews worked on behalf of victims of the Irish famine,[35] and were themselves lauding Irish society for its racial tolerance until late in the nineteenth century.[36]

What happens then, disastrously, is that, in certain nationalist quarters, as Jews enter Ireland in greater numbers, the Irish-Jewish identification traditional within the culture breaks down. Griffith, Moran, and others begin to identify the arriving Jews with invaders and thus with the colonizer. Not only do they appear wilfully to ignore the dire injustice of this conflation. They also seem oblivious to the fact that it effectively subscribes to the structure of a mythology (identifying Protestant and Jewish causes) that was being promoted by Unionism. For the nationalists in question, the Jew is a 'parasite', like the Irish landlord and his agents.[37] Jews are 'prosperous' and therefore privileged.[38] They threaten to 'plant their heels' on the people's necks and impose a worse 'slavery' than did Cromwell.[39] They are 'grinders' of the poor and in conspiracy with the English.[40] Nationalist discourse on Jewry thus splits. Griffith, Moran and others become anti-Semites. Nationalists like John Redmond, Fred Ryan, and, above all, Michael Davitt continue to condemn anti-Semitism in itself, outright, and to insist on both the allegorical significance and the material substance of the more traditional Irish-Jewish analogy.[41] In the terms of this discourse, the denunciation of Jews is not required by nationalist opposition to English rule. It is rather the result of a pathetic, even cowardly reluctance to face the realities of colonial power and the logic of the Irish predicament. This above all is Davitt's argument.[42]

---

[34] Keogh, *Jews in Ireland*, 6.   [35] Ibid. 7.

[36] The most famous example of this is Dr S. Hermann Adler's speech in Dublin in 1892. See below.

[37] Keogh, *Jews in Ireland*, 21. Cf. J. F. Moloney, *L* (Sat. 30 Apr. 1904), 148–50, esp. 149, on Jewish 'rapacity' in exploiting the Irish poor.

[38] As Davitt noted, this emphasis was part of Creagh's tactics in his Limerick sermons. See Michael Davitt, 'The Jews in Limerick', letter to the Editor, *FJ* (Mon. 18 Jan. 1904), 5.

[39] See Creagh's response to Davitt's letter, *FJ* (Wed. 20 Jan. 1904), 6.

[40] This was part of Griffith's argument. See Davison, *Joyce, 'Ulysses' and Jewish Identity*, 68–70.   [41] See Keogh, *Jews in Ireland*, 19–23.

[42] See Davitt's reply to Creagh in 'Jews in Limerick': 'Let me suggest a field for his reforming energies which will not require the invocation of any poisonous feeling of racial animosity or of un-Christian hate. Let him attack the English rule of Ireland which levies £12,000,000 taxes, every year, on our lives and industries, not to the good, but to the injury of our country.'

Remembering Thee, O Sion

Ulysses responds to this situation in various and complex ways. First, Joyce repudiates the English and Anglo-Irish construction which opposes reasonable, enlightened England and Unionist Ireland to bigoted, benighted Catholic Ireland. He knew it was a myth, not just where questions of tolerance in general were concerned, but where anti-Semitism itself was at stake. The first two major instances of anti-Semitism we encounter in the novel come from an Englishman and an Ulster Unionist. Joyce literally gives priority to English examples of anti-Semitism, or an anti-Semitism that refers back to an English context. This anti-Semitism was evident enough at the time. Haines's version of it echoes English worries about 'undesirable aliens' which led to the Aliens Act of 1905.[43] Jews (East European, rather than German) figured largely among the 'aliens' in question.[44] Balfour—who wanted to keep Britain 'Anglo-Saxon'—spoke of 'the undoubted evils which had fallen upon portions of the country from an alien immigration which was largely Jewish'.[45] Deasy echoes the same 'xenophobic attitude to the supposed "alien menace" threatening Britain' as expressed (according to Loughlin) by turn-of-the-century Ulster Unionists.[46] Here, again, the attitude was chiefly focused on Jewish refugees.

Joyce presents this English and Unionist anti-Semitism as the larger, determining frame for the Catholic anti-Semitism which will later emerge in the novel. Within a certain English and Unionist discourse, the Jews, like the Fenians, are the enemy of or at the very least a problem for the nation and state. They are 'the signs of a nation's decay', says Deasy: 'Wherever they gather they eat up the nation's vital strength. I have seen it coming these years. As sure as we are standing here the jew merchants are already at their work of destruction. Old England is dying' (2. 347–51). But the most significant instance of Deasy's anti-Semitism comes at the end of 'Nestor': 'Ireland, they say, has the honour of being the only country which never persecuted the jews. Do you know that? No. And do you know

---

[43] According to Jason Tomes, the Act was 'not intrinsically anti-Jewish'. See *Balfour and Foreign Policy: the International Thought of a Conservative Statesman* (Cambridge: Cambridge University Press, 1997), 201.   [44] Ibid.

[45] Quoted ibid.; cf. 203.

[46] James Loughlin, *Ulster Unionism and British National Identity since 1885* (London and New York: Pinter, 1995), 31.

why? . . .—Because she never let them in, Mr Deasy said solemnly'
(2. 437–42). From O'Connell to Davitt, what Deasy ironically calls
Ireland's 'honour' in this respect was a nationalist boast.[47] It was fa-
mously echoed by the Chief Rabbi of the British Empire, Dr S.
Hermann Adler, when consecrating the new headquarters of the
Dublin Hebrew Congregation in 1892.[48] Davitt himself cited the
Rabbi in denouncing Creagh and defending Irish and Limerick
Jewry.[49] Deasy is clearly also citing Rabbi Adler but with Davitt in
mind, mocking and distorting both the Catholic claim and the Irish-
Jewish analogy in the process. But the historical irony rebounds on
him: as Joyce surely knew, Deasy's jest and his anti-Semitism in general also flagrantly contradict the *Unionist* claim then current to solidarity with the Irish Jews. The chapter leaves it to the young
'fenian' Stephen Dedalus (2. 272) to defend the cause of the Jews as
best he can. In fact, 'Nestor' as a whole returns us to an established
nationalist alignment: Catholic and Jew on the one side, Protestant
and Unionist on the other.

The irony, of course, is that, amongst Catholics, it is Bloom who
must insist on the same alignment: 'And I belong to a race too, says
Bloom, that is hated and persecuted. Also now. This very moment.
This very instant' (12. 1467–8). Throughout the day, and above all in
'Cyclops', in the Catholic community, Bloom encounters the contemporary betrayal of the Irish-Jewish analogy. He comes up repeatedly against the anti-Semitism of the new nationalism. He likewise
confronts the nationalist identification of the Jew with the colonial
invader or the colonial exploiter evident in the writings of Griffith,
Moran, and others. In the citizen's diatribe, the new Jewish arrivals
in Ireland are not merely 'nice things . . . coming over here to Ireland
filling the country with bugs' (12. 1141–2).[50] They are also 'swindling
the peasants . . . and the poor of Ireland' (12. 1150), 'We want no
more strangers in our house', the citizen continues (12. 1151–2):
'—The strangers, says the citizen. Our own fault. We let them come
in. We brought them in. The adulteress and her paramour brought

[47] See Keogh, *Jews in Ireland*, 6, 26 and *passim*.
[48] 'You have come here, my foreign brethren, from a country like unto Egypt of old to a
land which offers you hospitable shelter. It is said that Ireland is the only country in the
world which cannot be charged with persecuting the Jews.' Quoted ibid. 19.
[49] 'Jews in Limerick'.
[50] Bernard McGinley points out to me that it is in fact the Cork sailor D. B. Murphy who
has brought the bugs, having picked them up in Bridgewater (16. 670–2). Bridgewater is a
town in England.

the Saxon robbers here' (12. 1156–8). The Jews fleeing from the European progroms are conflated with English despoilers. The citizen has only one type for the incoming arrival or alien intruder, and it is colonial. It is thus no accident that the two principal objects of the citizen's vituperations in 'Cyclops' are Jews on the one hand and British imperialism on the other. The coincidence of the same two targets was evident enough in Griffith's *United Irishman* and Moran's *Leader*. But the commonplace suggestion that Joyce understood both kinds of attack as informed by a similar racism is absurd. What he recognizes is a kind of colonial pathology according to which the invader's pitiless refusal to imagine otherness may be reduplicated and even intensified in the invaded. The capacity for any imaginative leap has been swallowed up by the polarized antagonisms of the colonial context. The other from elsewhere can only be the enemy.

Such intellectual paralysis left Anglo-Ireland and England free to appropriate the Jewish identification. In *Ulysses*, however, Joyce powerfully reasserts the traditional Irish-Jewish analogy. In effect, he reclaims it for a people in danger of disavowing and thereby surrendering it. The most obvious example of this is MacHugh's rendering of John F. Taylor's speech in 'Aeolus' (7. 828–70). The anti-colonial, Parnellite intensity of the speech emerges very clearly in the mimicry of the conqueror's voice:

—*Why will you jews not accept our culture, our religion and our language? You are a tribe of nomad herdsmen: we are a mighty people. You have no cities nor no wealth: our cities are hives of humanity and our galleys, trireme and quadrireme, laden with all manner merchandise furrow the waters of the known globe. You have but emerged from primitive conditions: we have a literature, a priesthood, an agelong history and a polity.* (7. 845–50)

The speech goes on to insist on the need to continue with the proud, indomitable, Parnellite tradition of resistance, not least as couched in '*the language of the outlaw*' (7. 861–9). The passage is extremely important for the novel as a whole. It was so important for Joyce that, when he was asked to record some of *Ulysses*, he selected this passage.[51] In doing so, he repeated Stephen's self-effacing homage

[51] See Sylvia Beach, *Shakespeare and Company* (New York: Harcourt and Brace, 1959), 170–3. Any doubts as to Joyce's feeling for Taylor's speech may be allayed by referring to John Wyse Jackson with Peter Costello, *John Stanislaus Joyce: The Voluminous Life and Genius of James Joyce's Father* (London: Fourth Estate, 1997), 396–7. Its importance for Joyce was clearly personal as well as political.

to the tradition Taylor represents ('me no more', 7. 883). He also chose, not only to give a privileged place to Parnell and Parnellism, but also to give the same privilege to the Irish-Jewish analogy. In effect, he was underlining the centrality of the latter to his larger project. But this is by no means the only moment at which *Ulysses* reasserts the Irish-Jewish analogy in more or less its traditional form. It reappears sporadically throughout the book, with Kevin Egan, for example: 'They have forgotten Kevin Egan, not he them. Remembering thee, O Sion' (3. 263–4); or with Stephen's injunction to '[his] people' to 'look forth upon the land of behest' in 'Oxen', whilst, as both Irish bard and scapegoat, he is left alone with the 'Egypt's plague' of 'the adiaphane in the noon of life' (14. 375–86).

But Joyce does not just reassert the Irish-Jewish analogy. He also makes it his own. He deepens it, as in Stephen's recollection of the Jews at the Bourse (2. 364–72). 'Not theirs', thinks Stephen, 'these clothes, this speech, these gestures' (2. 367). The Parisian Jews' condition echoes that of an Irish bard dressed in 'castoffs' whose earlier avatar asserted of the English Dean of Studies that 'his language, so familiar and foreign, will always be for me an acquired speech' (*P*, 205). So, too, intermittently throughout *Ulysses*, the Irish-Jewish analogy is expanded into a sustained meditation on the psychology and politics—the trauma—of cultural alienation and self-dividedness. Still more importantly, in 'Calypso', Bloom calls the Dead Sea to mind: 'It bore the oldest, the first race. A bent hag crossed from Cassidy's, clutching a naggin bottle by the neck. The oldest people. Wandered far away over all the earth, captivity to captivity, multiplying, dying, being born everywhere' (4. 223–6). That the Irish hag, the poor old woman should cross Bloom's path at this moment is doubly significant, reminding us of how far Jews and Irish are engaged in parallel struggles with a burden of history and historical consciousness. At the end of the passage, Bloom briefly experiences a sentiment of 'desolation' and 'grey horror' (3. 229–30). Quickly, comically, he also bounces back from it: 'Morning mouth bad images. Got up wrong side of the bed. Must begin again those Sandow's exercises. On the hands down' (3. 233–4). Here, in miniature, the issue of catastrophe and recovery from catastrophe—an issue that is important everywhere in *Ulysses* and is historical, political, cultural, and psychological together—is broached precisely in terms of the Irish-Jewish analogy.

An Anythingarian

The culturally split self and 'the traditional accent of the ecstasy of catastrophe' (17. 786): these are the two dominant emphases in the Irish-Jewish analogy that Joyce is most concerned to deepen. But he underlines differences as well as resemblances. In 'Calypso', Bloom swiftly recovers from a moment of 'vastation of soul' (CW, 80). So, too, throughout the novel, his psychological reflexes preserve him from any prolonged, melancholy immersion in catastrophe of the kind evident in the Irishmen in 'Sirens'. Furthermore, if Joyce opens up differences within the Irish-Jewish analogy by means of Bloom, he also opens it up *to* difference. In Bloom, he retrieves the figure of the Irish Jew from English and Protestant claims to a community of interests. He locates Bloom solidly where he evidently belongs, in the Dublin Catholic community. Bloom spends most of 16 June 1904 in its midst, and it is much more significant in his many memories even than Dublin Jewry. Not only that: in their own mild, distinctive, and sometimes ambivalent way, Bloom's politics are readily identifiable as the politics most prominent in the community in question, post-Parnellite, anti-British, sympathetic to Sinn Féin.[52] Yet, at the same time, Bloom is both a non-Jewish Jew who has been baptized both a Protestant and a Catholic, and a non-Irish Irishman. If Keogh's account is exact, he is not even a typical Jewish immigrant, since those who arrived before the 1880s—like Bloom's father—came from England, Holland, France, Germany, Poland, Russia, Galicia, Lithuania, and even Morocco, but apparently not Hungary.[53] The fact that Bloom is not kosher is pointedly drawn to our attention almost as soon as he is introduced (4. 45–6). 'Is he a jew or a gentile or a holy Roman or a swaddler or what the hell is he?' asks Ned Lambert in 'Cyclops' (12. 1631–2). Part of the answer comes in 'Circe': Joyce's Jew is an 'anythingarian' (15. 1712) or composite of many things. Joyce reaffirms and deepens the Irish-Jewish analogy, then, only to loosen it in a host of differentiations both between and within the Irish and Jewish sides of the equation. Bloom's Jewish identity is clearly central to Joyce's project. So, too, is his Irish Catholic identification. Yet Joyce also blurs and complicates both. Interestingly, when posed the question, Why Bloom?, it was not Bloom's Jewishness that

---

[52] See e.g. 18. 383–6, 1187–8. [53] Keogh, *Jews in Ireland*, 6.

Joyce first emphasized: 'Only a foreigner', he said, 'would do. The Jews were foreigners at that time in Dublin'.[54]

What can we make of this? Why does the Irish-Jewish identification seem to be both extremely important and rather insignificant? Why are the very principles of identification and analogy themselves so pervasively imperilled by nuance and concrete instance? As both foreigner in general and Jew in particular, Bloom is an effective weapon against the ideological and discursive formations of the two imperial masters in Ireland, for he is both intimate with those formations and yet, by virtue of his Jewishness and foreignness, the source of a doubly alienated and alienating perspective on them. At the same time, as Jew and foreigner, he is also alienated from the formations in question in a different way to the community with which he has most to do (whose alienation from the Roman Catholic imperium, in any case, is at best equivocal). He is alienated from colonial formations as someone to whom they are still foreign, and thus often a source of perplexity, common-sense surprise, amusement, or simple indifference. He has neither the intimacy nor the complicity with them that is bred of a tradition of profound hostility. Constructed in this fashion, Bloom becomes an extremely subtle and flexible instrument. Joyce uses his character to steer a delicate course between a range of political positions that are finally unpalatable as wholes. In doing so, he produces a complex, ironic, composite politics of his own.

Thus in 'Lotus Eaters', Bloom joins Maud Gonne and Griffith in a pungently critical view of the British military presence in Dublin (5. 70–3). But Joyce separates his tone from theirs, granting Bloom a measured detachment and wry, playful nonchalance at odds with their invective. Bloom avoids their 'big words'. In doing so, he also avoids their unhappiness (2. 264). His awareness of the colonial character of Irish culture, of the poor 'fit' between the cultural formations of colonizer and colonized that was so much a theme of contemporary nationalism, is similarly astute but insouciant ('They can't play it here', he notes, of cricket. 'Duck for six wickets', 5. 558–60). His sense of class can be antagonistic (notably where the gentry are concerned, 5. 99–106, 122, 268–70, 304–5). But he mainly

---

[54] Jacques Mercanton, 'The Hours of James Joyce', in Willard Potts (ed.), *Portraits of the Artist in Exile: Recollections of James Joyce by Europeans* (Dublin: Wolfhound, 1979), 205–52, at 208; quoted in Ira B. Nadel, *Joyce and the Jews: Culture and Texts* (Iowa City: University of Iowa Press, 1989), 139.

expresses his antagonisms cheerfully, unresentfully and in sexual terms ('Possess her once take the starch out of her', 5. 106). Bloom is shrewdly aware of certain aspects of the economic exploitation of Ireland, and the significance of questions of caste and power (5. 305–12). Here, again, he seems close to contemporary nationalists, politically if not rhetorically. But equally, his hilariously uncomprehending attitude to Catholicism and Catholic culture in the All Hallows sequence (5. 340–466) has an anthropological detachment from strange customs. He is indeed remote from the Church with which nationalism was so closely allied. Here if anywhere, Bloom becomes a powerful satirical tool, exposing the ideological effects of contemporary Irish Catholicism ('Stupefies them', 'Lulls all pain', 5. 350, 367–8), providing a comically down-to-earth account of its political complicities ('Wine. Makes it more aristocratic', 5. 387), remarking on its cultural power and insidious efficiency ('Wonderful organization, certainly, goes like clockwork', 5. 424–5), noting its rhetorical force and persuasiveness, the power of its trappings (5. 403–5), and its rapacity ('And don't they rake in the money too?', 5. 435).

'Lotus Eaters' may therefore be thought of as constructing a political position broadly sympathetic to nationalist anti-imperialism and the levelling tendencies within nationalism, but also as concerned to separate nationalism from the Church, to moderate its cultural exclusivity (5. 465, 549–50), and, perhaps above all, to endow it with a much more urbane and thoughtful tone. This in itself is quite an intricate formulation. In each of the subsequent chapters in which Bloom is a substantial presence, Joyce adds to it or makes it still more sophisticated. Thus 'Hades' is concerned, not only with a historically specific, funerary and elegiac Irish culture, but with the extent to which it has been determined and shaped by English influences. Joyce presents the Irish culture of death and the dead as partly a consequence of the ravages of the colonial vampire. He also presents it as partly a Victorian import, whilst making us recognize how far a Catholic and nationalist community historically steeped in catastrophics was disposed to be susceptible to the importation in question. Bloom is robustly indifferent to matters that Irish funerary culture tends to clothe in solemn garb. He thus becomes a paradigm for resistance to and freedom from the culture at issue ('They are not going to get me this innings', 6. 1004). In Joyce's hands, he becomes a means of destabilizing and, indeed, promoting a radically secular view of it. Similarly, in 'Lestrygonians', Bloom restates his alienated versions of questions of class (e.g. 8. 877–89), and of colonial power and forms of complicity with it (like the 'toady news', 8. 338–9). He also adds a disabused view of colonial economics and its effects (8. 1–4, 41–5). At the same time, however, he asserts a principle of relaxed flexibility in judgement—Sir Frederick Falkiner is after all a 'wellmeaning old man' (8. 1156)—in keeping with his distance from the community with which he nonetheless has most to do.

Like all the other Bloom-centred chapters, then, 'Lestrygonians' produces what is in effect a complex deliberation within a given set of political parameters. There have been various versions of Joyce's politics. Even the classic works like Manganiello's, however, have tended to describe an international modernist's interests and sympathies, with Joyce's reading chiefly in mind.[55] In fact, critics have repeatedly made Joyce's politics sound academic. There has been comparatively little reflection on how far *Ulysses* itself might be elaborating a distinctive political position relative to an Ireland on the threshold of independence.[56] This isn't surprising: the position in question is complex to say the least. Joyce develops it partly through Bloom. In the end, for Joyce, in the Dublin of 1904, as Jew and 'anythingarian', Bloom is perhaps as close as it is possible to get to a truly independent mind. He both belongs to the Dublin Catholic community and clearly does not belong to it. He can therefore open up a different perspective or line of thought, but from within the horizons of the community rather than—as has so often been assumed—outside them. He functions partly as a corrective to what Joyce takes to be certain limitations to Irish culture that are the legacy of the colonial past.

Chief amongst these is the logic of the new nationalist anti-Semitism. Joyce repeatedly turns this logic on its head. Griffith argued, for instance, that Jews were people who came to live amongst the Irish, but who never became Irish: the Jew, he claimed, 'remains among us, always and ever an alien'.[57] Bloom's position as both insider and outsider is a principal source of his sanity, openness, moderation, and psychological resilience. That, in effect, is Joyce's retort to Griffith. *The Leader* argued that Ireland could rid itself of its Jews if the Irish grew more like them: sober, thrifty, economical, shrewd

[55] Dominic Manganiello, *Joyce's Politics* (London: Routledge & Kegan Paul, 1980).
[56] But see Enda Duffy, *The Subaltern 'Ulysses'* (Minneapolis: University of Minnesota Press, 1994), 1 and *passim*.   [57] *United Irishman* (Sat. 23 Apr. 1904), 1.

and possessed of 'industrial morale'.[58] Joyce's Jew has the exemplary status of Moran's, but is not dragooned into service as the instrument of his own elimination. In the end, however, for Joyce, what is perhaps most important about Bloom's relation to the Catholic community is not alienation but possibility. He represents possibilities, possible change, even a possible future. More importantly still, since Joyce imagines Bloom as part of an actual, historical community, he clearly also presents the possibilities in question as compatible with a determinate set of historical realities, in this instance, at least. Wyse Jackson and Costello have demonstrated the many points of comparison between Bloom and Joyce's father and the similarities between their careers. Joyce subjects Bloom to much of John Stanislaus's historical experience. In doing so, he shows how far, in principle, it could have led to a different outcome, both psychologically and culturally.[59] In his very ordinariness—a complex, exquisite phenomenon that, at this historical moment, is quite beyond the scope of the traumatized culture in which it emerges—Bloom is even a utopian figure. In order to take on this significance, however, he has to be both Irish and Jewish and more than both. He has to have an identity and be irreducible to the identifications practised by those around him. In *Ulysses*, the habit of thinking determinate identities must collapse. For it is inseparable, not only from the anti-Semitism depicted in the novel, but from a set of Irish political mythologies and their history.

[58] *L* (Sat. 4 June 1904), 234–5. I am grateful to Deirdre Toomey for alerting me to this argument.
[59] See Wyse Jackson with Costello, *John Starislaus Joyce*, 184 and *passim*. The points of comparison include a list of shared friends (82); life in Ontario Terrace (98); loss of a baby son (100); connections with Goodwin (90); Drimmie's (106); Luke and Caroline Doyle (107); Alderman Hooper (133); Matt Dillon, his family, house and party (16); canvassing for ads and the crossed keys (190–3); *Tit-Bits* (213); the City Arms Hotel and work for Cuffe's (208); employment at Thom's (216); even interest in the Wonderworker (223).

CHAPTER THREE

Gentle Will is being Roughly Handled: 'Scylla and Charybdis'

The Shakespeare Controversy

The meaning of the title of the ninth chapter of *Ulysses* has been interpreted in so many different ways as to seem indeterminable. The principle of the chapter is opposition or fissure, and the fissures spread and are perceptible everywhere. As Len Platt has shown particularly effectively, political and cultural antagonisms are crucial to 'Scylla',[1] and the title's main point of reference is surely the pervasiveness of schism and confrontation in contemporary Irish cultural politics. So, too, the problem of how to steer between contending opponents recurs in Irish writing of the 1890s and 1900s.[2] Joyce evidently had this larger context in mind in composing the chapter. But one paradigmatic instance of major importance to 'Scylla' is the Irish literary controversy of the 1890s. Various such controversies lie just beneath its surface. The controversy of 1898 between Yeats and Eglinton over the use of heroic legends in poetry helps to elucidate the Wordsworth references at 9. 820, since Eglinton argued for a Wordsworthian model in poetry.[3] So, too, the controversy of 1901 between Yeats and Moran in *The Leader* provides an exact context for Stephen's reference to Burns at 9. 817.[4] But one particular controversy is of very specific relevance to the chapter, as Joyce makes clear from its first lines.

---

[1] *Joyce and the Anglo-Irish: A Study of Joyce and the Literary Revival* (Amsterdam and Atlanta, Ga.: Rodopi, 1998), 73–86.
[2] See e.g. A.E. (George Russell), 'Literary Ideals in Ireland', in John Eglinton et al., *Literary Ideals in Ireland* (London: T. Fisher Unwin, 1899), 49–54, at 49.
[3] See Yeats, *Collected Letters*, ii, 1896–1900, ed. Warwick Gould et al. (Oxford: Clarendon Press, 1997), 275–302, esp. 293 n. 1.   [4] See ibid. 562–9, esp. 564–5 n. 12.

The chapter begins in hesitation, with Lyster 'creaking to go, albeit lingering' (9. 9). There is an opening flurry of references, not only to Shakespeare, but to Goethe, Shelley, and Arnold. The figure immediately and prominently indexed here is Edward Dowden, Shakespeare scholar and professor of English literature at Trinity College, Dublin from 1867 to his death in 1913. There is good reason for Lyster to be talking about Goethe: he was a Goethe enthusiast and translated Dunster's *Life of Goethe*. So much is well known. But behind Lyster's work and his enthusiasm, as Joyce would certainly have known, stood Dowden. For it was Dowden above all who was both the Germanist—largely as a result of his work on German Shakespeare criticism—and the lover of Goethe. He gathered material on Goethe from the 1870s, lectured on him, and, in 1895, finally published five articles on him, including one on *Wilhelm Meister*, the Goethe text referred to at the beginning of 'Scylla', which Dowden himself brought into his discussions of Shakespeare.[5] He was also President of the Goethe Society for twenty-five years. Lyster was a friend and disciple of Dowden's, and Dowden's letters show him encouraging Lyster to work on Goethe from the late 1870s.[6] The Shelley reference at the beginning of 'Scylla' likewise indexes Dowden: after Shakespeare, the author with whom Dowden's name was most closely connected was Shelley. The book for which Dowden was best known—after *Shakspere: A Critical Study of his Mind and Art* (1875)—was his *Life of Shelley* (1886). In 'Last Words on Shelley' (1896), Dowden repeatedly muses on Arnold's judgement on Shelley: a 'beautiful and ineffectual angel, beating in the void his luminous wings in vain'.[7] That Lyster should refer to it in 'Scylla' (9. 9–10) is hardly surprising.

But a second figure is also of major importance from the first page of 'Scylla'. The chapter's first explicit allusion to Yeats is at line 28. But he is present from lines 9–10. In 'The Philosophy of Shelley's Poetry' (1900), without ever quite naming him, Yeats took issue with Dowden's robust, positivistic, and frequently sceptical account of Shelley. Yeats argues *contra* Dowden that Shelley was a

---

[5] See e.g. Dowden, *Shakspere: A Critical Study of his Mind and Art* (1875; London: Kegan Paul, Trench, Trübner & Co., 1901), 128–30, 149–50.
[6] See e.g. Dowden, *Letters* (London: J. M. Dent & Sons Ltd., 1914), 120–1.
[7] 'Last Words on Shelley', in *Transcripts and Studies* (London: Kegan Paul, Trench, Trübner & Co., Ltd., 1896), 75–111.

poet of mind, an intellectual, unworldly dreamer.[8] If Lyster dithers
at the beginning of 'Scylla'—'a sinkapace forward . . . backward a
sinkapace' (9. 5–6)—this is partly a figure for divided loyalties, since
the disciple of Dowden's was also a friend of Yeats's. Lyster had encouraged Yeats to write and guided him in his reading of
Elizabethan literature.[9] The Quaker librarian's problem lies in the
fact that, whilst Yeats and Dowden knew each other well—Yeats's
father was a close friend of Dowden's—they had become cultural
antagonists. Most importantly of all for 'Scylla', the quarrel had led
to a dispute about Shakespeare. In the first years of the century in
Dublin, Shakespeare's name was closely associated with this controversy, and the latter has a decisive effect on Joyce's chapter. To
understand the controversy aright, however, we should look first at
what Yeats called 'the Dowden controversy'.[10] In 1895, Dowden and
the revivalists had quarrelled in the columns of the Dublin *Daily
Express*. The issue was the Irish literary renaissance. Dowden had
long seemed at best indifferent to the Revival. When he commented
dismissively on a lecture by Roden Noel on Ferguson, his indifference became an issue of some weight. Yeats rounded on what he
took to be Dowden's scorn for 'the Irish Literature movement and
Irish literature generally'.[11] Others joined in, and the arguments
were eventually published as *Literary Ideals in Ireland* (1899). The
volume pits Yeats and Russell against William Larminie—and
Eglinton. For Eglinton was another of Dowden's disciples. He
called Dowden 'our saint of culture'[12] and wrote the preface to the
selection of his letters that was published after Dowden's death.
Thus if the Yeats–Dowden opposition is adumbrated at the beginning of 'Scylla', it is also represented inside the chapter, in the
figures of AE and Eglinton.

The central issue of 'the Dowden controversy' was the relationship
between English and Irish culture. Dowden, Eglinton, and Larminie
all refer approvingly to cultural 'cosmopolitanism'. Nonetheless,
Dowden's real concern was what he saw as the inferiority of Irish rel-

---

[8] See 'The Philosophy of Shelley's Poetry', in *Ideas of Good and Evil* (Dublin: Maunsel
and Co., 1905), 90–141.

[9] See Yeats, letter to an unidentified correspondent, 11 Mar. 1887, in *Collected Letters*,
i. *1865–1895*, ed. John Kelly and Eric Domville (Oxford: Clarendon Press, 1986), 9–10 n. 4.

[10] Ibid. ii. 446–7; and letter, 20 Jan. 1895, quoted in Kathryn R. Ludwigson, *Edward
Dowden* (New York: Twayne, 1973), 141.   [11] Ludwigson, *Edward Dowden*, 140.

[12] Quoted ibid. 21.

ative to English literature.[13] As far as he was concerned, English culture was deeply and ineradicably rooted in Irish soil. The significant
Irish culture *was* English. Significantly, from the late 1880s until his
death in 1913, Dowden worked tirelessly on behalf of the Unionist
cause. He lectured at patriotic meetings, attended Unionist demon-
strations and founded a Unionist club. He even requested a Unionist
song from Swinburne. He claimed to have spent months on 'nothing
but Unionist work'.[14] Most importantly of all, he served as president
of the Irish Unionist Alliance at a time when its publications exhibit
an almost hysterical fear of the shift in political and cultural power
towards the Catholic majority.[15] To Dowden the staunch Unionist,
however, Yeats counterposed himself as nationalist: they construed
their differences in these terms. For Yeats, the problem with Dowden
was that he just recycled 'the received categories of English
thought'.[16] Dowden was indomitably English-oriented, a defender of
middle-class, utilitarian, Victorian English assumptions. For
Dowden and his supporters, on the other hand, Yeats in his nationalism was merely a provincial admirer of the second-rate. Before long,
Yeats was attacking the very foundation of Dowden's reputation and
career, his work on Shakespeare. Yeats argued that Dowden wrote 'as
would any Englishman of Shakespeare and Shelley'.[17] He had turned
Shakespeare into a British Benthamite.[18] 'The more I read the worse
does the Shakespeare criticism become', Yeats wrote, in a letter of
1901. 'And Dowden is about the climax of it. I[t] came out [of] the
middle class movement & I feal [*sic*] it my legitimate enemy'.[19] The
antagonism finally helped produce Yeats's Shakespeare essay of
1901, 'At Stratford-on-Avon'.

Stephen's position in 'Scylla' can be situated exactly in relation to
Dowden's and Yeats's. For Dowden, the poet who wrote the great
tragedies was also 'practical, positive and alive to material

---

[13] Dowden's 'cosmopolitanism' was actually Anglocentric. This is partly indicated in
his assertion that the direction of his work was always 'Imperial or cosmopolitan'. See
E. A. Boyd, *Appreciations and Depreciations* (Dublin: Talbot Press, 1917), 156; quoted in
Declan Kiberd, *Inventing Ireland: The Literature of the Modern Nation* (London:
Vintage, 1996), 160.   [14] Ludwigson, *Edward Dowden*, 45.
[15] In fact, to set Dowden's 'civilized' criticism alongside the—frequently virulent—
publications of the Alliance during this period is to gain an important and devastating in-
sight into the pathology of Unionism.   [16] Kiberd, *Inventing Ireland*, 121.
[17] Ibid. 445.   [18] Yeats, *Letters*, i. 622.
[19] Letter to Lady Augusta Gregory, 25 Apr. 1901, in *Collected Letters*, iii. *1901–1904*, ed.
John Kelly and Ronald Schuchard (Oxford: Clarendon Press, 1994), 61.

interests'.[20] He was 'prudent, industrious and economical' and concerned with 'worldly prosperity'. He 'acquired property, about which
he cared much'.[21] At the beginning of 'Scylla', Lyster introduces the
word 'facts' (9. 10). 'Fact' was a key term in Dowden's criticism.
Shakespeare never lost his grip on the world of 'facts'. He is 'inexorable in his plays to all rebels against the fact',[22] like Hamlet and
Richard II. This inexorability lies at the heart of Shakespeare's virile
power: for Dowden, Shakespeare 'feared that he might falter from his
strong self-maintenance into a Hamlet'.[23] But he was able manfully
to resist the temptation to weaken. He is preoccupied with 'mastery',
failure being 'the supreme sin'.[24] For Dowden, then, Shakespeare 'evidently lived in no dream-world'.[25] For Yeats, on the other hand, the
playwright is irresistibly drawn to Hamlet, Richard II, Coriolanus,
and Timon. Shakespeare's sympathies are with men 'made useless to
the State' by their very spiritual 'abundance'.[26] The trouble with
Dowden is that he has lived in Ireland, 'where everything has failed'.
This makes him glorify 'the perfection of character which had, he
thought, made England successful'.[27] But it also blinds him to
Shakespeare's feeling for those who have 'nothing to give but some
contemplative virtue, whether lyrical phantasy, or sweetness of temper', 'dreamy dignity' or 'capricious fancy'.[28] In other words, Yeats's
Shakespeare sides with 'the beautiful ineffectual dreamer'.

The antagonism between Dowden and Yeats has a clear political
structure. Dowden's account of Shakespeare is quite blatantly political. Shakespeare expresses 'an exultant patriotic pride and an exhila-
rating consciousness of power' at a time of great national 'energy'.[29]
So, too, the 'spirit of Protestantism . . . animates and breathes
through his writings'.[30] Along with Hooker's Anglicanism—'an embodiment of the ecclesiastical wisdom of England'—and Bacon's
English science, Shakespeare's *rich feeling for positive, concrete fact*
is culturally foundational.[31] By contrast, Yeats's 'nationalist' reading
of Shakespeare produces an anaemic and politically impotent poet of
the Celtic Twilight. Stephen steers between these two positions. But
the route between Scylla and Charybdis is not the way of modera-

---

[20] *Shakspere: Critical Study*, 33.   [21] Ibid. 30–1.   [22] Ibid. 36.
[23] Ibid. 36–7.   [24] Ibid. 72–3.
[25] *Introduction to Shakespeare* (London: Blackie & Son, 1893), 34.
[26] 'On Stratford–on–Avon', in *Ideas of Good and Evil*, 142–67, at 154.
[27] Ibid. 156.   [28] Ibid. 158–9.   [29] *Introduction*, 44.
[30] *Shakspere: Critical Study*, 38.   [31] Ibid. 23.

tion. Circe warns Odysseus to steer well clear of Charybdis: 'take heed and swiftly draw nigh to Scylla's rock and drive the ship past'.[32] In fact, Stephen's account of Shakespeare is very much that of the 'fenian' Deasy takes him to be (2. 272), certainly, compared to Dowden's. At the same time, however, he also steers noticeably closer to Dowden than to Yeats.

Indeed, in some ways, Stephen's account of Shakespeare is closer to Dowden even than to the Shakespeareans (Brandes, Lee, Harris) on whom Joyce most famously drew. There are more echoes of Dowden in 'Scylla' than have so far been detected. More importantly, however, Stephen's tone and concerns are often close to Dowden's. What binds their accounts of Shakespeare together—and distinguishes them from Brandes, Lee, and Harris—is a specific mode of politicization. This is notably clear at 9. 738–60. Eglinton says that 'You cannot eat your cake and have it' (9. 738–9). Stephen wilfully interprets this ironically. The class that has long enjoyed political and economic power in Ireland is also making a pre-emptive bid for cultural supremacy—a bid to *represent* Irish culture itself—precisely at the historical moment when its political status is most gravely threatened. This cannot be permitted: 'Will they wrest from us, from me, the palm of beauty?', says Stephen to himself, of the Anglo-Irish (9. 740). He promptly follows this reflection with an account of an entrepreneurial Shakespeare. Here many of his emphases—on Shakespeare the 'cornjobber and moneylender' with his hoard of 'ten tods of corn' (9. 743), on Chettle's account of his 'uprightness of dealing' (9. 745) and the 'few bags of malt' (9. 746)—are also Dowden's. So is the interpretative use of nautical-military metaphor. Stephen refers to the Armada as Shakespeare's jeer in *Love's Labour's Lost* and then, in the next sentence, speaks of the Histories as sailing 'fullbellied on a tide of Mafeking enthusiasm' (9. 753–4). Dowden writes of the Histories that 'their trumpet-notes of patriotic *enthusiasm* . . . must have echoed gloriously in the hearts of men who had witnessed the recent overthrow of the Armada'.[33] Joyce got many of the details in this passage from Brandes and Lee. But the tone and inflection are not remotely like theirs. Stephen's construction of

---

[32] *The Odyssey of Homer*, done into English Prose by S. H. Butcher and A. Lang (London: Macmillan & Co., 1879), bk. 12, 195.

[33] *Shakspere: Critical Study*, 63; italics mine. Joyce, however, would have found the same emphasis in Raleigh's similarly patriotic account of Shakespeare, which I discuss below. See Walter Raleigh, *Shakespeare* (London: Macmillan, 1909), 169.

Shakespearean biography in terms of a more or less thinly disguised political agenda is the mirror image of Dowden's. Brandes and Lee devote sections of their books to Shakespeare's business interests. But for neither of them do the latter have any larger implications.[34] In other words, what both separates Dowden and Stephen off from the other Shakespeareans and most opposes them to each other is their insistence on thinking politics and culture together.

Drive the Ship Past

Stephen's account of Shakespeare tacks decisively away from Yeatsian or revivalist 'nationalism'. The latter is represented in 'Scylla' by Russell. Russell sneers at the dense factuality of Stephen's account of Shakespeare as 'interesting only to the parish clerk' (9. 184), and asserts that 'the movements which work revolutions in the world are born out of the dreams and visions in a peasant's heart on the hillside' (9. 104–6). This gives us an exact indication of the mixture of snobbery, elitism, and political unreality that, in Joyce's terms, hopelessly flaw the Revival. To Yeats's emphatic rejection of the idea that Shakespeare might judge men 'with the eyes of a Municipal Councillor weighing the merits of a Town Clerk', Stephen counterposes an eminently practical, bourgeois Shakespeare. In doing so, however, he sails very close to the Scylla of Dowden. He pushes away from and beyond Dowden in three principal ways: first, he massively beats Dowden at his own game. Behind Dowden's insistence on Shakespeare's grip of 'fact' lay Arnold's identification of the world of hard fact as characteristically English. For Arnold, the Celts were rebels against this world. Stephen's discourse is powered—stoutly and explicitly at 9. 147, after Eglinton has accused him of just wanting to tell a 'ghoststory' (9. 141)—by an indomitable resistance to the terms of the Arnoldian proposition. In resorting to Brandes, Lee, and Harris, for example, he resorts to a world of fact that is quite beyond

---

[34]   Dowden was not the first to stress the economic aspect of Shakespeare's life, but the emphasis is Victorian, and more or less contemporary with his emergence as a Shakespeare scholar. J. L. Styan associates the emergence of the theme with J. O. Halliwell-Phillipps, *Illustrations of the Life of Shakespeare* (1874). See Styan, *The Shakespeare Revolution: Criticism and Performance in the Twentieth Century* (Cambridge: Cambridge University Press, 1977), 41. Cf. also Gary Taylor, *Reinventing Shakespeare: A Cultural History from the Restoration to the Present* (London: Vintage, 1990), 215.

Dowden's command. There are more facts about Shakespeare in 'Scylla', and more quotations from a larger range of his work known in more intimate detail, than in the whole of Dowden's supposedly classic study. Stephen's superiority to Dowden is as decisive as his superiority to the Dean of Studies in *Portrait* (*P*, 189–94). His is a bravura performance. In terms of the 'palm' of cultural prestige, its implications are huge: Dowden was one of the first two professional academic professors of English in Britain.[35] His Shelley biography was regarded as definitive until the 1930s. When he applied for the Clark lectureship in English literature at Trinity College, Cambridge, his referees included Arnold, Rossetti, Hallam Tennyson, Furnivall, Masson, Stopford Brooke, and J. C. Shairp. In 'Scylla', his work gets trounced by a Fenian upstart.

Secondly, Stephen does not just beat Dowden at his own game. He turns Dowden's case on its head. In setting Shakespeare in a historical, economic, and political context, Stephen also develops a critique rather than a celebration of Shakespeare and his world.[36] He sets him in certain proportions, even diminishes his stature, though not as a 'lord of language' (9. 454). He strips Shakespeare of the cultural eminence and centrality which Dowden takes for granted. He emphatically resists Dowden's conflation of Shakespeare with an auratic Englishness. He counters Dowden's Protestant Shakespeare by repeatedly linking Shakespeare to Catholic writers and understanding him in Catholic terms.[37] Dowden produces what Gary Taylor calls a 'constitutional' interpretation of Shakespeare's psyche, in that he sees Shakespeare as holding artistic inspiration and practical, material interests in 'a system of checks and balances'.[38] By contrast, for Stephen, the key psychological components in Shakespeare's biography are pathology and disorder. Thirdly and lastly, sex: as Mulligan's part-quotation of the coy first sentence from his popular Shakespeare primer—'*All we can say is that life ran very high in those days*' (9. 733)[39]—helps emphasize Dowden's pragmatic, entrepreneurial Shakespeare is notably sexless. This is hardly surprising:

---

[35] The other was David Masson.

[36] According to Taylor, such accounts were also produced by some of 'the best American critics' of the time, including Whitman, to whom Stephen refers (9. 625–6). See Taylor, *Reinventing Shakespeare*, 202.   [37] See e.g. 9. 831, 835–45, 1006–8.

[38] *Reinventing Shakespeare*, 215, 229.

[39] See Dowden, *Shakspere* (1877; London: Macmillan, 1930), 5. Kenner was the first scholar to notice the quotation. See his *Ulysses* (London: George Allen and Unwin, 1980), 113.

Dowden's Shakespeare is interested in power, not sex. He is the very image of English mastery. To Shakespeare the English master, however, Stephen counterposes a Shakespeare whose art proceeds from sexual trauma, a sexual wound that will never heal. Joyce clearly owed the larger contours of this emphasis partly to Harris. For in Harris's account of him, too, Shakespeare is a man broken by 'passion and jealousy and madness'.[40] Stephen thus retains some of the features of Dowden's account of a 'strong' Shakespeare. But he also understands Shakespeare as 'strong' only in relation to a terrible and founding weakness. So, too, in his Defoe lecture, Joyce presents Robinson Crusoe as the 'true symbol' of English power, not only in his strength, but also in his 'sexual apathy' (*DD*, 24–5). The stress may fall differently, but the tactic is very much the same.

The Idol of the People

A structural opposition therefore emerges in 'Scylla' between what we might call Fenian and Unionist readings of Shakespeare. At the same time, however, the reverberations of Stephen's iconoclastic practice self-evidently go well beyond Dowden, Unionism, and the literary controversies of Dublin. Dowden was at the centre of the English as much as of the Dublin literary establishment. As such, he was highly significant within a developed cultural and discursive formation that, between 1880 and 1920, entered into a specific phase of its development. The formation in question is English bardolatry, as Shaw christened the phenomenon of Shakespeare-worship in 1901.[41] Within this formation, a passionate devotion to Shakespeare was inseparable from a certain political understanding of him and his work. The process of what Dobson calls the 'the making of the national poet' begins as the hopes of Catholic Ireland are ending: 'Shakespeare, in the course of the reformulation of British national identity which followed the Glorious Revolution, came to serve as part of the acceptable face of the national past, and ultimately, suit-

---

[40] Frank Harris, *The Man Shakespeare and his Tragic Life Story* (London: Frank Palmer, 1909), 407–8.

[41] In the preface to *Plays for Puritans*. Strictly speaking, 'bardolatry' tends to be used more to refer to popular or commercial manifestations of English Shakespeare–worship than to literary, academic, and scholarly traditions. But the two traditions were closely connected.

ably moralized, became by the 1760s one of the symbols of British national identity itself.'[42] The national identity in question was English-centred, and the Shakespeare at issue increasingly associated with the colonial enterprise, with British aspiration 'to world dominion'.[43] Throughout the eighteenth century, Shakespeare's critical reputation steadily gained ground. So did bardolatry, notably with David Garrick's Stratford Jubilee of 1769, which saw it become 'an organized evangelical movement'.[44] The process continued throughout the nineteenth century. The Romantics gave it a formidable new momentum. In Coleridge's famous lectures on Shakespeare, the pre-eminent, English bard even took on 'the idealized, and thereby dehistoricized, form of a universal genius'.[45] Joyce had a copy of Coleridge's *Lecture Notes on Shakespeare and Other English Poets* in Trieste. In *Characters of Shakespear's Plays*—which Joyce also possessed—Hazlitt was of course a good deal more radical than Coleridge. But Hazlitt's 'deeply personal and fiercely evangelical' commitment to Shakespeare nonetheless places him within the mainstream of bardolatry.[46] According to Bate,[47] the tradition ran from Hazlitt to Mrs (Anna) Jameson's *Shakespeare's Heroines* (1832), another book Joyce owned.[48]

The apotheosis of the tradition was what Gary Taylor describes as the extraordinary Victorian worship of Shakespeare.[49] Between 1880 and 1920, however, bardolatry expands, but is also differently inflected. First, the Second Reform Bill of 1867 quickly led in the direction of mass education. As a result, by the late nineteenth century,

---

[42] Michael Dobson, *The Making of the National Poet: Shakespeare, Adaptation and Authorship 1660–1769* (Oxford: Oxford University Press, 1992), 226.   [43] Ibid. 227.

[44] Graham Holderness, 'Bardolatry: or, the Cultural Materialist's Guide to Stratford–upon–Avon', in Holderness (ed.), *The Shakespeare Myth* (Manchester: Manchester University Press, 1988), 2–15, at 3. On the development of bardolatry in the 18th cent., see also Peter Martin, *Edmond Malone, Shakespeare Scholar: A Literary Biography* (Cambridge: Cambridge University Press, 1996), 25–7.

[45] Howard Felperin, 'Bardolatry Then and Now', in Jean I. Marsden (ed.), *The Appropriation of Shakespeare: Post-Renaissance Reconstructions of the Works and the Myth* (London: Harvester Wheatsheaf, 1991), 129–44, at 129.

[46] Jonathan Bate, *Shakespearean Constitutions* (Oxford: Clarendon Press, 1989), 187.

[47] Ibid. 154.

[48] Mrs Jameson [Anna], *Shakespeare's Heroines; Characteristics of Women Moral, Poetical, and Historical* (London: J. M. Dent, 1910). Anna Jameson was popularly believed to be related to the whiskey–making Jamesons. In fact, whilst she was born in Dublin, the family moved to England early in her childhood, and her husband was English.

[49] See Taylor, *Reinventing Shakespeare*, pp. 168–9; and Chris Baldick, *Criticism and Literary Theory: 1890 to the Present* (London and New York: Longman, 1996), 43.

English was rapidly developing into a serious academic subject. This meant that bardolatry took an academically more respectable direction. For it seemed obvious that Shakespeare should be the dominant component in the new subject of English literature. Shakespeare's plays were turned into textbooks for study and examination. They circulated in schools and universities, and among prospective civil servants.[50] Secondly, at the same time, Shakespeare's colonial and indeed global currency grew swiftly. Thirdly, more and more varied books on Shakespeare became available: mass literacy and the growth and proliferation of publishing houses produced a market flooded with academic, sub-academic, and popular studies. Joyce had all three kinds on his shelves: as well as Brandes and Lee's books, for example, he owned Ernest Law's account of a conservative, royalist Shakespeare in *Shakespeare as a Groom of the Chamber*, and Maurice Clare's *A Day with William Shakespeare*, another book on which 'Scylla' draws.[51] One effect of the Shakespeare boom was a generalized diffusion of bardolatry, if sometimes in diluted form. For instance, Joyce also possessed and drew on Thomas Ordish's *Shakespeare's London*. Even Ordish's mild-mannered, uncontentious, informative book performed the appropriate genuflections, referring to Stratford, for example, as 'the Mecca of the English race'.[52]

Fourthly, and most importantly in this context, English cultural nationalism 1880–1920 affected the tenor of bardolatry. The period sees the emergence of institutions like the British Empire Shakespeare Society and the London Shakespeare League. At a time at which there was so much concern for 'national renewal', accounts of England's greatest poet were bound to become increasingly nationalistic, if in various, and more or less subtle ways. Sidney Lee, George Saintsbury, Stopford Brooke, J. A. R. Marriott, Sir Arthur Quiller-Couch, and Sir W. W. MacCallum all produced such

---

[50] See Taylor, *Reinventing Shakespeare*, 194–5.

[51] Law, *Shakespeare as a Groom of the Chamber* (London: G. Bell & Sons Ltd., 1910), and Clare, *A Day with William Shakespeare* (London: Hodder & Stoughton, 1913). *Ulysses* 9. 626–8 and 651–2 would seem clearly to derive from passages in Clare (unpaginated). See also Richard Ellmann, *The Consciousness of Joyce* (London: Faber & Faber, 1977), 59–61.

[52] See *Shakespeare's London: A Commentary on Shakespeare's Life and Work in London* (London: J. M. Dent & Co., 1904), 133. For a preliminary indication of Joyce's borrowings from it, see William H. Quillian, 'Shakespeare in Trieste: Joyce's 1912 *Hamlet* Lectures', *James Joyce Quarterly*, 12/1–2 (Fall 1974–Winter 1975), 7–63.

accounts.[53] With the distinguished exception of the remarkable A. C. Bradley (who is of no direct significance for *Ulysses*), the Shakespeare criticism of the period did not provide interpretation, analysis, or philosophical investigation. As Baldick puts matters, it was rather inclined to celebrate 'the National Poet's many-splendoured breadth of mind'.[54] Perhaps the most notable example of such criticism was Walter Raleigh's *Shakespeare*, another book Joyce had on his shelves and used for 'Scylla'. Raleigh produced his book for Macmillan's *English Men of Letters* series, itself then 'attaining the rank of a traditional British institution'.[55] Macmillan wanted the Shakespeare volume to be the jewel in this crown,[56] and Raleigh saw himself as producing a national monument: 'I could not guess that I should be given the opportunity of designing a monument for the poet I love best, in the national cathedral church. The *English Men of Letters* series is not as other series are.'[57] Raleigh gave Shakespeare a 'noble ancestry' running back to Guy of Warwick and King Alfred.[58] He turned Shakespeare into a triumphantly imperial figure who, from the Folio Edition of 1623, had steadily advanced 'to the conquest of the world'.[59] Given such eminent grandeur, for Raleigh, it was only natural that the English should be bardolaters 'born and bred'.[60]

Anglo-Ireland had a peculiarly intimate and complex relationship with bardolatry.[61] Felperin remarks that 'the main line of descent of orthodox bardolatry' in the nineteenth century runs from Coleridge to Dowden.[62] Joyce was well aware of the parameters of the relationship in question, as 'Scylla' shows. The origins of bardolatry lay in a period of English triumphalism which not only witnessed the transition from Stuart to Hanoverian England but was notably significant for questions of power and culture in Ireland.[63] Equally, Dobson suggests that if, by the end of the eighteenth century, Shakespeare had

---

[53] See Peter Brooker and Peter Widdowson, 'A Literature for England', in Robert Colls and Philip Dodd (eds.), *Englishness: Politics and Culture 1880–1920* (London: Croom Helm, 1986), 116–63, at 118–19.   [54] *Criticism and Literary Theory*, 46; cf. 58.

[55] See John Gross, *The Rise and Fall of the Man of Letters* (Harmondsworth: Penguin, 1973), 123.

[56] See Terence Hawkes, *That Shakespeherian Rag* (London: Methuen, 1986), 56.

[57] Letter to Macmillan, 30 Aug. 1903, in Simon Nowell-Smith (ed.), *Letters to Macmillan* (London: Macmillan, 1967), 250.   [58] *Shakespeare*, 31.

[59] Ibid. 2.   [60] Ibid. 3.

[61] Bernard McGinley suggests to me that a full list of relevant names would include William Davenant, Edmund Kean, Charles Macklin, and Nahum Tate.

[62] *Bardolatry*, 139.   [63] See Dobson, *Making of the National Poet*, 8.

become 'representative of British constitutional conservatism', it was due to the efforts of Burke and Malone. The Anglo-Irish men of letters placed Shakespeare in opposition to 'the excessive liberty of revolutionary France'.[64] But the threat that weighed most heavily on their minds actually lay closer to home. Malone is a crucial figure. Margreta de Grazia writes of 'the interlocked imperatives in the study of Shakespeare' as having long been 'authenticity, periodization, individuation, chronology'. These 'imperatives' are still with present-day scholars. As de Grazia has brilliantly shown, they are the legacy of Malone's late eighteenth-century, scholarly revolution in Shakespeare studies.[65] Malone intended his apparatus to protect Shakespeare from error. He wanted to save Shakespeare's texts from what de Grazia calls 'contaminating mediation' and 'spurious materials',[66] and what Malone himself referred to as 'impositions', 'fabrications', 'modern sophistications and foreign admixtures'.[67] However, de Grazia overlooks a very important point: the Trinity-educated Malone was of Anglo-Irish, landowning stock, with an English mother from an aristocratic family. He moved to and established himself in England at the time of political stirrings in Ireland that were to lead to the upheavals of 1798. He remained implacably loyal to the English crown. He was a Unionist and opposed to Catholic emancipation. He thought of the Irish Catholic peasantry or 'lower Irish' as 'a cunning, false, perjured, ferocious and sanguinary people'.[68] A well-known anecdote tells of him informing the Prince of Wales in 1797 that 'the grievances of the Irish Catholics' were 'merely imaginary'. In his youth, he was friends with John Fitzgibbon, Earl of Clare, who, in 1789, was to become the much-execrated, anti-Catholic, despotic lord chancellor of Ireland. It is worth noting that Malone renewed this friendship in 1798.[69]

The cultural politics at issue in Malone's work were clear enough to Burke, who equated Malone's history of the stage with 'the history

---

[64] Dobson, *Making of the National Poet*, 228 n. 10.

[65] *Shakespeare Verbatim* (Oxford: Clarendon, 1991), 1. Peter Martin's recent attempt to call de Grazia's Foucauldian thesis into question cannot withstand rigorous theoretical scrutiny. See Martin, *Edmond Malone*, 25, 32, 48–9, 134, 137, 205.

[66] de Grazia, *Shakespeare Verbatim*, 225, 78.   [67] Quoted in ibid. 10, 109–10.

[68] Letter to William Windham, June 1798. Malone is urging Windham to be 'less moderate' in denouncing radicals. Even Malone's sympathetic biographer thinks the letter shows a 'remarkable' dislike 'for 'the Irish peasantry'. See Martin, *Edmond Malone*, 221.

[69] In correspondence. See Sir James Prior, *Life of Edmond Malone* (London: Smith & Elder, 1860), 59, 245–50.

of the [British] state'.[70] In his obsession with rescuing an 'authentic' Shakespeare from all 'contamination', the famously bookish and apolitical Malone was in fact conducting a campaign in England that reflected the more conservative tendencies in late eighteenth-century Ascendancy politics. If Malone is the most significant figure in the tradition of Anglo-Irish bardolatry, Dowden was partly his heir. Joyce engages with this tradition in his 1903 review of A. S. Canning's *Shakespeare Studied in Eight Plays* (*CW*, 137–8). Canning was an Ulsterman, a landowner, and an aristocrat (second son of the first Baron Garvagh). He wrote three kinds of book: literary criticism, and studies of religion and of history (especially Irish history). In Canning as in Malone and Dowden, Unionism and bardolatry coincide. However much Joyce knew about Canning himself, he was certainly aware of the book's cultural provenance and ideological disposition. He recognized it as a piece of contemporary bardolatry. So much is clear from his reference to the 'great bard', which ironically mimics Canning's standpoint (*CW*, 137). At the back of the book, he would have seen details of some of Canning's other books and quotations from reviews. He would also have noted Canning's admiration for the eminent Irish historian W. E. H. Lecky, and Lecky's comments on Canning's *Revolted Ireland: 1798 and 1803*, mailed from the Athenaeum. He would have set them alongside the substance of the book itself, a blatantly if feebly Unionist reading of Shakespeare. Canning's book is actually so poor that it hardly has 'themes' at all. But Shakespeare's 'loyalty' is a recurrent emphasis.[71] Joyce's review makes no explicit mention of Canning's political position. He simply provides an extravagant and supercilious demonstration of the intellectual poverty of Canning's book, its lack of any 'attempt at criticism', its 'meagre, obvious and commonplace' interpretations, its absurdities and blunders (*CW*, 137). Joyce would have noticed that, like Dowden, in England, Canning seemed to be regarded as eminently fair-minded and impartial. For his own part, Joyce deliberately refers to him as 'non-committal'. Worse, he makes it clear that Canning is 'non-committal' only out of sheer lack of intellect. He was right. The book has little to offer save dutiful platitudes, 'and even the pages are wrongly numbered' (*CW*, 138).

[70] Martin, *Edmond Malone*, 137.
[71] See A. S. Canning, *Shakespeare Studied in Eight Plays* (London: T. Fisher Unwin, 1903), 337, 4. Cf. 323, 340, and *passim*.

Sophistications and Admixtures

To some extent, Joyce stands in relation to Canning as the Stephen of 'Scylla' does to revivalists and bardolaters alike. Like Stephen, he knows that no advantage is to be gained from direct expressions of violent political antagonism, that they are tokens of vulnerability. Like Stephen, he recognizes the importance of cool superiority. The author of the review and the character in the novel both provide a concentrated, pre-emptive exposure of the intellectual slightness of the opposition, whilst also making it clear that their opponents are playing out a historical endgame from which they cannot possibly emerge as victors. Joyce undoubtedly recognized that Canning's book was a late, forlorn gasp of Unionist bardolatry. Indeed, along with the pungent relish of his ridicule, there is even a hint of tenderness for a book so pitifully thin and weak. In 'Scylla', however, Stephen's task is harder. Not only does Joyce pit him against Anglo-Irish readings of Shakespeare. He runs Stephen and the chapter counter to many of the principal insistences of the whole English and Anglo-Irish tradition of bardolatry. His books on Shakespeare would have made him very conscious of this tradition. Indeed, they would hardly have allowed him to escape from it. His very edition of the *Collected Works*, for example, would have told him that 'No writer ever so perfectly represented the entire genius of his country [as Shakespeare]; hence probably he is so especially the idol of the people; so completely identified with their modes of thought and feeling.'[72] Lofty amusement tinged with pity was unlikely to prove an adequate response to so imposing a formation.

Thus Stephen develops a set of wide-ranging, iconoclastic strategies. The first and most obvious is Shavian disparagement. Shaw was more than willing to call Shakespeare's reputation into question. He produced a scathing critique of bardolatry that he sometimes thought of as Irish in kind. For Shaw, his campaign against bardolatry was inseparable from his campaign on behalf of Ibsen, the 'new drama', and the spirit of Ibsenism in Europe.[73] When Eglinton quotes from Shaw's *The Quintessence of Ibsenism*, early in 'Scylla', he is indicating what he takes to be the provenance of Stephen's view

[72] *Collected Works of William Shakespeare*, (the 'Universal' Edn., London: Frederick Warne and Co., 1890), p. ix.
[73] See 'Introduction', *Shaw on Shakespeare*, ed. and introd. Edwin Wilson (Harmondsworth: Penguin, 1969), 11–13.

of the bard.[74] He is partly right. Some of Stephen's more caustic revaluations of Shakespeare's plays do indeed stem partly from Shaw, and Stephen's brusquely dismissive tone can also sound Shavian.[75] Secondly, where the Shakespeareans insisted on Shakespeare's 'identity with England', and even asserted that the argument was borne out by 'accurate scholarship',[76] Joyce responded by 'Europeanizing' Shakespeare, as he had done in his Defoe lecture (*DD*, 7). Thirdly, contemporary English Shakespeare studies were often characterized by a masculinism inseparable from the 'imperial' reading of Shakespeare as evident, above all, in Raleigh's 'phallic bard'.[77] Stephen rather offers a Shakespeare 'overborne' not overbearing, a Shakespeare who 'will never be a victor in his own eyes' (9. 456–7) and has the 'culpable interiority' attributed to him by Wilde and Harris.[78] Fourthly, contemporary Shakespeareans often emphasized the notion of Shakespeare the myriad-minded man, the artist of truly universal sympathies in whom the English spirit was thereby itself revealed as universal.[79] By contrast, Stephen presents us with a Shakespeare unable to escape from himself (9. 1023–4, 1041–6). Fifthly, 'to Dowden and his contemporaries, it seemed obvious that Shakespeare "grew in wisdom and in knowledge" from year to year'.[80] Stephen's Shakespeare, however, is left pointedly 'untaught by the wisdom he has written' (9. 477–8). Joyce also redeems the apocrypha of Shakespeare biography. From Malone onwards, scholars insisted that anecdotal evidence of Shakespeare's life should not be given the weight and authority of documentary evidence. Joyce strews his text with allusions to the anecdotes that they distrusted: the story of the Lucy incident (9. 1134), for example, of Burbage and the 'burgher's wife' (9. 632–7) and Shakespeare slaying calves in his father's butcher shop (9.130–2).[81] Finally, and perhaps most

---

[74] Compare the references to 'the fat boy in Pickwick' at 9. 142–3 and in *The Quintessence of Ibsenism*. See *Shaw on Shakespeare*, 249.

[75] Cf. e.g. 9. 77–8 and 990–2, and *Shaw on Shakespeare*, 222, 230–1, 266, 273–4.

[76] See Sidney Lee, *Great Englishmen of the Sixteenth Century* (London: Constable, 1907), 345. Joyce had this book in Trieste.

[77] On which see Hawkes, *Shakespeherian Rag*, 60, and Baldick, *Criticism and Literary Theory*, 60.   [78] Hawkes, *Shakespeherian Rag*, 43.

[79] See e.g. Raleigh, *Shakespeare*, 174, 228, and *passim*.

[80] Dowden, *Shakspere: Critical Study*, 43; quoted in Taylor, *Reinventing Shakespeare*, 174.

[81] See de Grazia, *Shakespeare Verbatim*, 70–2, 76. In Karl Elze's book on Shakespeare, Joyce would have found a case for crediting the story of the incident with Sir Thomas Lucy

strikingly of all, to the effusive and fulsome tone of much contemporary bardolatry, Stephen opposes an intellectual rigour that is consciously chilly and austere.

Of course, bardolatry was not a simple phenomenon. It was not without its critics and heretics. It even had its radical side.[82] So, too, an account of 'Scylla' as a Joycean retort to English and Anglo-Irish bardolatry will not explain the full variety and subtle complexity of the literary practices informing the chapter. As Joyce was well aware, the polar structure that opposes Stephen to Dowden and what he represents is also a token of their intimacy. What is necessary, as everywhere in *Ulysses*, is that the ferociously antagonistic politics in question be registered and elaborated, but also that its 'shape' be 'changed', as Stephen's cannot be.[83] The distinction between Stephen's treatment of Shakespeare in 1904 and the middle-aged Joyce's treatment of him in 1918–19 is therefore extremely important. The most significant difference lies in Joyce's handling of Shakespeare's language. Here, as repeatedly in the later chapters, politics is inseparable from aesthetics, from questions of style. Felperin points out that even the Shakespeare heretics—anti-Stratfordians, 'disintegrators', and other iconoclasts—resembled the worshippers they opposed in continuing to accept 'the massive cultural authority' of Shakespeare's plays.[84] Joyce, however, is altogether more daring.

For 'Scylla' sets to work on the plays themselves, redistributing and recasting their language. True, this might largely be thought of as Stephen's doing. But it has implications of which Stephen cannot be altogether conscious. Here, more immediately and pervasively than anywhere else in *Ulysses*, what Stephen says is inherently textual. The first point to make is that, where the structure of the opposition between Stephen and Dowden is clear and categorical, Joyce's aesthetic practice is complex and irreducibly multiple. Emulation, imitation, simulation, admiration, degradation, domination: all are aspects of what Joyce does with Shakespeare. Of course, 'Scylla' partly subverts

that was explicit in its disagreement with Malone. See Karl Elze, *William Shakespeare: A Biography* (London: George Bell & Sons, 1901), 99–112.

[82] See Bate, *Shakespearean Constitutions, passim*. His argument that 'there is a strand within bardolatry which turns Shakespeare against the power of the State and repossesses him in the name of liberty' is particularly notable (ibid. 7).

[83] Richard Ellmann, *James Joyce* (rev. edn. Oxford: Oxford University Press, 1982), 459. He is quoting from Frank Budgen, *James Joyce*, 107.   [84] 'Bardolatry', 135.

or perverts Shakespeare's language. Given Stephen's involvement, this is predictable enough. 'Gentle Will'—or genteel Will—was bound to be 'roughly handled' (9. 793) and even pissed on ('*Mingo, minxi, mictum, mingere*', 9. 762). A humorously irreverent or disparaging attitude to the bard can be found elsewhere in contemporary Irish nationalist culture.[85] 'Scylla' picks up on and amplifies it. Take for instance Joyce's twisting of the quotation from Enobarbus's famously beautiful speech—'Age has not withered it' (9. 1011)—so that it applies to Shakespeare's 'original sin' (9. 1008). The most obvious subversions give sexual connotations to innocent Shakespearean phrases: 'the swelling act' (9. 259), 'a bay where all men ride' (9. 452–3), 'mount and cry O' (9. 638). In this respect, if Raleigh conceives of himself as the designer of a monument to Shakespeare in the national cathedral church, Joyce is the vandal who desecrates it.

'Scylla' also contains some pastiche or ersatz Shakespeare. This produces 'reader traps':[86] can any 'Scylla' reader invariably tell the real Shakespeare from the fake? 'Chivvying her game of cygnets' (9. 161) looks Shakespearean but is not. The same is true of 'comether': the *OED* gives the earliest use as 1838 and associates the word with Ireland. Furthermore, the practices of pastiche, simulation, borrowing, and reworking are themselves historical and textual variables. 'Scylla' sets to work, for instance, not only on Elizabethan and Shakespearean English, but on Milton's, too. Joyce also 'catholicizes' Shakespeare's language, subsuming it within a discourse which is predominantly that of Catholic theology. He 'Irishises' it, inflecting it in relation to an Irish context. To adapt a phrase of Stephen's (9. 158), he also makes Shakespeare his accomplice. Thus the vengeful power of Hamlet's feelings about Claudius—'I should have fatted all the region kites with this slave's offal' (2. 2. 575–6)—feeds into and enhances Stephen's glowering resentment of the revivalists ('I will serve you your orts and offals', 9. 1094–5). Stephen produces a political critique of Shakespeare, partly as a purveyor of colonial ideology. Like his psychoanalysis of the poet, a set of textual and linguistic practices is crucial to the process.

---

[85] See e.g. the amusing 'Hamlet among the Celts' in D. P. Moran's *L*, 7/19 (2 July 1904), 300–2. *L* frequently provided little skits and playlets, complete with Dramatis Personae. The page display of Mulligan's *Everyman His Own Wife* (9. 1171–89) resembles them closely.

[86] For the concept of the 'reader trap' specifically in 'Wandering Rocks', see Clive Hart, 'Wandering Rocks', in Clive Hart and David Hayman (eds.), *James Joyce's 'Ulysses': Critical Essays* (Berkeley and Los Angeles: University of California Press, 1974), 181–216.

When related to Malone, such practices look very striking. Joyce doubtless had some knowledge of Malone's editorial principles and practices. They were evident, and sometimes explicit, in his various editions of Shakespeare's plays. Furthermore, in his copy of Karl Elze's *William Shakespeare: A Literary Biography,* he would have found an account of Malone's importance, a description of his methods, and attempts to dispute some of Malone's premises and findings.[87] 'Scylla' seems to set out deliberately to put the tradition inaugurated by Malone into reverse. Where Malone wanted to purge Shakespeare of fabrications, contaminations, modernisms, alien additions, Joyce deliberately introduces them. Where Malone's was a labour of purification, Joyce's is one of corruption. In this respect, 'Scylla' might be compared to the work of Fleay and the Victorian 'disintegrators', about whom, again, Joyce would have known.[88] The disintegrators argued that various Shakespeare texts were 'impure'. There was much more material by other writers in Shakespeare's plays than had commonly been recognized, for example.[89] The disintegrators' case 'created a series of notable scandals' in England.[90] But what to them was an observable, textual fact, in 'Scylla', becomes active, a practice. Thus some of what seems to be Shakespeare turns out to be from someone else, like Spenser, for example. Shakespeare does not necessarily suffer in the process of adulteration, however. There are occasions when Stephen even *beautifies* him: the word 'firedrake', for example, as in 'A star, a daystar, a firedrake, rose at his birth' (9. 928–9), is used only once in the plays, in *Henry the Eighth,* where it is applied to a man with pustules on his face. So, too, Joyce sometimes echoes and affirms Shakespeare's lyricism in applying it evocatively to the poet's life and mind. Via *Cymbeline,* for example, the phrase 'An azured harebell like her veins' (9. 652) evokes brothers contemplating a woman's naked body. In context, this summons up both a fleeting image from Stephen's version of Shakespeare's

---

[87] See Elze, *William Shakespeare,* 6, 13 n. 1, 99–112, 305–6, 557, 562, and *passim.* Joyce clearly drew on Elze's book in composing 'Scylla'. See Michael Gillespie, 'Sources and the Independent Artist', *James Joyce Quarterly,* 20/3 (Spring 1983), 325–6, 331.

[88] From Elze. See *William Shakespeare,* 114, 188, 307, 348, 350, and esp. 356. For an account of the 'disintegrators' and the outcry against them, see Hugh Grady, *The Modernist Shakespeare* (Oxford: Clarendon Press, 1991), 47–56; and 'Disintegration and its Reverberations', in Marsden (ed.), *Appropriation of Sheakespeare* 111–24.

[89] The 'disintegrators' did not intend their work to be subversive: they wanted to purify 'a sacred text whose "authentic" message had been adulterated with non–authentic matter'. Grady, 'Disintegration', 117.   [90] Ibid. 111.

psychodrama, and its connection with a moment in his art. At the same time, however, the passage actually subordinates Shakespeare's lyricism to Stephen's. 'Scylla' also pays tribute to what is rare and strange in Shakespeare's work. Stephen relishes choice words, words used once and once only in the whole of Shakespeare's oeuvre: 'behoof' (9. 142), 'cerecloth' (9. 169), 'reverbed' (9. 1026). Yet the chapter also contains an ersatz version of that very practice. Some words sound both Shakespearean and choice, but are not in fact to be found in Shakespeare: 'brooding' (9. 346), which is Miltonic not Shakespearean; 'afterwit' (9. 1137), which is Elizabethan but not Shakespearean; 'parafes' (9. 1116), which—according to the *OED*—can be found in Evelyn as 'paraffs', but is not in Shakespeare; and 'spatchcocked' (9. 991), for which the *OED* cites Mahaffy, no less.

If there is one strict principle at stake in so complex a practice, it is the unremitting imperative of both fidelity to and a betrayal of Shakespeare. To take a tiny example: Joyce knew that Shakespeare often used two nouns in apposition in a way that gave the first an adjectival force. He uses examples in 'Scylla'. But some of the Shakespearean nouns in apposition in Joyce's chapter, like 'coistrel' (9. 455), 'meacock' (9. 938), and 'miscreant' (9. 373) do not appear in apposition in Shakespeare's plays. Textually and linguistically, the 'Scylla'–Shakespeare relation is a continually shifting one, in which there is a ceaseless play of correspondence and difference. Joyce does not share the assumptions—of unity, homogeneity, self-identity, the purity of 'the original'—that are fundamental to the work of Malone and late nineteenth- and early twentieth-century Shakespeareans. His chapter does not proceed on such a basis. Thus, if there is 'fenian' subversion of Shakespeare in 'Scylla', there is also a lyrical identification with him, a celebration of the beauty of Shakespearean language, an attempt to emulate it, a wicked production of neo-Shakespeareanisms, a use of Shakespeare against revivalist and English culture. The structure of the Stephen–Dowden opposition may appear fixed and unchanging. 'Scylla' establishes a very different relationship between English and Irish culture or the English and Irish genius. It does so not only by means of language but within it. The Shakespeare of 'Scylla' is profoundly pluralized, multi-purpose if you like, a Shakespeare with whom it is always possible to play, a plaything but also a playfellow. It is through the principle of play— the production of a multiplicity of contexts that is also a multiplicity of mind—that Joyce's chapter decisively progresses, not only beyond

Scylla and Charybdis, but beyond the very mode of formulating political and cultural issues symbolized in the Homeric choice.

But what happens to Shakespeare in Joyce and Stephen's hands in 'Scylla' may also have its analogy in the fate of many of the English in Ireland before the Statutes of Kilkenny in 1366. They were assimilated, adopting Irish customs and styles of hair and dress. They often married Irish girls, and spoke a language almost unintelligible to their fellow Englishmen. They even became bilingual. This did not mean they were unloved. The Statutes of Kilkenny put in place a system of segregation and caste intended to call a halt to such degenerate practices. 'National degeneration', of course, was an anxious concern of Raleigh's, as of many Englishmen and women in the period 1880–1920. Joyce puts the system of thought and value underlying that concern into radical question. 'Scylla' offers a miniature model to Ireland of how to settle for a feature of its history. So, too, in the spirit of Richard Kearney's marvellous, recent projection of a political future ahead for Europe's offshore archipelago, it might even conceivably be read as offering white England a lesson in how to stop worrying and learn to love its lack of identity.[91]

[91] 'Towards a Postnationalist Archipelago', *Edinburgh Review*, 103 (2000), 21–34.

CHAPTER FOUR

A Look Around: 'Wandering Rocks'

Between Two Roaring Worlds

In 'Scylla and Charybdis', Joyce begins a kind of work on English culture and English discourses that will come to dominate *Ulysses*. In the next chapter, however, he pauses, steps back, and takes 'a look around', as Stephen puts it (10. 826–7). Stephen is calling Parnell to mind. When others encouraged the latter to enter politics, Parnell initially resisted, saying 'I must look more around for myself first; I must see a little more how things are going'.[1] So, too, Stephen pauses on the threshold of a momentous decision, of departure and commitment to his Irish art, and *Ulysses* pauses and surveys the scene before embarking on the political and aesthetic project that constitutes its second half. 'Wandering Rocks' functions as an anatomy of colonial, Dublin culture, and the relationship of the macro- to the micropolitical within it. It starts with one of Ireland's two 'imperial masters' and finishes with the other. Church and State enclose or contain the rest of the chapter. The enclosure is not merely formal. Conmee and the Viceroy serve as tokens of the determining conditions within which everything else in the chapter takes place. But 'Wandering Rocks' is also very much concerned with the politics of personal relations, even psychological processes, as they are grasped in the moment, as fleeting phenomena in everyday life. It is about power in both the political and the personal realms; the way in which the structures of power in the second realm replicate, reflect, or are otherwise determined by those in the first. The chapter cuts laterally, showing power synchronically, in a varied but more or less simultaneous manifestation. This produces a complex and subtle account of

---

[1] See R. Barry O'Brien, *The Life of Charles Stewart Parnell*, pref. John E. Redmond MP (London: Thomas Nelson & Sons, 1910), 50.

the effects of a colonial culture on the minutiae of psychic, social, and affective life.

Here, as anywhere, power exists in specific formations, and Joyce presents them as pervasive. They are evident in economic relations, of course, but also in gender relations, sexual relations, the family, friendships, street encounters, bodies, lifestyles. One obvious feature of power in 'Wandering Rocks' is its fundamental imbalance. The final sequence in the chapter is stark testimony to this. But the imbalance is repeated in relationships throughout the chapter: Kernan and Crimmins, Mulligan and Haines, Simon and Dilly Dedalus, Boylan and Miss Dunne. Joyce underlines this and draws our attention to it. It makes social negotiations tricky, delicate, difficult, or strained in particular ways. Within those negotiations, a given range of responses is possible. Most importantly, the same imbalance prevails in the relationship between Church and State. Critics have often treated these two as though Joyce presented them as politically equivalent, in the chapter. But they are in fact quite different entities. Joyce's presentation of the State in the last sequence is purely external or macropolitical. The viceroys were by no means mere figureheads. They wielded considerable power on behalf of the crown.[2] 'Wandering Rocks' deals with a symbol of a power that is not only remote from daily Dublin life, but also so clearly superior in the political sense that it need only be represented symbolically. In the case of the Church, however, power is represented in Conmee, the individual priest seen in the midst of his daily business. Here the terms of the macropolitical are also micropolitical. The chapter begins with an image of secondary or derived rather than absolute power, and is concerned as much with Conmee's social, intellectual, cultural, and political servility as with his authority.

Take for instance the significance for Conmee of Bernard Vaughan and Mrs David Sheehy. The details of Conmee's brief recollection of Vaughan at 10. 33–8 are largely accurate.[3] But the actual reasons for Vaughan's 'love' of (and frequent visits to) Ireland are particularly revealing. On the one hand, the family were landowners there.[4] On

---

[2] See ibid. 320. Parnell emphasized the power of the viceroys, referring to Lord Spencer's, e.g. as 'despotic and unlimited' (ibid.).

[3] Vaughan was indeed of 'good family' (10. 38; Herefordshire gentry; he was educated at Stonyhurst). He put on a fake Cockney accent when delivering sermons in the East End.

[4] Bernard's father owned Rosstucker Castle. See C. C. Martindale, SJ, *Bernard Vaughan, S.J.* (London: Longmans, Green & Co., 1923), 147.

the other, Bernard and his brother Cardinal Herbert Vaughan
were Catholic zealots. As such, they were instances of a new and distinctive phenomenon. When Conmee refers to Vaughan as 'zealous'
(10. 36), he is conscious both of the word as coming from outside an
established Catholic vocabulary, and of it being associated with the
Vaughans in particular.[5] For their 'zeal' was an index of a new,
proselytizing, evangelical temper in the English Catholic Church.
Cardinal Vaughan founded the Society for Foreign Missions, with its
project for 'the evangelization of the heathen races . . . a totally new
idea to English Catholics'.[6] Bernard Vaughan was a puritanical,
pragmatic, utilitarian evangelist, with a sympathy for practical, business people which Joyce of course recalled in 'Grace'.[7] Vaughan once
told an audience of advertising men that he was one of them, since
his work meant 'advertising God'.[8] He was also reactionary in politics, a friend of Edward VII, and an ardent patriot who declared that
'with a right-minded Catholic, loyalty to the throne . . . must live
with his life, grow with his growth, and be stronger than death itself'.[9]

Bernard Vaughan features in 'Wandering Rocks' because he represents the historically specific form of a late Victorian, puritan,
English Catholicism whose inroads into the Irish Church Joyce was
much concerned with. It fitted in very well with the directions the
Church had been taking under Archbishop Cullen and since his
death. The mid- and late nineteenth-century, Cullenite Church was
characteristically puritanical and increasingly practical in its orientation. It was obsessed with decency, the 'cheerful decorum' that
Conmee so likes (10. 121).[10] Since the Famine, it had also become
very concerned both to counter and to emulate Protestantism as 'the
religion of those who had their way to make in the world, and who
did so most successfully'.[11] Thus when Cullen appeared in official re-
galia at the Lord Mayor's banquet, the *Catholic Directory* purred

[5] See e.g. Revd Mgr. Bernard Ward, *Cardinal Vaughan* (London: Catholic Truth Soc.,
1903), 13.   [6] Ibid. 7, 10.
[7] See Vaughan, *The Sins of Society* (London: Kegan Paul, Trench, Trübner & Co.,
1905), pp. xiii–xiv and *passim*. Cf. the Revd M. O'Riordan, who wrote approvingly of
priests who 'show remarkable business gifts and habits, and carry business transactions
through with unqualified success'. See *Catholicity and Progress in Ireland* (London: Kegan
Paul, Trench, Trübner & Co., 1905), 210.   [8] Martindale, *Bernard Vaughan*, 230.
[9] Vaughan, *Her Golden Reign: A Sermon* (London: Burns & Oates, 1887), 3.
[10] See K. Theodore Hoppen, *Ireland since 1800: Conflict and Conformity* (London:
Longman, 1989), 144–52.
[11] D. George Boyce, *Nineteenth-Century Ireland: The Search for Stability* (London: Gill
& Macmillan, 1990), 135.

with pleasure at the fact that ' "a prince of the church" ' had now ascended the dais 'next to the Lord Lieutenant, having on his arm Lady Rachel Butler, sister to Earl Russell, and chatting pleasantly with Lady Abercorn'.[12] The passage exactly captures the complicity that so exercised Joyce. The late nineteenth-century Church was markedly susceptible to a certain kind of English influence. Indeed, James Connolly suggested—as Joyce does—that the Church in Ireland had become the political accomplice of the State. Connolly even provided a potted history of Catholic complicity with the English in Ireland from 1177 to the fall of Parnell.[13] It is clear from Joyce's work that he would have endorsed much of it. Joyce sees Conmee as embodying the kind of collusion of Church with State excoriated by Connolly. It is evident in Conmee's obsequiousness and snobbery; in his valuation of Cunningham as a 'good practical catholic' (10. 5–6); in his little, mercenary impulses; in his planned trip to Buxton 'for the waters' (10. 20).That he is introduced as 'the superior . . . John Conmee S.J.' (10. 1; my italics) is clearly significant. But, though Conmee's affectation of superiority is rooted in substantial power, it also masks an essential submission. Conmee has the illusion that he is his own legislator: the phrase 'he knew' recurs throughout the first two hundred lines of the chapter. But, ironically, English voices insistently haunt the movements of his mind. In fact, he is one of those Joycean oppressors who are also 'gratefully oppressed', to quote 'After the Race' (D, 36). 'Coactus volui', mutters Cashel Boyle O'Connor Fitzmaurice Tisdall Farrell ('Coerced I willed it', 10. 1113). The first word obviously refers to British rule, evoking the British policies of coercion and the 'emergency legislation' of Coercion Acts restricting political and civil liberties to which Ireland was subjected repeatedly in the nineteenth century.[14] The phrase is indicative of much in 'Wandering Rocks'. Conmee is the type of its embodiment.

---

[12] W. E. Vaughan (ed.), A New History of Ireland, v. Ireland under the Union 1: 1801–1870 (Oxford: Clarendon Press, 1986), 737–8; quoted in Boyce, Nineteenth-Century Ireland, 136.

[13] See 'Labour, Nationality and Religion', in Selected Writings, ed. P. Berresford Ellis (Harmondsworth: Penguin, 1973), 57–117, esp. 60–4.

[14] According to Mrs Parnell, fifty Coercion Acts were passed between the Act of Union and 1882. See Katharine O'Shea, Charles Stewart Parnell: His Love Story and Political Life (2 vols., London: Cassell & Co., 1914), i. 273. Joyce had both volumes in Trieste. The most infamous of the Acts—and the one chiefly identified with coercion—was Forster's Bill of 1881. It suspended Habeas Corpus and substantially fuelled the Parnellite cause.

Various historical viceroys are lurking in the background of 'Wandering Rocks'. Conmee is especially conscious of the Talbot family, which was much associated with the viceregal position (10. 155–7). He recalls their title, 'Lord Talbot de Malahide, immediate hereditary lord admiral of Malahide'. But Joyce was surely also aware that the family were actually granted the title because John Talbot, Earl of Shrewsbury was notably ruthless and effective in 'reducing the turbulent Irish septs to submission' under Henry V and Henry VI.[15] Not surprisingly, Conmee's sentimental reflections ignore this fact. Conmee is the latest historical incarnation of the 'compromise bargain' that, for Joyce, as for Connolly, Séan O'Faolain, and others, the Church had repeatedly made with the Ascendancy and/or the British throne. The 'bargain' was made at the expense of the Irish people, and was itself a second-order replica of the British tradition of partial union of Church and State.[16] It had taken on a new dimension with the deals Peel had done with the Catholic hierarchy in the 1840s to undermine O'Connell. Peel expressly sought to 'Anglicize the Hierarchy'.[17] In a similar fashion, Gladstone had conducted clandestine negotiations with the Church behind Parnell's back in the 1880s.[18] Joyce hears the 'compromise bargain' in a tone and language—Conmee's—that are paradigmatic, as the *Irish Catholic Directory and Almanac* for 1904 amply demonstrates.[19] Conmee's genteel exchange with Mrs David (Bessie) Sheehy (10. 18–29) is fitting. For there are precise analogies between the progress of the Church under Cullen and the progress of Mr David Sheehy MP. Sheehy moved from being a member of the Irish Republican Brotherhood and an ardent Parnellite to taking the Catholic and clericalist position on Parnell. In *States of Ireland*, Sheehy's grandson, Conor Cruise O'Brien, actually imagines Bessie as persuading her husband into his act of betrayal.[20] Sheehy went on to become a Redmondite and 'a respectable, Victorian Catholic' father of

---

[15] William Francis Collier, *History of Ireland for Schools* (London: Marcus Ward & Co., 1884), 82–3. Joyce had Collier's book in his Trieste library.

[16] See Paul Blanshard, *The Irish and Catholic Power* (London: Derek Verschoyle, 1954), 63–5.

[17] R. Barry O'Brien, *Dublin Castle and the Irish People* (2nd edn., London: Kegan Paul, Trench, Trübner & Co., 1912), 57.   [18] See O'Shea, *Parnell*, ii. 13.

[19] Note e.g. its mixture of religion and English commerce, its unctuous account of Edward VII, and the coy references to Cardinal Logue's connections with Westminster. See *The Irish Catholic Directory and Almanac* (Dublin: J. Duffy and Co., 1904), 439, 441, 442, and *passim*.   [20] See *States of Ireland* (St Albans: Panther, 1974), 33–5.

a family.[21] That family was a part of a rising, national, bourgeois elite that had been developing since the 1870s and was heavily English-influenced. It had been kept from real power by the Protestants, but was also detested by many nationalists.[22] Its logical ally was therefore the Catholic hierarchy, and Joyce points to their intimate complicity.

But the elite in question was deeply compromised. With 'the overthrow of the landlord garrison', wrote Francis Sheehy-Skeffington, England was simply 'building up for herself a new garrison in the Catholic hierarchy'. Thus, at the turn of the century, the ecclesiastical power 'was ranged on the side of England'.[23] Joyce is much concerned with this collusion as represented in the figure of Conmee. By contrast, the end of the chapter is a bald summation of the power that winds through the lives of the Dubliners as the cavalcade winds its way through the city. That power has already been visible in many details, like the collocation at Trinity of British soldiery—the Scotsmen rendered as 'gillies', faithful retainers to a landowning class, 'smuggling' their 'implements of music' into a beleaguered fort—and 'carfuls' of 'palefaces' (English tourists, 10. 340–66).[24] The Dubliners respond to the cavalcade in various ways. But what is most important about it is simply the fact that it traverses Dublin. It is there for everyone, however they choose to respond to it, and they are tightly constrained by what it represents.

The constraints operate in different ways, however. There are those who simply work for the State, like Kelleher, or 'Castle Catholics' such as Cunningham, who is sufficiently identified with State power to get an obsequious salute from the policeman as he passes 'out of the Castleyard gate' (10. 957). There are also those who exhibit the same servility as Conmee, if in different forms. One of the principal symbolic figures in 'Wandering Rocks' is the 'lacquey' viewing himself in a mirror (10. 643–4). The point about Mulligan,

---

[21] *States of Ireland* (St Albans: Panther, 1974), 35.

[22] See Michael J. F. McCarthy, *The Irish Revolution*, i. *The Murdering Time, from the Land League to the Present* (London and Edinburgh: William Blackwood & Sons, 1912), 31. Joyce had McCarthy's book in Trieste.

[23] Quoted in Blanshard, *Irish and Catholic Power*, 64.

[24] Joyce is alluding to Trinity College's long, historical connection with the English garrison (for which see Brigid Redmond, *The Story of Dublin: City and County* (Dublin: Browne and Nolan, 1921), 89) and its historical usefulness as a loyalist stronghold. He may also have been thinking of its strategic significance during the Easter Rising. See another book he had in Trieste, John F. Boyle, *The Irish Rebellion of 1916: A Brief History of the Revolt and its Suppression* (London: Constable & Co., 1916), 70.

in this respect, is summed up in the fact that, in his eagerness to please Haines, he even helps the waitress 'to unload her tray' (10. 1081), momentarily becoming her fellow servant. Joyce harps on Mulligan's dandyish primrose waistcoat for two reasons. The first is to remind us that Mulligan is replicating Wilde's servile role as court jester to the English. The second is to tell us that he is yellow-bellied (as, in 'Scylla', Joyce uses Dante to inform the reader that Eglinton is talking through his arse: '*Ed egli avea del cul fatto trombetta*', 9. 34). Ned Lambert is equally concerned to curry favour with the Protestant clergyman Hugh C. Love in a context strewn with reminders of the colonial presence, from Love's interest in historical members of the Fitzgerald family, to the 'floats' (10. 434–5) whose self-advertisement in English was once required by colonial legislation.[25] Tom Kernan is similarly afflicted: he recalls his interview with the Protestant Crimmins[26] as a triumph of obsequiousness and fake gentility in which he 'sirred' Crimmins as repetitively as Lambert sirs Hugh C. Love, seeking deftly to play on what he takes to be Crimmins's anti-agrarian prejudices ('Those farmers are always grumbling', 10. 723–4). Indeed, in so far as Kernan owes his high spirits to anything but gin, it is to his desperate conviction that he can play posh with the best. He deems his coat 'stylish' enough (10. 743), for example, to have attracted the attention of John Mulligan, 'the manager of the Hibernian bank' (10. 746). Joyce simply lets Kernan undermine himself: his belief that he has the bearing of a '[r]eturned Indian officer' (10. 756) is due partly to his 'high colour' (10. 755), and therefore to nothing classier than an alcoholic past.

Must Dress the Character

For Kernan, Mulligan, and many others, what is at issue is partly the question of *advantage*. In a colonial society in which, in the most important respect, significant power is all on one side—in which, for the majority, the reality is disempowerment—social relations involve

---

[25] That Lambert should have a '*pliant* lath' that he raises 'in salute' may clearly be pointedly contrasted with Stephen's ashplant with 'ferrule . . . *squealing*' (10. 401–2; cf. 1. 627–8; my italics).

[26] On Crimmins's Protestantism, see Don Gifford with Robert J. Seidman, '*Ulysses*' *Annotated: Notes for James Joyce's* 'Ulysses' (rev. edn., Berkeley and Los Angeles: University of California Press, 1988), 273.

constant little calculations of or tussles for advantage: tussles for power through financial gain, however small, or through claims to status, however trivial. Such tussles are determined by a context in which chronic disadvantage is the norm. As has often been remarked, *Ulysses* shows little overt awareness of Dublin's urban poor as such. This might seem to be the more striking in that, as commentators of the time pointed out, they were scarcely to be avoided. 'In most cities', remarked the *Report upon the State of Health in the City of Dublin for the Year 1903*, 'the purlieus are in a limited number of districts, but in Dublin they are to be met with everywhere'.[27] The report stressed that, in Dublin, unlike other British cities, there was little sense of the poorer classes being segregated or screened off from other citizens. From the Famine onwards, the poor, homeless, rural families arriving in Dublin had not gravitated towards a ghetto or ghettos, but had often taken over the grand houses left untenanted by wealthier and more powerful families after the demise of the Irish parliament.[28] The poor were likely to be down any alley and round every corner. In one respect, though, at least, the closeness of dereliction and destitution is vividly evident in *Ulysses* as a whole and 'Wandering Rocks' in particular. The contemporary reports on public health were compiled by the Sir Charles Cameron who features in 'Wandering Rocks' (10. 538). Many of what they identify as the problems of impoverished, working-class life in Dublin were either incipient or real problems for the declining middle class, and the chapter alludes to a range of them. Tuberculosis accounted for nearly twice as many deaths as all other infectious diseases combined, and showed no sign of the long-term decline evident everywhere else in Britain.[29] Respiratory complaints were the most common form of illness in Dublin.[30] Hence the references to Flynn's snuffle (10. 479), Lenehan's wheezing (10. 544) and his 'shrinking' body (10. 565), the shopman's coughing (10. 632), the phthisic O'Molloy's 'white careworn face' (10. 236), Barlow's asthma, and so on. Apart from respiratory and circulatory illnesses, the most common causes of death were 'convulsions and other diseases of the brain and nervous sys-

[27] Sir Charles A. Cameron, *Report upon the State of Health in the City of Dublin for the Year 1903* (Dublin: John Falconer, 1904), 100.   [28] See Redmond, *Dublin*, 86.
[29] See Ruth Barrington, *Health, Medicine and Politics in Ireland 1900–1970* (Dublin: Criterion Press, 1987), 13.
[30] See Cameron, *Report upon the State of Public Health in the City of Dublin for the Year 1904* (Dublin: John Falconer, 1905), 31–2 and *passim*.

tem' as instanced in the chapter by Farrell. The major Dublin diseases were often alcohol-related, and the public health reports repeatedly connected the dietary, nutritional, and health problems of the poor with a preference for alcohol over 'wholesome and abundant food'.[31] Here we have Simon Dedalus's shaking hand (10. 700) and the memory of a 'boosed' Paddy Dignam (10. 1167–9). The reports also stressed deformities resulting from poor seating in schools, like 'curvature of the spine'[32] which Simon Dedalus sees as likely to be Dilly's problem (10. 662; cf. Doran's 'humpiness', 10. 985; and Dollard's 'bockedy' gait, 10. 897). Dental problems and eye problems are likewise referred to in the chapter: Rochford's eyes,[33] the shopman's 'ruined mouth' (10. 596–7) and 'eyes bleared with old rheum' (10. 640). Dublin 'was very unhealthy indeed, with a much higher death rate than the worst English or Scottish cities'.[34] Thus 'Wandering Rocks' presents a world of the fragile, handicapped, or ailing. Lack of power is a literal, physical fact. Here, if anywhere, in Foucauldian terms, is a stark, Joycean 'anatomo-' or 'bio-politics'.[35]

The lack of adequate clothing was repeatedly noted as a cause of ill health. As 'Wandering Rocks' makes us aware, the use of second-hand clothes was very common. It aided the spread of disease.[36] Another worry was insanitary practices, of which the shopman would presumably be a good example (10. 632–6). The widespread habit of casual spitting increased the spread of tuberculosis.[37] Yet another concern was poor arrangements for sewage, a cause of enteric fever.[38] It is significant that Simon Dedalus finally offers to treat Dilly to a glass of milk (10. 706–7): insufficient supplies of milk, or milk that was tainted, were common causes of sickness, especially among children.[39] The reports even comment at length on the culture of the

---

[31] Cameron, *Report upon the State of Public Health in the City of Dublin for the Year 1902* (Dublin: Cahill & Co., 1903), 30. The reports suggested that the preference stemmed in large measure from the urge to escape appalling living conditions for the relative warmth, comfort, and spaciousness of the pub. [32] Cameron, *Report 1904*, 94.

[33] Rochford's damaged sight is not referred to directly in the section of the chapter in which he features (10. 465–503), but the recurrent use of 'see' and the references to him 'ogling' and 'peering' are clearly allusions to it.

[34] Mary E. Daly, *Dublin, the Deposed Capital: A Social and Economic History 1860–1914* (Cork: Cork University Press, 1984), 2.

[35] For these terms in context, see Michel Foucault, *The History of Sexuality*, i. *Introduction*, trans. R. Hurley (Harmondsworth: Penguin, 1990), 139 and *passim*.

[36] See Cameron, *Report 1902*, 42–3. [37] See Barrington, *Health*, 13.

[38] See Cameron, *Report 1902*, 73; cf. *Ulysses*, 10. 1197.

[39] See Cameron, *Report 1904*, 74.

pawnshop as a damaging factor in the life of the poor. For many, the trips to the pawnshop were part of a weekly cycle which allowed them to live a few days in advance of their wages.[40] The auction, by contrast (as in 'Wandering Rocks'), was a sign that a family was definitively on the slide.

The possibility of infection decidedly lurks in the nooks and crannies of 'Wandering Rocks'. The 'porksteaks' with which young Patrick Dignam is trotting home (10. 1121–3) may well have come from one of the many pigs kept in Dublin backyards, about which the health inspectors complained. Since they were collected on 'unwholesome sandflats . . . breathing upward sewage breath' (3. 150–1), even the eleven cockles in the 'midwife's bag' (10. 820) are likely to be polluted, another danger about which the reports warned. ('Poor man O'Connor wife and five children poisoned by mussels here', Bloom reflects, in 'Nausicaa'. 'The sewage. Hopeless', 13. 1332–3.) The spectre of social disaster is uncomfortably close to many of the characters. The end of the chapter makes us aware of a social gulf: Dudley was a Tory appointment and immensely affluent, even by viceregal standards. His wife was socially strikingly success- ful, and turned 'the Dublin season' into 'one of splendour'.[41] In fact, wealth and social glamour were the two features most associated with Dudley's tenure. The concluding sequence in 'Wandering Rocks' alludes to this. Here a social division is confirmed and made absolute. But in crucial respects there is also strikingly little real dif- ference between Joyce's characters and the class supposedly 'be- neath' them. The gap between a small elite and others is beyond all closing. But otherwise, class difference is a fragile or notional con- struction. Class distinction is *itself* a phantom production, an insub- stantial replica of power relations whose 'truth' is elsewhere. Justice and decency are subject to the same irony, the same phantasmatic re- fraction. It is not surprising that the Lord-Lieutenant is setting out to open a bazaar to raise funds for Mercer's Hospital. The health report for 1904 specifically identified it as in need of 'modernization'.[42] Joyce deliberately put the cavalcade into the novel, though none had

---

[40] See Cameron, *Report 1903*, 102–3. Interestingly, however, Cameron actually defends the pawnbrokers.

[41] See Charles O'Mahony, *The Viceroys of Ireland* (London: John Long, 1912), 323.

[42] Cameron, *Report 1904*, 54. The *Report* mentions the bazaar. The other hospital identified as in urgent need of improvement was Holles Street (ibid. 55–6), which had a dispensary next to the mortuary.

taken place. The point is that this colonial administration makes insignificant, token gestures towards repairing a situation for which the greater power it represents must also be held partly responsible, not least economically.

To return to Connolly again: his ideas and vocabulary are most likely to have reached Joyce between 1897 and 1903.[43] In that period, one of Connolly's terms for the condition of colonial Ireland was misery.[44] The same word bursts into Stephen's mind at a psychologically crucial moment in 'Wandering Rocks' (10. 880). In a culture intrinsically so perverted, the spectre of misery is never far off. Gaining or sustaining an advantage may often merely mean avoiding brutalization, staving off complete dereliction, or maintaining sufficient face to function. Thus in 'Wandering Rocks', minds tend to dwell on fantasies of rank or social elevation. Indeed, the micropolitical formations evident here are partly questions of certain modes of fantasy. The chapter is much concerned with the colonial imaginary. Miss Dunne, for instance, is reading *The Woman in White*, presumably having expected it to be a sentimental romance. But it is evidently above her head and she finds it irksome (10. 371–2). Her choice of it, however, is connected to her interest in Shannon and 'the boatclub swells' (10. 385).[45] She has apparently no interest in the image of a resourceful, independent-minded woman provided by Collins's Marian Halscombe, but likes the novels of 'Mary Cecil Haye' (10. 372). Her preference, here, is surely for works like *Nora's Love Test*. Nora is an ordinary Irish girl who longs for England but is deemed to know 'no more than an English servant' and promises to be an object of mirth to English ladies. However, she finally and triumphantly discovers that she is in fact the daughter of an English lord, and ends the novel happily united

[43] See Peter Costello, *James Joyce: The Years of Growth 1882–1915* (London: Kyle Cathie, 1992), 214–15. Like Joyce's, Connolly's project partly involved opening up nationalist tradition insofar as it was monolithic. He insisted that the interests of the poor and working classes were not necessarily identical with those of republican nationalism, as they appeared to be in the late 19th cent. See Desmond Fennell, 'Irish Socialist Thought', in Richard Kearney (ed.), *The Irish Mind: Exploring Intellectual Traditions* (Dublin: Wolfhound Press, 1985), 188–208, esp. 199–204.

[44] See e.g. Connolly, 'Socialism and Nationalism', in *Selected Writings*, 121–4, at 122; and 'Socialism and Irish Nationalism' in *Selected Writings*, 125–8, at 125.

[45] The 'swells' may very well belong to the Royal Yacht Club, the Royal St George, or the Royal Irish, all of which were located at Kingstown. See Samuel A. Ossory Fitzpatrick, *Dublin: A Historical and Topographical Account of the City* (London: Methuen, 1907), 336. Alternatively, they may be Trinity oarsmen from the Dublin University Boat Club.

with an English gentleman who wears 'that unequivocal stamp of lofty society'.[46] Joyce's point is that Miss Dunne's fantasy of social ascent spells self-division and the adoption of contradictory agendas. The colonial subject is alienated in the image of another she not only aspires to be but also seeks to mimic. Dilly Dedalus's equivalents of *The Woman in White* are her Chardenal's French primer and poignant 'pinchbeck bracelet' (10. 860–1). The pathos of ornamentation—and the desperate thinness of the imaginary it represents—are starkly evident, here. It is cruelly ironic that Dilly should finger the bracelet as a 'late lieabed under a quilt of old overcoats' (10. 860), in a parodic version of a posture of indulgent ease. In reality, the family is disintegrating as an economic unit. Dilly is a 'late lieabed' simply to stay warm, and her 'quilt' is a makeshift substitute for proper bedclothes.

So, too, characters dress poverty up or deck it out in the trappings of affluence, if only by way of language or conceits: 'What's the time by your gold watch and chain?' Lenehan asks M'Coy, to which the latter replies by peering 'into Marcus Tertius Moses' sombre office, then at O'Neill's clock' (10. 507–9). Unsurprisingly, a page later, in his account of the Glencree reformatory dinner, Lenehan rapidly promotes himself from 'chief bottlewasher' to an invited guest ('Lashings of stuff we put up: port wine and sherry and curaçoa to which we did ample justice', 10. 546–8). Bloom is no different: the point about *Sweets of Sin* is the intimate combination of sexual with social and economic markers in the fantasy it purveys. That Bloom turns to a passage describing lavish expenditure on a woman with '*opulent* curves' whose attractiveness is partly to do with her '*sabletrimmed wrap*' and '*queenly shoulders*' is no accident (10. 612–16). In 'Wandering Rocks', 'advantages' are either depressingly mean, or exist only in fantasy. Yet they are nonetheless keenly pursued. Indeed, the urgency with which characters chase small, temporary gains in money, power, and even identity is in direct proportion to their distance from real power. The pawnshop—for Stephen, one symbol of Ireland (2. 47)—is a metaphor for this. In 'Wandering Rocks', it is not only very important in the lives of the Dedalus family. Significantly, the very pawnbroker who has disappointed Boody and Maggie Dedalus (10.

---

[46] Mary Cecil Hay, *Nora's Love Test* (London: John Maxwell and Co., 1878), 40, 149.

266–9) shares a moment of formal, social recognition with Conmee, and has a 'queenly mien' (10. 61–7).[47]

The more powerlessness is a condition of social life, the more the little remnants of power come to matter. Thus the different Dubliners in 'Wandering Rocks' strike their own forms of 'compromise bargain' with the State. That the characters seem ordinary and likeable and yet their temporizations so questionable is exactly the point. In a culture that is intrinsically pathological and extreme, definitively riven, exposed to bizarre distortion by the colonial intrusion, the most mundane engagements are likely to assume outlandish dimensions. Take gender relations: Boylan deploys his 'gallantry' briefly to exploit the 'young pullet' in Thornton's and apparently get something for nothing (10. 327–36). Similarly, Lenehan comforts himself with a story at Bloom's expense that also involves a fantasy of having half-seduced Molly. It even entails an amusing but pathetically nostalgic recollection of phallic power ('The lad stood to attention anyhow, he said with a sigh', 10. 566). As often, a small claim to 'strength' immediately reverses into its opposite. The memory of sexual excitement begins to stimulate Lenehan again, only to usher in a religious vocabulary (10. 559–60). Furthermore, the comfort he derives from his tale is so slight that the merest fear that M'Coy might disapprove is enough to make him change tack (10. 578–83). More painfully, the confrontation between Simon and Dilly involves them trying to outbid each other in the power stakes, both claiming that the other is a public embarrassment and a disgrace, Dilly occupying the moral high ground, Simon appealing to caste and finally resorting to threats and patriarchal brutality. Even little Patrick Dignam turns out to be calculating his advantages, recognizing how much freer he is likely to be, now his father has died ('I could easy do a bunk on ma', 10. 1137).

The discourse of the chapter, however, is not moralistic but diagnostic. 'Wandering Rocks' shows how far Joyce worked in a different direction to the moralists of the English novel ('I have little or nothing to learn from English novelists', he wrote, to Stanislaus, *Letters* ii. 186). The chapter does not ask us to peer down on its Irish characters with Olympian scorn, as a not-so-venerable critical tradition

---

[47] The reference to 'cess' is surely not coincidental: the word originally referred to a form of English levy or taxation. See Collier, *History of Ireland*, 121. The Irish 'cess' was first imposed by the Tudors, and blatantly favoured the crown and its representatives.

sometimes used to suggest. It rather ostentatiously brackets its Dubliners' predicaments between representatives of institutional structures. It gives precise indications of the political context most relevant to the various characters' manoeuvrings. 'Wandering Rocks' is concerned with the politics of the personal, the forces at work in the minutiae of social relations in a given historical society and culture. Joyce articulates the relevant micropolitical structures of power partly through parallels or sequential replications. O'Molloy, for example, is trying to borrow from Lambert the money he couldn't get from Crawford in 'Aeolus', so the structure of the relationship between Love and Lambert is effectively replicated in that between Lambert and O'Molloy, but with Lambert in the position of power and playing the dominant role. We might be reminded of 'Counterparts', where Farrington's humiliation at the hands of his Protestant boss leads to his violent humiliation of his own child. In both cases, Joyce's concern is with a micropolitical *formation* determined by the parenthesis which has Conmee at one end and the Viceroy at the other. This is the principal significance of a narrative technique involving fragmentation, but also simultaneity and an 'interfolding' of the fragments, the circulation or permutation of repetitive elements. The technique corresponds to a representation, not only of the political hegemony of the two 'imperial masters', but also of a kind of false community that results from it, a community whose determining condition is complicity, and whose more pronounced features therefore include disintegration, alienation, false consciousness, the failure of real community.

Cold Specks of Fire

In this respect, the Dublin of the Parnellite 1880s hangs like a shadow over the chapter. For there had been a radical shift in the political culture of the metropolis. For much of the 1880s, the political life of Dublin was characterized by a dynamic conflict triggered by Parnell that must have seemed remote enough, by 1904. Above all, the Castle administration and Dublin Corporation repeatedly collided. The importance of street names in 'Wandering Rocks' has been noted.[48]

⁴⁸ See Len Platt, *Joyce and the Anglo-Irish: A Study of Joyce and the Literary Revival* (Amsterdam and Atlanta, Ga.: Rodopi, 1998), 88.

What the narrator calls 'O'Connell bridge' (10. 599), for example, is 'Carlisle bridge' to Kernan (10. 747), as is appropriate, given the latter's own kind of 'compromise bargain'. So, too, Simon Dedalus's reference to 'the gutter in O'Connell street' (10. 703)—not Sackville Street, as loyalists and residents had it—is an index both of his political allegiances and his prospects.[49] The significant context, here, is the struggle over street names that began in December 1884, when the Corporation decided to rename certain Dublin streets after nationalist patriots. According to McCarthy, street names had previously indicated 'the continuous loyalty of its Corporation to the English connection' and were 'almost a complete index to the Lords-Lieutenants'.[50] Nationalists wanted them changed. The very struggle over the issue indicated a historically decisive shift: Mansion House and the Corporation had come under popular control. Ordinary Dubliners could now feel that they had a share in political power. Hence the importance of memories of the Glencree Reformatory dinner both in 'Wandering Rocks' (10. 536 ff.) and *Ulysses* as a whole.[51] The result of the shift in power was that the democratically inclusive Mansion House emerged as a political rival to the socially exclusive Castle. When the Dublin Metropolitan Police at one point went on strike, the Lord-Lieutenant and Lord Mayor issued separate proclamations enrolling special constables. Both loyalists and nationalists went out on the beat, and there were hostile encounters between them.[52] In 'Wandering Rocks', by contrast, the relaxed if furtive exchange between Kelleher and Constable 57C (10. 217–26) indicates the corrupt, heavily politicized, 'military prone' police force that was mostly characteristic of late nineteenth- and early twentieth-century Dublin.[53]

Of course, the shift from the riven but politically vital Dublin of the 1880s to the Dublin of 1904 is represented in a council meeting

---

[49] On the politics of O'Connell Street, see McCarthy, *Irish Revolution*, i. 364.

[50] See ibid. From the 1880s, the renaming of streets appeared to be an important symbol of the retreat of loyalist power.

[51] The dinner took place in 1894 (8. 158–60), which makes it look like a late token of fast receding hopes for greater democracy and the breaking down of political barriers. It is the sense of a new dispensation—even if crumbling—that makes Molly so impressed by the luxury of the occasion (18. 427–34). Paddy Dignam, Ben Dollard, and Simon Dedalus could hardly have hoped to attend such an occasion in 1904.

[52] See McCarthy, *Irish Revolution*, i. 285.

[53] On which see Séamus Breathnach, *The Irish Police from Earliest Times to the Present Day* (Dublin: Anvil, 1974), 45 and *passim*.

with 'nothing in order' and the Mayor 'in Llandudno' (10. 1008–10). But Joyce is not principally concerned with a declension into political paralysis. He is rather interested in a continuity which his novel massively aids and abets. 'Wandering Rocks' is less about the miserable failure of the politically recalcitrant spirit that had been evident in Dublin in the 1880s than its mutations in the less hopeful years that followed. Many of the political preoccupations of the Dublin of the 1880s are still evident in the chapter: the 'ejectment' of tenants for non-payment of rents, for example, an issue in rural Ireland, but also one into which civic figures were repeatedly drawn, and another source of conflict between Castle and Corporation.[54] It had ample urban parallels. Thus 'Wandering Rocks' evokes the ' "antipathy to a bailiff or process-server" ' that had long been traditional as a result of rural evictions (10. 934–6).[55] The insistent emphasis on the 'outriders' to the cavalcade (10. 794) and their 'clatter of horsehoofs' (10. 1031) likewise summons up a controversy of the 1880s. It was Spencer who first introduced a viceregal military escort which 'surrounded' him in his 'excursions through the streets of Dublin'.[56] It was hated by Dubliners, for whom it was a token of his alienation from and distrust of themselves.

It might nonetheless seem as though, in 1904, any continuity with the Dublin of the 1880s is largely submerged in complicities. Connolly offered a sober assessment of the 'neo-colonial' condition of Irish political culture at the turn of the century.[57] He argued that colonialism had so deeply pervaded Irish life that the end of colonial rule would not signify an end to English political and cultural power. England would still dominate Ireland 'through the whole array of . . . institutions she has planted in this country'.[58] There was no question of the noble Irish rising up triumphantly from under an ignoble yoke. The colonial 'enslavement and subjection' of the Irish had meant a

---

[54] See McCarthy, *Irish Revolution*, 83–6.

[55] See ibid. 85. He is quoting a Mr Shaw, 'nominal leader of the [Home Rule] party and chairman of the Munster Bank'. [56] O'Brien, *Parnell*, 321.

[57] Anderson sees Connolly as an early witness to 'the process that is now known as neo-colonialism'. W. K. Anderson, *James Connolly and the Irish Left* (Blackrock: Irish Academic Press, 1994), 43.

[58] *The Workers' Republic*, 16, (13 Oct. 1900), 6. The two most significant 'institutions' of this kind were class divisions and private property, which Connolly saw as alien impositions on Brehon law and the communal structures of Gaelic civilization. See 'Socialism and Nationalism', 124; and Kieran Allen, *The Politics of James Connolly* (London: Pluto, 1990), 35–6.

profound subjugation, to which reconstruction would be the only plausible response. The glorious tradition of heroes and martyrs was much less important than a 'distinct and definite' set of responses 'to the problems of the present'.[59] For Connolly, of course, the answer lay in the Irish proletariat, which—for all his emphasis on the reconstruction of the Irish—he understood to be already constituted as such. Joyce's view was different: the Irish proletariat had still 'to be created' (*Letters* ii. 187). He anticipated the emergence of an authentic proletariat as an index of a modernized, industrialized, independent Ireland. But he also saw that an Irish proletariat would have to be *sui generis*, that its distinctive Irishness still remained to be 'forged'.

For the emphasis on the *creation* of Ireland is persistent in Joyce's work. It surely underlay his choice of aesthetic rather than political labour. He recognized how crucial aesthetic activity might be to postcolonial Ireland, to its emancipation and political prospects. It might serve as a paradigm, might even *produce* the difference that could not be guaranteed as a consequence of liberation or political revolution. Joyce's and Connolly's projects were obviously distinct. But in some ways, 'Wandering Rocks' moves in Connolly's direction, affectively if not ideologically. To overemphasize this, however, is again to pitch the chapter too much in the mode of negative critique. For it also flickers with resistance to the political and cultural authority of the colonial power. For all his antipathy to dissidence, for example, at one point, Kernan is momentarily caught up in thoughts of Lord Edward Fitzgerald and rebellion (10. 785–90). Any attraction to Fitzgerald that Kernan is capable of feeling is largely snobbish and sentimental. Fitzgerald was 'on the wrong side' (10. 789–90). Nonetheless, the suggestion is that false consciousness is never total. Its relations with what it seeks to smother are heterogeneous, and ensure the survival of a residue of the subversive impulse, if only in alien form. There is a similar contradiction between John Wyse Nolan's affected 'elegance' of manner and his 'unfriendliness' towards the viceregal procession (10. 980, 1036); between Simon Dedalus's heterodoxy and his snobbish disdain for family 'inferiors' (10. 657–9, 695, 715–16); and between Lambert's obsequious attitude to Love and the zest with which he tells the story of the Great Earl and Cashel Cathedral (10. 444–6). Haines argues that 'the sense . . . of

---

[59] Connolly, 'Socialism and Nationalism', 121.

retribution' is missing in the Irish (10. 1083–4). But 'Wandering Rocks' suggests the reverse: the will to retribution is precisely what survives beneath the ashen surface of post-Parnellite Dublin. The flickers of recalcitrance are indicative of a space in which the possibility of disruption, upheaval, even change or transformation continues to exist.

There is in fact an irregular pattern of tiny refluxes in the chapter, little pockets of defiance of the larger powers. In this context, the Geraldines sentimentalized by Hugh C. Love are important figures, especially Silken Thomas. Several features of the latter's rebellion are relevant, here. In the council chamber at St Mary's, in a famous gesture, Thomas flung the sword of state on the table in front of the assembled archbishops and English dignitaries. He thus renounced all allegiance to the English monarch. He also took Church as much as State as his enemy, notably in the person of John Allen, Archbishop of Dublin and special friend of Cardinal Wolsey. More flagrantly than the Great Earl, whom Lambert also mentions (10. 447–8), Thomas defied the two 'imperial masters'. His rebellion appeared to spell the collapse of English rule in Ireland. Conversely, up until Silken Thomas's rebellion, English power had been narrowly confined. In 1515, the Pale was merely sixty miles by thirty. The rebellion left Henry VIII with no choice. He had either to quit Ireland or to conquer, subdue, and 'plant' it.[60] Silken Thomas is therefore a key figure in Irish history.[61] He is significant, too, in another respect: by the time of his rebellion, the Fitzgeralds had become striking examples of the 'degenerate English' whom I mentioned at the end of Chapter 3, that is, Anglo-Normans who had been 'Irishised'.[62] They married Irish girls, fostered their children with Gaelic families, and employed Gaelic harpers.[63] Silken Thomas spoke Irish—his supporters did not understand English.[64] He thus represents the reverse of the process that has moulded so many of the characters in 'Wandering Rocks': where their identity is heavily overdetermined by the colonizer's culture, the Fitzgeralds were assimilated by the Irish. Silken Thomas

---

[60] Brian FitzGerald, *The Geraldines: An Experiment in Irish Government 1169–1601* (London: Staples Press, 1951), 228.

[61] The name was still familiar enough to serve as a soubriquet. The Thomas O'Hagan of 'Aeolus', e.g. was known as 'Silken Thomas', partly because he was 'silvertongued' (7. 707). See McCarthy, *Irish Revolution*, i. 207.

[62] Of course, strictly speaking, and significantly, the Geraldines were Cambro-Normans, half-Celtic from the start (FitzGerald, *Geraldines*, 228).

[63] See ibid. 228–9.   [64] See ibid. 206.

was thrice a rebel: like other Geraldines, he joined the Irish in opposing attempts made by the feudal English monarchs and English merchants to dominate Ireland politically. He resisted English attempts
to proscribe Irish habits in the Anglo-Irish, identified the Church
with English power, and fought both together.

So much was also true of the Great Earl, which is surely one reason
why Joyce has Lambert tell his anecdote about Cashel Cathedral.
The Great Earl was often linked to Parnell.[65] Both were referred to as
'The Uncrowned King of Ireland'.[66] The Great Earl and Silken
Thomas were viceroys of a very different kind to Dudley. In important respects, the Fitzgeralds were decidedly not the 'personable' figures on whom Love fondly meditates (10. 930). They were proud,
unregenerate, intractable, and sometimes wild in their refusal of the
English yoke. This is relevant to 'Wandering Rocks' in that it is much
concerned with a vestigial, contemporary residue of this spirit of revolt. The latter is most obviously represented in Stephen. His principal concern in his part of the chapter (10. 800–80) is the political,
historical, and cultural power of the two imperial masters and its destructive effects: 'I between them. Where? Between two roaring
worlds where they swirl, I. Shatter them, one and both. But stun myself too in the blow. Shatter me you who can. Bawd and butcher were
the words. I say! Not yet awhile. A look around' (10. 823–7). Stephen
is still much concerned with the need to kill the inner priest and king,
but also aware of his own complicity with them, and therefore also of
the enormity of his task. It is between these two poles—resistance
and the problematic awareness of complicity—that the rest of
Ulysses will in some sense operate. Here, the dominant tone is one of
adamant rebellion. It is reinforced as such by Stephen's dismissive
mimicry of what he imagines to be Haines's polite surprise at his
thoughts ('I say!'), and by his sober homage to Parnell. It continues,
too, as Stephen, having been reminded of George Russell by his
namesake the 'lapidary' (10. 800), casts himself as a mocking
Hamlet, deriding the first of the two as a Polonius-figure and a
pompous anachronism (10. 828–9; cf. 9. 207). To Stephen, Russell is
one of the landed Anglo-Irish who discourses on timeless 'spiritual
essences' and 'eternal wisdom' (9. 49, 52), but is both affluent and

---

[65] The Great Earl also qualified as another court jester to the English. One of his great
(and politically advantageous) talents was for making Henry VII laugh (ibid. 148).

[66] O'Brien, *Parnell*, 268.

practical enough to sport a watch (10. 828; cf. 9. 269–70). Here as in 'Scylla', Stephen thinks of him as an exploiter, a 'grandfather ape gloating on a stolen hoard' (10. 813–14; cf. 9. 272), a member of a class historically committed to economic and cultural dispossession together.

Stephen's response to being left out of the Anglo-Irish revivalist's 'sheaf' of verses (9. 291) is one of determined resistance. To that small sheaf, in Traherne's phrase, he will counterpose a harvest of 'Orient and immortal wheat standing from everlasting to everlasting' (10. 816–17). Elsewhere in 'Wandering Rocks', resistance is ruder, livelier, and less grandiose. One of the key effects of the arrival of Parnell on the Irish political scene was a spread and intensification of the democratic *attitude*, a continuing shift in ordinary people's responses to power. Simon Dedalus is the very type of this. Parnellism 'destroyed the old-time respect of the people for mere titles and positions, causing them to regard Viceroys, Chief Secretaries and cabinet ministers as common men to be judged solely on their merits'.[67] Parnell did much to make Irish nationalism more egalitarian or, at least, more thoroughly disrespectful of formality and established authority. By 1904, the shift in question had suffered a check. But 'Wandering Rocks' demonstrates that it is nonetheless still alive. In the 1880s, the Viceroy's appearances on his public rounds were frequently received with 'manifestations of disloyalty'.[68] There are similar manifestations in 'Wandering Rocks'. The 'disloyalty' is still apparent, even if often in a mixed and muted mode. Hence the number of mere stares the procession gets in the final section, and the fact that the salutes on Northumberland and Landsdowne roads are so 'rare' (10. 1277–9). Hornblower is singled out as the one 'loyal king's man' (10. 1264). So, too, the John Howard Parnell who 'understood his [brother's] every fibre'[69] continues to gaze 'intently' at his chessboard (10. 1226), ignoring the viceregal presence.

But what matters most, here, for Joyce, is how art can supplement, refashion and transmogrify such 'manifestations'. The end of 'Wandering Rocks' is concerned not only to memorialize but to sustain, amplify, and also to subtilize the dissident spirit. The Dubliners may be on their guard. According to O'Brien, at least, at this time, any

---

[67] McCarthy, *Irish Revolution*, 75.   [68] O'Brien, *Parnell*, 321.

[69] The phrase is Joseph Carroll's and is self-evidently an exaggeration; but John Howard quotes it himself in his memoir of his brother. See John Howard Parnell, *Charles Stewart Parnell: A Memoir* (London: Constable & Co., 1916), 290.

public expression of political animus could on principle constitute grounds for a political as opposed to a non-political arrest and lead to a question in the House of Commons.[70] But Joyce has no reason to hold back, and the chapter itself provides the expressions of offensive irreverence that the Dubliners watching the procession might have felt it unwise to show in public. Thus at 10. 1197, Joyce makes the River Poddle hang out 'in fealty' its 'tongue of liquid sewage'.[71] For a moment, at least, Simon Dedalus's penis might be quite close to hanging out in fealty, too (10. 1200–1), and little Patrick Dignam's shirt collar springs up in what looks like an obscene or at least a dismissive gesture (10. 1267–8). These details form part of a sequence of 'retaliations' that has been emerging throughout the chapter. Part of the irony, for example, of Lambert's tribute to Love's historical knowledge (10. 439) is that his own account of the Great Earl's well-known words is actually quite faithful to extant accounts, give or take a racy, colourful flourish or two which surely enhance rather than diminish the plausibility of the rendition (10. 445–6). On the other hand, Love's version of the Fitzgeralds' address is at the very least disputable (10. 416).[72] Perhaps the toughest and most sardonic of such ironies, however, lies in the fact that, in a chapter in which Silken Thomas is so important, Conmee should be making for Artane. For the Industrial School itself had been built on the site where John Allen, the Archbishop of Dublin who was Silken Thomas's great enemy, was killed.[73]

The 'retribution' in question will be gigantically and often hilariously magnified and diversified in much of what follows in *Ulysses*. As Love, the 'refined' Protestant clergyman to whom Lambert is so subservient, enters the novel with a plum in his mouth, so he will end

---

[70] See *Dublin Castle*, 98–9. However, this was principally true for the Constabulary. According to O'Brien, a more relaxed state of affairs prevailed for the Metropolitan Police and in Dublin.

[71] The Poddle's homage is specifically metropolitan: it became a sewer from the spot where it entered the city proper. See Dillon Cosgrave, *North Dublin: City and Environs* (Dublin: Catholic Truth Society of Ireland, 1909), 35.

[72] According to the great Dublin historian John T. Gilbert, the Fitzgeralds' 'mansion' or family home was not in 'Thomas court' but in Skinner-row. See Gilbert, *A History of the City of Dublin* (Dublin, 1854–9), introd. F. E. Dixon (3 vols. Shannon: Irish University Press, 1972), i. 172. Joyce was familiar with Gilbert's book and wanted to have it with him in Trieste. See *Letters*, ii. 194.

[73] See E. MacDowel Cosgrave and Leonard R. Strangways, *The Dictionary of Dublin* (Dublin: Sealy, Bryers and Walker, 1895), 114. The detail is frequently given in contemporary books on Dublin.

with a carrot up his arse (15. 4704–6).[74] The remaining chapters of *Ulysses* richly exploit the space that has partly been opened up by the practices I have noted, here. The closing section of 'Wandering Rocks' provides a foretaste of this. For it takes a public English discourse—the contemporary gazette—and exposes it to a 'double reading'. The reference to Miss Douce and Miss Kennedy 'admiring' the cavalcade, for example (10. 1198–9), means one thing within the discourse of the gazette and quite another in the novel. A few pages later, 'Sirens' will tell us that the girls were actually admiring clothes ('pearl grey and *eau de Nil*', 11. 67) and a man ('the fellow in the tall silk', 11. 70). A gap appears between an (English) form of representation and a clandestine set of indications as to 'what is really going on' in an Irish context. The result is subversive and wickedly funny. Significantly, too, the discourse at stake gets distorted; as though— like the Fitzgeralds—its tie to its origins were being 'corrupted' or radically loosened in a process of assimilation. From 'Wandering Rocks', we move into a series of chapters where such effects will be among the most notable features of *Ulysses*.

[74] Interestingly, Love is the only character in the novel whose accent is actually specified as being 'refined'.

CHAPTER FIVE

History, All That:
'Sirens', 'Cyclops'

Most Trenchant Rendition

Having scanned the Dublin of 1904, Joyce embarks on a particular kind of treatment of English and Anglo-Irish discourses that is to a large extent responsible for producing the famous 'styles' of *Ulysses*. To continue with my theme from the previous chapter: the practices in question are retributive, but with many complications. The beginnings of these practices have been evident earlier in the novel, above all, in 'Scylla and Charybdis', a chapter which allows us to see Joyce's project in the later part of the novel emerging out of Stephen. Now, however, Joyce separates his stratagems decisively from the melancholy of the young man, giving them an independent life. Like Bloom, they follow on logically from Stephen, but also challenge and transform much that is still rigid in Stephen's thought.

In their different ways, both English cultural nationalism and 'constructive Unionism' worked to close the gap between England and Ireland, to draw the lesser closer to the greater power politically and culturally and, in doing so, to continue to limit its autonomy. In a different way, this was also the case with Anglo-Irish revivalism, whatever its claims to the contrary. That it flourished during the period in question was no coincidence. To some extent, its ambivalences resembled those of 'constructive Unionism', even Haines's. F. S. L. Lyons has shown how far the Anglo-Irish revivalists were intent on forging a unity, on producing the 'fusion of cultures' for which Yeats worked.[1] The project was based on three principles. First, it assumed the special role of the Anglo-Irish: 'educated, leisured, self-confident', they would naturally 'take the lead in the cultural sphere'. Secondly, it assumed a broad area of common

---

[1] See *Culture and Anarchy in Ireland 1890–1939* (Oxford: Clarendon Press, 1979), 57.

ground between Anglo-Irish Ireland and Irish Ireland on which increasing collaboration could be built, Thirdly, it took for granted the notion that cultural fusion and regeneration 'were the agreed objectives of a society which had laid aside its political differences'.[2] These three principles underpinned the whole plan to recover the traditions of ancient Ireland. Samuel Ferguson had asserted that the Anglo-Irish needed to unearth an authentically Irish past with which they might identify, to consolidate their position in the unsettling wake of Catholic emancipation. He allied himself with the schol-ars—Petrie, O'Curry, O'Donovan—who had already begun to sal-vage something of that ancient Irish culture. In doing so, he saw himself as making that culture his own. He described himself as 'no rootless colonist of alien earth' but a man aspiring 'to link his present with his Country's past | And live anew in knowledge of his sires'.[3] From Ferguson's point of view, his enterprise was syncretic, unifying. From Joyce's point of view, on the other hand, the 'union' in question effectively spelt continuing dispossession and subordination, not least, at a time of intensifying nationalism at the centre of the Empire. This is reflected in Stephen's anxiety as to whether the Anglo-Irish will 'wrest from us . . . the palm of beauty' (9. 740).

History and music were two key revivalist preoccupations. If Joyce pits *Ulysses* against the Anglo-Irish Revival, he does so most notably in two consecutive chapters much concerned with those themes, 'Sirens' and 'Cyclops'. Harry White has argued that, throughout the nine-teenth century in Ireland, music was a profoundly political issue.[4] This dates back at least as far as 1831, when, in his anthology of Gaelic lyrics, *Irish Minstrelsy*, Catholic nationalist James Hardiman attacked the Anglo-Irish as alien exploiters. Ferguson duly responded, significantly, by translating some of the same lyrics, thus staking a rival claim to the tradition in question.[5] But musical revivalism emerges most conspicuously in Irish culture in the 1890s, as is evident in the appearance of the Irish Musical Festival or Feis Ceoil. In 1894, T. O'Neill Russell wrote a letter to the *Evening Telegraph* in which he protested against what he took to be the lack of Irish music in Ireland.

[2] Ibid., 57.

[3] 'Mesgedra', in *Lays of the Red Branch*, introd. Lady Ferguson (London: T. Fisher Unwin, 1897), 23–34, at 32–3.

[4] 'Music and the Irish Literary Imagination', in Gerard Gillen and Harry White (eds.), *Irish Musical Studies*, iii. *Music and Irish Cultural History* (Blackrock: Irish Academic Press, 1995), 212–27, esp. 213.   [5] Lyons, *Culture and Anarchy*, 30.

Thus originated a movement which led at length to the first Feis, held in Dublin in May 1897. The intention was to revive the Annual Musical Congress of Ireland supposed to have 'decayed with the fall of the bards and their privileges', and thus to connect with 'the early ages which, brightened by the halo of romance, have been described as the golden age of Erin'.[6] The constitution of the Feis specifically stated that, apart from 'the general cultivation of music in Ireland', its objects were the promotion of 'the study and cultivation of Irish music' and the collection and preservation of 'the old [Irish] airs'.[7]

With the inauguration of the Feis, Ferguson seemed to have triumphed over Hardiman. For in the context of Irish cultural politics, the agenda that lay behind the Feis was unmistakable. It was Anglo-Irish and genteel. Those most closely associated with the Feis—some as early members of the Executive Committee—included Douglas Hyde, Edith Oldham, George and Dora Sigerson, Annie Patterson, George Coffey, A. P. Graves, John McGrath, and Edward Martyn. The programmes provided long lists of frequently patrician guarantors and subscribers. The compilers of the programmes reassured their readers of the historical importance of Irish music by citing English approval, pointing out, for example, that 'Queen Elizabeth had her Irish harper (named Donell)'.[8] Something of the particular social and cultural flavour in question can be gained from the inaugural programme. The very first item on it was 'The Gol and Irish Caoine or Lament', performed by one Mrs Scarff-Goodman, complete with 'chorus and band of harps'.[9] (A Mrs Scott-Ffennell was listed among the other performers: Feis programmes tend to sound like roll-calls for society ladies in 'Circe'.) Later items included Irish songs like 'Here in Cool Grot' by the eighteenth-century Irish composer the Earl of Mornington.[10] Yeats wrote enthusiastically to John O'Leary of the first Feis Ceoil (a name he had trouble spelling) as 'by all accounts a great affair'.[11] He remained an ardent supporter, seeing the Feis as an opportunity for the promotion of a 'Celtic theatre' and asserting that its loss would be 'very serious'.[12] By contrast,

[6] *Programme*, Feis Ceoil (Irish Music Festival), Dublin, 17–22 May 1897, 3.
[7] *Syllabus of Prize Competitions*, Feis Ceoil, Dublin, 18–23 May 1903, 9.
[8] *Programme*, 8.   [9] Ibid. 7.   [10] Ibid. 10.
[11] Letter to John O'Leary, 30 May 1897, in *Collected Letters*, ii. *1896–1900*, ed. Warwick Gould et al. (Oxford: Clarendon Press, 1997), 105–6.
[12] See e.g. letter to the Guarantors for a 'Celtic Theatre', before 16 July 1897, ibid. 123–5; letter to Lady Gregory, 18 July 1897, ibid. 125–6; and letter to Alice Milligan, ?28 July 1897, ibid. 128.

Griffith 'dreaded' the example set by what he took to be the 'West-Britishness' of the Feis.[13]

Joyce's attitude was closer to Griffith's than Yeats's, but was less anxious, more one of contemptuous amusement. According to Eglinton, he 'once persuaded himself to enter as a competitor' in the Feis. 'When a test-piece was handed to him', however, 'he looked at it, guffawed and marched off the platform'.[14] 'Sirens' sustains, diversifies, and massively amplifies that original guffaw. In a sense, the chapter stages Joyce's own Dublin Music Festival, the whole spirit of which runs radically counter to that of the Feis. The key item in 'Sirens', for instance, is a rebel ballad. Where the first Feis took place in the Royal University Buildings, Joyce's chapter takes place in a bar. 'Sirens' is dense with European music (though in the prize competitions at the Feis, unlike the concerts themselves, European music was quite common; indeed, the material performed was surprisingly diverse and wide ranging). More importantly, as White puts it, in composing 'Sirens', Joyce drew upon 'that vast demotic culture of song which characterised middle-class life', using music as a means not only of 'imagining the past' but of 'modifying the present' and proving 'the contingency of music in Ireland'.[15] The result is dissonance, a host of clashing sounds. Where the revivalists dreamt of an unreal harmony, Joyce insists on cacophony, on radical discord. But most significantly of all, 'Sirens' is not actually made of music. It is made of language, the English language warped, distorted, even brutalized, twisted out of true by the countervailing pressure of music. It is interesting to find Tom Kernan, in another (failed) effort to sound posh, praising Dollard's 'rendition' of 'The Croppy Boy' as 'most trenchant' (11. 1148). The adjective is usually applied to 'cutting' or critical observations, remarks, or phrases. Trenchancy is verbal: the *OED* stresses the point. But in 'Sirens' it is *music* that cuts into *language*:

Forgotten. I too. And one day she with. Leave her: get tired. Suffer then. Snivel. Big spanishy eyes goggling at nothing. Her wavyavyeavy-heavyeavyevyevyhair un comb:'d. . . .
Miss Douce, miss Lydia, did not believe: miss Kennedy, Mina, did not believe: George Lidwell, no: miss Dou did not: the first, the first: gent with

---

[13] According to Yeats. See letter to George Russell (AE), c.9 Aug. 1901, *Collected Letters*, iii. *1901–1904*, ed. John Kelly and Ronald Schuchard (Oxford: Clarendon Press, 1994), 103–4, at 104 and n. 2.
[14] *Irish Literary Portraits* (London: Macmillan, 1935), 138.   [15] 'Music', 221.

the tank: believe, no, no: did not, miss Kenn: Lidlydiawell: the tank. (11. 807–9, 811–20)

Words are repeatedly deformed, wrenched, truncated, severed, shorn apart. Joyce thus reverses the relationship between English and music that was central to the revivalist project. As Seamus Deane puts matters, the translators and collectors of Irish songs sought to effect 'some ultimate reconciliation' between the English language and the essential Irish spirit as represented in music.[16] But Joyce will have no truck with such a union. Whatever music is or represents, it is not to be reconciled with English save through a process of anamorphosis of which the victim is English itself.

Heroic History

It is in 'Cyclops', however, that Joyce's assault on Anglo-Irish revivalism is most pronounced. From Hugh Kenner onwards, scholars have recognized that 'Cyclops' develops a 'critique' of what Kenner himself calls the 'neo-Celtic movement' and its 'pseudo-histories'.[17] They have named some relevant names.[18] But they have also tended to see this aspect of 'Cyclops' as of secondary importance alongside its criticism of the citizen and his brand of nationalism, and Bloom's stout resistance to him.[19] In fact, 'Cyclops' engages in a sustained assault on Anglo-Irish, revivalist historiographies and constructions of Irish history, and the politics and aesthetics implicit in them. The forms of historical imagination in question are those chiefly familiar from the work of Ferguson, O'Curry, Yeats, Lady Gregory, Douglas Hyde, and, above all, Standish O'Grady. An anti-revivalist animus is central to 'Cyclops' and is the determining context for the chapter's

---

[16] 'Poetry and Song 1800–1890', in Deane, with Andrew Carpenter and Jonathan Williams, *The Field Day Anthology of Irish Writing* (3 vols., Derry: Field Day Publications, 1991), i. 1–9, esp. at 5.

[17] See *Dublin's Joyce* (London: Chatto and Windus, 1955), 254–5, 357.

[18] See e.g. ibid. 191, 255; Phillip F. Herring (ed.), *Joyce's Notes and Early Drafts for 'Ulysses': Selections from the Buffalo Collection* (Charlottesville, Va.: University Press of Virginia, 1977), 134–5; C. H. Peake, *James Joyce: The Citizen and the Artist* (London: Edward Arnold, 1977), 237; and Daniel R. Schwarz, *Reading Joyce's 'Ulysses'* (Basingstoke: Macmillan, 1987), 177, 224.

[19] See e.g. Michael Mason, *James Joyce: 'Ulysses'* (London: Edward Arnold, 1972), 52; Patrick Parrinder, *James Joyce* (Cambridge: Cambridge University Press, 1984), 172; and Schwarz, *Reading Joyce's 'Ulysses'*, 175–6.

other themes, rather than a more or less incidental embroidery upon them. It is important to remember, here, that Joyce's 'initial impulse' was 'in the direction of the parody passages' rather than that of the chapter's 'first person naturalistic narrator' or its naturalistic narrative.[20]

Ferguson's insistence on the need for an Anglo-Irish accommodation with the Gaelic past led him to translate an old Irish poetry that contained the legends and sagas of the pre-Christian, heroic age.[21] But it was in O'Grady's work that Ferguson's insistence most notably flowered. O'Grady's effort to put together the narrative of the Red Branch or Ulster Cycle, the two volumes of the *History of Ireland* (1878–80), is the most crucial work of Irish historiography of the period. Its importance in the culture Joyce knew can hardly be underestimated.[22] It was enormously influential on Yeats, and on Lady Gregory, whose *Gods and Fighting Men* and *Cuchulain of Muirthemne* sustain its mode of historical imagination. It had a similar influence on Hyde, as he turned to peasant, oral traditions for a dimension of history otherwise beyond the reach of the educated. Again and again, the emphasis is on history as retrieval, the 'disclosure' of an 'ancient tradition', as Lady Gregory put matters, that also asserts a connection with it.[23] O'Grady claimed that part of his purpose was 'to express the whole nature of a race or nation'.[24] Young Stephen's concern with the conscience of the race in *Portrait* is both a product of and a reaction to this kind of Anglo-Irish project. For revivalist historiography was an appropriation of a past by those to whom it did not truly belong.

If Anglo-Irish, revivalist historiography is concerned with the ancient heroic past, then, it is also concerned with the relation between that past and the present and future. 'The gigantic conceptions of heroism and strength', O'Grady wrote, 'with which the forefront of Irish history is thronged, prove the great future of this race and land'.[25] But in between the heroic past and the present and future, there yawned a huge gap which made revival history seem much less

[20] Michael Groden, *'Ulysses' in Progress* (Princeton: Princeton University Press, 1977), 118.   [21] See Lyons, *Culture and Anarchy*, 28–31.

[22] See ibid. 33–5.

[23] *The Kiltartan Poetry Book: Prose Translations from the Irish* (Dundrum: Cuala Press, 1918), p. vi.

[24] *History of Ireland: Critical and Philosophical*, vol. i (London: Sampson Low & Co., 1881), 57.   [25] Ibid. 58.

than an 'expression' of a 'whole nature'. In particular, the revivalists minimized the place and importance of Ireland's Christian history and traditions.[26] O'Grady thought that the advent of Christianity had 'ruined' the ancient culture.[27] It had also ended 'the golden age of bardic composition'.[28] Medieval Ireland had surrendered to a 'rationalism and logic' which had been 'primarily responsible for the cloud which hangs over our early history'.[29] So, too, for Lady Gregory, part of the excitement of reading Hyde's translations of the *Love Songs of Connacht* was a sudden sense of connection with a pre-medieval era and a tradition that 'existed in Ireland before Chaucer lived'.[30] For O'Grady, the 'scholastic Irish were great in annals and chronology, but the functions of the poet and maker were not theirs, nor vividness of perception, nor sympathy, nor grandeur of thought'.[31] The choice between Oisin and Patrick was clear. This choice—a choice between the heroic past and Irish Catholic traditions—was also a choice between ways of imagining history. O'Grady's historical imagination establishes itself partly in idealizing reaction to Catholic historiographers 'great in annals and chronology'. By contrast, the Joyce of *Ulysses* clearly asserts a certain kinship with them.

The Anglo-Irish, revivalist imagination blurs the borderlines between history and mythology, legend, folklore. In Lady Gregory's phrase, it was concerned with 'myth turned into history, or history into myth'.[32] She herself clearly relished the tendency of oral tradition not to preserve historical fact but to de-historicize the historical. She noted, for example, that O'Connell, though dead for 'only sixty years', had 'already been given a miraculous birth, and the power of a saint' was 'on its way to him'.[33] O'Grady likewise rejected 'mere history', the 'merely archaeological'.[34] 'In history', he wrote, 'there must be sympathy, imagination, creation'.[35] The exercise of the historical imagination was more than merely individual. For 'century after century', the mind of Ireland had been 'inflamed by the contemplation of ... mighty beings'.[36] O'Grady saw his own

[26] Cf. Len Platt, *Joyce and the Anglo-Irish: A Study of Joyce and the Literary Revival* (Amsterdam and Atlanta, Ga.: Rodopi, 1998), 22–30.
[27] *History of Ireland: The Heroic Period* (2 vols., London: Sampson Low & Co., 1878–80), vol. i, p. xv.   [28] Ibid. ii. 24.
[29] O'Grady, *Ireland: Critical and Philosophical*, 63.
[30] *Poets and Dreamers: Studies and Translations from the Irish* (London: Hodges, Figgis & Co. Ltd., 1903), 47.   [31] *Ireland: Critical and Philosophical*, 166.
[32] *The Kiltartan History Book* (Dublin: Maunsel & Co., 1909), 49.   [33] Ibid. 51.
[34] *Ireland: Heroic*, ii. 17; vol. i, p. iii.   [35] Ibid., vol. i, p. iv.   [36] Ibid., p. vi.

historiography as an extension but also a reawakening of this mind, of a national historical imagination capable of returning to a people its own mythology. This would be achieved, not through 'the labours of the patient brood of scholars' but by a recasting of the old 'heroic history' in 'a literary form'.[37] For O'Grady, this is the only truly useful history: one that represents 'the imagination of the country', expresses 'the ambition and ideals of the people', takes on 'a value far beyond the tale of actual events and duly recorded deeds', and thereby becomes 'that kind of history which a nation desires to possess'.[38]

It is a history that requires and creates heroic forms. It encourages and thrives on exaggeration. Lady Gregory praises the legends of Finn precisely because they are 'the most exaggerated of the tales' of the Fianna and therefore those 'most often in the mouths of the people'.[39] The exaggeration is equally present in her own *Cuchulain of Muirthemne*, for which, as Declan Kiberd notes, Joyce felt 'a deep aversion'.[40] In O'Grady's terms, history requires 'gigantic treatment', in the spirit of the bards.[41] 'Gigantism' is the authentically Irish way. Thus, for example, 'in the statue which fronts Trinity College, we have represented Grattan in twice or three times his natural size'.[42] Gigantism goes hand in hand with a flight from and distaste for the actual. 'The distant in place and the distant in time', writes O'Grady, 'have ever been the chosen realms of the imagination'.[43] Hence a certain indifference to questions of accuracy: 'historical or not', says O'Grady, of the Fenian heroes, 'they are real'.[44] Lady Gregory is similarly paradoxical and cavalier. 'The history of England and Ireland was shut out of the schools', she writes, 'and it became a passion'. She herself aims merely to record that impassioned history as it already exists 'in "the Book of the People"'. At the same time, she will not 'go bail for the facts'.[45] Indeed, like O'Grady's, her logic dictates that history must float free of factuality. The politics of this historiography are evident enough. O'Grady was

[37] *Ireland: Heroic*, ii. 40.   [38] Ibid. 22.   [39] *Kiltartan History Book*, 49.
[40] 'The Vulgarity of Heroics: Joyce's *Ulysses*', in Suheil Badi Bushrui and Bernard Benstock (eds.), *James Joyce, An International Perspective: Centenary Essays in Honour of the Late Sir Desmond Cochrane*, foreword by Richard Ellmann (Gerrards Cross: Colin Smythe, 1982), 156–69, at 157. R.F. Foster remarks on a traditional Ascendancy 'culture of exaggeration' running back to the 18th cent. See his *Modern Ireland 1600–1972* (London: Penguin, 1989), 194.   [41] *Ireland: Heroic*, ii. 110.
[42] *Ireland: Critical and Philosophical*, 236.   [43] Ibid. 22.   [44] Ibid. 355.
[45] *Kiltartan History Book*, 51.

an Ascendancy man, hostile alike to the Irish *demos*, the levelling tendencies in Parnellite nationalism, and the *canaille* or commercial classes.[46] Phillip Marcus points out that, for enthusiasts, a chief attraction of the old legends was the refuge they offered from a seemingly sordid present.[47] But the legends also needed to be purged of more sordid, vulgar, and even obscene elements of their own. Ferguson and O'Grady disliked these. They were not alone in doing so. 'We want the Irish spirit, certainly, in Irish literature', wrote T. W. Rolleston, 'but we want its gold, not its dross'.[48] For O'Grady, the legends were and had to be an idealized haven to which 'the intellect of man, tired by contact with the vulgarity of actual things' and the world of common men, could return 'for rest and recuperation'.[49] By contrast, D. P. Moran suspected that all the talk of 'ancient glories', of the Irish being 'a fine people long ago' that he saw as sanctioned 'by O'Curry and others' was arrant evasion of political reality.[50] Certainly, in retrospect, it is hard not partly to interpret such talk as at the very least an escapist reaction to the decline in Ascendancy power.[51]

Revival historiography sought to revitalize or rather to reinvent not only the ancient legends but ancient modes of history-telling, specifically, those of the bards. O'Grady did not merely use 'bardic story'. He also wanted to use 'the actual language of the bards, and as much as possible their style and general character of expression'.[52] Indeed, he thought of his own method as bardic and saw his work as a continuation of bardic history, in which 'the legendary' continually blends 'with the historic narrative'.[53] Lady Gregory was similarly fascinated by the bard as historian and, indeed, as teacher of history.[54] To some extent, the revivalists even identified with the bards as a privileged class 'entrusted with the preservation of the literature and history of the country'.[55] Hyde provides an obvious example of this fascination with the bard. Like Lady Gregory, Yeats, and Martyn, he was particularly interested in Raftery. He saw the latter as a

---

[46] See E. A. Boyd, *Standish O'Grady: Selected Essays and Passages* (Dublin: The Talbot Press, n.d.), 16, 166; quoted in Phillip L. Marcus, *Yeats and the Beginning of the Irish Renaissance* (Ithaca, NY and London: Cornell University Press, 1970), 238. Cf. Lyons, *Culture and Anarchy*, 33–5. [47] *Yeats*, 224.

[48] 'Shamrocks', *The Academy* (9 July 1887), 19; quoted in Marcus, *Yeats*, 231.

[49] *Ireland: Heroic*, i. 22.

[50] *The Philosophy of Irish Ireland* (Dublin: James Duffy & Co., 1905), 39.

[51] Cf. Lyons, *Culture and Anarchy*, 72. [52] *Ireland: Heroic*, vol. i, p. x.

[53] Ibid. 19. [54] See e.g. *Poets and Dreamers*, 10.

[55] O'Grady, *Ireland: Heroic*, ii. 50.

bardic historian who kept the Irish appropriately conscious of Ireland. He praises Raftery's 'Story of the Bush' as 'a concise and intelligible history of Ireland' (and apparently partly a true one, too).[56] As a founder of the Gaelic League and its president until 1915, a believer in 'Gaelicism' and the de-Anglicization rather than the de-Davisization of Irish literature, Hyde stands apart from the other writers I have just been discussing. But as a Trinity-educated Protestant, a friend and collaborator of Yeats and Lady Gregory who was firmly intent on keeping the League apolitical, he stands on their side, too. Though his own grasp of Irish history as reflected in his *Literary History of Ireland* was very different to O'Grady's, it is likewise reductive, and for similarly polemical purposes. Like O'Grady (and the bards, in O'Grady's view) Hyde relies on ancient native sources and argues for that reliance. Like O'Grady, too, he is happy to 'leave verifiable history behind'.[57] His work cannot simply be separated off from other aspects of revival historiography. He shared and fed attitudes to Irish history emergent in the work of others, and this is particularly evident in his contribution to the cult of the bard.

One of the most striking contradictions in the revivalist historical imagination lies in its relation to English culture. In part, the Anglo-Irish revivalists wanted to draw further away from that culture and closer to an indigenous one.[58] O'Grady repeatedly states that this is one of his purposes. But in point of fact, Englishness is constantly perceptible within the enterprise. That in itself reflects its compromises and its predicament. Marcus points out how earnestly Victorian Ferguson's conception of literature was.[59] The traces of England are apparent throughout O'Grady's *History*, with its epigraphs from Shelley, Byron, and Keats and its outlandish stylistic oscillations between the plain-historical, the pseudo-bardic, the high-Shakespearean, and the would-be Miltonic. Moran argued that the new historical enthusiasms in Ireland had actually been accompanied by an increase in the Anglicization of Irish culture.[60] Indeed, contradiction was always bound to haunt the historiographical project in question.

---

[56] 'Raftery's Poems', in Douglas Hyde (ed., trans., and annot.), *Songs Ascribed to Raftery* (Dublin: Gill agus a Mhac, 1903), 3–61, at 19. Cf. also Lady Gregory, 'Raftery' and 'West Irish Ballads', in *Poets and Dreamers*, 1–46, 47–65.

[57] *A Literary History of Ireland from Earliest Times to the Present Day* (London: T. Fisher Unwin, 1899), 239.

[58] See Oliver MacDonagh, *Ireland: The Union and its Aftermath* (London: Allen and Unwin, 1977), 72. [59] *Yeats*, 233.

[60] *Philosophy*, 39.

It sought to bridge gulfs, to heal divisions. It attempted to minimize differences. Hence Lady Gregory's effort to imagine Irish tradition as a unity 'born of continuity of purpose' rather than a succession of disparate epochs ('The names change from age to age, that is all').[61] In reality, however, it was a historiography produced by a dominant but threatened class. Divided within itself, such writing could only exacerbate the differences it sought to overcome.

Satirical Effusions

Revival historiography, its politics and aesthetics were bound to seem anathema to Joyce. As a middle-class Catholic intellectual, an ironic realist with a satirical intelligence and a devouring passion for exactitude, a radical, and a nationalist, if of a distinctive kind, with a powerful feeling for the demotic, he was hardly likely to find the revivalist conception of Irish history congenial. *Ulysses* is itself a historical work that battles fiercely to reverse the emphases of revivalist historiography and reclaim Ireland and its past for Joyce's own culture. To O'Grady's idealist principles, Joyce counterposes a stubbornly realist aesthetic that insists on the significance of almost numberless historical particulars. To O'Grady's 'escape from positive history and unyielding despotic fact'[62] he opposes a clear-eyed and resolute factuality (hence, in part, Stephen's struggle: the 'nightmare' is irreducibly 'despotic'). Where O'Grady dwells on ancient history and ignores the Catholic past, Joyce drastically economizes on allusions to ancient Ireland and fills his novel with accounts of and references to the history and culture of Irish Catholicism. To O'Grady's dismissal of the Middle Ages, Joyce opposes his own medievalism. O'Grady disparages what he takes to be the medieval 'thirst for minuteness, chronology and succession, co-ordination and relation'.[63] Joyce's Dantean aesthetic—his Dantean architectonics—promotes all these as values. Where O'Grady gives us the heroic, a history cleansed of meanness, squalor, and vulgarity, an art of gigantic inflation, Joyce offers the anti-heroic, the dirty, trivial, and obscene, an art of deflation. Where O'Grady purges history of terror, Joyce is everywhere alert to its oppressive consequences. Where O'Grady's writing is

---

[61] *Kiltartan Poetry Book*, p. iii.   [62] *Ireland: Critical and Philosophical*, 57.
[63] Ibid. 63.

pervasively contaminated by the very Englishness it seeks to resist, Joyce is both acutely conscious of contamination and acutely concerned to reverse its vectors. Most strikingly of all, O'Grady sought to connect Ireland with ancient Greece, especially Homer. He insistently associates Irish bards with Homer and presents himself as writing the Irish equivalent of Homeric epic. In *Ulysses*, Joyce counters O'Grady's Homeric analogies with a (wickedly ironic) one of his own. In this respect, his practice supplies an important context for understanding the famous Homeric parallel.

Joyce's critique of Anglo-Irish, revivalist historiography begins with the 'Telemachiad'. Stephen recasts and reinterprets the role of the bard. He devises an eerie poem about the invader as vampire that echoes Hyde's translation of 'My Grief on the Sea' (7. 522–5).[64] So, too, the 'Telemachiad' is dominated by a mode of historical imagination very different to that of the Revival. Stephen is both concerned with a different Irish history to that of the Revival, and with giving episodes from that history a different form. But he has also been contaminated by O'Grady. His tone and prose style are sometimes remarkably close to O'Grady's (if notably superior versions). Even as late as 'Oxen', Stephen can sound very like O'Grady:

In my heart, too, are empty chambers, and I knock at doors which never shall be opened. To me the sun at noon tide is black, and pale memories dim for me the banquet-hall.[65]

Stephen's evocation of 'the adiaphane in the noon of life'—'my moon and my sun thou hast quenched for ever'—sounds very like this passage, particularly at 14. 375–80. Stephen is young and, as in *Portrait*, his 'blood' is easily 'wooed by grace of language' (7. 776). But his susceptibility leaves the cultural and political critique of revivalism in the 'Telemachiad' looking somewhat less than resolute. In the later chapters of *Ulysses*, Joyce therefore necessarily conducts the critique in a different manner. As far as the historical imagination is concerned, this is very much the case in 'Cyclops'.

If there is 'parody' in 'Cyclops', its most important targets are the styles of Revival historiography and related poetry and translation. The very title of the chapter and its 'technic' ('gigantism', at least, according to the 1921 schema) refer us to O'Grady. Like 'gigantic',

[64] Cf. Hyde (ed., trans., and annot.) *Love Songs of Connacht* (London: T. Fisher Unwin, 1893), 29–31.   [65] *Ireland: Heroic*, ii. 250–1.

'Cyclopean' was among his favourite adjectives. Joyce offers a mocking critique of Revival simulations of bardic history and discourse as found not only in Ferguson, O'Grady, Hyde, and Lady Gregory but in McCarthy, Samuel Lover, et al. Some of the 'parodies' in the chapter allude to a composite set of mock-bardic styles and devices, many of which have long been recognized as such: the double epithets, for instance (as at 12. 152–5) and the exaggerations of size; the lists or— to adopt the appropriate term as used by Hyde—'runs'.[66] Joyce provides a comic 'fish-run' (12. 71–4, 81–2) and the list of Nolan's wedding guests at 12. 1269–79 is an outrageously eccentric burlesque of a 'tree-run'. Joyce also compounds the hilarity—and the subversion—by giving us a 'clergyman-run' (12. 927–38) and Catholic runs, including a 'saint-run' (12. 1676–1719). The list at 12. 176–99 begins as a characteristic chronological run of names (and then develops quite aberrantly). Elsewhere, we get the eulogistic catalogue of place names, the *dindsenchas* that was common in bardic topography and Revival versions of it (12. 110–12, 12. 1451–61).[67] It is not surprising to find a comic passage in 'Cyclops' that treats of Hyde, Raftery, and the cult of the bard (12. 712–39). Here, the humour of Garryowen's 'recitation of verse' (12. 719) is directed less at Raftery than at Hyde's translatorese (which can certainly be laughable). It is no accident, either, that Joyce humorously couples Raftery with Donal MacConsidine as a master of 'satirical effusions' (12. 728). MacConsidine was in fact no bard but the 'fine Irish scholar' referred to fleetingly in both *Love Songs of Connacht* and *Beside the Fire* as a transcriber of Gaelic poems.[68] Once again, the emphasis is on versions of the original, mediators and mediating forms.

Of course, there are moments when Joyce seems to be making fun of O'Grady's style (12. 1183–9, for instance). He wryly introduces words favoured by O'Grady, like 'puissant' (12. 1184). He picks up on some of O'Grady's preferred designations: 'Banba' for Ireland, for example (12. 375), and Clanna Rury for the Red Branch (as in

[66] Hyde (ed., trans., and annot.), *Beside the Fire: A Collection of Irish Gaelic Folk Stories*, (London: D. Nutt, 1890), pp. xxv–vii.

[67] On the *dindsenchas*, see Foster, *Modern Ireland*, 5; and Maria Tymoczko, *The Irish 'Ulysses'* (Berkeley and Los Angeles: University of California Press, 1994), 121–2, 153–9, 169, 263–4, 291–3, and *passim*. Curiously, Tymoczko does not consider the relationship between 'Cyclops' and the *dindsenchas* in any detail.

[68] See Hyde (ed., trans., and annot.), *Love Songs of Connacht* 11, 115, and *Beside the Fire*, p. xxxiii. MacConsidine appears to have been little more than a scribe.

'O'Bloom, the son of Rory', 12. 216).[69] There are clear echoes in Joyce's introduction of the citizen of O'Grady's manner of introducing his heroes (12. 151–67).[70] Joyce also engineers subtle gratings of gear, awkward little shifts in level that echo similar incongruities in O'Grady. One or two of the 'parodies' even switch into a more Anglicized mode, especially when a certain sort of English subject matter is around, as if, again, a comment is being passed on O'Grady's kind of historical writing and its allegiances (12. 290–9, 12. 1593–1620). 'Cyclops', then, owes much to O'Grady's *History*, and to similar heroic Revival texts like *Gods and Fighting Men* and *Cuchulain of Muirthemne*. Thus the citizen is very obviously placed as a Cuchulain figure.[71] He has his Garryowen with him, as ancient heroes often have their hounds (notably Finn and his Bran).[72] A comic voice gives him a spear and a 'strong growth' of hair, familiar attributes of ancient heroes (12. 157, 200). It also dwells on 'the reverberations of his formidable heart' (12. 164–7), as O'Grady says of Cuchulain that 'like the sound of a mighty drum his heart beats'.[73] The throwing of the biscuit-tin is reminiscent of various flights of various missiles in the *History* and elsewhere. The ancient heroic duel finds its comic counterparts in 'Cyclops' in Bloom's dispute with the citizen and the Bennett–Keogh fight (12. 960–87). The account of the catastrophe in 'Cyclops' (12. 1858–96) partly makes fun of similar accounts, like that of the catastrophe surrounding Cuchulain's death, in the *History*.[74] Bloom's departure down the Liffey and his surprise elevation to glory are comic versions of similar occasions in O'Grady and elsewhere. Finally, Bloom is set in a 'chariot' (12. 1911) which is partly Joyce's version of the ancient hero's war-car that, according to O'Grady, played such 'a vital and intimate' part in cyclic literature.[75]

Joyce picks up on other motifs, too: Ireland's fruitfulness (12. 102–17), its rich forestation (12. 1266–79), sport (12. 897–926), brewing (12. 280–6), and the ancient law (12. 1111–40). The fact that they are motifs is important. In 'Cyclops', it is not detailed allusions that really count, nor a particular butt, not even O'Grady. Hence my

[69] O'Grady clearly prefers Banba to the comparable alternatives (Fohla and Eire).
[70] See e.g. *Ireland: Heroic Period*, ii. 215.
[71] Cf. Schwarz, *Reading Joyce's 'Ulysses'*, 178.
[72] Cf. Herring (ed.), *Joyce's Notes*, 134–5. He quotes an appropriate passage from O'Grady. [73] *Ireland: Critical and Philosophical*, 232.
[74] *Ireland: Heroic*, ii. 342. [75] *Ireland: Critical and Philosophical*, 31.

reservations about the use of the term 'parody'. The chapter is rather a massive recycling of a stock-in-trade. Joyce was making light of a whole mode of discourse that speciously presented itself as a form of historiography. The 'making light' was a conscious tactic. In a period that witnessed the aggressive promotion of a supposedly 'unifying' English cultural nationalism, Anglo-Irish, revivalist history effectively colonized a set of narratives. It appropriated an indigenous, bardic tradition for its own ends. Whilst claiming that it was bodying forth the soul of Ireland, it relied heavily on English and Anglo-Irish cultural constructs. Linguistically, much of the humour in 'Cyclops' is at the expense of clumsy attempts to match Gaelic idiom with a sort of 'approximate English'. It was that 'approximation' where there was and could be no real unity that Joyce would have no truck with. His laughter refuses to accept the validity of the revivalist enterprise. Rather, it pushes that enterprise back, relativizes it, mockingly demonstrates its cultural shallowness. Into the formulas to which Revival historiography resorted, Joyce introduces precisely what it sought to exclude: Catholicism, the Middle Ages, the colonial past and present. He also strews his chapter with all kinds of references to matters English. In effect, he emphasizes the actual, compromised, adulterated character of a history and culture that the Revival had attempted to purify, but only at the cost of evasion and massive omission. As for Joyce heroic and gigantic forms required deflation, so too the forms of an idealist history had to be defaced with the marks of what they had sought to hold at bay.

There is another important way, too, in which the process at work in 'Cyclops' is a fiercely and deliberately corrupting one. O'Grady was by no means altogether enthusiastic about the original narratives from which he derived so much. He found them often 'wild and improbable', 'weird with incursions', full of 'the shifting chaos of obscure epic tale'. By contrast, he himself wished 'to mould all into a harmonious and reasonable form'.[76] At the very outset of the *History*, he explicitly refuses simply to 'pile up' a mass of bardic material. For such a mass would be 'without harmony, meaning, or order'. The 'valuable and the valueless', he writes, would be promiscuously mingled together, and the whole 'would be utterly incondite, inorganic', strewn with incongruities and probably 'unreadable'.[77] Rather, the old bardic narratives must be purged, condensed, shaped.

---

[76] Ibid. 202–3.   [77] *Ireland: Heroic*, vol. i, p. ix.

Phillip Marcus has shown in detail how far this process often went in Revival versions of the ancient tales.[78] They were moralized, cleansed of various elements originally intrinsic to them: the obscene, the comic, the fantastic, grotesque, monstrous, and frivolous. The original Cuchulain, for example, was an extraordinary figure. According to John Rhys, his contortions were so many and various that they 'won for him the nickname of the *Riastartha*, or the Distorted One'.[79] But none of this appears in the *History*. In the effort to provide a 'good story', O'Grady, De Vere, and P. W. Joyce all modified the plots of the tales and tidied up their characterization.[80] In doing so, they produced a much more homogeneous and orthodox form of narrative than that of the tales themselves.

Again, Joyce works in the opposite direction. He introduces into his 'Cyclops' narrative the very qualities in bardic literature that the Revival writers had so often sought to excise from their texts: vulgarity, grotesqueness, prodigious bizarrerie of a kind wholly absent from the work of O'Grady or Ferguson. Karen Lawrence has argued that 'Cyclops' is Joyce's most Rabelaisian chapter.[81] The reason for this should be obvious: Joyce is using a Rabelaisian 'gigantism'—a medieval and Catholic one—to criticize, modify, and indeed transform its revivalist equivalent. In effect, he returns the latter to something closer to the spirit of the original tales. He also restores heterogeneity as a narrative principle, in the 'alternating asymmetry' that was one of the 'technics' he ascribed to the chapter;[82] the abrupt slides into nonsense, irrelevance, or triviality, as in the case of the Black Liz passage (12. 846–9); the casual confusions of the grandiose and the insignificant in some of the lists (as at 12. 176–99), like those in similar lists in 'Story of the Bush';[83] the multiplicity of the 'parodies' and their styles, and the variable relation between the 'parodies' and the styles to which they allude. All make 'Cyclops' look the very antithesis of—say—*Gods and Fighting Men*, with its smooth, flat prose and its uniform point of view. Again, where O'Grady aspired to concord, Joyce dwells on dissonance. Historically, of course, he

[78] *Yeats*, 227–37.
[79] *Lectures on the Origin and Growth of Religion as Illustrated by Celtic Heathendom* (London: Williams & Norgate, 1888), 438.
[80] See Marcus, *Yeats* 227–37.
[81] *The Odyssey of Style in 'Ulysses'* (Princeton: Princeton University Press, 1981), 109.
[82] According to the Linati schema. See Ellmann's comparison of the Linati and Gorman-Gilbert schemas in his *'Ulysses' on the Liffey* (London: Faber & Faber, 1972), 187–9.   [83] See Hyde (ed., trans., and annot.), *Songs Ascribed to Raftery*, 121.

was right. But the insistence is also an expression of political and cultural allegiances. For in his resistance to Anglo-Irish appropriation, Joyce also revitalizes or finds a modern equivalent for some of the properties of bardic narrative itself. In effect, he wrests a tradition back from the hands that have sought to seize it.

The Green Hungarian Band

But for Joyce, nationalists like Griffith and the citizen had not been able or prepared to do as much. He therefore takes issue with their attitudes to history, as well. Behind a posture of ferocious defiance, he detects a residual complicity. Joyce's treatment of nationalism in 'Cyclops' is best understood in such terms. The chapter provides a humorous commentary on Griffith's Hungarian-Irish 'parallel', for example. The key text, here, is Griffith's *The Resurrection of Hungary* (1904). The book describes the Hungarian nationalists' successful attempt—in the mid-nineteenth century—to establish a dual monarchy with Austria within the Austro-Hungarian Empire. Griffith gives a brief account of Hungarian history up to 1848. He then concentrates on the period 1848–67 leading up to the *Ausgleich*. This was the agreement whereby Hungary and Austria were defined as two separate and independent states united under a single monarch. Griffith used his account of recent Hungarian history to develop an extended parallel to the situation of Ireland within the British Empire. The result was advocacy of a 'Hungarian policy' for Ireland. It envisaged 'passive resistance leading to a dual monarchy or the restoration of the 1782 constitution'.[84]

Joyce's interest in Griffith's 'parallel' was not merely scholarly. Nor was it one of Olympian detachment. He was passing comment on a political movement and the historiography it relied on. For *The Resurrection of Hungary* was not just a minor, quirkily parochial text. Griffith was not the sole begetter of the Hungarian-Irish parallel. Indeed, there was really 'nothing new' in it.[85] It had been part of Irish republican thinking since at least 1848. Thomas Davis, William Smith O'Brien, John Mitchel (in the famous *Jail Journal*), Michael

---

[84] Richard Davis, *Arthur Griffith* (Dundalk: Dundalgan Press, 1976), 11.
[85] Ibid. 8.

Doheny, and others had all resorted to it.[86] O'Connell, Parnell, and
Davitt had suggested similar arrangements to those proposed by
Griffith.[87] It was *The Resurrection of Hungary*, however, that gave
fullest expression to such ideas. It proved to be Griffith's most important work. Padraic Colum described its publication as 'an event in
Irish history'.[88] Tom Kettle hailed the Hungarian policy as 'the
largest idea contributed to Irish politics for a generation'.[89] For upon
its basis 'Sinn Féin was constructed'.[90] The policy became common
currency. Sinn Féin was actually known, in D. P. Moran's phrase, as
'the Green Hungarian Band'.[91] The Hungarian parallel underpinned
Sinn Féin's policies of self-reliance and passive resistance. This was
true even after the Rising of 1916, when there was still 'a strong feeling' in favour of the Hungarian policy being applied 'in its entirety'.[92]
The position enshrined in *The Resurrection of Hungary* remained
valid for many as late as 1919.[93] The Treaty with England that finally
emerged in 1921—and that Griffith helped to negotiate—partly
resembled the *Ausgleich*.

The 'Hungarian policy' thus had far-reaching effects. Aladar
Sarbu is surely right to suggest that Joyce's interest in Hungary was
very largely due to Griffith and the 'parallel'.[94] He works to subvert
both the 'parallel' and the Irish valuation of it. This is the point to
Bloom's being a Hungarian Jew (more Hungarian than he is Jewish,
in fact, since his mother was apparently born to a Hungarian father,
17. 536–7). Griffith argues that the Hungarian statesman Count
Istvan Széchenyi 'led his country within sight of the promised
Land'.[95] Like Hungary before it, Ireland needs a Moses to bring it
out of captivity. Joyce wryly provides his own version of such a figure. Given Griffith's anti-Semitism, the irony here is precise: the

[86] See Thomas Kabdebo, *The Hungarian-Irish 'Parallel' and Arthur Griffith's Use of his Sources* (Maynooth: St Patrick's College, 1988), 32–3.
[87] See Virginia Glandon, *Arthur Griffith and the Advanced-Nationalist Press in Ireland, 1900–1922* (New York: P. Lang, 1985), 16.
[88] *Arthur Griffith* (Dublin: Browne & Nolan, 1959), 78.   [89] Quoted ibid. 77.
[90] Calton Younger, *Arthur Griffith* (Dublin: Gill and Macmillan, 1981), 22.
[91] See Kabdebo, *Hungarian-Irish 'Parallel'*, 25.   [92] Davis, *Arthur Griffith*, 21.
[93] By 1919, however, Sinn Féin policy had begun to change. See Kabdebo, *Hungarian-Irish 'Parallel'*, 26–8.
[94] 'Literary Nationalism: Ireland and Hungary', in Wolfgang Zach and Heinz Kosok (eds.), *Literary Interrelations: Ireland, England and the World* (3 vols., Tubingen: Gunter Narr Verlag, 1987), iii. *National Images and Stereotypes*, 19–26, at 21.
[95] *The Resurrection of Hungary: A Parallel for Ireland* (Dublin: James Duffy & Co., 1904), 16.

Jewishness of Griffith's Moses was purely symbolic. Bloom is the obverse both of Griffith's Moses and of his dignified, idealistic, statesmanlike, exemplary Hungarian hero. He is a Chaplin to Griffith's Széchenyi or Deák (Ferenc Deák being the liberal politician who led Hungary in passive resistance to Austria). So, too, in 'Circe', Joyce has Bloom claim that he comes of heroic Hungarian stock, with a 'progenitor of sainted memory' who 'wore the uniform of the Austrian despot in a dank prison' (15. 1662–3). He gives Bloom a mock-coronation (15. 1439, 1546) which, in part, humorously alludes to Griffith's account of the coronation of Francis Josef in Buda-Pesth in 1867.[96] This was the coronation which set the official seal on the dual monarchy. Joyce also gives Hungarian names to Bloom, his father, and grandfather, and provides Bloom with a great-uncle who lives in the traditional royal seat of Szesfehervar (17. 1887).[97]

All this involves a double swipe at Griffith. His ideas themselves are burlesqued, but Joyce also travesties them in linking them to qualities (Jewishness, royal blood) that Griffith detested. However, the humour at the expense of the 'Hungarian parallel' finds its most sustained form in 'Cyclops'. The chapter suggests, for example, that Bloom was the real source of the 'parallel' itself (12. 1573–9). It attributes Griffith's grandiose idea to a singularly unheroic Jew. Once again, the effect is comic, especially at lines 1575–6. The contumely heaped on Bloom at this point effectively constitutes another ironic riposte to Griffith. It underlines how little any Hungarian reality is likely to matter to Griffith's fellow nationalists, and enters a reservation about the raw material with which an Irish Deák would actually have to work. Joyce also gives fleeing Bloom a humorous send-off as a Hungarian hero cheered on his way by adoring Irish supporters (12. 1814–42). The 'select orchestra' strikes up with '*Come Back to Erin*, followed immediately by *Rakóczsy's March*' (12. 1827–8), a mocking fusion of Irish and Hungarian. Indeed, in 'Cyclops', even the Hungarian language seems to get 'Irishised'. Most of the snatches of Hungarian to be found in the chapter contain errors.[98] The fact that, at the same time, Joyce is also able to include a quite sophisticated

---

[96] cf. ibid. 74–6.

[97] I am grateful to Ferenc Takács for these points, and to other Hungarian scholars for confirming them.

[98] According to Ferenc Takács, most of the Hungarian in *Ulysses* is incorrect, though sometimes only slightly.

Hungarian joke suggests that the mistakes are deliberate.[99] In effect, 'Cyclops' both plays with and comically repudiates Griffith's identification of the two nations, his insistence on their symmetrical relation.

Joyce's attitude to Griffith was complex, and by no means primarily critical.[100] Yet the Hungarian 'parallel' clearly roused him to derisive mirth. He was by no means alone in poking fun at it. It was 'often lampooned' in contemporary Ireland.[101] Yet Joyce's main objection was surely to the mode of historiography on which it was based. This is why Hungary figures to such an extent in 'Cyclops'. In *Stephen Hero*, Stephen had already poured scorn on 'analogies built haphazard on very little knowledge' and used the Hungarian 'parallel' as an example (*SH*, 66–7). But Joyce also noticed how closely Griffith's historiographical principles resemble those of the revivalists. Griffith oversimplifies, omits facts not favourable to his case, and introduces errors.[102] He is reluctant to look too closely at the 'chronological, social, institutional or even economic details' of Hungarian history.[103] In the *Resurrection* as in O'Grady's *History*, indifference to certain questions of accuracy goes hand in hand with a stress on unity rather than conflict and division. Griffith sees Catholics and Protestants as forming 'a common nation' both in Hungary and in Ireland.[104] He ignores or explicitly minimizes 'distinctions' of 'class' and 'party'.[105] He praises Swift for his desire to unite 'the old Irish and the new'.[106] As a de-Anglicizer, he is critical of the 'séoinin Magyars' in Hungary.[107] But he is also intent on possible compromise. Significantly, he is actually more sympathetic to an Anglo-Irish tradition of resistance (Swift, Molyneux, Charles Lucas) than to a Catholic one (as in the case of O'Connell).[108] The result once again is a heroic, idealist historiography. Griffith's 'statistics of an 18 million

---

[99] 'Százharminczbrojúgulyás-Dugulás' (12. 1818) is not in fact a place name. It means 'Constipation caused by one hundred and thirty portions of veal goulash'. See Ferenc Takács, 'Joyce and Hungary', in Zach and Kosok (eds.), *Literary Interrelations*, iii. *National Images*, 161–7, at 161–2. According to Takács, the joke suggests at least a moderately sophisticated knowledge of Hungarian. Joyce may have relied on the help of Hungarian friends like Theodor Mayer.

[100] See e.g. Richard Ellmann, *James Joyce* (rev. edn., Oxford: Oxford University Press, 1982), 238; and Dominic Manganiello, *Joyce's Politics* (London: Routledge & Kegan Paul, 1980), 118–19, 124–7. [101] Younger, *Arthur Griffith*, 22.

[102] See e.g. Kabdebo, *Hungarian-Irish 'Parallel'*, 12, 17, 18; and Davis, *Arthur Griffith*, 19. [103] Kabdebo, *Hungarian-Irish 'Parallel'*, 12.

[104] *Resurrection of Hungary*, 6. [105] Ibid. 38. [106] Ibid. 86.

[107] Ibid. 21. [108] Ibid. 86–7, 90.

strong Hungary' enjoying 'an economic boom' entirely ignore 'the abject poverty of the over 3 million agrarian labourers'.[109]

The Citizen and the Nameless One

As Colum suggests, *The Resurrection of Hungary* was not history but 'a myth—an arousing myth'.[110] Joyce clearly quarrelled with both its form and its substance. He saw in it a kind of historiography that, even while protesting its will to independence, actually remained subservient, not least in its collusion with the dominant mode of Irish historiography as established by the Anglo-Irish revivalists. Hence the mockery to which he subjects it in 'Cyclops'. This finally provides us with a useful perspective on Joyce's treatment of the citizen. Joyce was prepared to use various weapons against Revival historiography. Historical particularity is one of the most obvious. Where O'Grady rejects 'minuteness' on the one hand and 'despotic fact' on the other, the historical allusions in 'Cyclops' are frequently extremely precise, in the spirit of the provocatively hard-edged account of Shakespeare with which Stephen challenges Russell and Eglinton. Thus the passage that alludes to the Creed, for example, is exact in its reference to the contemporary controversy over naval discipline (12. 1354–9).[111] Such historical precision also partly serves as an antidote to the citizen's often generalized, hyperbolic, inaccurate rhodomontade. Here, again, Joyce's acerbic view of the colonial power has a steely exactitude missing from the citizen's denunciations. Joyce adopts the same strategy to counter both the citizen's historical discourse and Revival historiography. This shouldn't surprise us. Emer Nolan has rightly taken the critical tradition to task for its more or less uniformly negative account of the citizen, and the lack of political acuteness and historical awareness

---

[109] Kabdebo, *Hungarian-Irish 'Parallel'*, 21. Kabdebo, who seeks to defend Griffith, calls Griffith's fixing of evidence 'an optimal representation of available facts' (ibid. 24). Joyce, of course, was no enthusiast for 'optimal representations'.

[110] *Arthur Griffith*, 78.

[111] See R. M. Adams, *Surface and Symbol: The Consistency of James Joyce's 'Ulysses'* (New York: Oxford University Press, 1962), 227; and Don Gifford with Robert J. Seidman, *Ulysses Annotated: Notes for James Joyce's 'Ulysses'* (rev. edn., Berkeley and Los Angeles: University of California Press, 1988), 357. For some other examples, see F. L. Radford, 'King, Pope and Hero-Martyr: *Ulysses* and the Nightmare of Irish History', *James Joyce Quarterly*, 15/4 (Summer 1978), 275–323.

that has frequently been at the root of it.[112] The most common view
has been that, through Bloom on the one hand and irony on the other,
Joyce subjects the citizen and nationalism—or at least, violent
nationalism—to a severe but warranted, liberal-humanist (or, more
recently, postmodern-liberal) critique.[113] By way of rejoinder, it is
worth remarking that there is an element of crude satire and indeed
of crude insult in the writing of 'Cyclops' itself that markedly closes
the gap between Joyce and the citizen (as in the case of 'sir Hercules
Hannibal Habeas Corpus Anderson', 12. 1893–6). Similarly, Nolan
has recalled some of the connections and similarities between Joyce
and the citizen, and convincingly argued, contrary to orthodoxy, that
'in some respects' their views 'may actually *coincide*'.[114]

But, helpful though this argument may be, it nonetheless still
approaches Joyce in terms of his 'judgement of' and/or 'sympathy' or
'lack of sympathy' with his creation. So, too, whether humanistic or
postmodern, the dominant interpretation of the citizen continues
largely to rely on a tired old Leavisite construction of the text that
bears little or no relevance to Joyce's endeavour. As Nolan says herself, it is necessary rather to address the relation between 'the citizen's
discourse and the other kinds of writing' in the chapter.[115] The crucial point is that Joyce understands the citizen (historically), rather
than judging him, and invites a certain understanding of him by plac-
ing him in a particular discursive context. To return to my point
about the twin uses of a single strategy: Joyce recognizes how far, like
Griffith's, the citizen's view of history as articulated in 'Cyclops' is an
extension of and conditioned by the view of history so frequently
adumbrated in the 'parodies'. The areas of historical concern may be
different. Nonetheless, it is important to stress, once again, how
deeply complicit the new nationalism was with the older revivalism,

---

[112] See her *James Joyce and Nationalism* (London: Routledge, 1995), 91–113.

[113] For liberal humanist accounts, see e.g. Parrinder, *James Joyce*, 172; S. L. Goldberg,
The Classical Temper: A Study of James Joyce's 'Ulysses' (London: Chatto & Windus,
1961), 282–3; Matthew Hodgart, *James Joyce: A Student's Guide* (London: Routledge &
Kegan Paul, 1978), 101–2; and Ellmann, *'Ulysses' on the Liffey*, 116. For a view of Joyce as
an (oddly virulent) postmodern-liberal moralist in his treatment of the citizen, see Joseph
Valente, *James Joyce and the Problem of Justice: Negotiating Sexual and Colonial Difference* (Cambridge: Cambridge University Press, 1995), 42–3. For an early version of this
kind of reading, see Colin MacCabe, *James Joyce and the Revolution of the Word*
(London: Macmillan, 1978), 93, 101. See also Nolan's pointed critique of MacCabe, *James
Joyce*, 94.   [114] Nolan, *James Joyce*, 100.
[115] Ibid.

and how relevant that is to *Ulysses*.[116] 'Cyclops' makes such complicity clear. It partly does so in simple ways. Thus traces of the 'composite style' evident in the 'parodies' also appear in what the citizen has to say: the double epithets (12. 1198–1200), the choice and archaic vocabulary (12. 1374), the place-list (12. 1302–3), the 'run' (12. 1240–54). The citizen's habits of imprecision (12. 1240) and exaggeration (12. 1199–1205) resemble O'Grady's and Griffith's. The historical lacunae are different, of course, but the tendency to leave lacunae is itself a shared one (12. 1364–75). Thinking in terms of polar opposites (12. 523–4) or fixed categories is likewise a habit that O'Grady, Griffith, and the citizen all have in common, as is the resort to mythology (12. 1306–10). Some of the themes in the 'parodies' and their sources are equally themes of the citizen's: sport (12. 889–90), Irish forestation (12. 1262–4), the fruitfulness of Ireland (12. 1242–54). More importantly, the 'gigantism' of Revival historiography spills over into the citizen's nationalist account of history. The fondness for heroics is still there (12. 1372–5), along with the same rather grandiose nostalgia (12. 1248–54), and the same grandly improbable view of the future (12. 891). Joyce was well aware of the connections binding the emergent nationalist culture to Revival culture.[117] He was also well aware of the latent continuities between their respective views of history. The relationship between the two cultures partly resembled that between Revival culture and English culture. The demands were repeatedly for purity. The reality, again and again—as Joyce underlines—was interinvolvement.

Almost everything else in 'Cyclops' can be fitted around its central concerns as I have described them: the burlesque of Russell and theosophical discourse, for instance (another revivalist rejection of 'the vulgarity of actual things', and of history along with it, 12. 338–60); the humour at the expense of certain journalistic styles (displaying their Anglicized character even as they deal with nationalist subjects, 12. 897–926). Joyce's seriocomic treament of Bloom in 'Cyclops' also makes more sense in this context. It remains perplexing only if we insist on seeing Bloom and the realist narrative as central to the

---

[116] Cf. Kiberd, 'Vulgarity of Heroics', *passim*; Seamus Deane, '"Masked with Matthew Arnold's Face": Joyce and Liberalism', in Beja et al. (eds.), *James Joyce: The Centennial Symposium* (Urbana, Ill.: University of Illinois Press, 1986), 9–21; and G. J. Watson, 'The Politics of *Ulysses*', in Robert D. Newman and Weldon Thornton (eds.), *Joyce's 'Ulysses': The Larger Perspective* (London: Associated University Presses, 1987), 39–59.

[117] Cf. Lyons, *Culture and Anarchy*, 85–8.

meaning of the chapter. Take the historical theme and the 'parodies' as a starting point, and it becomes clear that Joyce's presentation of Bloom is ambiguous and playful partly because he can afford to let it be so. There is only a limited amount at stake. In a certain way, Joyce probably takes what Bloom says seriously—that is, he means it—but it is clearly not intended to be largely significant within the chapter. Finally, once we take the ramifications of the historical theme fully into account, the distinctive contribution made by its nameless narrator to 'Cyclops' becomes clearer. In tone and manner, he is the antithesis of the imaginative world of O'Grady, Yeats, and Lady Gregory (particularly of its anti-democratic cast). He is equally obviously set at a difficult angle to the citizen's, Griffith's, or Pearse's view of the Irish.[118] Critical responses to him have surely been too prim and proper.[119] In comparison, not only to the citizen, but to the literature the 'parodies' respond to, he is a liberatingly comic relief. His limitations are doubtless conspicuous. But for Joyce, in contrast to a whole historiography—a whole mode of the historical imagination—he has and represents an irreducible, unregenerate, vulgar, and vital presentness. He may lack any sense of history himself. But he and his discourse embody Joyce's wicked challenge to the historical imagination of others. If he lacks a name, it is chiefly within all extant Irish historical and political discourses, constrained as they remain by the colonial past. But here, Joyce is saying, is an actual Irishman, living in history, and you must take him with all his imperfections.

[118] In the case of Griffith, one might recall his responses to Synge, *In the Shadow of the Glen* and *The Playboy of the Western World.*

[119] For examples of this, see e.g. Ellmann, *The Consciousness of Joyce* (London: Faber & Faber, 1977), 21, and *'Ulysses' on the Liffey*, 110–11; Peake, *James Joyce*, 234; and Stanley Sultan, *The Argument of 'Ulysses'* (Columbus, Oh.: Ohio State University Press, 1964), 234–6.

CHAPTER SIX

Waking Up in Ireland: 'Nausicaa'

An English Usurper

In *The Lady's Own Novelette* for 24 June 1903, there is a story entitled 'An English Usurper'.[1] It is set in Ireland. The O'Donovans, grandfather and granddaughter, are being pursued by 'money-lending Jews' and their English creditors, the France family of Birmingham. In a climate of political unrest, they cannot raise loans, and must abandon their ancestral estate at Rossmore. Young Harry France travels to Ireland to occupy the property. He arrives at the village, where he encounters dreary landscapes and depressing scenes. The whiskey is bad. There is no room for English Harry at Joyce's hotel (no less). He has to cope, not only with the drunkenness, sloth, and incompetence of the locals, but also with their peculiar brogue. Delia O'Donovan hates young Harry on principle and on sight, and duly incites a boycott against him. However, Harry sets her right: her father has been an improvident manager of his own estate. For their part, the Frances have been generous and tolerant in all their dealings with the O'Donovans. Delia swiftly repents. Too late, however: the dangerous and illiterate 'Capen Moonlite' (aka Dennis Toomey) has already sent Harry a death threat. Delia seeks feebly to excuse this, with some interesting shifts in pronouns: 'They don't understand it like that [as murder]. They think we have been wronged. Round here we don't reason things out logically and soberly as you do'.[2] An ambush is laid for Harry. Delia gets wind of it, and rides out to save him. The bullet strikes her rather than the young man. Happily, however, the wound is not fatal. Harry and Delia confess their love, marry, and divide their time between England and Rossmore. 'Capen Moonlite' meets his nemesis, dying 'bruised and disfigured' after a fall.[3] At the

---

[1] *LON* 762 (24 June 1903), 3–12.   [2] Ibid. 11.   [3] Ibid. 12.

end of the number is an advertisement for Thomas Holloway's Pills and Ointment, 'used wherever the white man has set his foot'. It includes a picture of a grateful 'Masai warrior' with a jar of 'HOLLOWAY'S OINTMENT' ornamentally welded into one earlobe.

The story is arresting, for several reasons. First, in certain ways, it gives a relevant account, albeit a loaded one, of the structure of the political and cultural relations between England, Anglo-Ireland, and Catholic Ireland which *Ulysses* addresses. Secondly, 'An English Usurper' is very obviously a Unionist allegory in popular form: sane, prudent, commercially-minded but generous and tolerant England saves a lovable but insecure Anglo-Irish gentry from alliance with a feckless, faintly disgusting but menacing Catholic Ireland. In the process, the Englishman renews the failing Anglo-Irish heritage. Hence the story's relevance to 'Nausicaa': it shows how far, in the first decade of the century, popular women's magazines and magazine fiction could articulate a markedly ideological account of contemporary Irish society and culture.[4] Thirdly, so far as I know, in this respect, the sustained, ideological coherence displayed in 'An English Usurper' is unique in the women's magazines of the period. But some of its elements are evident elsewhere: the 'characteristic Milesian', for example, the charming Irish gentleman afflicted with lassitude and lacking purpose and direction;[5] the stereotypical presentation of the common Irishman or woman. As Irene Dancyger has amusingly shown, not only did Ireland provide useful material for a 'patronizing genre' of fiction in nineteenth-century women's magazines. Such stories also traded in 'near-imbecilic stock characters'. As Shaw noted, says Dancyger, they spoke a tongue unknown to the Irish themselves.[6] The genre was still around in 1904. Fourthly, in its material context, the magazine itself, 'An English Usurper' shows how far popular publications for women insistently confirmed not only class and gender but also racial hierarchies, and helped to keep them in mass circulation. In *The Lady's Own Novelette* for 24 June 1903, the

---

[4] The 'condition of Ireland' was an established theme in popular fiction from the Victorian period onwards, featuring in Victorian series like the *Parlour Library* and the *Railway Library*, e.g. See Margaret Dalziel, *Popular Fiction A Hundred Years Ago* (London: Cohen & West, 1957), 81.

[5] The quotation is from 'Honour Above All', *LON* 2 (Mar. 1889), 15.

[6] Dancyger, *A World of Women: An Illustrated History of Women's Magazines* (Dublin: Gill and Macmillan, 1978), 47. The readers used in the national schools in Ireland often dealt in similar stock types. See Janet A. Nolan, *Ourselves Alone: Women's Emigration from Ireland 1885–1920* (Lexington, Ky.: University of Kentucky Press, 1989), 38.

appropriate distinctions between the English, Irish gentlefolk, Jews, Irish peasants, and Masai warriors are made very clear.

Imperial, colonial, and racial discourses were a routine if sometimes low-level feature of popular women's magazines between 1880 and 1920. Joyce could not have failed to be aware of this: it would have been starkly evident to any politically sensitive, Irish reader. The writing of the Gerty MacDowell section of 'Nausicaa' (13. 1–770) develops partly in relation to the discourses in question. The most significant and popular women's magazines of the period were published in London. In fact, they largely emanated from a square mile, Fleet Street and environs. Their provenance was self-evident: the society and gossip columns, for instance, were frankly London-centred. But the magazines also had a colonial readership, were aware of it, and explicitly addressed it. 'Nausicaa' refers in particular to one 'penny dreadful', *The Princess's Novelettes* (13. 110). This contained a section called 'All About People' which was about life in the colonies. 'The colonies' included Ireland: members of the Anglo-Irish gentry featured alongside the colonial classes in more far-flung lands.[7] 'Nausicaa' also alludes to a 'quality' magazine, *Lady's Pictorial* (13. 151), which provided columns of colonial anecdote and discussions of colonial issues. It contained an 'Irish Letter' which offered regular news of the Irish well-to-do or the 'Irish galaxy of fashion' (largely the Anglo-Irish gentry and aristocracy).[8] It provided accounts of the balls, bazaars, and literary events they attended.[9] One particular number included a loyalist view of Edward VII's visit to Ireland.[10]

Not surprisingly, when the publisher of *The Princess's Novelettes* advertised his list, it included *The Empire Novels* and *Boys of the Empire: An Up-to-Date Boy's Journal*. Some issues also advertised the *Empire Bouquet Novels*. The *Novelettes* told 'colonial readers' how they in particular might obtain copies of the patterns for clothes that were a regular feature.[11] This kind of instruction was common: the editor of *The Lady's Own Novelette* addressed 'my readers in all parts of the world' and constantly reminded them not to use foreign stamps on stamped addressed envelopes.[12] Many of the stories in the novelettes

---

[7] See e.g. *PN* 36/905 (22 June 1903), 32.
[8] See e.g. *LP* 45/1, 140 (3 Jan. 1903), 25; and 154 (11 Apr. 1903), 761.
[9] See e.g. the account of the celebration of the Moore Centenary, *LP* 45/1, 163 (13 June 1903), 1344.   [10] Ibid. 1326.
[11] See e.g. *PN* 37/954 (20 May 1904), 398.   [12] *LON* 811 (1 June 1904), unpaginated.

at least touched on colonial life. Heroes were often given some experience of the colonies, to make them more glamorous. In this respect as in others, the stories in *The Princess's Novelettes* often overlapped with 'All about People' and those in *Lady's Pictorial* with its vignettes of colonial life. So, too, the advertisements often had a colonial flavour, whether they were for malaria cures or the Annual Balaclava Dinner.[13] What Anne McClintock has called 'commodity jingoism' was common in the magazines, as in advertisements for products like 'Oriental Toothpaste' and ' "Imperial' Curlers'.[14] When non-white races featured, they summoned up colonial contexts or the power relations that obtained in them: the 'Coon Songs' in *The Princess's Novelettes*, the pictures of Indian women in *Lady's Pictorial*, the 'commodity racism' of grinning Chinese or black faces in advertisements.[15]

The magazines were partly responding to a contemporary insistence within English cultural nationalism. The assumption that England suffered from a 'surplus' of women was common from the 1880s onwards. Women were therefore increasingly encouraged to settle in the colonies.[16] The number of organizations 'devoted to encouraging such emigration, and to training women for colonial life' expanded significantly and rapidly.[17] Women became a crucial part of the 'civilizing mission'. For women could 'ensure the survival' of Anglo-Saxon ideals and the national heritage in an alien environment.[18] The magazines reflected this drive. Indeed, they were particularly responsive to it in the first decade of the century.[19] Thus in the

---

[13] See e.g. *LON* 796 (17 Feb. 1904), 31; and 778 (14 Oct. 1903), 29.

[14] See e.g. *LP* 47/1, 207 (16 Apr. 1904); 211 (14 May 1904); and 212 (21 May 1904). For the concept of 'commodity jingoism', see McClintock, *Imperial Leather: Race, Gender and Sexuality in the Colonial Contest* (New York: Routledge, 1995).

[15] See e.g. *LON* 805 (20 Apr. 1904), unpaginated. For a particularly striking example of imperial propaganda involving different races in *LP*, see the picture ' "Sisters": Delhi, New Year's Day, 1903', 45/1, 141 (10 Jan. 1903), 51. 'Commodity racism' is McClintock's term. McClintock provides an important account of late Victorian advertising as taking 'scenes of empire into every corner of the home', mediating 'the Victorian poetics of racial hygiene and imperial progress', and helping to 'reinvent and maintain British national unity in the face of deepening imperial competition and colonial resistance' (*Imperial Leather*, 209). See esp. ch. 5, 'Soft-Soaping Empire: Commodity Racism and Imperial Advertising', pp. 207–31.

[16] See Sara Delamont, 'The Contradictions in Ladies' Education', in Sara Delamont and Lorna Duffin, *The Nineteenth-Century Woman: Her Cultural and Physical World* (London: Croom Helm, 1978), 134–63, esp. 139.

[17] Jane Mackay and Pat Thane, 'The Englishwoman', in Robert Colls and Philip Dodd (eds.), *Englishness: Politics and Culture 1880–1920* (London: Croom Helm, 1986), 191–229, at 203.   [18] Ibid. 203.

[19] Ibid. 205.

Lady's Pictorial for 18 June 1904, 'Ella Hepworth Dixon' argued the case for inducing 'the superfluous women who congregate in these islands [note the plural] to go . . . to our more flourishing Colonies'. Colonial British men might otherwise be tempted to marry native women.[20] The content of the magazines was inflected by English nationalism in other ways, too. In particular, their domestic concerns were determined by Victorian and Edwardian 'domestic ideology', and their concern with health by the contemporary drive for 'national fitness'. Both the ideologies in question were crucial to the development of 'girls growing up' in late Victorian and Edwardian England and Ireland.[21] The 'national efficiency' movement and the anxieties that lay behind it helped produce an emphasis on the virtue of motherhood, domesticity, and self-sacrifice. These were women's duties, not only to men and the family, but also to the State. Evolutionary theorists, social-Darwinists, eugenicists, clergymen, and the medical profession all propounded theories about 'the social and biological inadvisability of women deserting their "responsibilities to the race" by selfishly developing their own intellects at the expense of reproduction'.[22] At the same time, there was widespread, contemporary concern that the English race might be undergoing a 'physical deterioration'. *Times* readers in 1904—like James Joyce—could hardly not be aware of it. Indeed, 1904 saw the much-bruited publication of the *Report of the Physical Deterioration Committee*. The national welfare itself appeared to require that women develop their domestic skills.[23] The woman who proved to be a good housewife was the more likely to be an effective weapon against the threat posed to both family and nation by poverty, squalor, enfeeblement, and drink.[24] Thus 'a large body of literature' with 'a strident, imperialist vocabulary' urged women, not only to maintain their health and fitness, but to regard the preservation of their health 'as a moral duty' owed 'to the Empire and the Race'.[25]

[20] LP 47/1, 216 (18 June 1904), 1140.

[21] See Carol Dyhouse, *Girls Growing Up in Late Victorian and Edwardian England* (London: Routledge & Kegan Paul, 1981), *passim*; and Sara Delamont, 'The Domestic Ideology and Women's Education', in Delamont and Duffin, *Nineteenth-Century Woman*, 164–87.

[22] Dyhouse, *Girls Growing Up*, 121. Dyhouse points out that this formed part of an argument that feminism in particular was 'dysgenic', a threat to social efficiency and racial progress (ibid. 154). [23] See ibid. 162.

[24] See Dyhouse, 'Good Wives and Little Mothers: Social Anxieties and the Schoolgirl's Curriculum, 1890–1920', *Oxford Review of Education*, 3/1 (1977), 21–35, esp. 22.

[25] Mackay and Thane, 'Englishwoman', 136.

The *Lady's Pictorial* for 11 June 1904 has a number of connections with *Ulysses*, notably an account of the Mirus bazaar and a full-page picture of the Alake of Abeokuta (cf. 12. 1514–33). It also contains a feature entitled 'A Healthy Suggestion'. This suggested that 'naturally we English are a sturdy and hardy race'. At the same time, however, the English should not hide from themselves 'the unpleasant truth that we are not what we were in times past'. Those who formed 'the backbone of the nation' were showing signs of 'physical deterioration'. If the nation were to remain strong, then the people must be educated 'in the gospel of health'. This was a matter especially for women. For women could serve as 'health missionaries' in the home.[26] *Pearson's Weekly*—another journal to which 'Nausicaa' explicitly refers (13. 291–2)—ran features like 'How to keep a Husband Healthy: To a Great Extent the Wife can Regulate his Physical Well-Being'.[27] That *Lady's Pictorial* ran a regular column called 'The Home' alongside frequent 'healthy suggestions' is indicative. The ideology of 'national fitness' and the 'domestic ideology' often went hand in hand. The advertisements and advice columns in the magazines told women how to improve their health and fitness. At the same time, the stories, advertisements, and features all insisted that a girl's destiny was romance, marriage, and a 'nice snug and cosy little homely house' (13. 239). Such a destiny brought her round in a full if narrow circle, depositing her back in the English home to which she had always in any case belonged.

The magazines therefore served as points of intersection between colonial and racial discourses, the 'domestic ideology' and the ideology of 'national fitness'. The emphasis on fitness, for example, led to a concern, not just with the healthy body, but with a 'normative' (white, European, chiefly English) body. *Pearson's Weekly* regularly ran pieces like 'Folks Who Fake Features: How Japanese Eyes, Jewish Noses and Other Awkward Features Are "Corrected" ', and 'Making Black Men White: Wonders that Radium is Capable of Doing'.[28] 'Freaks' were an object of boggle-eyed curiosity. The *Weekly* ran a column called 'Odd Beings'. The 'beings' in question included Irishmen like the 'limbless trunk', MP Arthur McMurrough Kavanagh.[29]

---

[26] LP 47/1, 215 (11 June 1904), 1102.
[27] PW 718 (week ending 21 Apr. 1904), 783.
[28] PW 716 (week ending 7 Apr. 1904), 735; and 719 (week ending 28 Apr. 1904), 797.
[29] See 'Freak M.Ps: Odd Beings Who Have Sat in the House of Commons', PW 712 (week ending 10 Mar. 1904), 663.

Commentators on 'Nausicaa' have often dwelt on Joyce's concern with the ideological construction of Gerty.[30] Thomas Richards argues that here, 'for the first time', a writer confronted advertising 'not just as a social space for displaying commodities but as a coercive agent for invading and structuring human consciousness'.[31] The 'coercions' in question, however, were not those of a generalized 'commodity culture'. They were quite specifically English, imperial, and nationalistic—or were at least inflected in those directions—and belonged to a specific phase of English (and Irish) history.

'Nausicaa' is thus much concerned with the relationship between Gerty and a set of discourses that produce a serviceable model of English and colonial womanhood. The model had a contemporary, political significance. Joyce discreetly but exactly indicates how far the ideological features of Gerty's historical situation are implicit in the magazines she reads. It is no accident, for example, that the reader of 'Nausicaa' immediately encounters two small boys dressed in English sailor suits, with the name of a British naval vessel 'printed on both' (13. 15). Such suits, or patterns for them, were part of a contemporary, commercial romance of the British navy, and were often advertised in both *Lady's Pictorial* and *The Princess's Novelettes*.[32] Joyce clearly signals, not only the fact of colonial importation, but also the vectors of colonial power that underlie it. In 'Nausicaa', the detail also promptly fits into a larger context. The point, at once, is that the 'Irishman's house' is not 'his castle' (13. 46–7). The boys' argument over whether the sandcastle might be 'architecturally improved by a frontdoor like the Martello tower had' (13. 44–5) reintroduces a familiar symbol of 'the British presence in Ireland'.[33] That presence is decisively indicated from the start of the chapter, as it is from the start of the novel. So, too, is the involvement of the colonial power in the construction of young Irish minds (at least, in so far as

[30] See e.g. Bonnie Kime Scott, *James Joyce* (Brighton: Harvester, 1987), 62–7; Patrick McGee, *Paperspace: Style as Ideology in Joyce's 'Ulysses'* (Lincoln, Nebra.: University of Nebraska Press, 1988), 85–99; Suzette Henke, *James Joyce and the Politics of Desire* (London: Routledge, 1990), 138; and Katie Wales, *The Language of James Joyce* (London: Macmillan, 1987), 97.

[31] *The Commodity Culture of Victorian England: Advertising and Spectacle 1851–1914* (London: Verso, 1991), 207.

[32] See e.g. *PN* 36/906 (29 June 1903), 45; *LP* 45/1 (11 Apr. 1903), 154, where one advertisement refers to them as 'Man o' War' suits; and *LP* 47/1 (11 June 1904), 215.

[33] Cf. Tom Paulin, 'The British Presence in *Ulysses*', in *Ireland and the English Crisis* (Newcastle: Bloodaxe, 1984), 92–100, esp. 92.

learning English is concerned, 13. 26–8). Joyce's use of the women's magazines is directly related to these two themes.

The British presence is a determining force in Gerty's understanding of matters of class, gender, and race. First, Gerty's reading has generated fantasies of elevation to the ranks of the English (or Anglo-Irish) aristocracy or gentry. Secondly (and not altogether consistently), it has also been a principal point of transmission for the 'domestic ideology'. Gerty is 'womanly wise', and recognizes that one of her main tasks is to supply a man with 'that feeling of hominess' (13. 223–4). The ideology of personal fitness is likewise evident in the chapter, if poignantly and ironically, in Gerty's efforts to remedy her bodily 'fragility' (13. 84). The same ideology underlies her effort to improve her appearance and thus (she supposes) her chances in the marriage market. Physical self-improvement is also a racial issue. Gerty repeatedly stresses the attractions of pure whiteness: she imagines having a face of 'ivorylike purity' (13. 88), hands of 'alabaster' (13. 89), arms that are 'white and soft' (13. 341). She also dreams of having tapering fingers, which *The Princess's Novelettes* would have told her were a sign of purer or more 'aristocratic' blood.[34] Equally, her concern with being physically 'flawless' (13. 583) reflects the magazines' emphasis on the importance of a 'faultless' body,[35] and their corresponding valuation of racial purity. Gerty's reference to improving the nose (13. 114) also echoes advertisements with racial overtones. So does her conviction of her own refinement as compared to 'Madcap Ciss with her golliwog curls' (13. 270). The image in Gerty's mind, here, comes from the soap advertisements that featured black women's faces.

But if 'Nausicaa' is caught up in a particular discursive formation, it also resists it, often in small, fleeting, and subtle ways. In her innocence, for example, Gerty frequently deflects and disarms the racial discourses in question. She remarks of nose improvement, for example, that 'that would suit Mrs Dignam because she had a button one' (13. 114–15).[36] So, too, whilst the magazines traded in a fixed semi-

[34] See e.g. 'Sir Arthur Hanaford's Revenge', *PN* 37/952 (16 May 1904), 353–64, at 354.
[35] See e.g. the advertisement for F. Cecil Russell's *Corpulency and the Cure* in *PN*, 36/908 (13 July 1903).
[36] Note, however, that Mayhew refers to 'button noses' among the London street-Irish as though they were a common Irish feature. See Henry Mayhew, *London Labour and the London Poor*, selected and introd. Victor Neuburg (Harmondsworth: Penguin, 1985), 56–60.

otics of race, 'Nausicaa' stresses the changeability and inconstancy of skin colour. Gerty follows the magazines and makes a fetish of whiteness. But Joyce deliberately emphasizes that skin tints change. Gerty flushes (13. 120, 365), crimsons 'up to the roots of her hair' (13. 454), and turns 'scarlet' (13. 518). Bloom 'colours', too (13. 743). Such details also subvert that mythological entity, the perfect body. 'Nausicaa' insists on the reality of imperfection (Gerty's lameness, Edy's squint, 13. 521; Cissy's 'skinny shanks' and 'long gandery strides', 13. 478–9, 483–4). It also repudiates the concept of a hard, static body implicit in the notion of flawlessness. Bodies in 'Nausicaa' are notably in process: flushing, blushing, pissing (13. 75–7, 395), vomiting (13. 611), dribbling (13. 612), ejaculating (13. 705–6), menstruating (13. 562), leaking tears and snot (13. 399, 529). They are also liable to 'rushing' sensations, sudden irritations (13. 560–1), a whole variety of comings and goings which make questions of perfection irrelevant. The chapter also counters the genteel values routinely purveyed by the magazines. In this respect, the rumbustious figure of Cissy is clearly important. Cissy's comic version of the genteel hostess at afternoon tea—'would you have some more Chinese tea and jaspberry ram' (13. 271–2)—subverts another stock magazine image. Cissy is strikingly resistant to the 'domestic ideology'. So, too, 'Nausicaa' insistently reminds us of what actual domesticity is likely to mean for Irishwomen: the strain that has produced Mrs MacDowell's 'raging splitting headaches', for example (13. 327). Furthermore, Gerty's position in the MacDowell household sometimes seems closer to the servant's than that of the cosily domestic woman projected by the magazines. Mona Hearn's list of the tasks of domestic servants in Dublin between 1880 and 1920 includes a number of Gerty's chores (firelighting, and looking after the lavatory and gas).[37]

'Upstart Journals' and the Starved Soul of Womanhood

To a large extent, then, Joyce makes Ireland, Irish girlhood, and 'Nausicaa' itself seem recalcitrant to a set of discursive formations

---

[37] See 'Life for Domestic Servants in Dublin, 1880–1920', in Maria Luddy and Cliona Murphy (eds.), *Women Surviving: Studies in Irish Women's History in the Nineteenth and Twentieth Centuries* (Dublin: Poolbeg, 1990), 148–70, at 153.

imported from the dominant culture. He does so in a host of little touches. If the touches are slight, that is because they must seem plausible within the drastically restricted sphere of women's lives in turn-of-the-century Dublin. The two points that follow, however, will seem to cut directly across my argument so far. First, the chapter equally indexes *Lady's Pictorial* and *The Princess's Novelettes*. The two certainly shared a number of common features. But they were also different kinds of magazine, and attracted very different reader-ships. Like *The Lady, Ladyland, The Queen, The Young Ladies' Journal*, and *The Gentlewoman, Lady's Pictorial* was an upmarket or 'quality' magazine. It appealed predominantly to the middle and upper classes. The fantasy world it constructed was not altogether remote from the real lives of its readers. The latter tended to *be* the kind of women mentioned in columns like 'Women's World of Sport', 'At the Play', 'Boudoir Gossip', 'London Fashions', 'Ladies Who Hunt', 'The Social Biograph', and 'Court News'. By contrast, 'All About People' in *The Princess's Novelettes* was precisely not about the women who read it. The novelettes—*Princess's, Lady's Own, Royal, Mayflower, Duchess, Countess*—traded in a romance of social elevation. They were aimed at 'the mill-girl, the shop-assistant and the lady's maid', and peddled what Cynthia White calls a 'spurious gentility'.[38] In this respect, they often became targets of mockery. To an editor of *Ladyland*, they showed 'no more intimate knowledge of the domestic life of the upper and middle classes than might be gleaned from a surreptitious conversation with Sarah Jane at the back-garden gate'. Their 'high-sounding titles' notwithstand-ing, they would never 'reach the realms of "ladyland" '.[39] In fact, they were doomed to the status of 'upstart journals'.[40] Gerty's section of 'Nausicaa' may be made up of disparate elements. But her imaginary and her position relative to the magazines are substantially those of the novelette reader. They are not those of the reader of the 'quali-ties', nor, *a fortiori*, of the other kinds of women's magazine then available (the 'sensible' magazines, the magazines for educated women, the magazines that gave space to women's rights).[41]

[38] *Women's Magazines 1693–1968* (London: Michael Joseph, 1970), 70. My distinction derives from White's extremely informative book, 65–71.
[39] *Ladyland* (1898), preface to launch issue; quoted in White, *Women's Magazines*, 70.
[40] The phrase is White's. See *Women's Magazines*, 71.
[41] On the first two, see White, ibid. 73. On the third, see Mirabel Cecil, *Heroines in Love 1750–1974* (London: Michael Joseph, 1974), 115.

My second point is this: there is undoubtedly a fair amount of laughter at the expense of the novelettes, in 'Nausicaa'. But Joyce's attitude to them is not one of patrician derision. Dowden saw the popular press as providing 'a mincemeat that requires no chewing'.[42] In doing so, he was reproducing a snobbery already well established in English intellectual culture. It stemmed from Matthew Arnold, who described popular fiction as 'hideous and ignoble of aspect' and only for those with 'a low standard of life',[43] and was to run to F. R. Leavis and well beyond. But Joyce does not share Arnold and Dowden's superciliousness. In particular, it is not clear that Joyce is really *parodying* anything specific. He certainly does not parody the staple, fictional style in *The Princess's Novelettes*, which is rather different to the one in Joyce's chapter (and much less fun).[44] The sentimental style in the first half of 'Nausicaa' actually seems closer to some of the fiction in other magazines. But no particular target was obviously uppermost in Joyce's mind. In any case, the language of sentimental fiction in general was too differentiated for 'Nausicaa' to be based on a stock, homogeneous model. Significantly, too, the chapter also draws on other styles from other parts of the magazines, like the fashion columns.

The most important point is surely the sheer extent to which the *particularities* of Gerty's mind come from the magazines. Richards notes, for instance, that, at lines 148–87, Gerty virtually runs through the details of a full ensemble from *Lady's Pictorial*.[45] The references to Gerty's 'wealth of wonderful hair'—'dark brown with a natural wave in it'—derive from the magazines (13. 116–17). The latter almost invariably contained pictures of young women with luxuriant tresses, an image that was also frequent in the stories. At the turn of the century, auburn was the preferred colour, a trend set by the Gibson girl.[46] 'Nausicaa' covers most if not all of the points listed in advertisements for books like *How to be Beautiful; or, Articles on a Lady's Toilet*.[47] Gerty's 'selftinted' blouse (13. 150) calls to mind the patterns for home-made blouses provided by the

---

[42] 'Hopes and Fears for Literature', *Fortnightly Review*, 45 (1889), 166–83, at 169–70.

[43] 'Copyright', *Fortnightly Review*, 27 (1880), 319–34, at 327–8.

[44] In particular, Gerty's somewhat intermittent but vivid awareness of her body affects her style in a manner quite unlike the novelette fiction, which largely screens out physical feeling and the senses.   [45] See *Commodity Culture*, 215.

[46] See Cecil, *Heroines in Love*, 124.   [47] See PN 37/955 (6 June 1904), 417.

magazines, especially in 'the latest fashion'.[48] Her concern with 'blushing scientifically cured and how to be tall increase your height' (13. 113–14) derives from magazine advertisements. So does her interest in powders that cure 'the drink habit' (13. 291) and in nostrums and panaceas like 'the Widow Welch's female pills' (13. 85–6).[49] So do her interest in cheap or sentimental poetry (13. 645–6), her interest in exotic foreigners (who frequently featured in the stories, 13. 416–17), and, more largely, her banal concepts of 'manliness' and 'womanliness' (13. 210, 435, 439).[50] So does the present she imagines giving Father Conroy ('perhaps an album of illuminated views of Dublin or some place', 13. 465: the magazines traditionally and frequently offered their readers photographic albums of views).[51] Even Gerty's moments of superstition (13. 119, 179, 185) may stem less from her 'Irishness' than from English magazines. *The Princess's Novelettes*, for instance, featured *The Princess's Infallible Fortune Teller*, and the numbers for June 1904 advertised a book entitled *Love Spells and Marriage Forecasts*.

Some extremely specific details derive from the magazines. Gerty's dream of having 'jewels on her brow' (13. 102) comes from *The Princess's Novelettes*: the cover sported a picture of 'the princess', tiara on forehead. But the magazines are also a more general and diffuse source of some of the chapter's features: the interest in dye (13. 150) and disinfectant (13. 333), both of which were advertised in *Lady's Pictorial*; the references to the 'pushcar' (13. 21), bicycles, clocks, and watches (which were all often advertised in the magazines); the scattering of French words (associated with class, style and fashion); the concern with avoiding social gaffes (13. 265);[52] the concern with 'keeping up' socially (13. 164–5), with maintaining appearances or 'holding one's own' (13. 124–5, 487–8), not least, in front of other women (13. 99–102). Gerty's account of making

[48] See *PN* 37/947 (11 Apr. 1904), 284.
[49] Cf. the pills 'for all female complaints' advertised in *The Countess Novelette*, 1/1 (15 Feb. 1897). On the treatment of the problem of drink in the magazines, see Dancyger, *World of Women*, 108.
[50] See e.g. the endearing and sometimes hilarious *Original Poetry* section in *LON*, and the poems published regularly in *PW*. The number for the week ending 16 June 1904 contained one with the title 'By the Sea'.
[51] See e.g. many of the numbers of *LON* for 1895, and esp. the advertisement for 'Beecham's Photo-Folio' in *PN* 37/942 (7 Mar. 1904), 193.
[52] See Dancyger, *World of Women*, 86, for an account of the importance of this theme in Victorian women's magazines.

'queen Ann's pudding' sounds like the recipes in *Pearson's Weekly* (13. 225–8). If pictures and pictorialism are important in 'Nausicaa'—the *'Tableau'* (13. 486), the 'spectacle' (13. 285), 'engravings' and photographs (13. 231–2)—this is because the pictorial element was so important in the magazines. Certain images in Joyce's chapter derive from the magazines' pictorial repertoire, like the image of Gerty 'gazing far away into the distance' (13. 80).

Gerty's conception of the world is thus deeply and densely embedded in the world of the magazines. Much of this is already familiar. But the sheer abundance of such particularities is nonetheless significant, and worth stressing. For they make up the substance of Gerty's cultural imaginary (as distinct from her consciousness). There is simply not very much more to be found there, apart from religious deposits. In fact, Joyce is chiefly concerned, not with a fictional style, but with the magazine culture as a whole. More importantly, to suggest that stylistic parody is central to 'Nausicaa' is to minimize the significance of the style as a composite entity. The discourse in the first half of the chapter is actually a rickety and even outlandish construction, a hybrid mix of disparate or incongruous materials.

Here as throughout this study, what David Fitzpatrick refers to as methodological 'particularism' is a very important tool. The particularist works to uncover what is specifically Irish in a historical process (like 'modernization'). For such processes are easily generalized and stripped of cultural specificity, not least, by theoretical discourses.[53] For Joyce, Gerty is a historically particular instance of cultural aspiration and psychological survival. As such, she is reliant on the very imported forms of the colonizer's culture that 'Nausicaa' subverts. To understand this seeming contradiction, we need to be as exact as possible about Gerty's historical situation as a young, disadvantaged Irishwoman from an impoverished, Dublin Catholic background in 1904. Since the Famine, the average age for marriage in Ireland had risen rapidly. There had also been a marked decline in female employment and women's opportunities for economic

---

[53] Fitzpatrick, 'The Modernization of the Irish Female', in O'Flanagan et al. (eds.), *Rural Ireland 1600–1900: Modernization and Change* (Cork: Cork University Press, 1987), 162–80, esp. 162. It is perhaps 'particularism' above all, in Fitzpatrick's very precise sense, that separates my work off from that of others it might seem to resemble, like Cheryl Herr's and Trevor Williams's. See Cheryl Herr, *Joyce's Anatomy of Culture* (Urbana, Ill.: University of Illinois Press, 1986), and Trevor L. Williams, *Reading Joyce Politically* (Gainesville, Fla.: University Press of Florida, 1997).

independence.[54] The incidence of celibacy had gone up sharply. Between 1841 and 1901, the number of Irish nuns increased eightfold.[55] Prior to the Famine, Irish popular culture had frequently emphasized the erotic and romantic aspects of marriage. After the Famine, however, this emphasis disappeared, partly because of the growth in Church power and the more puritan direction the Church was taking.[56] In Rosemary Cullen Owens's term, there was a marked 'desexualisation' of Irishwomen.[57] In the post-Famine period, the Irish family also developed a more patriarchal orientation. Daughters were more likely to occupy a subservient position and to be seen as economically superfluous.[58] The historians repeatedly emphasize the bald fact that, in the second half of the nineteenth century, on the whole, Irishwomen's status declined and their lives grew decidedly narrower.[59] This was particularly true in the case of celibate women. All too often, 'the life of the unmarried Irishwomen, increasingly cut off from male companionship as well as independent employment, was one of humiliation and despair'.[60]

It is important, however, to set another, more positive trend alongside this grim set of circumstances. As George Russell put it, women were also 'waking up in Ireland'.[61] Recent women historians have repeatedly used this trope.[62] By the turn of the century, the 'modernization' of Irishwomen had begun.[63] This was partly the result of emigration and the desires it bred in those who remained behind, not least because of emigrants' letters.[64] In some ways, Irishwomen gained in status during the period 1880–1920. So much is evident

[54] See Nolan, *Ourselves Alone*, 12, 26, and *passim*; Rita M. Rhodes, *Women and the Family in Post-Famine Ireland: Status and Opportunity in a Patriarchal Society* (New York and London: Garland, 1992), 194; and C. L. Innes, *Woman and Nation in Irish Literature and Society 1880–1935* (London: Harvester Wheatsheaf, 1993), 39. David Fitzpatrick suggests that in 1901, 'Ireland was competing with Iceland for the honour of heading the European celibacy league'. See his 'Marriage in Post-Famine Ireland', in Art Cosgrove (ed.), *Marriage in Ireland* (Dublin: College Press, 1985), 116–31, at 117.

[55] Catríona Clear, 'The Limits of Female Autonomy', in Luddy and Murphy (eds.), *Women Surviving*, 15–50, at 21. [56] See Nolan, *Ourselves Alone*, 32–6.

[57] *Smashing Times: A History of the Irish Women's Suffrage Movement 1889–1922* (Dublin: Attic Press, 1984), 16. [58] See Rhodes, *Women and the Family*, 194, 229.

[59] See Nolan, *Ourselves Alone*, 37, 42. [60] Fitzpatrick, 'Modernization', 173.

[61] *Irish Homestead* (19 Feb. 1910); repr. in Henry Summerfield (ed.), *Selections from the Contributions to the Irish Homestead* (2 vols., Gerrards Cross, Colin Smythe, 1978), i. 220.

[62] See e.g. Owens, *Smashing Times*, 19–34.

[63] See Fitzpatrick, 'Modernization', *passim*.

[64] See Nolan, *Ourselves Alone*, for a helpful account of this, esp. at 42. See also Fitzpatrick, 'Modernization', esp. 175–6.

from the Married Women's Property Acts and the Contagious Diseases Acts (1864, 1866, 1869); the emergence of the Dublin Women's Suffrage Association (1876; later the Irish Women's Suffrage and Local Government Association, 1901); the formation of the Ladies' Land League and a women's trade union; and the opening of Trinity College to women (1904). The Irish Local Government Act (1885), the Poor Law Guardian Act (1896), and, perhaps above all, the Local Government (Ireland) Act (1898) all tended to empower women, a pattern accelerated in the last years of the century. More women—including Catholic women—were elected to positions of power and responsibility in local government. They joined Poor Law Board and Urban District Councils.[65] As I stress elsewhere in this book, in the phrase of Mrs Maurice Dockrell, the 1898 Act was particularly important in transferring 'the governing power in local [Irish] affairs . . . from the unionists to the nationalists.[66] (It is also particularly significant for Joyce studies.) Its consequences for women seemed far-reaching enough to merit triumphant announcement at the International Congress of Women in 1899. Above all, the drive for women's education was developing and spreading swiftly. In England, the Education Act of 1870 led to the creation of a national education system and an ensuing drive towards mass education and mass literacy.[67] In Ireland, the Intermediate Education Act of 1878 made for similar transformations, causing 'a revolution in female education'.[68] The 'modernization' in question gained some of its momentum from the decline in opportunities for female employment.[69] But it was nonetheless Irishwomen who benefited most from the rapid growth in literacy. Before the Famine, existing schools had catered almost exclusively to a male clientele. By the end of the century, however, the average Irishwoman was more literate than the average Irishman.[70]

---

[65] See Cliona Murphy, *The Women's Suffrage Movement and Irish Society in the Early Twentieth Century* (London: Harvester, 1989), 14–15.

[66] Mrs Maurice Dockrell, 'Irishwomen in Local Government', in Countess of Aberdeen (ed.), *Women in Politics: The Transactions of the International Congress of Women, 1899*, v (London: T. Fisher Unwin, 1900), 87–9, at 88.

[67] See White, *Women's Magazines*, 59; and Marjorie Ferguson, *Forever Feminine: Women's Magazines and the Cult of Femininity* (Aldershot: Gower, 1985), 16.

[68] Eibhin Breathnach, 'Women and Higher Education in Ireland (1879–1914)', *The Cranebag* (1980), 48.   [69] Fitzpatrick, 'Modernization', 164.

[70] See Rhodes, *Women and the Family*, 195–6.

According to Russell, at the beginning of the new century, the 'starved soul of [Irish] womanhood' was crying out 'for an intellectual life'.[71] Journalism helped prompt the cry and seemed partly to assuage the craving. In England, 'the last two decades of Victoria's reign' saw an explosion of journals and newspapers.[72] So, too, in Ireland, the increase in literacy and the availability of newspapers and magazines was turning the Irish into a newspaper-reading public. This seemed to some to be directly linked to a growth in political awareness.[73] Newspapers and magazines expanded people's sense of possibilities. As Rhodes puts it, at the turn of the century, popular journalism was exposing Irish people 'to political and social alternatives' as never before, exerting 'a powerful appeal for change'.[74] This was particularly the case with the growing body of literate women between Ascendancy women and the peasantry who increasingly hoped 'for wider horizons'.[75] Historians repeatedly trace a conflict, intensifying towards the end of nineteenth century, between Irishwomen's aspirations and rising expectations, and their chronically limited real-life prospects.[76] As 'Nausicaa' puts it, women were indeed likely to end up 'hoping against hope' (13. 179–80). In Gerty MacDowell, Joyce captures this conflict and its relation to popular English journalism. Up to a point, Russell was an admirable supporter of Irishwomen's causes. But his sympathies were limited by questions of class. He complained, for example, that every farmer's daughter was now yearning 'to move up the social scale, and to be a postmistress or lady's companion'.[77] Joyce, however, was free of the Anglo-Irishman's misgivings. For him, the aspirations—the very fact of aspiration itself—were portentous.

In some measure, Gerty is therefore representative of Irish girlhood on the threshold of modern consciousness. As such, her significance is more progressive than parodic. Joyce was preoccupied with

[71] IT (8 Apr. 1903); quoted in Jenny Beale, Women in Ireland: Voices of Change (London: Macmillan, 1986), 36.   [72] White, Women's Magazines, 58–9.
[73] David. B. King provides an example of this. See The Irish Question (London: W. H. Allen and Co., 1882), 293; quoted in James S. Donnelly, The Land and the People of Nineteenth-Century Cork: Studies in Irish History, 2nd ser. (London: Routledge & Kegan Paul, 1975), ix. 249.   [74] Women and the Family, 51–2.
[75] Roger Sawyer, We are but Women: Women in Ireland's History (London: Routledge, 1993), 46.
[76] See Nolan, Ourselves Alone, 42 and passim; and Sawyer, We are but Women, 45. Cf. Fitzpatrick on the late 19th-cent. contradiction 'between the growing rigidity of Irish social institutions and the growing cosmopolitanism of their members', 'Modernization', 163.   [77] Irish Homestead (3 Mar. 1906); repr. in Summerfield (ed.), Selections, 161.

the figure in question. The woman of Davin's story in *Portrait*, for example, is both 'a type of her race' and 'a batlike soul *waking to the consciousness of itself* in darkness and secrecy and loneliness' (*P*, 198; my italics).[78] The girl from Jacob's biscuit factory—who presumably might well also be a reader of 'upstart journals'—serves as another 'figure of the womanhood of her country' and attracts the same phrasing (*P*, 239–40). In her autobiography, Joyce's friend Mary Colum tells of the fascination magazine fiction could hold for a growing Irish girl and stresses the importance it might have in her development.[79] So, too, for Joyce, the beginnings of modern 'consciousness' could manifest themselves in many different ways. That they sometimes clothed themselves in cheap, imported forms was not *ipso facto* a token of their degradation.

In a historical context, Gerty's fantasies therefore represent a principle of political and cultural creativity. They conspicuously defy the rule of endogamy in class, religion, and birthplace that was the norm in Ireland before the twentieth century.[80] This is particularly significant in the case of Gerty's 'daydream of a marriage' to Reggy Wylie (13. 195), unpromising though that 'daydream' may be in other respects. Not only is Reggy's background more affluent than hers: it is also Protestant. Before the late nineteenth century, mixed marriages had been problematic in Ireland. Indeed, until 1871, mixed marriages celebrated by a Catholic priest were void in civil law.[81] Gerty's fantasy is thus an index of modernity. The same may possibly even be true of her awareness of sex. Recent research has suggested that the levels of Irishwomen's ignorance in sexual matters at this time could be extraordinary.[82] For all Joyce's undoubted suspicion of the 'domestic ideology', there may also be a positive side to Gerty's domestic fantasies. The disadvantages of the shift to housewifery in late nineteenth- and early twentieth-century Irishwomen's culture were

---

[78] For an interesting reading of this passage which raises some of the same issues as my own, see Innes, *Woman and Nation*, 65. Innes's interpretation depends on ignoring the words 'type' and 'waking'.   [79] *Life and the Dream* (Dublin: Dolmen Press, 1966), 6.

[80] See Fitzpatrick, 'Marriage', 122–5.

[81] See Patrick J. Corish, 'Catholic Marriage under the Penal Code', in Cosgrove, (ed.), *Marriage in Ireland*, 67–77, at 75.

[82] See the oral evidence collected by the National Union of Public Employees, Women's Committee, Northern Ireland, *An Oral History of Women's Health in Northern Ireland, 1900–1990* (Dublin: Attic Press, 1992), 20, 95–104. In comparison with the girlhoods described by some of the Irishwomen interviewed here, Gerty's has left her relatively knowing.

evident enough. But Joanna Bourke has recently argued that, in this specific historical context—one comprehensively occluded by the post-war conviction of the alienation and deprivation of house-wives—the shift could sometimes also be relatively empowering. It was useful for women to have skills in the more specialized forms of domestic labour. They could thereby 'improve the quality of their lives' and 'increase their status' in a society where, otherwise, their options were drastically curtailed.[83] It may be status as much as pathos that is at stake in Gerty's ability to do her 'griddlecakes . . . to a goldenbrown hue' and smartly to recite her pudding recipe (13. 224–8).

Gerty also gets a rudimentary vocabulary for aspiration, longing, frustration, dissatisfaction, and even reproof from the magazines. In the absence of better alternatives, she derives the terms of her spiritual and moral self-awareness from them. Here, again, Joyce places her on the threshold of modernity. Gerty's 'yearning tendency' (13. 106) is 'strange', not only to herself, but as a modern form of sensibility newly articulate in women of her class. Its finds a bleak and equally 'strange' corollary in the 'dull aching void in her heart sometimes' (13. 136–7). To a limited extent, Gerty's expression of her desires and frustrations even produces a recognition of injustice. It may be impossible to tell whether, if Gerty had 'only received the benefit of a good education', she 'might easily have held her own beside any lady in the land' (13. 100–2). But the very fact that the possibility is raised underlines her relative deprivation. Religious influences may partly lie behind Gerty's disapproval of men caught in 'the clutches of the demon drink' (13. 290). But so do the magazines, especially *Pearson's Weekly*. The same is true of Gerty's censure of male violence against women (13. 297–302). The magazines have made Gerty large-minded enough to imagine loving 'a sinner' (13. 433) and to value the 'intellect' and 'culture' she detects in Bloom (13. 416, 548). They have supplied her with a basic aesthetic vocabulary, too (13. 332–9, 627–9, 648–9). Her moments of intellectual curiosity (e.g. 13. 342–4) are also tiny signs of 'waking'. Of course, her progress is limited. She risks certain thoughts only swiftly to withdraw them. When she imagines loving Bloom 'even if he was a protes-

---

[83] See Bourke, *Husbandry to Housewifery: Women, Economic Change and Housework in Ireland 1890–1914* (Oxford: Clarendon Press, 1993), quotations from 271. Bourke argues brilliantly that the politics of housewifery in pre-war agricultural societies, British and Irish in particular, has mistakenly been conflated with its post-war equivalent.

tant or methodist', for example, she immediately adds that 'she could convert him easily if he truly loved her' (13. 433–4). But the limits are exactly the point: unlike many of her critics, Gerty is not modern in all her ways. She is poised on modernity's edge. In reality, beyond question, Gerty's prospects would have been starkly and depressingly limited, like those of Joyce's sisters.[84] Joyce nonetheless presents her at a moment of relatively developed consciousness that is also a moment of precise historical significance.

Walker's *and the Hoydens*

I have in fact set up what appear to be two colliding perspectives on 'Nausicaa'. But the delicate course between Scylla and Charybdis which I have argued is the most apposite figure for Joyce's negotiations in the sphere of cultural politics is frequently traced with such subtlety as to seem full of contradictions. Joyce was clearly aware of the imperial, English discursive formation in the women's magazines, and treated it critically. But he also recognized that the magazines were an important and even enabling feature of Gerty's development as a young Irishwoman at the turn of the century. The magazines, of course, formed part of a colonial culture which was coming under fire from both nationalists and the women's organizations associated with nationalism, like Inghinidhe na hÉireann.[85] But Joyce would no doubt have agreed with his friend Hanna Sheehy-Skeffington when she declared that 'the disabilities of Irishwomen today' were only partly 'the result of Anglicization'.[86] What exactly would Gerty be without the latter? Joyce identifies an inescapable double-bind in which the colonizer held the colonized: in many spheres of life, his culture was the chief if not the only source of anything resembling advanced cultural formations.

The double-bind was insidious: the historians have suggested that, in the short term, the benefits of literacy to Irishwomen were at best

---

[84] On the narrowing of opportunities for women immediately after independence, see Carol Coulter, *The Hidden Tradition: Women and Nationalism in Ireland* (Cork: Cork University Press, 1993), 3.

[85] See e.g. the account of the Inghinidhe na hÉireann meeting in *United Irishman* (13 Oct. 1900), and their statement of aims, quoted in Maria Luddy (ed.), *Women in Ireland 1800–1918: A Documentary History* (Cork: Cork University Press, 1995), 300–1.

[86] 'Sinn Féin and Irishwomen', *Bean na hÉireann* (Dec. 1909), repr. in Luddy (ed.), *Women in Ireland*, 301–4, at 302.

ambiguous. For literacy often made for a more efficient ideological construction of subjectivity.[87] In principle, for the most part, the cultivated, educated, well-read woman was also 'feminine' and 'ladylike' (in other words, English-genteel).[88] Here, again, 'Nausicaa' provides some spirited resistance to the discourses of the magazines. The laughter in the chapter is not principally at the expense of a supposedly pathetic, dim-witted Gerty.[89] Rather the reverse: it stems chiefly from the fact that, in many respects, Joyce's Irish girls turn out to be obstinately if largely unconsciously immune to the terms of the imported culture and discourses. In 1904, contemporary English commentators were complaining about the wayward tendencies of lower-class girls. They deplored their 'individualism' and 'excitability', their love of 'pleasure' and of 'crudities', their easy surrender to degrading 'influences', even their lack of any sense of responsibility toward 'the life of the State'.[90] It is the traces of this indomitable vitality that Joyce relishes in Gerty, Edy, and Cissy. Their 'motherwit' (13.75) keeps on bursting back into the discourses that would smother it, chiefly via a set of distinctive idioms. It warps the discourses in question, taking them in unexpected directions, entering into new, surprising, and often hilarious relationships with them. It infects them with terms, flourishes, attitudes, and kinds of experience that the discourses would in principle exclude.

Thus the vernacular is an intrusive presence, in 'Nausicaa': words like 'plucks' (13.24), 'scatty' (13.32), 'dote' (13.34), 'hominess' (13.224), 'dredge' (13.226), 'brack' (13.501), 'streel' (13.506), 'kinnatt' (13.601), and 'rossies' (13.688); phrases like 'black out at daggers drawn' (13.93), 'something off the common' (13.143), 'the very it' (13.159), 'never would ash, oak or elm' (13.166–7), 'drew the jugs' (13.272), 'right go wrong' (13.43; which Gerty shares with Ned Lambert, 12.1033), 'Wait till I catch you for that' (13.52–3), 'those

[87] See e.g. J. J. Lee, 'Women and the Church since the Famine', in Margaret MacCurtain and Donncha Ó'Corrain (eds.), *Women in Irish Society: The Historical Dimension* (Dublin: Arlen House, 1979), 37–45, at 41.

[88] See Delamont, 'Contradictions', 145–8.

[89] For the opposite view, see Marilyn French, *The Book as World: James Joyce's 'Ulysses'* (London: Abacus, 1982), 156–68; and Bernard Benstock, *Narrative Con/Texts in 'Ulysses'* (London: Macmillan, 1991), 105. Contrast Richard Ellmann, *'Ulysses' on the Liffey* (London: Faber and Faber, 1972), 130–1.

[90] See e.g. Lily H. Montague, 'The Girl in the Background', in E. J. Urwick (ed.), *Studies of Boy Life in Our Cities, Written by Various Authors for the Toynbee Trust* (London: J. M. Dent & Co., 1904), 233–54, 233–4, 235, 238, 243–5.

cyclists showing off what they hadn't got' (13. 436–7), and 'his ownest girlie' (13. 440). This language is an expression of a demotic sensibility that refuses to be overpowered by imported, genteel idioms, and worms its way back into consciousness in spite of them. As Joyce points the Poddle's 'tongue of liquid sewage' at the viceregal cavalcade (10. 1197), so, too, in 'Nausicaa', little, rude tongues of language stick out constantly at the magazine style. The tone of street gossip runs up directly against the stilted confections of gossip columns. According to Richard Altick, from the mid-nineteenth century onwards, the English popular press had seldom if ever tolerated 'an improper expression'.[91] By contrast, 'Nausicaa' revels in a number of different forms of impropriety:

Cissy was a past mistress in the art of smoothing over life's tiny troubles and very quickly not one speck of sand was to be seen on his smart little suit. Still the blue eyes were glistening with hot tears that would well up so she kissed away the hurtness and shook her hand at Master Jacky the culprit *and said if she was near him she wouldn't be far from him*, her eyes dancing in admonition. (13. 57–62; italics mine)

In the italicized phrase, an alien idiom collapses, and can no longer be sustained. The result is an awkward but significant, composite formation. Raucously lively Dublin erupts into an inert, English gentility. Gerty looks down on the 'brats of twins' as 'little monkeys common as ditchwater' (13. 466–8). But there is an invigorating amount of common girl in Gerty herself. In *Portrait*, Stephen was 'shouldered' into the ditchwater *(P*, 14). In 'Nausicaa', it threatens to overflow and soil the chapter's whitewash.

In 'Nausicaa', 'dignity' is often troubled by 'inclination' (13. 124–5). This is also the case with Gerty's attitudes to sex. Part of her recoils from 'everything in the least indelicate' (13. 660), exhibiting the 'dignity' required of her by Victorian England and Cullenite Catholicism together. But she exhibits other things, too. She is quite shrewd in her awareness of what Bloom and the 'gentleman lodger . . . out of the Congested Districts Board' (13. 702–3) may be getting up to. Before the Famine, observers often commented on what they took to be Irishwomen's lack of physical modesty. De Tocqueville suggested, for example, that Irishwomen 'took less trouble to hide

---

[91] *The English Common Reader: A Social History of the Mass Reading Public 1800–1900*, foreword by Jonathan Rose (2nd edn., Columbus, Oh.: Ohio State University Press, 1998), 364.

themselves than in any other country in the world'.⁹² The Famine and
the Cullenite Church reversed this tendency. In 'Nausicaa', however,
it shows signs of reappearing as part of an emergent modernity: in effect, in the phrase of Archbishop McCabe, Gerty 'so far disavows her
birthright of modesty as to parade herself before the public [or at
least, Bloom's] gaze'.⁹³

Gerty's determination to live the 'untrammelled' life (13. 673) may
be painfully ironic. But she is nonetheless capable of moments of
spontaneous release, like her 'joyous little laugh' (13. 126–7). Finally,
however, my point about 'inclination' is best summed up by counter-
posing *Walker's Critical Pronouncing Dictionary*—which Gerty herself recalls consulting (13. 342–3)—with the notion of the hoyden. In
nineteenth-century Britain, *Walker's Dictionary* was a major text.
Parts of the nation were threatening to 'vitiate' the English language'.⁹⁴ The *Dictionary* aimed to regularize the latter and suit it to
the 'polite ear'.⁹⁵ It laid down 'rules' to be 'observed' by the backward
(chiefly Londoners and 'provincials, particularly the Irish, Scotch
and Welch').⁹⁶ The rules would help these unfortunate transgressors
avoid their 'Respective Peculiarities'. Walker presented the *Dictionary* as part of a process of the refinement and homogenization of
English usage that had begun 'in Queen Anne's time'⁹⁷ and continued
through Jones's *New Art of Spelling*, Steele's *Grammar*, the work of
Johnson, Sheridan, Robert Lowth, James Elphinston, William
Kenrick, and many more. I shall return to this process in Chapter 9.

Walker's Dictionary was overtly political and its apparatus chau-
vinistic.⁹⁸ It reprehended a 'thousand insensible deviations'.⁹⁹ By
contrast, 'Nausicaa' revels in the impulse to deviation itself. It re-

⁹² *Journeys to England and Ireland*, ed. J. P. Mayer, trans. George Lawrence and J. P.
Mayer (London: Faber & Faber, 1958), 121; quoted in S. J. Connolly, 'Marriage in Pre-
Famine Ireland', in Cosgrove (ed.), *Marriage in Ireland*, 78–98, at 90.
⁹³ *FJ* (12 Mar. 1881); quoted in Luddy (ed.), *Women in Ireland*, 263.
⁹⁴ John Walker, *Walker's Critical Pronouncing Dictionary and Expositor of the English
Language, to which are Prefixed Principles of English Pronunciation; Likewise, Rules to
be Observed by the Natives of Scotland, Ireland, and London, for avoiding their Respective Peculiarities, and Directions to Foreigners, for Acquiring a Knowledge of the Use of
This Dictionary*, corrected and enlarged with upwards of three thousand words by Revd
John Davis (Belfast: Simms and McIntyre, 1830), p. vi.   ⁹⁵ Ibid. 186.
⁹⁶ Ibid. 14.   ⁹⁷ Ibid. 629.
⁹⁸ To quote a single example: of 'espionage', Walker comments that it is 'a perfect
French word, signifying the practice of a spy. . . . That our language is without this word,
is a compliment to our government' (ibid. 186). Cf. the *Dictionary's* various other engagements with what it calls 'revolutionary words' (ibid. 282).   ⁹⁹ Ibid. p. ix.

sponds to English linguistic nationalism by celebrating the discourse of the Irish hoyden. The hoyden was a rude and ill-bred girl. She was boisterous, noisy, and a romp. In the first instance, she was working class, emboldened to insolence by recent, democratic trends. But middle-class girls who picked up bad habits from working-class girls were also hoydens.[100] Unlike good girls, the hoyden was psychologically robust: spirited, ebullient, spiteful, sharp. In 'Nausicaa', Cissy's vigour and lack of inhibition mark her out in particular as a hoyden. But there is quite a lot of hoyden in Gerty and Edy, too, not least, in their needling aggressions. T. W. Rolleston and other Anglo-Irishmen sentimentally associated a 'magic' of feminine co-operation with Irishwomen and their work.[101] But Joyce's girls show no such inclinations. In 1904, of course, there were very good reasons why young Dublin women might feel aggressive towards others and seek to get the better of them. The pressures of economic and sexual competition were considerable. Since the Famine, there had been a 'continuous influx' into the capital 'of country girls who would work for a pittance'.[102] This tended to generate rivalry. In the end, Joyce's 'seaside girls' are not equipped or even truly disposed to conform either to Walker's rules or to the discourses of the magazines. Whatever the compromises she has made with the dominant culture, the Irish hoyden will not be subdued.

[100] Baden-Powell worried about the 'hoydenism' of girls gatecrashing his Boy Scout Movement, e.g. See Mary Cadogan and Patricia Craig, *You're a Brick, Angela!* (London: Gollancz, 1986), 140.
[101] Quoted in 'The Home as Workshop', in Countess of Aberdeen (ed.), *Women in Industrial Life: The Transactions of the International Congress of Women, 1899*, vol. vi (London: T. Fisher Unwin, 1900), 145–51, esp. 147.   [102] Owens, *Smashing Times*, 75.

CHAPTER SEVEN

An Irish Bull in an English Chinashop: 'Oxen of the Sun'

Let All Malthusiasts Go Hang[1]

Commentators on 'Oxen' have tended to see it as partly the work of an 'advocate of fertility'.[2] Of course, not all critics have taken the 'advocacy' seriously.[3] But few have doubted that it is central to the chapter. Yet this central place raises another question, which is why Joyce bothered with the theme at all. Richard Brown has argued that Joyce ironizes the fertility theme in the interest of expressing a different and more progressive conception of sexuality. But the problem still remains as to why the expression requires so oddly indirect a vehicle. Why should Joyce's great modernist achievement include a chapter that celebrates procreation, whether seriously, ironically, or mock-heroically? The theme seems faintly stuffy and banal, anachronistic, even unmodern; all the more so, given the modern turn in Europe to the regulation of fertility by birth control. Economists call this the 'fertility transition'. In the opening decades of the century, it was steadily transforming the population debate, and its effects were being felt in Ireland.[4]

---

[1] For a more developed version of some of the argument in the first two sections of this chapter, see my '"Let All Malthusiasts Go Hang": Joyce's "Oxen of the Sun" and the Economists', *Literature and History*, 10/2 (autumn 2001), 62–78.

[2] Robert Janusko, *The Sources and Structures of James Joyce's 'Oxen'* (Ann Arbor: UMI Research Press, 1983), 55.

[3] See esp. Richard Brown, *James Joyce and Sexuality* (Cambridge: Cambridge University Press, 1985), 70, 77; Mark Osteen, *The Economy of 'Ulysses': Making Both Ends Meet* (New York: Syracuse University Press, 1995), 247–8; and Robert Spoo, *James Joyce and the Language of History: Dedalus's Nightmare* (Oxford: Oxford University Press, 1994), 145–6.

[4] On the 'fertility transition' with reference to Ireland, see Cormac Ó Gráda and Niall Duffy, *Fertility Control Early in Marriage in Ireland c.1900: Some Local Contrasts* (Dublin: University College, 1983), e.g. 1–7; and Ó Gráda, *Ireland Before and After the Famine:*

In a ground-breaking study, Mary Lowe-Evans has indicated the importance of a historical approach to Joyce's treatment of the fertility theme. In an Irish context, the theme takes a specific form. Here as in so many other respects, again, 'particularism' is crucial: the Ireland Joyce grew up in turns out to constitute 'a special case' of a given issue.[5] The history and politics of a colonial culture are what make it 'special', in a way that Lowe-Evans cannot quite see. She has drawn attention to the importance of Malthus for 'Oxen',[6] and Malthus is indeed important. More precisely, the discourses of nineteenth-century English political economy—in particular, classical economy, and notably the Malthusians—provide a strikingly significant context for Joyce's chapter. That the chapter refers to economic discourses on fertility and population increase might itself seem surprising. In the late nineteenth and early twentieth century, they were being steadily replaced by psychological and sociological discourses.[7] The important point, however, is that, for the economists, Ireland was a key instance.[8] Joyce described the chapter's first passage of connected prose as 'Sallustian-Tacitean'.[9] Sallustian-Tacitean or not, however, one principal point of reference for it is nineteenth-century economic discourse. The vocabulary of one or more of the economists—'continuance' (14. 15), 'bounty' (14. 21), 'increase' (14. 21), 'abundance' (14. 30), 'prudence' (14. 56), and, above all, 'subsistence' (14. 49)—is evident throughout the passage. The same is true of habits of style attributable to one economist or another.[10] Style and ideology were often not separable. The passage

---

Explorations in Economic History 1800–1925 (2nd edn., Manchester: Manchester University Press, 1993), 197–202.

[5] The assimilation of such cases to their modern European or English versions repeatedly appears to be problematic. A good example of an awareness of this question is Mark Finnane's *Insanity and the Insane in Post-Famine Ireland* (London: Croom Helm, 1981). Finnane asserts the need for a recognition of the specificity of the discursive construction of insanity in post-Famine Ireland as opposed to elsewhere (particularly England and Scotland).

[6] Lowe-Evans, *Crimes against Fecundity: Joyce and Population Control* (Syracuse, Kan.: Syracuse University Press, 1989), *passim*. Osteen has also given a brief but interesting account of the relevance of Malthus to 'Oxen', pointing out, e.g., that the notesheets show Joyce to have been familiar with Malthus and concerned with his thought as he composed the chapter. See *Economy of 'Ulysses'*, 237–9.

[7] See D. E. C. Eversley, *Social Theories of Fertility and the Malthusian Debate* (Oxford: Clarendon Press, 1959), 12.   [8] See ibid. 60–1.

[9] In his oft-cited letter to Frank Budgen of 20 Mar. 1920. See *Letters*, i. 139.

[10] Some of the more cumbersome sentences and recherché Latinisms in the passage, e.g., read like a parody of the Thomas Newenham whom Malthus took to task. See

begins with the adverb 'universally'. This probably constitutes an ironic homage to Malthus himself: it is common in his *Essay on Population*, and he liked beginning sentences with it.[11] The connection between the passage and the economists' discourses is not simply localized. Rather, the opening of 'Oxen' advertises its relationship to a set of historically specific English (and sometimes Anglo-Irish) discourses that were, politically, highly charged, above all, in an Irish context. 'Oxen' sporadically alludes to these discourses elsewhere, if usually not at length. They serve as a base from which much of the rest of the chapter can be more clearly understood.

The exact impact of the discourses of political economy is still debated. But they were immensely important in nineteenth-century British thought and culture.[12] Political economy had a particular character and set of functions and meanings relative to Ireland. The 'Malthusian spectre' hangs heavily over 'popular perceptions of Irish history'.[13] In the 1780s, the population of Ireland began rapidly to increase. The increase continued until the Famine and finally amounted to four million.[14] It was chiefly associated with Catholic Ireland.[15] From the seventeenth century, English and Anglo-Irish observers had been noting that the Irish Catholics appeared to have 'a general Custom (which has been of vast Service to repair the great Losses in this Island by War &c.) of marrying very early, and consequently breeding fast'.[16] The growth in population from the 1780s,

Thomas Newenham, *A Statistical Inquiry into the Progress and Magnitude of the Population of Ireland* (London: C. & R. Baldwin, 1805). Compare e.g. 1 and 103–4 with *Ulysses*, 14. 7–70. On occasions, the vocabularies are also strikingly close.

[11] T. R. Malthus, *An Essay on the Principle of Population* (London: Ward, Lock & Co., 1890), *passim*.

[12] Indeed, Boylan and Foley have recently suggested that political economy has claims to being 'the master public discourse of nineteenth-century Britain'. See Thomas A. Boylan and Timothy P. Foley, 'A Nation Perishing of Political Economy?', in Chris Morash and Richard Hayes (eds.), *Fearful Realities: New Perspectives on the Famine* (Dublin: Irish Academic Press, 1996), 138–50, at 138.

[13] L. A. Clarkson, 'Famine and Irish History', in E. Margaret Crawford (ed.), *Famine: The Irish Experience 900–1900: Subsistence Crises and Famines in Ireland* (Edinburgh: John Donald, 1989), 220–36, at 220.

[14] Recent work, however, has in fact shown that 'Irish birth rates were dropping in the twenty years before the famine'. Mary Daly, *The Famine in Ireland* (Dublin: Dundalgan Press, 1986), 34.

[15] It was also sharply in excess of the comparable increase in England. See K. H. Connell, *The Population of Ireland 1750–1845* (Oxford: Clarendon Press, 1950), 1.

[16] Samuel Madden, *Reflections and Resolutions Proper for the Gentlemen of Ireland* (Dublin: G. Ewing, 1738), 98.

however, coincided with increasing English attention to the 'Irish problem'. The combination of these factors attracted the attention of the economists.[17] From Malthus onwards, classical economics identified the growth in the Irish population as the fundamental cause of Irish poverty.[18] In Ireland, the economists asserted, population increase had far outpaced the growth of capital. Thus the average wage had fallen to the level of minimum subsistence. Combined with the absence of any work other than agricultural, the fall had created intense competition for land and resources. For many economists, a fundamental condition of Irish economic development was therefore an alteration of the arithmetical ratio of population to capital, 'either through an increase in capital, a reduction in population, or a combination of the two'.[19] As Lowe-Evans has emphasized, in practice, the economists' case tended to lead to arguments for emigration.[20] Bolstered by economic thought, assisted emigration became one of the three major planks in British goverment policy regarding poverty and the 'surplus population' in Ireland.[21] The case for emigration was endorsed with dismaying ardour by Anglo-Irish enthusiasts for political economy, like Richard Whately, as also by many Irish landlords.[22] As matters turned out, Ireland was ultimately to witness an unparalleled and unplanned reduction of population. This was the result of a combination of famine, wholesale emigration, and the practice of Malthusian 'moral restraint' to 'a degree far exceeding Malthus's most optimistic expectations'.[23]

[17] Malthus himself toured Ireland in 1817, and other economists had more direct connections with the country: Ricardo e.g. served as MP for Portarlington.

[18] Jacob Viner, Foreword, in R. D. Collison Black, *Economic Thought and the Irish Question* (Cambridge: Cambridge University Press, 1960), pp. v–viii, at pp. vi–vii. The classical school was virtually unanimous in this view of Ireland until the later writings of John Stuart Mill.

[19] Boylan and Foley, 'Nation Perishing', 141. To liberals and humanitarians, at least, this looked like a promulgation of 'the revolting doctrine' that the Irish poor 'should be left to starve, lest they should propagate their numbers too rapidly' (Collison Black, *Economic Thought*, 96).

[20] Ricardo did not agree with this particular case, however, and nor, initially, did Malthus, though he was later converted to it. See ibid. 203.

[21] Daly, *Famine in Ireland*, 43.

[22] See Collison Black, *Economic Thought*, 213. Whately was a sufficiently ardent supporter of political economy to found a chair in it at Trinity College in 1832. Trinity College was crucial to the promotion of political economy in Ireland. Along with Whately himself, some of the former holders of the chair even defended Malthusian principles during the Famine (Boylan and Foley, 'Nation Perishing', 138–40).

[23] Viner, Foreword, p. vii. For evidence of the voluntary practice of 'restraint', see Ó Gráda, *Ireland Before and After the Famine*, 180–206, esp. 193.

Malthusian theory was often seized on 'by a privileged class who, having been stripped bare of rational justifications by the philosophers of the eighteenth century, saw in it an almost miraculous restoration of their position'.[24] This was notably the case in Ireland, where the proposals of the economists appeared to coincide with the interests of the landlords and conservative ideological positions.[25] But there was another aspect to the covert politics of discussions of Irish population levels. Malthus did not say much about Ireland in the *Essay on Population*. But in two essays for the *Edinburgh Review*, he expressed an alarm at Irish fertility rates which was clearly political. Following Newenham, he emphasized the fact that any growth in the Irish population meant an increase in Catholic relative to Protestant numbers. Since Irish Catholics were much more fertile than Protestants, so too the 'physical force' of the former was 'rapidly increasing'. This would logically mean a growing threat to the Union and an increasing chance of insurrection. 'The increasing strength of Ireland', he wrote, in a phrase significant for 'Oxen', 'is the increasing weakness of England'.[26] Other economists were particularly concerned about this, particularly Anglo-Irish ones.[27] In Malthusian terms, the growth of the Catholic population spelt the possible triumph of barbarism. To deploy a key term in the economists' arsenal, civilized man was *prudent*. He knew how to control himself and the size of his family. Barbarians multiplied heedlessly.

[24] Harold A. Boner, *Hungry Generations: The Nineteenth-Century Case against Malthusianism* (New York: King's Crown Press, 1955), p. vi. To see Malthus simply as 'the arch-apologist of the ruling classes', however, is far too reductive. Eversley makes this point convincingly. See *Social Theories of Fertility*, 256. In England, the political economists were often regarded as the champions of the urban middle class, as radicals.

[25] See Collison Black, *Economic Thought*, 243.

[26] 'Newenham and Others on the State of Ireland', *Edinburgh Review* (July 1808), repr. in *Occasional Papers on Ireland, Population and Political Economy*, ed. and introd. Bernard Semmel (New York: Franklin, 1963), 33–52, at 47. For the argument as a whole, see 40–7. It is important not to demonize Malthus himself relative to Ireland. Although a clergyman of the Established Church and opposed to the relief of the Irish tenantry from exorbitant rents, he recognized that political oppression was the original source of the predicament he described, supported Catholic emancipation, argued that landlords should be taxed rather than tenants, and wanted to see an end to restrictive legislation subordinating Irish commercial enterprise to England. Malthus matters less, here, than the discourse of Malthusianism.

[27] Population increase was also a political issue in 19th-cent. Ireland, and was feared by the landlords, because the Poor Laws had made them responsible for half the rate. See Isaac Butt, *Land Tenure in Ireland: A Plea for the Celtic Race* (Dublin: John Falconer, 1866), 33.

Eminent figures were fiercely critical of Malthus and the Malthusians: Coleridge, Byron, Cobbett, Godwin, Dickens. In an Irish context, there were also more humanitarian and unorthodox economists, both English and Anglo-Irish, who took 'a rejection of the Malthusian doctrine as their starting-point'.[28] But the critics frequently gave with one hand only to take away again with the other. For in dealing with Ireland, the economists tended automatically to assume the importance of a closer assimilation of the less to the more developed economy.[29] Carlyle and Mill's critiques of the Malthusian case on Ireland, for example, are made problematic if not vitiated by their unquestioning acceptance of the need to maintain the Union.[30] Yet the authority of Malthusianism might seem to have been in retreat long before 1904, let alone the time at which 'Oxen' was written.[31] Authority is one thing, currency another. Malthusian strains remain perceptible in Mill, Carlyle, Arnold, Spencer, Wells. Darwin described his thought as 'the doctrine of Malthus applied with manifold force to the whole animal and vegetable kingdoms'.[32] Vulgarizations of Malthus were common currency, and clung on well into the early twentieth century. Lowe-Evans points out that the Malthusian League was not disbanded until 1927.[33] Most importantly, the mid- and late nineteenth-century status of Malthusianism in England was by no means the same as its standing in Ireland, where the political stakes were higher or more dramatic. *The Character and Logical Method of Political Economy*, by John Elliot Cairnes, one of the string of professors of political economy at Trinity, was in many ways ultra-Malthusian, and appeared as late as 1857.[34] It is sobering

[28] The list would include such figures as James Warren Doyle, J. B. Bryan, Michael Thomas Sadler, and G. Poulett Scrope. See Collison Black, *Economic Thought*, 94–6.

[29] See ibid. 240.

[30] Both Carlyle and Mill accepted the arguments for emigration. In some ways, however, Mill was a fine critic of Malthus. See Eversley, *Social Theories of Fertility*, 156–8.

[31] Boner, e.g., has suggested that the cultural power and discursive prestige of Malthusian economics were under pressure in England from the mid-19th cent. on and decisively in retreat by 1860 (*Hungry Generations*, 128).

[32] Darwin's enthusiasm for Malthus continued into the 1870s. See Charles Darwin, *On the Origin of Species (1859)*, in *The Works of Charles Darwin*, ed. Paul H. Barrett and R. B. Freeman, xv (London: William Pickering, 1988), 47. The sentence remains in the 1876 edn. See *On The Origin of Species (1876)*, in *Works*, xvi (London: William Pickering, 1988), 53. See also *The Descent of Man, and Selection in Relation to Sex, Part One*, with essay by T. H. Huxley, in *Works*, xxi (London: William Pickering, 1989), 48–51; and Lowe-Evans, *Crimes against Fecundity*, 27.   [33] *Crimes against Fecundity*, 25.

[34] John Stuart Mill supplies clear evidence of how strong the Malthusian view of Ireland still was in the late 1860s. See 'England and Ireland' (1869), in *Collected Works*, vi.

to note that, in 1867, Isaac Butt was attacking a viceroy for publicly declaring—after the Famine and decades of accelerating emigration—that the Irish population was 'somewhat in excess' of what 'the rules of economic principles allow'.[35] It is more sobering to note that—according to Wilfrid Scawen Blunt, at least—in 1892, the very politician who spoke of killing Home Rule with kindness, Gerald Balfour, on the basis of Darwin's 'law' of the survival of the fittest, declared that 'they [the Irish] ought to have been exterminated long ago . . . but it is too late now'.[36]

Remember, Erin, Thy Generations

There were Irish discourses, however, that ran counter to the political economists. The poetic affirmation of fertility had been traditional in Irish culture. For Yeats and others, the theme had its origins in fertility rituals.[37] But it is its political inflection that is most important: as Murray Pittock has demonstrated, from at least the seventeenth century onwards, the fertility theme was never simply literal. It also had an allegorical significance relative to the fortunes of the nation, national prosperity, and national renewal. The theme of Ireland as devastated land awaiting its redeemer was widespread in Irish Jacobite poetry and the eighteenth-century *aisling*. The redeemer was conceived of as a fertility god, a means to regeneration.[38]

Essays on England, Ireland and the Empire, ed. John M. Robson, introd. Joseph Hamburger (Toronto: University of Toronto Press and Routledge & Kegan Paul, 1982), 502–32, at 528.

[35] Butt, *The Irish People and the Irish Land* (Dublin: John Falconer, 1867), 141. The viceroy in question was the Marquis of Abercorn. In Collison Black's words, there can be no doubt that the Malthusian attitude to Ireland 'played a significant part in forming the social philosophy, and so the social policy [in Ireland], of the whole period from 1817 to 1870 and beyond' (*Economic Thought*, 94).

[36] Wilfrid Scawen Blunt, *My Diaries* (London: Martin Secker, 1919), 69–70; quoted in Andrew Gailey, *Ireland and the Death of Kindness: The Experience of Constructive Unionism 1890–1905*, Studies in Irish History (Cork: Cork University Press, 1987), 30.

[37] See Yeats, e.g., on the relation between the pagan ritual tradition in Ireland and *The Midnight Court*. Yeats, Preface, in Brian Merriman, *The Midnight Court and the Adventures of a Luckless Father*, trans. Percy Arland Ussher (London: Cape, 1926), 5–12, 8. Future refs. are to this edn.

[38] With James II e.g. in Irish Jacobite poetry, 'the Stuart cause and its leader are typically seen in terms of fertility and renewal, the good king bringing light and life to a starving land'. Pittock, *Poetry and Jacobite Politics in Eighteenth-Century Britain and Ireland* (Cambridge: Cambridge University Press, 1994), 45. The redeemer figure was sometimes pluralized as the (returning) 'wild geese'. For examples, see Patrick Mac Gearoit, 'The

So, too, the loss of children was directly linked to 'the ruin of dark slaughters' visited on Ireland by the invader.[39] The fertility theme wound its way into the political *aisling* of the nineteenth century.[40] It thus became an item in an armoury of nationalist tropes.[41] Perhaps the most significant instance of the tradition is Brian Merriman's *The Midnight Court*, the eighteenth-century poem that Standish Hayes O'Grady referred to as 'the best poem written in Gaelic'.[42] Speakers in *The Midnight Court* exhort their fellows to 'unite' in 'love'. The Irish race is 'apace decreasing' because 'lads and lasses have left off breeding'.[43] Here, again, as Yeats said and as Joyce surely knew, the theme had a political meaning:[44] '[Merriman] wrote at a moment of national discouragement, the penal laws were still in force though weakening, the old order was a vivid memory but with the failure of the last Jacobite rising hope of its return had vanished, and no new political dream had come.'[45] The argument for procreation is thus equally a political argument for the social and cultural renewal of Ireland. Ireland is oppressed and sunk in poverty and misery, its wealth 'destroyed', its land 'purloined' and left 'untilled' and 'unsown'.[46] More fertility will 'restore to Erin the spirit of old | And rear a race of heroic mould'.[47] The lament for 'the dearth and decrease of our nation' and 'our sickly and sad generation'[48] seemed readily open to

Spirit of Song', in George Sigerson, *Bards of the Gael and Gall: Examples of the Poetic Literature of Errin* (London: T. Fisher Unwin, 1897), 253–5.

[39] The phrase is from Féilim MacCarthy, 'The Caoiné of the Children', in Sigerson, *Bards of the Gael and Gall*, 313–19, at 318.

[40] In the 19th-cent. *aisling*, however, figures like O'Connell replace that of the returning king (Pittock, *Poetry and Jacobite Politics*, 190).

[41] Pittock draws attention to the close connection between the theme and the characterization of Ireland as Cathleen ni Houlihan in the nationalist literature of the late 19th and early 20th cents. (ibid. 189).

[42] Quoted in Yeats, Preface, 12. The view of Merriman's poem as representative both of a tradition and a culture can be found in Daniel Corkery. See *The Hidden Ireland* (Dublin: M. H. Gill and Son, 1926), 233, 249.   [43] *Midnight Court*, 118–19.

[44] The poem was in English trans. as early as 1880, with a verse trans. appearing in 1897 and a German prose trans. by L. C. Stern in *Zeitschrift für Celtische Philologie* in 1905. Joyce could have come across an account of the poem in Hyde's *A Literary History of Ireland* (1899). See also Maria Tymoczko, *The Irish Ulysses* (Berkeley and Los Angeles: University of California Press, 1994), 249–50. But *The Midnight Court* was 'a famous— even an infamous poem'. See David Marcus, Preface, in Brian Merriman, *The Midnight Court*, trans. D. Marcus (Dublin: Dolmen Press, 1953), unpaginated. Gogarty was aware of the poem in the opening years of the century, and expected others to be so, too. See Oliver St John Gogarty, *Tumbling in the Hay* (London: Constable & Co., 1939), 282.

[45] Preface, 9.   [46] Merriman, *Midnight Court*, 18.   [47] Ibid. 42.
[48] Ibid. 40.

appropriation by a post-Famine and indeed a post-Parnellite Ireland. Joyce was surely conscious of this in invoking the tradition in 'Oxen'.

Alongside this tradition, from the Famine onwards, there was a strain of Irish resistance to Malthusianism and its Anglo-Irish proponents.[49] The 1840s saw the emergence of what its authors themselves refer to as an Irish political economy. It picked its quarrel principally with the English economists. In a famine-stricken or post-Famine Ireland, the central issue was a population decline presented as so drastic as to spell the end of a people. Isaac Butt, for instance, explicitly defied the Malthusians, asserting the political urgency of the issue of the continued existence in its own land of a seemingly threatened race.[50] At the extreme end of the spectrum, John Mitchel stridently denounced both the British government and the landlords as aiming to 'extirpate the Irish nation'.[51] For Mitchel, that project was inseparable from the perverted economics practised by 'English professors of political economy'.[52] For Lalor, too, post-Malthusian political economy was 'quackery' (CW, 152). Lalor, Mitchel, other Young Irelanders, and Butt all argue for the priority of political over economic conditions. Ireland's problems—they assert—have primarily been caused by the colonial power and the landlord class.[53] The Famine increased Irish hostility to England. Mitchel, Lalor, and Butt held England and Anglo-Ireland responsible for the Irish plight and were impatient with the arithmetical ratios of the Malthusians. Lalor in particular came close to producing an argument for the repopulation of Ireland. For economic reinvigoration to take place, he suggested, 'the powers of vitality but require to be set in movement, and the contrivances of nature left free to act' (CW, 21). Beneath the Victorian reticence, this is evidently enough an anti-Malthusian argument, and forms part of a discourse which 'Oxen' in some sense sustains.

[49] For opposition to Anglo-Irish economy, see Lalor's view of Whately's arguments as 'poison', e.g. James Fintan Lalor, Collected Writings (Poole, Washington DC: Woodstock Books, 1997), 153.

[50] Irish People, 137–46, and Land Tenure, 64–6, 73, 101.

[51] The History of Ireland from the Treaty of Limerick to the Present Time (New York: D. and J. Sadlier & Co., 1868), 599. For his argument as a whole, see ibid. 544–5, 597–9.

[52] Mitchel, Preface, Irish Political Economy, by Jonathan Swift, Dean of St. Patrick's, and George Berkeley, Bishop of Cloyne (Dublin: William Holden, 1847), pp. iii–vi, at p. iv.

[53] On Lalor's conception of social as opposed to political economy, see David N. Buckley, James Fintan Lalor: Radical (Cork: Cork University Press, 1990), 63–4. John Smurthwaite reminds me that the young Bloom was an adherent of Mitchel and Lalor. See Ulysses, 17. 1647–8.

Ireland had to wait until the 1880s, however, for a cogently argued and amply elaborated opposition to English political economy. The key figure was not Irish but American, the popular economist Henry George. George was a progressive and in some ways socialistic thinker who was also a fierce opponent of Malthus and Malthusianism, which he saw as still enjoying 'general acceptance'.[54] He 'electrified' Ireland when he arrived there in the early 1880s, soon after the publication of his best-known book, *Progress and Poverty* (1879).[55] George's Irish reception was partly connected with his view of Malthus. He argued that Malthus had furnished a philosophy 'by which Dives as he feasts can shut out the image of Lazarus who faints with hunger at his door'.[56] His success was also due to his vigorous denunciations of British rule in Ireland ('the most damnable government that exists today outside Russia').[57] He was scathing about 'the wrong-headedness of Englishmen who attributed mischief in Ireland to some inherent racial or national characteristics'.[58] But what most gripped Ireland was the determination with which George insistently linked the population issue to the question of landlordism. In Ireland, George wrote, 'the bounty which the Creator intended for all' had become 'the exclusive property of some'.[59] This fundamental injustice was the source of Irish poverty and misery. By 'property', George meant land. Insofar as property was a question of land—and only to that extent—a redistribution of wealth was essential. The simplicity of this (expressly anti-Marxist) position brought a curt dismissal from Marx himself ('Theoretically the man is utterly backward').[60] But it also made George hugely popular in Ireland, where the argument was exactly right for the mood of the times.[61] George was especially influential on his friend and ally Michael Davitt. The

---

[54] See *Progress and Poverty* (New York: D. Appleton & Co., 1880), 81. Boner has argued that, in fact, George held 'a singularly exaggerated notion of the prevalence of Malthusian views' (*Hungry Generations*, 188).

[55] The word is Bernard Semmel's. See his introd. to Malthus, *Occasional Papers on Ireland*, 4–29, at 19. The word 'electrifying' can be found in other accounts of George and his work.   [56] *Progress and Poverty*, 88.

[57] Quoted in Charles Albro Barker, *Henry George* (New York: Oxford University Press, 1955), 347.   [58] Quoted ibid. 347.

[59] *The Irish Land Question* (New York: D. Appleton & Co., 1881), 62.

[60] Letter to Friedrich A. Sorge, 30 June 1881; quoted in Barker, *Henry George*, 356.

[61] As Steven B. Cord puts it, 'the headline-making "land for the people" agitation that had just begun in Ireland . . . served to make *Progress and Poverty* appear very timely indeed'. Cord, *Henry George: Dreamer or Realist?* (Philadelphia: University of Pennsylvania Press, 1965), 34.

influence is perceptible in Davitt's *The Fall of Feudalism in Ireland* (1904), a book Joyce had in Trieste. It includes an account of George's arrest and 'trial' at Athenry which appears to take it for granted that any reader will know who George is.[62] Irish nationalist discourse sustained and extended George's anti-Malthusian position. It was significant for Davitt, for the Irish land agitation in the 1890s, and for Griffith. So, too, was George's insistence on a bountiful nature whose operations have been impeded by the injustice of colonial social structures.

There are several key emphases in the fledgling discourse of Irish political economy. It considers the Irish economic situation politically. The classical English economists commonly did not. It understands that situation—if often crudely—in terms of power, class, distribution of wealth, and colonial occupation. Most importantly for 'Oxen', it refuses to accept the Malthusian analysis of the Irish predicament, in which overpopulation becomes the most important determining factor. It suggests, instead, that an Ireland free to arrange its own affairs might be empowered to feed its own. Above all, it edges towards an argument for replenishing a decimated people. That it does so hesitantly and ambivalently is hardly surprising, given both the traumatics of reproduction that followed the Famine and the simultaneous dominance of a peculiarly puritan form of Victorian Catholicism. It nonetheless constitutes a tradition. This tradition gains an additional momentum from its conflation with an older one which presented fertility and an abundant population as a trope for Irish political power, self-confidence, and independence. Together, they are crucial to understanding 'Oxen'.

Joyce's treatment of the population and fertility themes clearly connects up with the tradition of Irish political economy. This is particularly clear early in the chapter, in the argument that

by no exterior splendour is the prosperity of a nation more efficaciously asserted than by the measure of how far forward may have progressed the tribute of its solicitude for that proliferent continuance which of evils the original if it be absent when fortunately present constitutes the certain sign of omnipollent nature's incorrupted benefaction. (14. 13–17)

The equation of populousness with 'prosperity' directly addresses the question of the state of the Irish nation and is blatantly opposed

---

[62] See *The Fall of Feudalism in Ireland* (London and New York: Harper & Bros., 1904), 421–6. The inverted commas are Davitt's, but seem appropriate.

to the Malthusians. But equally, in the chapter as a whole, the recurrence of the word 'bounty' and the references to nature's (beneficent) 'ends' (14. 228), nature's 'benefaction' (14. 17), and 'the bounty of the Supreme Being' (14. 879) all recall the founding premiss of George's anti-Malthusianism.

The traditional emphasis is chiefly present at the start of the chapter. It serves as a containing structure for much of what follows. The chapter touches, for example, on the stark historical context which the subject of population was bound to summon up: on Ireland as a country of 'lean kine' (14. 1476) with but a 'fraction of bread' for 'them that live by bread alone' (14. 283–4). So, too, it alludes to many of the supplementary issues that both the English and the Irish political economists discussed: Irish dietary habits (14. 281–5); infant mortality (14. 1239 ff.); poor sanitary conditions (14. 1242–50); infanticide (14. 962, 1261); 'neglect, private or official' (14. 1259–60); and medical provision. It also contains a number of casual little sideswipes at some of the Malthusians' emphases: their concern with voluntary sexual restraint (14. 669–70); their frequent racism (14. 671, 1250); the connection between the discourse of political economy and the doctrine of natural selection (14. 1277–85). Joyce also refers to some of the contexts that the Irish writers thought were so important, particularly through Stephen: colonial injustice (14. 624–5); English checks on the development of Irish agriculture (14. 609–18); emigration as the result of colonial rule (14. 639–46).

Yet such touches are usually small. The connections are often indirect, and the tone is light. 'Oxen' does not systematically 'parody' the discourses of English political economy. Joyce establishes a comic and ironic but vigorous insistence opposed to those discourses. He then reworks and redistributes a scattering of items associated with them. Yet again, he both admits the power of a set of historical circumstances and, at the same time, relativizes and displaces it. For the discourse on fertility in 'Oxen' is to some extent hopeful and future-oriented. Joyce connects it to the prospects of the nation, to the theme of 'a land flowing with milk and money' (14. 377). The chapter proposes an increase in population as part of a drive away from the trauma of the Famine and its aftermath. This drive will take Ireland towards modern independence and modern political and cultural health. 'Oxen' clearly emerges out of the Irish tradition of political economy. It places the population issue in an Irish political context and produces an anti-Malthusian discourse. But at the same time, it also supplements or radically extends the Irish tradition, most obviously in its playfulness. It separates itself off, not just from the Malthusians but from Lalor's sullen wrath, Mitchel's screams of rage, Davitt's stern anger, a tradition characterized, above all, by its obsession with a history of wrongs. It does this most effectively by laughter. Joyce recognizes 'the piteous vesture of the past' (14. 1354), but refuses to be clothed in it. He is concerned with a release from 'congenital defunctive music' (14. 1428). 'Oxen' precisely *contains* Stephen's bitter, melancholic mode of thought. The chapter designates its will to modern independence in its very insouciance. Its breezy cockiness or cavalier offhandedness is very important. So is its ease with itself, its capacity for making fun of itself. In Joyce's hands, an Irish discourse becomes so self-confident that it can afford not to take itself very seriously at all.

A Parcel of Brats of Boys

At this point, it is important to consider the young men in 'Oxen'. For their significance in the context of Irish history and contemporary Irish culture is a good deal more complex than has commonly been recognized. Furthermore, it cuts directly across the fertility theme. The group at the centre of the chapter is largely composed of students, particularly medical students, and is largely Catholic Irish, though it includes outsiders. Their animated, inventive, and often witty if increasingly drunken exchanges are of course refracted through the styles. But the exchanges nonetheless constitute the chapter's verbal and substantial 'ground'. Unsurprisingly, the young men are not much interested in having children. Their talk is boisterously sexual and more concerned with contraception and birth control. Any 'affirmation of fertility' they offer is satirical, burlesque, or disingenuous, as in the case of Buck Mulligan's proposal for a 'national fertilising farm' (14. 651–712).

The students should be placed in relation to the cultural history of Irish medicine, not least because a sense of the larger outlines of that history clearly underlies the chapter. There had of course been an indigenous tradition of Irish medicine. ('Among the Celts', as 'Oxen' puts it, 'the art of medicine' was 'highly honoured', 14. 34–5.) Physicians were one of the professional learned orders distinctive within the kin-based society of Gaelic Ireland.[63] Brehon law defined the place, rank, responsibilities, rules of practice, and even fees of the medical practitioner in Gaelic society.[64] Medical practice was a family affair and involved a hereditary appointment: hence Joyce's mention of 'the O'Shiels, the O'Hickeys, the O'Lees' (14. 37).[65] It was a learned tradition.[66] Each medical family had its book, in which its medical knowledge was transmitted from one generation to another: that is why Joyce refers to the practitioners having 'sedulously set down the divers methods by which the sick and the relapsed found again health' (14. 37–8).[67] The Gaelic medical tradition fused classical medicine with a learned tradition that ran from Aristotle to the Islamic medico-philosophers, notably Avicenna and Averroes (cf. 14. 246–7). Even in the sixteenth and seventeenth centuries, the Gaelic physicians were 'staunch Arabians'.[68] By then, however, they represented what Bannerman calls 'the conservative wing of the European medical spectrum'.[69] The reasons for their decline were political and cultural: Anglicization, the growth of colleges and universities as established medical training grounds, the end of patronage for the old schools of physic. Though Joyce's treatment of the tradition is unarguably light in tone, he surely knew of its fate. The career of Owen O'Shiel is symptomatic. The distinction of the O'Shiels is referred to in the *Annals of the Four Masters*.[70] But their lands were confiscated during the Elizabethan wars, and they were forced to move. In the early seventeenth century, Owen O'Shiel served as a 'wild goose' with the Spanish army. Returning to Ireland in 1620, he found himself excluded 'by the political bias of his times' from 'the

---

[63] See John Bannerman, *The Beatons: A Medical Kindred in the Classical Gaelic Tradition* (Edinburgh: John Donald, 1986), 1.

[64] These definitions held good in medieval Ireland. See J. B. Lyons, *Brief Lives of Irish Doctors* (Dublin: Blackwater, 1978), 11–12.

[65] On the families in question, see ibid. 12, 28, 35.   [66] See ibid. 12.

[67] The O'Shiels' book and what appears to have been the O'Lees' book are preserved in the Royal Irish Academy. For an account of the O'Lees' book, see Roderic O'Flaherty, *A Chorographical Description of West or H'Iar Connacht*, with notes and illustrations by James Hardiman (Dublin: Irish Archaeological Society, 1846), 71, Hardiman's note.

[68] H. O'Grady, *Catalogue of Irish Manuscripts in the British Museum*, 1 (1926), 175; quoted in Bannerman, *Beatons*, 91.

[69] *Beatons*, 91. See also ibid. 89–97. On 'the demise of the classical tradition', see ibid. 120–33.

[70] Murtough O'Shiel, e.g., is referred to in the *Annals of the Four Masters* as 'the best physician of his years in the neighbourhood'. See *Annals of the Kingdom of Ireland, by the Four Masters, from the Earliest Period to the Year 1616*, ed. and trans. John O'Donovan (7 vols., Dublin: Hodges and Smith, 1848), v. 1509.

patronage of the English notabilities'. In 1642, he joined the forces of the confederate Catholics, and fell in battle in 1650.[71]

Joyce was clearly unsentimental about this tradition. 'Oxen' does not even directly lay the blame for its decline at the door of the colonizer. The chapter rather points to an 'inverecund' (i.e. shameless, irreverent) Irish habit that 'gradually traduced the honourable by ancestors transmitted customs' (14. 25–6). But it also recalls how important the physicians were in times of widespread distress: of plague, fever epidemics, and, above all, famine (14. 35–40). The 'leperyards' Joyce refers to are presumably the celebrated Leper Hospitals of Armagh, 'supposed to antedate by several centuries all similar foundations in Europe'.[72] Above all, the references to the 'trembling withering' and 'flux' (14. 39–40) and to relapsing (14. 38) are to medical features of famine fever.[73] Owen O'Shiel died four years before the foundation of the Fraternity of Physicians in Dublin, a development which spelt the end of the tradition he represented and the emergence of 'a new type of Irish doctor'.[74] The new type was Anglo-Irish. From the late seventeenth to the early twentieth century, the medical profession and medical institutions in Ireland were heavily and usually exclusively Protestant-dominated. During the nineteenth century, however, there was a slow but steady erosion of this dominance. The repeal of 'some of the more repressive anti-Catholic legislation . . . opened up new opportunities' in medicine for Catholics such as the redoubtable Dominic Corrigan.[75] Similarly, the

---

[71] Lyons, *Brief Lives*, 28.

[72] They are now known never to have existed. See Sir William McArthur, 'Famine Fevers in England and Ireland', *Journal of the British Archaeological Association*, 3rd ser. 9 (1944), 66–71, at 70. There was a mistake in a translation from Gaelic to Latin.

[73] For details of famine fever and the debate around it, see Laurence M. Geary, '"The Late Disastrous Epidemic": Medical Relief and the Great Famine', in Morash and Hayes (eds.), *Fearful Realities*, 49–59. See also McArthur, 'Famine Fevers', 67. 'Trembling withering' alludes to the combination of feverish shivering and what Corrigan called 'emaciation, from the increased activity of secretion and excretion' that was brought on by famine fever. See D. J. Corrigan, *Lectures on the Nature and Treatment of Fever* (Dublin: J. Fannin and Co., 1853), 45. 'Bloody flux' was also associated with famine fever. See Connell, *Population of Ireland*, 144. Connell says that the typical famine fever was accompanied 'by trembling' and 'relapses were frequent' (ibid. 228–9). In Joyce's Ireland, famine was by no means a feature of an increasingly remote past. There were incidences in the west of Ireland in the 1890s, the last and most notorious being in 1897–8. See T. P. O'Neill, 'The Food Crisis of the 1890s', in Crawford (ed.), *Famine*, 176–97, at 177. On the almost complete collapse of Ireland's medical resources during the Great Famine—to which Joyce may also be ironically referring—see Geary, 'Late Disastrous Epidemic', esp. 52–8.

[74] Lyons, *Brief Lives*, 12.

[75] Davis Coakley, *The Irish School of Medicine* (Dublin: Town House, 1988), 57.

rise of a Catholic bourgeoisie had as one of its consequences the establishment of Catholic hospitals, like St Vincent's and the Mater Misericordiae, in complement to the well-established Protestant hospitals that largely dated back to the eighteenth century.[76] From the 1880s in particular, Catholics from schools like Clongowes were busily invading the Protestant professional strongholds like medicine as never before.[77] Joyce himself considered a medical career. All the same, before the twentieth century, Corrigan cuts a most unusual figure.[78] To the end of the nineteenth century, medicine was intimately associated with Protestant political and cultural power. As late as the 1890s, the Irish Unionist Alliance could boast that 'out of all the eminent medical men in the Irish capital there is only one who has ever shown the slightest leaning towards Home Rule'.[79] Yet at hospitals like the Rotunda, for instance, 'compared with the urban population as a whole, Roman Catholics were overrepresented among patients'.[80]

The National Maternity Hospital (where 'Oxen' takes place) was thus a particularly important institution. Its very name is significant. It opened in 1894. According to Farmar, its founding members were determined to create a Catholic maternity facility under Catholic management for a largely Catholic population. This distinguished it from the comparable, Protestant-run hospitals already existing, the Rotunda and the Coombe. The intention was to have it cater specifically to the needs of poor and under-privileged Catholic mothers.[81] Thus when one of the narrative voices in 'Oxen' declares that 'In Horne's house rest should reign' (14. 332–3), the observation should not be heard as a neutral generality. One of the principal points of policy in the National Maternity Hospital, as is clear from its being a *lying-in* charity, was that it was supposed to give tenement mothers the rest that middle-class mothers could get at home.[82]

[76] Ruth Barrington, *Health, Medicine and Politics in Ireland 1900–1970* (Dublin: Criterion Press, 1987), 15.

[77] See Tony Farmar, *Holles Street 1894–1994: The National Maternity Hospital—A Centenary History* (Dublin: A. & A. Farmar, 1994), 38.

[78] A quick scan through Coakley's *Irish Masters of Medicine* makes this very clear. Cf. Mary Daly, *Dublin, the Deposed Capital: A Social and Economic History 1860–1914* (Cork: Cork University Press, 1984), 127.

[79] *Publications of the Irish Unionist Alliance*, I (1891), 247.

[80] W. Peter Ward, *Birth Weight and Economic Growth: Women's Living Standards in the Industrializing West* (Chicago and London: University of Chicago Press, 1993), 73.

[81] See Farmar, *Holles Street*, 7–9.   [82] See ibid. 8.

Joyce was evidently precisely conscious of the political significance of the Hospital. He is even slyly ironical about one or two
aspects of its policy and work. The presence of the Scotsman
Crotthers among the students may well be significant. From the mid-
eighteenth century onwards, the Rotunda maternity hospital had
always specified Protestant staff and management. So, too, the
founders of the National Maternity Hospital declared that 'the management of the hospital be exclusively Catholic'. The masters, doctors, resident pupils, nurses, and all intern servants and assistants
were Catholic, the only exception being students.[83] In a piece of historical realism that is also a gesture of resistance to sectarianism,
Joyce emphasizes the mixed character of his group, and adds Bloom
and Lenehan, for good measure. Similarly, one of the points about
working at the Holles Street hospital was that, whilst the institution
catered to the poor, the doctors were picking up 'a breadth of experience and prestige that could easily be transmuted into considerable
fees in private practice'.[84] In one respect, the hospital aimed to close
a gap between classes. In others, it repeated and perpetuated such
gaps. It maintained the condescension of charitable patronage, for
example, which had been so very largely the principle of medicine in
Ireland from the eighteenth century onwards. When Joyce refers to
'A. Horne' as 'lord' of the hospital (14. 74), he does so with a wicked
sense of fact. Horne was upper middle class, enjoyed the lifestyle
of the most eminent Protestant doctors, including a big house in
Merrion Square, and would arrive at the hospital in top hat, frock
coat, and a long black overcoat with astrakhan collar.[85] For all the
charitable exertions of the hospital, the future for the tenement
mothers was commonly grim. Thus a harsh irony lies just beneath
Joyce's Carlyle-narrator's obtuse and callous celebration of Mrs
Purefoy as 'a hoary pandemonium of ills, enlarged glands, mumps,
quinsy, bunions, hayfever, bedsores, ringworm, floating kidney, Der-
byshire neck, warts, bilious attacks, gallstones, cold feet, varicose
veins' (14. 1424–7). In his famous account of the chapter to Frank
Budgen, Joyce recounted his engagements with the cultural wealth of
the English and Anglo-Irish literary tradition. He ended with a stark,
single-sentence paragraph: 'How's that for high?' (*Letters*, i. 139). He
meant 'high' partly in the sense of 'high class', and the tone, again, is
heavily ironical.

---

[83] Ibid., 11, 24.   [84] Ibid. 8.   [85] See ibid. 6, 10, 18.

Medically, at the start of the twentieth century, Ireland stood on the very threshold of modernity. The years 1903–11 saw an intense scrutiny of medical facilities, particularly of medical relief for the poor.[86] In 1904, the British Medical Association examined medical conditions in Ireland and made proposals for the reorganization of the Poor Law medical service into a State one. This initiated a process that culminated in Lloyd George's Health Insurance Bill of 1913. The Bill spelt the beginning of major reform of the Poor Law in Ireland. The emphasis shifted towards providing medical services to all who needed them, in other words, towards a modern health service. Here, yet again, the Local Government (Ireland) Act of 1898 is significant. For one of its consequences was the transfer of power within the medical administration of Ireland from a Protestant elite to 'the [very largely Catholic] democracy'. In the words of the distinguished, English medical observer whom I have just cited: 'It was practically a social revolution in Ireland. . . . a democracy not well trained in medical, sanitary or other administration—and certainly without any practical experience—came at once to the throne'.[87] Subtract the Englishman's misgivings, and this registers an important new franchise within a modern political and cultural dispensation. The medical students in 'Oxen' represent a new, trained, and educated generation of young Catholics who can expect to be prominent in their profession. Furthermore, they are rising to prominence in a sphere in which political and managerial power is passing into Catholic hands.

That the young men are disrespectful, have no manners, are raucously ill-behaved, is therefore a large part of the point. They are part of an emergent political culture. But at the same time, as far as the Dublin medical establishment is concerned, they are also Irish 'aborigines', to recall Mahaffy's phrase, jumped-up versions of 'the corner-boys who spit in the Liffey'.[88] Mahaffy's patrician attitudes were traditional amongst the Dublin medical elite. Dr William Collum, for example, the master of the Rotunda from 1766 to 1773, opposed the spread of medical education on the grounds that it would 'afford instruction to a parcel of Brats of Boys, the

---

[86] See Barrington, *Health*, 24–38.

[87] G.J.H. Ewatt, *British Medical Journal: A Report on the Poor-Law Medical System of Ireland* (London: British Medical Association, 1904), 52.

[88] Gerald Griffin, *The Wild Geese: Pen Portraits of Famous Irish Exiles* (1938); quoted in Richard Ellmann, *James Joyce* (rev. edn.; Oxford: Oxford University Press, 1982), 58.

Apprentices of Surgeons and Apothecaries'.[89] This had been very much the tone adopted by the newly emergent, Protestant medical establishment as it closed down the older medical tradition, seeking 'to prevent illiterate persons from practising physic'.[90] Furthermore, the boisterous irreverence so evident in 'Oxen' was a historically specific phenomenon. For 'young [medical] aspirants' at this time, 'the interests of personal advancement, religion and nationalism were mixed in a heady brew that led to frequent clashes with the establishment'.[91]

Thus the fact that the students are there at all represents a triumph over the exclusivity traditional within Irish medicine. At the same time, it centres the chapter around an attitude of more or less flagrant political and cultural dissidence. The 'mettlesome youth' (14. 871) of the students represents the power of the new and looks to the future. As such, it directly conflicts with the historical discourses in the chapter. Stephen articulates the contrast between two historical worlds, if—ironically—in a language that seems to belong to the older one. His theme is the watershed that is so important for 'Oxen' itself:

Look forth now, my people, upon the land of behest, even from Horeb and from Nebo and from Pisgah and from the Horns of Hatten unto a land flowing with milk and money. But thou hast suckled me with a bitter milk: my moon and my sun thou hast quenched for ever. (14. 375–8)

As opposed to what Stephen calls the 'days of old' (14. 367), of which he still feels himself to be a prisoner, the 'land of behest' is clearly new, modern, and democratic. The young men represent a modern principle of lively difference and dispute, a democratic 'strife of tongues' within which 'discursiveness' seems 'the only bond of union' (14. 952–4). Joyce's choice of that last word, in a context where democracy and difference are at issue, is deliberate and not without irony. But the students' modernity is most evident in the various discussions of modern medical issues: 'the gravest problems of obstetrics and forensic medicine' (14. 977–8); Caesarian section

[89] Quoted in Robert F. Harrison, 'Medical Education at the Rotunda Hospital 1745–1995', in Alan Browne (ed.), *Masters, Midwives and Ladies-in-Waiting* (Dublin: A. & A. Farmar, 1995), 66–76, at 67.
[90] The phrase is from a request to London for parliamentary assistance made by the Dublin College of Physicians in 1725. See Gerard O'Brien, 'Scotland, Ireland and the Antithesis of Enlightenment', in S. J. Connolly et al. (eds.), *Conflict, Identity and Economic Development: Ireland and Scotland 1600–1939* (Preston: Carnegie Publishing, 1995), 125–34, at 133.   [91] Farmar, *Holles Street*, 38.

(14. 956–7); artificial insemination (14. 969–70); the relationship between sanitary and working conditions and health (14.1243, 1258); improvements in antenatal care (14. 1251–6). The concern about the relative rights of mother and child to life (14. 202–63) was both contemporary and local. The agenda had been set by no less a person than Horne himself.[92] Intermittently, as at 14. 1250, such issues are cast as national issues.

The students' concern with modern developments in medicine is clearly related to their modern, scientific, secular view of the world. 'Believe-on-Me' is 'nought else but notion'. The young men can 'conceive no thought of it' (14. 459–60). Their scepticism and materialism separates them off from almost all the other characters in *Ulysses*. It is also evident in their frank, straightforward attitudes to sex and their casual way of discussing it (as in the case of Mulligan's proposal, 14. 651–712). Their concern with contraception is likewise modern. As I said earlier, Ireland at the turn of the century was witnessing the 'slow beginnings' of the 'fertility transition'. In urban, middle-class Ireland, at least, family planning was becoming more common, and not just among Protestants.[93] The modern solution to 'the spectre of over-population' was contraception.[94] Humanist and feminist critics have sometimes felt uncomfortable at the frivolous tone in which the students talk about sex. But Joyce was registering the laughter of minds freeing themselves from historical bondage. After the Famine, one of the principal manifestations of such bondage was a traumatic melancholy regarding sexual activity.

It is here that these modern young men seem most clearly to collide with the politics of the 'affirmation of fertility'. Commentators on 'Oxen' have often felt notably superior to Stephen and his friends.[95] But there is no indication in the text that Joyce either sits in judgement on his students or expects his readers to. The 'mature' discourse on fertility is not clearly elevated above the more 'adolescent'

---

[92] See ibid. 28–30. In a paper given to the Obstetrics Section of the Royal Academy of Medicine in Ireland in 1902, Horne emerged as a modern advocate of the Caesarian section.

[93] See Ó Grada and Duffy, *Fertility Control*, 1–7; *idem.*, 'The Fertility Transition in Ireland and Scotland c.1880–1930', in Connolly et al. (eds.), *Conflict*, 89–102; and Ó Grada, *Ireland Before and After the Famine*, 195.   [94] Eversley, *Social Theories*, 11.

[95] See e.g. Stanley Sultan, *The Argument of 'Ulysses'* (Columbus, Oh.: Ohio State University Press, 1964), 286–7; Richard Ellmann, *'Ulysses' on the Liffey* (London: Faber and Faber, 1972), 133–40; and David Hayman, *'Ulysses': The Mechanics of Meaning* (new edn., rev. and expanded, Madison: University of Wisconsin Press, 1982), 30, 74.

emphasis on sex and contraception. But then what are we to make of the fact that two themes apparently so contradictory are both present in the chapter? If Joyce's young, Catholic Irishmen are modern and democratic in spirit, this is partly reflected in their 'inverecundity', their frank and carefree disparagement of solemn authority. Their targets are largely connected with Church, State, and the more privileged classes. One obvious example would be the clever, satirical, joint account of Irish colonial history (14. 580–650). Some of the narrators reproach the young men as 'votaries of levity' (14. 900–1) or members of 'a generation of unfledged profligates' (14. 932–3). But the prim and pompous voices in question are English and Anglo-Irish, and Joyce is clearly underscoring a conflict of cultures.

It is thus no accident that the young men in 'Oxen' are carousing together at the same time that a (presumably largely Anglo-Irish and more sober) group of young revivalists is congregating at George Moore's (14. 779–80; cf. 9. 273–4). Nor is it an accident that Stephen has ended up with the group in Holles Street (or that Mulligan shuttles from one to the other). Stephen was snubbed by the revivalists. But the students recognize him as *their* 'bard', if teasingly and light-heartedly ('All desire to see you bring forth the work you meditate. . . . I heartily wish you may not fail them', 14. 1120–2). In Joyce's terms, it is the young men at Holles Street rather than those at Moore's who represent new, modern forces and new possibilities in Irish culture. Joyce knew very well that the Ireland represented by the traditions of Gaelic medicine was properly dead. He also knew that the traditional Anglo-Irish domination of the medical profession was under siege. Thus if 'Oxen' expands the traditional Irish fertility trope and the discourses of an Irish political economy, it combines that practice with an emphasis that runs radically counter to both. A fertile Ireland was both a literal desideratum and a metaphor for political renewal. Joyce presents us with a group of young men who do indeed belong to a more hopeful future imaginable in terms of national regeneration. But they themselves are wholly unserious about fertility both literal and metaphorical. They are nationalists without being either grandiose or solemn in their nationalism. Here as elsewhere in *Ulysses*, Joyce suggests that Irish traditions be enlarged to include their self-betrayals, their will to self-sabotage. He interrogates any inclination to reverence. 'Oxen' maintains a degree of respect for certain Irish traditions. But it is also 'inverecund', and willing to 'traduce' them (14. 25). It even suggests that the usable tradition *is* that of irreverence.

To Flout and Witwanton

In fact, 'Oxen' is an outsize Irish bull. More particularly, however, it is 'an Irish bull in an English chinashop' (14. 581). It is far less concerned to traduce Irish than English traditions. In effect, Joyce 'writes back' at the stranger and his culture. 'Writing back' is the most conspicuous practice in the chapter. It is also the dominant one, subsuming and focusing the practices that I have described so far. Joyce 'writes back' in different modes. Some passages in 'Oxen' read like parodies of the records of meetings of the Anglo-Irish-dominated Obstetrical Society of Dublin.[96] The chapter contains jokes at the expense of particular Anglo-Irish medical figures, notably Purefoy. Joyce gave the name of a well-known and distinguished Anglo-Irish Dublin gynaecologist, ex-master of the Rotunda and posh friend of Gogarty's father, to a prolific but doddery head of a large and impoverished family who goes 'dapping' for fish 'off Bullock harbour' (14. 519–20) and is urged to suckle himself at his wife's breasts (14. 1433–4).[97] 'Oxen' also satirizes the magnanimous, philanthropic discourses about the health of the poor on which Arthur Griffith was pouring nationalist scorn during the first decade of the century.[98] It equally mocks the speciousness, pomposity, and evasiveness of mid- and late nineteenth-century discourses on the Famine. These often drew a veil of language over appalling facts, and figures like Corrigan complained bitterly about them (14. 33–49).[99]

Joyce also 'writes back' at the discourses of English political economy. Take two literary examples, his reworkings of Carlyle and Arnold. For Joyce, one of the chief points of transmission of English economic doctrine was undoutedly the 'soft Malthusianism' in Culture and Anarchy, a book he owned. Arnold puts forward a Malthusian argument against liberals and free-traders who have suggested that an increase in population is a sign of social and economic

---

[96] Cf. e.g. the Dublin sections of *Obstetrical Journal*, vols. 7 and 8 (Apr. 1879–Dec. 1880).

[97] On Richard Dancer Purefoy, see Peter Costello, 'James Joyce, *Ulysses* and the National Maternity Hospital', in Farmar, *Holles Street*, 208–16, at 213. On the relationship between Purefoy and the Gogartys, see J. B. Lyons, *James Joyce and Medicine* (Dublin: Dolmen Press, 1973), 52.

[98] Griffith satirized the campaign against tuberculosis mounted by do-gooders like the Countess of Aberdeen, e.g. See Daly, *Dublin*, 267.

[99] See D. J. Corrigan, *On Famine and Fever as Cause and Effect in Ireland* (Dublin: J. Fannin & Co., 1846), 23–5.

health: 'the enlarged conception of what is included in subsistence does not operate to prevent the bringing into the world of numbers of people who but just attain to the barest necessities of life or who even fail to attain them'.[100] Joyce parodies this passage in his evocation of an Irish tradition according to which care was provided not solely 'for the copiously opulent' mother 'but also for her who not being sufficiently moneyed scarcely and often not even scarcely could subsist' (14. 47–9). In general, 'Oxen''s emphases are strikingly anti-Arnoldian. Arnold argues that the 'increase of population . . . must not be mechanically pursued' like a 'fetish'.[101] 'Oxen' playfully pursues it as such. Arnold asserts that a growing population is no 'absolute proof of national prosperity'.[102] Joyce reverses the argument. Arnold suggests that one 'ought not to call the State well-managed and prosperous merely because its manufactures and its citizens multiply'.[103] 'Oxen' proposes something close to the opposite view.

Most importantly, however, Joyce turns Arnold's own language against him. As repeatedly elsewhere, he revels in twisting an English discourse to his own ends. In effect, he injects it with an auto-destructive principle. His treatment of Carlyle is another example of this. Carlyle was genuinely and bleakly horrified at what he saw of the Famine. But his attitudes to Irish Catholics were not uplifting. He loathed O'Connell, saw Catholicism as 'a religion of sloth and mediaeval corruption, and the Irish [as] a race of inferior Celts'.[104] Carlyle's views on Ireland were always staunchly Unionist, and his solution for the Famine was emigration. By contrast, Joyce's 'Carlyle' is a rumbustious figure who cheerily dismisses 'Malthusiasts' (14. 1415) and argues that one should drink one's 'udderful' of 'Mother's milk' (14. 1433). The 'Carlyle parody' (14. 1407–39) is both remote in tone from the oracular *gravitas* so common in the work of the Victorian sage, and produces an argument directly opposed to his.

But the discourses most at issue in 'Oxen' are those implicated in the chapter's styles. Scholars and critics have long been aware of two principal sources for them, William Peacock's anthology *English*

---

[100] Matthew Arnold, *Culture and Anarchy* (1869; New Haven and London: Yale University Press, 1994), 125.   [101] Ibid. 128.

[102] Ibid. 131.   [103] Ibid.

[104] See Fred Kaplan, *Thomas Carlyle: A Biography* (Cambridge: Cambridge University Press, 1983), 339, 343.

Prose from Mandeville to Ruskin and George Saintsbury's *A History of English Prose Rhythm*.[105] Janusko added Annie Barnett and Lucy Dale's *An Anthology of English Prose* and A. F. Murison's *Selections from the Best English Authors*.[106] H. A. Treble's *English Prose* and John Dover Wilson's *Life in Shakespeare's England: A Book of Elizabethan Prose* should also be included.[107] However largely Joyce borrows from original texts, the anthologies are the mainstay of the chapter. But do the styles really engage with the history per se of English literature or English prose, as has often been supposed, in the past?[108] Joyce's main concerns are surely more precisely focused. The tradition of English literature is less important for understanding 'Oxen' than a knowledge of the politics of the anthology itself in the period 1880–1920. Indeed, 'Oxen' is itself constructed like an anthology, though an anthology that turns out to be an anti-anthology, after all.

As I said in my introduction, in the period 1880–1920, English academics, critics, novelists and poets, men and women of letters, publishers, even politicians and parliamentarians[109] engaged in a range of activities intended to foster and promote the national literary culture. The market was flooded with series and cheap editions of classics and English literature handbooks: primers, anthologies, histories, textbooks, guides. Some individuals, like Saintsbury and Treble, virtually became solo industries. Publishers like Macmillan

---

[105] W. Peacock (ed.), *English Prose from Mandeville to Ruskin* (London: Grant Richards, 1903; 4th imp., London: Oxford University Press, 1912). The two editions have the same pagination. George Saintsbury, *A History of English Prose Rhythm* (London: Macmillan & Co., 1912). Strictly speaking, Saintsbury's book is less an anthology than a primer.

[106] Annie Barnett and Lucy Dale (eds.), *An Anthology of English Prose (1332 to 1740)*, pref. by Andrew Lang (London: Longmans, Green and Co., 1912); and A. F. Murison (ed.), *Selections from the Best English Authors (Beowulf to the Present Time)* (London: W. & R. Chambers, 1907). See Robert Janusko, 'Another Anthology for "Oxen": Barnett and Dale', *James Joyce Quarterly*, 27/2 (Winter 1990), 257–81; and 'Yet Another Anthology for "Oxen": Murison's *Selections*', *Joyce Studies Annual*, 1 (1990), 117–31.

[107] H. A. Treble (ed.), *English Prose: Narrative, Descriptive and Dramatic* (London: Oxford University Press, 1917); and J. Dover Wilson, *Life in Shakespeare's England: A Book of Elizabethan Prose* (Cambridge: Cambridge University Press, 1911). Joyce bought Treble's book in 1919, not long before starting 'Oxen'. Dover Wilson's book contains a glossary which Joyce used for both 'Scylla and Charybdis' and 'Oxen'.

[108] Robert Spoo's is the most convincing of such arguments: 'Oxen' qualifies and ironizes 'the voices of the fathers, subtly eroding the historicoliterary progression'. See *James Joyce*, 148.

[109] I am thinking, e.g., of the extent to which men like Acland, Asquith, and Balfour shared the presidency of the English Association with men and women of letters.

and Oxford University Press grew keenly aware of the imperial market, and many of their books—including anthologies—went rapidly into colonial circulation, not least, in Ireland.[110] If the colonies were a key market for the anthology, schools were another. The publications of the English Association between 1907 and 1922 that are specifically concerned with schools, libraries, and the teaching of English frequently recommend anthologies and primers.[111] Saintsbury and Peacock were among the most familiar names.[112] Peter Brooker and Peter Widdowson suggest that anthologies served as 'the barometers of the contemporary taste and judgement which worked to forge the English literary tradition'.[113] But Quantrill goes further, arguing that the anthology was 'one of the principal instruments' by which national identity was increasingly invested in the literary tradition.[114] In an age that sees a rapid extension of the educational franchise and a rapidly expanding mass readership, the anthology became a crucial point of transmission of the national literary tradition to a newly literate public. Indeed, it was doubly useful in promoting national unity, since it both presented a seemingly homogeneous tradition and was aimed at readers of diverse backgrounds and beliefs. Palgrave himself had been animated by the desire to produce a 'true national Anthology'.[115] Indeed, this kind of project seemed to have the sanction of no less a figure than Arnold himself.[116]

---

[110] On the relevant development in policy at Macmillan's and Oxford University Press, see Esther Quantrill, 'Anthological Politics: Poetry and British Culture 1860–1914' (Ph.D. thesis, University of Texas at Austin, 1995), 215. My discussion of anthologies is indebted to this singularly brilliant piece of work.

[111] The use of anthologies in schools was in fact a much-debated issue, but the very heat of the debates is an indication of how important they had become. See ibid. 39. See also J. H. Fowler, 'De Quincey as Literary Critic', English Association Pamphlet, 52 (July 1922), 3.

[112] Other names and titles familiar to Joyce scholars also recur in the publications of the English Association: Saintsbury, Lee, Dowden, Lamb's Tales from Shakespeare, and Butcher and Lang, who were seen as furnishing the British schoolboy with his authorized version of Homer.

[113] 'A Literature for England', in Robert Colls and Philip Dodd, Englishness: Politics and Culture 1880–1920 (London: Croom Helm, 1986), 116–63, at 120–1.

[114] 'Anthological Politics', p. xviii. Quantrill actually specifies the poetry anthology, but her argument holds good for other kinds of anthology and their cultural function.

[115] See ibid., p. ix. Interestingly, Palgrave initially developed his project in reaction to an anthology compiled by an Irish poet, William Allingham's Nightingale Valley (1859).

[116] Quantrill points out that Arnold's important and influential 'The Study of Poetry' was initially published as the introductory essay to Humphry Ward's hugely successful anthology The English Poets (1880). See ibid.

Prose anthologies were as much in demand as anthologies of poetry. But prose *fiction* was not particularly important. This is clear from 'Oxen' itself. Chris Baldick argues that 'generic inclusiveness' was 'by far the most important feature' of the canon in the period before 1918.[117] Both anthologies and literature syllabuses included 'historical', 'imaginative', 'descriptive', and 'biographical' along with fictional prose. Non-fictional prose was a clearer and more efficient if less subtle vehicle for the transmission of ideology. The ideological formation of English cultural nationalism was pervasively evident in the anthologies Joyce used, if with marked variations and in more or less compact or diffuse form. Joyce could hardly have opened John Dover Wilson's *Life in Shakespeare's England*, for example, with its opening section on 'England and the English' and its section on 'Colonization', its selections with titles like 'Hakluyt Extols England's Greatness at Sea', without directly and immediately confronting the formation in question. The same is true of Barnett and Dale's anthology, which includes Froissart's account of the Black Prince taking Limoges; Raleigh on the exploration, conquest, and defence of Guiana; and, most importantly, Spenser's attack on the Irish bards and recommendations for the government of Ireland. But the most blatantly ideological of the prose anthologies Joyce owned was actually Peacock's, the one to which he most frequently resorted. Peacock selected Malory's Arthur defying Rience, king of Ireland, and declaring his determination to humble him. He selected Raleigh's chillingly patriotic account of Sir Richard Grenville's last fight on the *Revenge*. He chose Hakluyt's account of Martin Frobisher's second voyage to America, in which Frobisher and his men scare the wits out of the Orkney islanders, sail on to do battle with American natives, discover riches in the American mountains, and take 'possession' of the country in the name of God and Queen.[118] He chose Burke on 'the Nature of England's hold of Her Colonies' as 'promoting the wealth, the number, the happiness of the human race'.[119] He included Kingsley's young boy listening to tales of colonial adventure ('as the Spaniards are the masters of the Indians, we're the masters of the Spaniards').[120] Again and again, Peacock's selections turn out to be nationalistic, militaristic, enthusiastically

---

[117] *Criticism and Literary Theory: 1890 to the Present* (London and New York: Longman, 1996), 57. [118] Peacock (ed.), *English Prose*, 48.

[119] Ibid. 236.   [120] Ibid. 368.

royalist, class-based, and anti-democratic. Above all, they are patently selections from the literature of a great imperial nation, the major moments of whose literary history Peacock conceives of as expressions of imperial power.

It is inconceivable that Joyce should not have recognized this aspect of Peacock's anthology. On occasions, he even reworks Peacock's material in a manner that suggests that he was well aware of its implications. He transplants phrases, for example, from Raleigh's account of the embattled *Revenge* to an apparently Swiftian and therefore strictly inappropriate passage in 'Oxen'.[121] In the passage in question (14. 639–46), Stephen presents an imaginative version of Irishmen emigrating to America, not only as a result of English intervention in Ireland, but in the same historical period as Grenville's last stand. In small part, then, Joyce's treatment of the anthologies involved a practice of recontextualization. But this is a complex matter: the anthologies Joyce used were not always politically close to one another. Set Murison alongside Peacock and it is clear enough that the professor from University College, London is a considerably more liberal anthologist than the civil servant from the Home Office. Murison chooses an extract from More's *Utopia* on the Utopians' contempt for gold. He also selects one from Bishop Latimer's *First Sermon before Edward VI* to which he gives the title 'Better Days for the Humbler Classes'. It suggests that the rich have too much property. There was a 'soft' as there was a 'hard' anthological politics during the period.[122]

But it is doubtful whether Joyce was much interested in such distinctions.[123] What he surely understood was the cultural politics represented by the contemporary prose anthology as genre. This is the crucial defining context for the styles in 'Oxen', and Joyce responds to it with a number of different literary (and political) strategies. On the one hand, there is straightforward mockery, as, for example, in the Macaulay 'parody' (14. 1198–1222). Its point of reference is a

---

[121] See Janusko, *Sources and Structures*, 110.

[122] In this respect, Joyce had two interesting books on his shelves: Edgar R. Jones, *Selected English Speeches* (London: Oxford University Press, 1913) and Sidney Lee, *Great Englishmen of the Sixteenth Century* (London: Thomas Nelson, 1907). Both attempt to balance a liberal agenda with the familiar nationalistic one.

[123] He told Jacques Mercanton, however, that the Newman 'parody' was distinct from the others. See Jacques Mercanton, 'The Hours of James Joyce', in Willard Potts (ed.), *Portraits of the Artist in Exile: Recollections of James Joyce by Europeans* (Dublin: Wolfhound, 1979), 206–52, at 217.

passage from Macaulay's essay *Warren Hastings*. The essay, and indeed the passage in question, was a *locus classicus* for late nineteenth- and early twentieth-century anthologists. As so often with the anthologies, this was a question of content as well as style. The whole point about Hastings's trial was the occasion. Joyce probably found the passage in Saintsbury, together with Saintsbury's analysis of it. He may well have noticed it in Treble's anthology, which provides a longer excerpt, and consulted his copy of Macaulay's *Critical and Historical Essays*, which contained the essay in full.[124] At any rate, there are elements in Joyce's 'parody' that can only be fully explained if we assume that he read beyond the point at which Saintsbury stops. Both Saintsbury and Treble begin with Macaulay's evocation of 'the great hall of William Rufus' in which the trial took place.[125] The passage then moves on to an account of those who attended the trial, followed—in Treble—by an account of Hastings himself and his advocates and accusers. The passage is an act of homage to a glorious ruling class: royalty, the aristocracy, the judiciary, military leaders, 'great dignitaries', the members of Macaulay's 'brilliant society' in all its splendour.[126] But those who pay the Empire tribute or acknowledge its sway are almost as important:

There were gathered together, from all parts of a great, free, enlightened, and prosperous empire, grace and female loveliness, wit and learning, the representatives of every science and every art. . . . There the Ambassadors of great Kings and Commonwealths gazed with admiration on a spectacle which no other country in the world could present.[127]

In fact, the passage as a whole is a classic hymn of praise to the pillars of the English imperium as it moves towards the zenith of its power. Furthermore, it is an account of a great empire affirming its probity and the morality of the imperial project not only in trying one of its most distinguished servants for corruption, but in transforming the occasion into a peculiarly solemn and awesome ritual. Hugh Kenner suggested that, stylistically, the 'parody' was actually constructed on quite unMacaulayesque principles.[128] But this is not what matters

[124] Thomas Babington Macaulay, *Critical and Historical Essays* (London: Longmans, Green, Reader and Dyer, 1874), 602–67. Michael Gillespie suggests that Treble's anthology is 'a strong candidate for the origin of the Macaulay parody'. See *Inverted Volumes Improperly Arranged: James Joyce and his Trieste Library* (Ann Arbor: UMI Research Press, 1983), 85–6.   [125] Treble (ed.), *English Prose*, 367.
[126] Ibid. 367–8.   [127] Ibid. 368.
[128] *Joyce's Voices* (London: Faber & Faber, 1978), 106–8.

most. Joyce retains enough of the structure and style of the relevant passage to indicate the exact provenance of his 'parody'. He mimics Macaulay's introduction to the debate, his evocation of the solemn grandeur of the scene, and his account of those who are to speak:

The debate which ensued was in its scope and progress an epitome of the course of life. Neither place nor council was lacking in dignity. The debaters were the keenest in the land, the theme they were engaged on the loftiest and most vital. The high hall of Horne's house had never beheld an assembly so representative and so varied nor had the old rafters of that establishment ever listened to a language so encylopaedic. A gallant scene in truth it made. Crotthers was there ... (14. 1198–1204)

It is the one *occasion* that is a parody of the other. The spirit of the 'impudent mocks' indulged in by Joyce's 'young sparks' (14. 846–8) is reproduced and extended in the passage, in that they themselves are made to function as a *reductio ad absurdum* of Macaulay's array of English grandees.

But Kenner is also right. As far as *style* is concerned, Joyce's passage hardly seems to qualify as 'parody' at all. It seems wilfully to eschew the possibility of expert parody offered, not least, by Saintsbury's detailed attention to the mechanisms of Macaulay's prose. Something else is going on here, apart from mockery. The more relevant term is arguably treachery. What Joyce does, in effect, is to establish his passage in a relationship of correspondence to (and therefore dependence on) the English writer, and then work his way towards a freedom from it. He refuses the subservience of parody, its residual structure of fidelity to the master text: fidelity, in this instance, to Macaulay's grandiose rhetoric and his stately periods. Yet the tie of the betrayer to the object of his betrayal remains. The movement towards freedom is uncompleted. This, in miniature, is Joyce's response to those of his nationalist contemporaries who argued for a radical separation of Irish from English culture. The radical break from established forms risks a replication of their cardinal features in the very posture of diametric opposition. This is the case throughout the chapter. Joyce is less concerned with parody or pastiche than with a strategy of adulteration.

David Lloyd has written brilliantly of the importance of the concept of adulteration to an understanding of Joyce. In Lloyd's terms, nationalism is intent on a singular, unitary, national identity. It wishes to transcend antagonisms, contradictions, social differences, cultural hybridity. By contrast, *Ulysses* insists on them. It is the citizen who wants purity. 'Cyclops' dramatizes the reality of adulteration as the condition of colonial Ireland at every level.[129] But Lloyd neglects the Joyce who understands the citizen but seeks to move beyond the limits of his political imagination. Joyce's conviction of the 'ignobility' of the forces against which he is ranged is incalculably more intense than his creature's.[130] Where the citizen wants to insist on cleansing Irish culture of the effects of adulteration, Joyce sees such a project as unambitious. He seeks actively to reverse the colonial vector of cultural power, to put the process of adulteration into reverse. In other words, he is intent on cultural retribution, on style as revenge. But he also practises retribution with a nonchalant ease and gaiety which establishes itself in contradistinction to the citizen's posture of ferocious antagonism. For Joyce, that posture is finally too cowed. The monument is firmly 'lodged' in place (2. 50). It is not simply to be blown up or done away with. The revenge of the disempowered is defacement, a graffiti-work which, if carried out with sufficient ardour and determination, develops a different, rival splendour of its own.

Much of Joyce's practice in 'Oxen' is actually an 'Irishisation' of things English, to adopt Hyde's term, the invasion of the invader's preserve.[131] This is a predictable effect of the relationship between English styles and Irish subject matter. The styles are repeatedly adulterated and distorted by Irish voices, Hiberno-English, Irish wit: Lenehan's quip about Mrs Purefoy 'expecting each moment to be her next', for example, serves as a conspicuous interruption of the Malory parody (14. 178). But English literature is also betrayed in its historical dimension: anachronism is one of Joyce's principal strategies. J. S. Atherton rightly pointed to a deliberate 'confusion of [historical] margins' in the episode.[132] Material from some of Joyce's sources constantly appears in his imitations of others. He copied the

---

[129] Lloyd, *Anomalous States: Irish Writing and the Post-Colonial Moment* (Dublin: Lilliput, 1993), *passim*, esp. 105–7.

[130] For Joyce on Ireland's 'belief in the incurable ignobility of the forces that have overcome her', see CW, 105.

[131] For Hyde's concept of 'Irishisation', see 'The Necessity for De-Anglicizing Ireland', in Sir Charles Gavan Duffy et al., *The Revival of Irish Literature* (London: T. Fisher Unwin, 1894), 115–61, at 135.

[132] 'The Oxen of the Sun', in Clive Hart and David Hayman (eds.), *James Joyce's 'Ulysses': Critical Essays* (Berkeley and Los Angeles: University of California Press, 1974), 313–39, at 323.

word 'relentment' out of Browne's *Hydrotaphia* into his notesheets, for instance.[133] But he used it in what is commonly referred to as the Gibbon parody (14. 968). Sterne's phrase 'a cap-full of wind' is apparently the source of Joyce's phrase 'a capful of light odes',[134] but occurs in his Landor passage (14. 1119). Burton's phrase 'a proper man of person' leaves its traces on the 'parody' of Steele and Addison (14. 713–14).[135] Any idea that 'Oxen' is seriously concerned with the 'organic' development of English literature and its resemblance to the development of the embryo in the womb collapses, here.[136] The chapter works as a sly corruption of the tradition as promoted by the anthology and its supposed historical shape.

Stylistically, 'Oxen' is also a gleeful celebration of ersatz. If Joyce appears to have captured the flavour of the prose of a given writer or period, that flavour is likely to turn out to be partly bogus. Joyce copied the phrase 'a world of' from Sterne's *A Sentimental Journey*.[137] But his use of it actually makes it sound considerably more recherché than it does in the original (14. 756). The phrase 'approved with' in the 'parody' of the Elizabethan Chronicles sounds right. Elizabethan meanings of the verb included 'confirm', and it could be followed by the preposition 'with' if used in that sense. But even with that sense in mind, the phrase doesn't really fit into its context (14. 360). Both these details have the air of adroit but finally unconvincing fakes. An allusion to a regiment known as the Fencibles might seem plausible enough in the Steele-and-Addison passage (14. 655). But the *OED* gives the date of the first reference to that regiment as 1795. Some of Joyce's apparently archaic turns of phrase are invented. Others are adulterations of the original. In the Defoe 'parody', Joyce uses the phrase 'what belonged of women'. But the phrase he actually copied down from Defoe was 'what belonged to a woman', which sounds altogether more ordinary (14. 534).[138]

Everywhere, the rule appears to be contamination: contamination, that is, of the ostensibly homogeneous with what does not belong to it, or what Karen Lawrence calls the 'strange mélange'.[139] This is the case with the many lapses into modern idiom. In Sterne's

---

[133] See Janusko, *Sources and Structures*, 133. [134] See ibid. 144.
[135] See ibid. 112.
[136] For a detailed account of criticism that has taken the concept of 'the embryological framework' seriously, see ibid. 39–54. [137] See ibid. 140.
[138] See ibid. 138.
[139] *The Odyssey of Styles in 'Ulysses'* (Princeton: Princeton University Press, 1981), 139.

Sentimental Journey, Yorick tells of an occasion when he 'popp'd upon Smelfungus'.[140] Joyce's echo—'out popped a locket'—sounds much more commonplace (14. 754). Some of the parodies are infected with the deliberate clumsiness that finds its apotheosis in 'Eumaeus'. The pretence to imitation may also yield to Joyceanisms. 'Twikindled', for example—as in 'twikindled and monstrous births' (14. 974)—may be a Joycean coinage, deriving from the word 'twikin', a variant form of the dialectal 'twokin', meaning two apples growing on the one stem.[141] Joyce sometimes mixes material from his sources with phrases from other parts of *Ulysses*. Boylan's 'seaside girls' refrain, for instance, crops up comically in the De Quincey parody, as Stuart Gilbert first noted (14. 1107).[142] So, too, Bloom's familiar preoccupation with metempsychosis surfaces hilariously in a sentence whose cadences are Johnsonian (14. 897).

Contamination in 'Oxen' is partly—and quite blatantly—contamination with the opposite. Joyce laces Junius's style, for example, with something like the style Junius most abhorred. Junius prided himself on having the style of 'a plain unlettered man'. It was free, he said, of the 'mazes of metaphorical confusion' to be found in the prose of his antagonist Sir William Draper.[143] But Joyce's parody of Junius itself lapses into something rather like 'metaphorical confusion', and Joyce actually transferred bits of Draper's letters to Junius into his Junius parody.[144] The Swift of *Polite Conversation* reviles abbreviations and compressions, giving 'incog.' for 'incognito' as one of his examples.[145] Joyce works 'Incog!' into *Ulysses* (15. 4308) and scatters similar compressions about in 'Oxen', mocking Swift's conservatism in matters of language, his distaste for improprieties and barbarisms. So, too, in his essay *On Conversation*, Cowper reprehends the use of oaths like 'Gad's bud'.[146] Lynch employs that very oath (14. 808). In the same vein, when Joyce includes the word 'ascendancy' in his 'parody' partly of Burke (14. 861), he spells it with a second *a*. Burke himself always preferred an *e*, as Joyce would have known from the *OED*.

---

[140] See Janusko, *Sources and Structures*, 141.

[141] Fritz Senn objects that the word simply combines 'twi' and 'kindle'. In my reading, the word carries more suggestion of babies physically joined.

[142] *James Joyce's 'Ulysses': A Study* (London: Faber & Faber, 1930), 300.

[143] Letter to Sir William Draper, Knight of the Bath, 3 Mar. 1769; Junius, *Letters*, ed. John Cannon (Oxford: Clarendon Press, 1978), 51. Cf. Janusko, *Sources and Structures*, 148–9.   [144] See Janusko, *Sources and Structures*, 148–9.

[145] See *Polite Conversation*, introd. with notes and commentary by Eric Partridge (London: Andre Deutsch, 1963), 33.   [146] Peacock (ed.), *English Prose*, 241.

This kind of waywardness is more than mere perversity: it is an expression of deep recalcitrance, of a refusal to be *governed*. Recontextualization, mockery, treachery, adulteration, anachronism, ersatz, graffiti-work: these are some of the terms that are surely most relevant to what Joyce is doing in 'Oxen'. How aware he was of such practices is less important than the ferocious intentness that produces so many of them and so casually, some of them as incidental spin-offs, like the lapse into modern cockney at the end of a passage whose chief source is usually deemed to be Goldsmith (14. 840–4). Brian Doyle writes, again, of the widespread English fear of national 'degeneration' during the period,[147] Baldick of the fear of 'foreign contamination' of the national literature.[148] 'Oxen' is itself an exercise in 'foreign contamination'. Contamination becomes an active cultural practice, part of a cultural politics. This is not to suggest that the chapter is necessarily engaged in an active denigration of English literature. Rather, in the period that, more than any other, sees the production of the imperial English monument, 'Oxen' is committed to what I have called a practice of defacement. Yet if Joyce produces an anti-anthology, he knows that it can never altogether escape the form of the monument that is its determining condition. The logic of 'Oxen' is paradoxical, and its necessary resolution is partly laughter. Here again it functions as an Irish bull in an English chinashop. Joyce thrusts the bull back into English literature: in the reference, for example, in the Dickens 'parody', to Mrs Purefoy as the 'brave woman' who had 'manfully helped' (14. 1312–13). As a comically inconsistent proposition, the bull is a strategy for managing contradiction. We'll return to it with 'Eumaeus'. 'Oxen' is a tissue of contradictions: between history and modernity, the fertility trope and 'inverecundity', a seemingly ineradicable, dominant culture and the imperative of resistance. Critics have often described the chapter as unified, as though everything in it could in principle be fitted together. In fact, it is an extraordinary and outlandish hybrid. As such, it not only exposes colonial history and culture as themselves productive of monstrous incongruities, but also negotiates those incongruities, in a manner that Joyce intended to be exemplary.

---

[147] *English and Englishness* (London and New York: Routledge, 1989), 17.
[148] *Criticism and Literary Theory*, 59.

CHAPTER EIGHT

Strangers in My House, Bad Manners to Them!: 'Circe'[1]

Ce bordel où tenons nostre état

Like 'Wandering Rocks', but unlike all the other later chapters in *Ulysses*, 'Circe' does not chiefly rework English (or Anglo-Irish) discourses that are traceable to printed texts. Fragments of a variety of the kind of discourses I've described appear in the chapter. But it is not primarily a treatment of them. For 'Circe' is a chapter of voices. In 'Circe', people speak, and the effects of colonial power are heard in what they say, and how they say it. If the chapter cannot principally be read off against a set of discourses, it nonetheless exposes the pervasiveness and complexity of the effects of colonization as much as any other chapter in *Ulysses*. It tells us a lot more than we have so far learnt about how the British have left their mark. 'Circe' turns Dublin—and the account of Dublin that has preceded it—inside out. In doing so, it insistently reveals the 'stranger' in places where we had not previously noticed him. To a large extent, this is the result of the chapter's 'hallucinatory' form, which licenses more immediate representations of the stranger's presence than might otherwise be feasible. Rumbold can actually appear (15. 1177–83). Bloom can feature as a schoolboy or in a (partly English) coronation ceremony. J. J. O'Molloy can be heard sounding oddly English in his barrister's harangue (15. 938–55).

In 'Circe', then, specific discourses are less important than a sense of the extent of the English presence in Dublin and its culture; in effect, of the colonization of the Dublin unconscious, a theme which

---

[1] For an extended version of this chapter, see my ' "Strangers in my House, Bad Manners to Them!": England in "Circe" ', in Gibson (ed.), *Reading Joyce's 'Circe'* (European Joyce Studies, 3; Amsterdam and Atlanta, Ga.: Rodopi, 1993), 179–221.

critics have largely overlooked.[2] This is therefore a good point at which to consider the contemporary Anglicization of Ireland, and Irish resistance to it, in rather more general and contextual terms. In 'Circe' as in 'Wandering Rocks', Joyce clearly indicated the general relevance of the theme by adopting a 'parenthetical' structure: at the beginning of the chapter, two British redcoats are marching *'un-steadily'* through Dublin's nighttown (15. 49), past assorted evidence of poverty, deprivation, and human squalor. A young Irish poet passes them, and they poke uncomprehending fun at him ('What ho, parson!', 15. 67). At the end of the chapter, the soldiers confront the poet and accuse him of insulting their girl and their king. Surrounded by a Dublin crowd of mixed sympathies, including figures present at the beginning of the chapter, one of the soldiers hits the poet and knocks him down (15. 4747–78). The young poet, of course, is a 'wildgoose' (15. 635), and will shortly flee Ireland.

This sets out the basic frame within which other parts of 'Circe' operate. The British presence in Dublin's 'nighttown' encloses the chapter. That the soldiers are in 'nighttown' at all is significant. In the first few years of the century, Maud Gonne and others had been protesting about Irish girls consorting with 'enemy soldiers' (often as prostitutes). Army enrolment in Ireland had dropped markedly with the onset of the Boer War.[3] To make recruiting easier, the Army therefore dropped its rule of obliging the men to sleep in barracks. According to Gonne, O'Connell Street was soon full of redcoats walking with their girls, 'with the result that almost every night there were fights'. Indeed, 'fighting soldiers became quite a popular evening entertainment with young men'.[4] In 1904, Maud wrote to the newspapers endorsing 'an official Dublin complaint about the patronizing of the Tyrone and O'Connell streets prostitutes by five thousand British soldiers'.[5] The British military presence was unusually conspicuous on the streets of Dublin.[6] Joyce remembered this,

[2] Critics of 'Circe' have tended to operate within certain parameters. For a relevant account of the principal concerns of 'Circe' criticism that runs up to 1993 but is still largely representative, see my 'Introduction' to *Reading Joyce's 'Circe'*, 3–32.

[3] See e.g. Margaret Ward, *Unmanageable Revolutionaries: Women and Irish Nationalism* (London: Pluto Press, 1983), 53.

[4] Maud Gonne MacBride, *A Servant of the Queen: Reminiscences* (Bury St Edmunds: Boydell and Brewer, 1983), 292.

[5] Samuel Levenson, *Maud Gonne* (London: Cassell, 1976), 224.

[6] Together with other members of Inghinidhe na hÉireann, Maud Gonne campaigned to stop relations between Irish girls and British soldiers. Joyce himself clearly saw that the

and clearly wanted to be exact about it.[7] He makes Bloom recall it in 'Lotus Eaters'.[8] He may have had his own reasons for keeping it in mind. He appears himself to have been knocked down in circumstances similar to Stephen's, in June 1904. Richard Ellmann suggests that the incident coalesced in his mind with the later fracas with Henry Carr in Zurich, when Joyce found himself blatantly pitted against British authorities.[9] In 'Circe', the presence and behaviour of the soldiers serves as a literal image of a determining condition, a crucial context for events. There are 'strangers in [the] house' (15. 4586). Not surprisingly, thus, when Bloom first appears in the chapter, his image is mixed up with those of *'gallant Nelson'*, *'grave Gladstone'*, and *'truculent Wellington'* (15. 145–50). In *'ce bordel où tenons nostre état'* (15. 3536), the traces of the 'brutish empire' are present everywhere (15. 4569–70).

But 'Circe' is primarily concerned not with a military or political but with a cultural English presence barely noted by critics. From the late nineteenth century, Irish Ireland gave particular prominence to the question of Anglicization.[10] 'Allied with a still powerful and articulate Catholicism',[11] the forces of resurgent nationalism insisted that 'the distinctively Irish element' in 'outward forms of life' was under pressure from English 'modes and habits', and in decline.[12] The emphasis was already familiar: from the 1870s, under Archbishop

---

sexual needs of British soldiers provided a useful boost to the Dublin economy, which is why the Bawd supports Carr and Compton against the Virago (15. 4519–20).

[7] His two soldiers are meant to sound right, e.g. The accuracy with which Joyce renders their tone and vocabulary is borne out by echoes in contemporary vignettes. See Hanna Sheehy-Skeffington's account of her husband's murderer, Capt. Bowen-Colthurst, esp. Bowen-Colthurst's use of the phrase *'Bash him'* (cf. 15. 4410–11), in 'British Militarism as I Have Known It', in Francis and Hanna Sheehy-Skeffington, *Democracy in Ireland since 1913* (n.p.: n.pub., 1917), 69–91, 71. 'The Boarding House' makes it clear that certain words were regarded as 'soldiers' obscenities' (*D*, 67).

[8] 'Redcoats . . . Maud Gonne's letter about taking them off O'Connell street at night: disgrace to our Irish capital. Griffith's paper is on the same tack now: an army rotten with venereal disease: overseas or halfseasover empire' (5. 68–72).

[9] See *James Joyce* (rev. edn., Oxford: Oxford University Press, 1982), 161, 426–9. Ellmann does not specify a soldier. Peter Costello gives the date of the incident as 22 June. See his *James Joyce: The Years of Growth 1882–1915* (London: Kyle Cathie, 1992), 226.

[10] On Irish Ireland, see F. S. L. Lyons, *Culture and Anarchy in Ireland 1890–1939* (Oxford: Clarendon Press, 1979), esp. ch. 3. For some interesting indications of how a revision of accounts of Joyce's relationship to Irish Ireland might proceed, see Coílín Owens, 'The Mystique of the West in Joyce's "The Dead" ', *Irish University Review*, 22/1 (Spring–Summer 1992), 80–92, at 80–2.   [11] Lyons, *Culture and Anarchy*, 57.

[12] Oliver MacDonagh, *Ireland: The Union and its Aftermath* (London: Allen and Unwin, 1977), 73.

Cullen's influence, the Catholic hierarchy in Ireland had been denouncing imported English amusements—theatrical productions, 'improper dances' like the waltz and the polka.[13] But it grew to prominence in the 1890s with what R. F. Foster calls 'the need of the Irish intelligentsia for self-definition', and the 'cultural revival' that answered that need.[14] From the 1890s onwards, the Gaelic culture found itself in full revolt against the dominant English culture, and the Revival gave it particular encouragement. The perception of Irish culture as contaminated found eloquent expression in Douglas Hyde's famous lecture of 1892, 'The Necessity for De-Anglicizing Ireland'. Hyde argued that the once learned and cultured Irish had allowed themselves to be overtaken by English culture to the point where they were prepared to imitate, not what was best in English culture, but anything English, simply because it was English. 'Within the last ninety years', he asserted, 'we [the Irish] have, with an unparalleled frivolity, deliberately thrown away our birthright and Anglicized ourselves'.[15] Quoting Jubainville, he argued that England '"has definitely conquered us, she has even imposed upon us her language, that is to say, the form of our thoughts during every instant of our existence"'.[16] Hyde of course was principally concerned with the question of language. But the lecture also amply complained, in general terms, of the 'shameful corruption' and 'West-Britonizing' of Irish culture, the invasion of 'penny dreadfuls, shilling shockers, and still more, the garbage of vulgar English weeklies like *Bow Bells* and the *Police Intelligence*'.[17] There was a 'constant running to England for our books, literature, music, games, fashions, and ideas'.[18] In their lack of any adequate cultural independence, the Irish had become 'the most assimilative' people in Europe.[19]

Eoin MacNeill, the Gaelic League, and the Gaelic Athletic Association were all similarly concerned about the English contamination of Irish culture. As Foster points out, so, too, were Irish feminists.[20] Maud Gonne's Inghinidhe na hÉireann remarked on 'the reading and

---

[13] See K. Theodore Hoppen, *Ireland since 1800: Conflict and Conformity* (London: Longman, 1989), 149.

[14] *Modern Ireland 1600–1972* (London: Penguin, 1989), 456.

[15] 'The Necessity for De-Anglicizing Ireland', in Sir Charles Gavan Duffy et al., *The Revival of Irish Literature* (London: T. Fisher Unwin, 1894), 115–61, at 135.

[16] Ibid. 135. A substantial account of the politics of the representation of consciousness in *Ulysses* has yet to be written. This quotation provides an excellent starting point.

[17] Ibid. 151, 154, 159.   [18] Ibid. 161.   [19] Ibid. 160.

[20] See *Modern Ireland*, 449.

circulation of low English literature, the singing of English songs, the attending of vulgar English entertainments at the theatres and music-hall'.[21] In the early years of the new century, both Griffith and Sinn Féin and D. P. Moran and *The Leader* harped on the same theme. Sinn Féin and Griffith wanted the Irish 'to recover their identity as a separate people', which meant ceasing 'to take both their goods and their opinions ready-made from England'.[22] *The Leader* attacked everything in Irish culture that seemed to bespeak a slavish obeisance to England.[23] Like Joyce, Moran viewed Ireland as a land of 'torpor and decay'. 'We only preserve a national colour,' he wrote, 'about the manner in which we don't do things'.[24] Like Joyce again, he felt that the Irish lacked pride, contempt, a 'fiery hate of subjection'.[25] This was especially true of the distinguished literary figures who had 'made a market' out of 'the "Celtic note" '. They had treated their achievement as 'a grand symbol of an Irish national intellectual awakening', when in fact it was a gift given to the enemy, to English literature.[26] But what was true of them was all the more true—according to Moran—of the philistine bank clerk class, reading their copies of *Tit-Bits*, turning constantly to England and 'her tittle-tattle periodicals'.[27] It was true of the 'thousands filing into the circulating libraries and the penny novel-ette shops for reams of twaddle about Guy and Belinda'.[28] It was also true of the 'well-to-do' and ' "respectable" ' natives, 'those who send, or would like to send, their children to English schools for good-breeding'.[29] It was true of 'Irish fashionable society', too.[30] All were complicit in their own enslavement to England.

Play Cricket

'Circe' foregrounds the invaded and adulterated nature of the culture as described by Irish Ireland, from the Bluecoat Schoolboy (15. 1535–6) to Bella Cohen's son at Oxford (15. 1289, 4306) to Bloom on the 'English invention' to quieten snoring (15.3275) and Stephen's

---

[21] Ward, *Unmanageable Revolutionaries*, 51.   [22] Lyons, *Culture and Anarchy*, 58.
[23] Moran thought the Irish were so far gone in servility as to be almost beyond saving, and he was little more enthusiastic about Fenian tradition than he was about England. Nationalists were just 'sulky West Britons'. D. P. Moran, *The Philosophy of Irish Ireland* (Dublin: James Duffy & Co., 1905), 9. See also Foster, *Modern Ireland*, 455.
[24] Moran, *Philosophy*, 2.   [25] Ibid. 3.   [26] Ibid. 22.
[27] Ibid. 6.   [28] Ibid. 80.   [29] Ibid. 9.
[30] Ibid. 7.

comment on 'the age of patent medicines' (15. 4470–1). Its form allows it to do so with marked directness and vividness. There is much more of the *sound* of Englishness here, for example, than anywhere else in the book. The chapter is full of decent, respectable, prim, and outraged English and Anglo-Irish voices seldom heard elsewhere. People in 'Circe' often don't sound like themselves. The most improbable figures may suddenly drop into an uncharacteristically English-sounding idiom: the jurors, for example (15. 1139–43).

If the chapter exposes far more evidence of Anglicization than we have so far had in *Ulysses*, and far more explicitly, many of the allusions back to earlier chapters have this function. The phantasmagoria denaturalizes and defamiliarizes everyday experience and allows us to see its (often grotesque) colonial dimension for the first time. Thus Edward VII singing the coronation song (15. 4562–4) alerts us to and comments on the significance of Mulligan's singing it in 'Telemachus' (1. 300–5). But perhaps the most striking example is Beaufoy, contributor to *Tit-Bits*. In 'Circe' we actually see him, genteel and 'palefaced' (15. 814), snottily declaiming against the 'bally pressman johnny' Bloom (15. 836–7) as a 'rotter' (15. 852), 'no born gentleman' (15. 820), a 'soapy sneak' (15. 822) who 'has not even been to a university' (15. 837–8). It is only then that we are likely vividly to register the full force of what was so innocently tucked away in 'Calypso': Beaufoy's address ('Playgoers' Club, London', 4. 503). We can now see why Joyce wanted Bloom to wipe his arse with Beaufoy.[31]

'Circe' particularly exposes the Anglicized or imported nature of Irish popular culture. This is the case, for instance, with the various echoes of the tones, the vocabulary, even the scenarios of Victorian melodrama,[32] and the stock-in-trade of Victorian iconography, as at 15. 3548–51. Much of the laughter at sentimental idealism turns out to be laughter at an alien (Victorian) construct at odds with Dublin's nighttown and its inhabitants. 'Circe' gives a concrete form to such incongruities. One good example of this is the dance supervised by

---

[31] The irony is that Beaufoy is probably no 'born gentleman' himself. According to Bernard McGinley, the real-life model was in fact Philip Beaufoy Barry (b. 1878). Barry worked as a journalist for various organs, including the *Daily Express* and the *Daily Mail*, and published a number of books, including *Amateur Acting from a New Angle*, *Twelve Monstrous Criminals*, and *Sinners Down the Centuries*. None of this suggests any very eminent social status. In the case of the fictional Beaufoy, this is evident in the very fact that he writes for *Tits-Bits*. He is caught up in the same kind of posturing as many of the other characters in 'Circe'.

[32] See e.g. 15. 1988, 2063–6, 3191–2.

Professor Maginni (15. 4016–4109). The music is 'My Girl's a Yorkshire Girl' (15. 4027), and Maginni is imagined in terms of Mr Turveydrop in Dickens's *Bleak House*. Katty Lanner of 'the Katty Lanner step' (15. 4044) was London-based. The whole ethos summoned up in Goodwin's 'court dress' (15. 4018), in 'calisthenics' (15. 4042) and 'deportment' (15. 4043), in the delicacy, grace, and prettiness of '*the morning hours*' (15. 4054) and their '*curchycurchies*' (15. 4083) clashes violently with the situation at Bella Cohen's. The sequence underlines a cultural discord. It opens up a rift between what is actually happening in the brothel, and what supervenes on it, or comes in from outside.

What is true of popular culture also partly goes for 'high culture', in two different ways. There are plenty of references to English literature in 'Circe'. But the effect is often comically anomalous, as when Philip Drunk and Philip Sober appear to Stephen '*masked with Matthew Arnold's face*' (15. 2514) to fight their brief, unreal battle over his soul, the one armed with moral saws and practical advice, the other with Byron and Swinburne (15. 2512–27). Scraps of English literature constantly appear in the characters' speech, usually incongruously, as when Bloom waxes Shakespearean after having been pelted with rubbish by Mother Grogan and the Dorset Street shopkeepers (15. 1768–9). English literature even invades the substance and style of the chapter itself, as when, before Bloom 'takes exception' to Beaufoy's banal Miltonism—'hand in hand'—the stage directions start to sound Miltonic ('*with hangdog meekness glum*', 5. 829–30). But perhaps the most noticeable thing about allusions to English literature in 'Circe' is the extent to which they recycle it at the level of popular culture. For the fragments of English literature in the chapter are largely tags and clichés, bromides: 'a thing of beauty' (15. 2254, 3268), 'Theirs not to reason why' (15. 4397). The chapter is strewn with trivial little adaptations and distortions of literary phrases, most notably from Shakespeare.[33] The references are often less to the actual writers or works in question than to a second-order version of them, to stereotypes or caricature: thus with Kipling, Kipling tags, and Kiplingese (15. 780–98). The 'literary world' in question is closer to that of the anthologies in 'Oxen' than might first seem to be the case. All this is actually the reverse of grandiose, Eliotic, or modernist allusiveness. The references to English literature in 'Circe' suggest a hand-me-down

---

[33] See e.g. 15. 952–3, 3522, 3655.

culture of 'orts and offals' (9. 1094–5), rags and scraps, the crumbs that have dropped from the rich man's table.

The manifestations of Anglicization in 'Circe' are often literal and commonplace. Take Freemasonry, for example.[34] Before 'Circe', the theme of Freemasonry is raised only intermittently or furtively. Bloom's own membership has been hinted at but not confirmed (8. 184).[35] In 'Circe,' however, Freemasonry and Bloom's Masonic connections are blatantly foregrounded. Once again, the chapter reveals an underside to colonial, Dublin culture. 'Circe' stresses the Englishness of Freemasonry in Ireland, consciously places it as an English incursion. It is no accident that Edward VII appears in the chapter as what he had been until 1901, grand master of the Grand Lodge of England.[36] 'Circe' repeatedly emphasizes the connections between Freemasonry and power, privilege, affluence, status, and influence (especially legal influence). Bloom is imagined as wearing the '*blue masonic badge in his buttonhole*', for instance, when proposing the toast at an elegant, expensive, formal dinner (15. 450–1). He attempts to beg off the Watch by clandestine, masonic means (15. 758–60).[37] He tries to pacify Bella and get Stephen off the hook by simultaneously making '*a masonic sign*', turning Stephen into 'a *Trinity* student' (italics mine) and spontaneously fabricating some highly respectable credentials for him ('Nephew of the vicechancellor', 15. 4297–9).[38] In colonial Dublin, it helps to have certain connections, and they are connections whose cachet is an Anglicized one.

It is therefore understandable enough that the theme of race (or relative whiteness) should be given some prominence in 'Circe'. Here,

[34] How far Freemasonry as a whole can be associated with Anglicization in Ireland is a complicated historical question. See Gibson, 'Strangers in my House', 190–1, n. 21. See also W. J. Chetwode Crawley, *Caementaria Hibernica* (Dublin: M'Gee, 1895); W. Fred. J. W. Crowe, *The Irish Master Mason's Handbook* (London: Kenning, 1909); J. H. Edge, *A Short Sketch of the Rise and Progress of Irish Freemasonry* (Dublin: Ponsonby and Gibbs, 1913); and John Herron Lepper and Philip Crossle, *History of the Grand Lodge of Free and Accepted Masons of Ireland*, i. (Dublin: Lodge of Research C.C., 1925).

[35] Bloom's membership shouldn't surprise us, of course. Edge, e.g., particularly stresses the contributions to Freemasonry of the 'great Israelitish people' and their 'marvellous energy, talents and financial enterprise'. See *Short Sketch*, 12.

[36] Cf. 5. 74–5. See Gibson, 'Strangers in my House', 190–1, n. 21, for an account of the political significance of Edward VII in Irish Freemasonry.

[37] Here as elsewhere, 'Circe' is playing on the traditional strength of the connection between the Masons and the forces of law and order.

[38] From the start, Irish Masons were closely associated with Trinity. See Lepper and Crossle, *History of the Grand Lodge*, *passim*.

to demonstrate one's irreproachability or to allay the authorities is also to prove one's whiteness. 'I treated you white', Bloom says to Mary Driscoll (15. 876). 'I regard him as the whitest man I know', says J. J. O'Molloy, pleading Bloom's cause (15. 980). On the other hand, when he decides to suggest, instead, that Bloom is 'irresponsible for his actions', his submission is that Bloom 'is of Mongolian extraction' (15. 954–5), whereupon Bloom promptly turns into a coolie '*in lascar's vest and trousers*' with '*tiny mole's eyes*', shrugging in '*oriental obeisance*' and speaking pidgin (15. 957–64).[39] The more English you look and sound, the more you appear to deserve your place in the sun. By the same token, Anglicization means self-division, a kind of colonization of the soul. This is evident above all in the treatment of the theme of decency and respectability in the chapter. 'Circe' exposes a rift between the literal situation it describes and the (frequently defensive) posturing that goes on within that situation. The postures are often Anglicized ones. If the characters repeatedly resort to Englishness, English idioms, English modes of self-presentation, that is because they find themselves under certain sorts of pressure or scrutiny, and involved in self-justification. This is most obviously the case with Bloom, and his evasive responses to others' challenges. The 'scamp', for instance, whom Mrs Breen joyously catches 'down here in the haunts of sin' (15. 395–6) tries desperately and rather incompetently to bluff his way out with a few fragments of banal, genteel, English-sounding exchange: 'How do you do? It's ages since I. You're looking splendid. Absolutely it. Seasonable weather we are having this time of year . . . Short cut home here. Interesting quarter. Rescue of fallen women. Magdalen asylum. I am the secretary.....' (15. 399–402). This kind of oscillation between sin and genteel pretension is one of the commonest patterns in 'Circe.' Compare for example Bloom's hilariously Anglicized military gentleman's manner with the watch (15. 743–4) or the coy 'teapot' exchange with Josie Breen (15. 457–8).

So, too, in 'Circe', efforts at a kind of linguistic propriety are frequently indexes of something else. That they are often uncertain or rather inept efforts only confirms the point. 'Circe' exposes the

---

[39] Cf. 14. 1448, where some of Bloom's companions seem to be jeeringly addressing him in pidgin, in crass recognition of his racial otherness. He is also derisively addressed in black dialect e.g. at 14. 1555–7.

extent to which, in colonial Dublin society, forms of Englishness can be thought of as acting as seals of respectability, guarantees of proper conduct. Thus Bloom will tell Mary Driscoll to '[p]lay cricket' (15. 878), inform the Watch that his 'club' is 'the Junior Army and Navy' (15. 730), and plead his father-in-law's impeccable credentials (15. 775–81).[40] In one way or another, many figures truckle to or traffic with England. Bella has 'her son in Oxford' (15. 1289, 4306), and Zoe emphatically denies that she is 'a Dublin girl' ('No bloody fear. I'm English', 15. 1344–7). Again and again, Englishness means status, even safety. Adopting English tones, styles, and manners is a way of laying claim to the moral, social, cultural, and political high ground. It is not surprising that, when Bloom attempts to help Stephen, he promptly tries to sound posher, more English, and more pro-British (15. 4606–7).

The degree to which a colonial culture necessarily promotes self-fabrication and self-alienation together thus becomes very clear. Self-division is perhaps the most prominent feature of the Dublin unconscious as it is dramatized in 'Circe'. Again, this is evident above all in language, idiom, and tone. Characters are constantly shifting back and forth between (often dirty, vulgar, or slangy) local idioms and Anglicized, more respectable ones. They repeatedly turn out to be double-voiced, shifting from one idiom to another, sometimes within the course of a single sentence. The penitent Kitty-Kate, for example, desperately trying to pull bogus rank, can't quite keep up the tone ('My mother's sister married a Montmorency. It was a working plumber was my ruination when I was pure', 15. 2228–9). The point is especially clear towards the end of the chapter, where Bloom addresses the Watch in one voice (15. 4838–41) and Kelleher in another (15. 4808–9, 4858). This kind of doubleness is everywhere in 'Circe'. It reflects a form of entrapment, bears witness to interior splits that, at one and the same time, are gaping wounds and sources of great mirth. The truly disruptive Other in 'Circe' is not the Freudian id. It is the alien idiom. At one point or another, almost all the characters stop sounding like themselves: Paddy Dignam (15. 1230–5), Theodore Purefoy (15. 1741–2), the young doctors (15. 1775–1810), the whores (15. 2233–4, 2288–9), Boylan (15. 3763),

---

[40] But of course the Circeanly feminized Bloom claims to be son-in-law, then *daughter* (15. 778). 'Circe' repeatedly works in this way: the pretensions can't be sustained.

Nosey Flynn (15. 1640), Chris Callinan (15. 1656), Crofton (15. 1679), and Larry O'Rourke (15. 1673–5).[41] If the occasion appears to demand it, all these Dubliners adopt a more or less 'marked' and incongruous 'refinement of phraseology' (to quote Biddy the Clap, who's doing the same herself at the moment she says it, 15. 4443). Even the stage-directions have something of this divided tone, as when Bloom feels '*his occiput dubiously with the unparalleled embarrassment of a harassed pedlar gauging the symmetry of* [*Zoe's*] *peeled pears*' (15. 1993–4). Hence the chapter is also strewn with numerous little errors, muddles, botches in tone and locution, as characters attempt a posher manner and don't quite pull it off, or run conflicting idioms together.

The situation in 'Circe' can be expressed in a nutshell: in 'The King versus Bloom' (15. 859), Bloom has to be on both sides; or rather, he can only promote his own 'side' by trying to join the other side, too. In this respect, the Dublin unconscious is not so much wild or turbulent as *subdued*, and therefore in large measure conformist. It is caught in contradictions and complicities. Similarly, the phantasmagoric imagery in 'Circe' is not primarily an example of modern irrationalism (expressionist, surrealist). It is a literalization of the outlandish incongruities produced by and within a colonial culture. Take Nannetti quoting Emmet on the deck of the *Erin's King*, for example, whilst travelling to England to ask about foot and mouth 'on the floor of the house of commons' (15. 3382–8, 12. 851); or the '*roar of welcome*' that greets Edward VII and his bucket (15. 4457).[42] As comic saviour, Parnell-figure, and Hungarian hero *à la* Griffith, Bloom is also simultaneously reimplicated in the ways of the two imperial masters (15. 1398–1449).[43] This is very much the point with regard to the Coronation sequence as a whole (15. 1353–1752).

---

[41] One notable exception here would be Simon Dedalus, who exhibits no marked change, and shows the others up by contrast. See 15. 2663–91.

[42] The 'roar of welcome' was of course a historical fact. See F. L. Radford, 'King, Pope and Hero-Martyr: *Ulysses* and the Nightmare of Irish History', *James Joyce Quarterly*, 15/4 (Summer 1978), 275–323, esp. 292.

[43] The passage in question would seem partly to be a further ironic exposition of some of the contradictions in Griffith's *The Resurrection of Hungary*, esp. the gap that yawns between Griffith's libertarianism and his lengthy, detailed, and indulgent descriptions of Francis Josef's coronation and Hungarian 'enthusiasm' for it. See Arthur Griffith, *The Resurrection of Hungary: A Parallel for Ireland* (Dublin: James Duffy and Co., 1904), 74–6. The contradiction at issue was implicit in Griffith's acceptance of the principle of the dual monarchy.

194   'CIRCE'

Bloom starts on his elevation to glory with an attack on 'Sir Walter Ralegh' and English colonial trade (15. 1355–61), and partly continues with the attitude of resistance. But he is also repeatedly dragged back into the patterns and connections he seeks to resist. For all the references to Hungary and Turkey, the *depth* of reference in the Coronation sequence is to the signs and symbols of English colonialism, from the *'sirdars, grandees and maharajahs bearing the cloth of estate'* (15. 1417–18) to Ladysmith (15. 1526), the Koh-i-noor diamond (15. 1499–1500), and 'The Charge of the Light Brigade' (15. 1527–30). Figures partly representative of Irish cottage industries (15. 1426–36) are promptly followed by various royal officials from the English court (15. 1436–9). So, too, the dominant modes of the actual ceremony are English, and echo the English one. The Coronation Oath (15. 1480–5) and the Oath of Fealty (15. 1498) clearly echo the English equivalents.[44] Bloom's Ireland is even given 'territories', on the model of colonial England. After Bloom has been welcomed as '[s]uccessor' to Parnell (15. 1513–14) and appeared to echo John F. Taylor, he promptly lapses into the tones of English military triumphalism (15. 1525–30). The 'new Bloomusalem' ends up looking suspiciously like the Crystal Palace (15. 1548 ff.). The fantasy of liberation may be Bloom's. But here he functions primarily as a representative Dubliner. Joyce is concerned with Irish culture as caught in a particular historical configuration. At this historical juncture, dreams of social and political transformation cannot escape the constraints they seek to transcend. They remain compromised or 'infected', to use one of Seamus Deane's terms.[45] They fail to move beyond the Anglicized context from which they sprang.

In its emphasis on self-division, contradictions, and complicities, 'Circe' ends up telling us that this specific colonized culture is partly a culture of imposture. In this respect, though its tone is very different to Moran's, its anatomy of Dublin partly resembles his. For Moran saw Irish culture as beset by 'shams and impostures'.[46] He was unremittingly hostile to *ráiméis*, or cant. He thought it 'stifled nearly every kind of constructive activity in Ireland', and 'found it nearly

---

[44] For details, see Don Gifford with Robert J. Seidman, *'Ulysses' Annotated: Notes for James Joyce's 'Ulysses'* (rev. edn., Berkeley and Los Angeles: University of California Press, 1989), 473–4.
[45] 'Joyce and Nationalism', in *Celtic Revivals: Essays in Modern Irish Literature 1880–1980* (London: Faber, 1985), 92–107, at 94.   [46] *Philosophy*, 94.

everywhere'.[47] Moran attacked 'brag', 'bluster', sentimentality, and humbug as either ministering to English influence or the consequence of it.[48] The brag and bluster hid timidity, a conviction of smallness and weakness. The sentimentality and humbug concealed base, dirty, ignoble, and impoverished realities.[49] The Anglicized façades were one thing, the Irish facts another. 'Circe' dramatizes the same division. It suggests that England's bequest to Ireland has been a culture of, on the one hand, chronic privation and, on the other, euphemism and fraudulent pretension. The recourse to sham gentility and bogus respectability is *ráiméis* in action. This is the point to be made even of some of the theatricality in 'Circe'. The acting out of roles conveys a sense of self-disjunction, not least within language. Characters repeatedly project themselves into imported forms of representation. For these provide a second self that is comfortingly distant from oppressive realities. Even the narrator gets in on the act, dressing up tawdry facts and using the stage directions to give scenes a more polished or grandiose air, as when the ice cream float becomes a '*gondola*' (15. 5), or the brothel floor is discovered as a '*mosaic of jade and azure and cinnabar rhomboids*' (15. 2043) and the walls as '*tapestried with a paper of yewfronds and clear glades*' (15. 2046–7). In effect, *ráiméis* is deeply and guilefully written into the chapter as a whole.

Why Go I Mourning?

This then is the substance of Joyce's anatomy of colonial Irish culture in 'Circe.' Stephen is still struggling with England and English domination, 'battling against [the] hopelessness' they appear to impose (9. 828). That is why, on the one hand, 'Circe' presents us with his father urging him on—'Are you going to win?' (15. 3946–7, the reference presumably being to Stephen's inward struggle)—and, on the other, with English Philip Drunk and Philip Sober offering their 'fool's advice' ('Keep in condition. Do like us', 15. 2516, 2539). On his way to 'Georgina Johnson, *ad deam qui laetificat iuventutem meam*'

---

[47] *Philosophy*, 87.   [48] Lyons, *Culture and Anarchy*, 58.

[49] I am simplifying here, of course. It is needless to say that Joyce also presents the realities beneath the humbug as vital (sexual, animal, and subversive) ones, too. One common pattern in 'Circe', e.g., is the breakdown of the language of fraudulence and imposture under the pressure of sexual excitement. See e.g. 15. 2320–35.

(15. 122–3) Stephen also echoes the Psalmist's prayer for delivery from the oppression of his enemies. The prayer begins:

Judge me, O God, and plead my cause against an ungodly nation: O deliver me from the deceitful and unjust man.

For thou art the God of my strength: why dost thou cast me off? Why go I mourning because of the oppression of the enemy?[50]

The irony, of course, is that Georgina Johnson has absconded with 'Mr Lambe from London' (15. 3636).

Stephen has nonetheless made progress. He has resisted his own depressed conviction of imprisonment within ineluctable conditions, and reasserted the project of an open art, one dedicated to the exploration of possibilities (15. 2087–93). Paris has helped loosen his relation to language. He can now burst into a kind of wild franglais or 'parisian clowneries' (15. 3886), a liberating, hybrid pidgin (15. 3881–3916).[51] As Zoe recognizes, he is clearly poised to 'fly' (15. 3687, 4256). But he must also submit to various, final confrontations. These have to do with colonial power and its traces, or Irish collusion in and subservience to colonial power. Colonial power is partly what is at stake in his last battle with his mother's spirit. For all the strength of his love and pity, Stephen must oppose her pathos and resist a Catholic culture of sacrifice which can only mean continuing in servitude and dereliction. He must refuse the 'bitter milk' with which his mother has 'suckled' him (14. 377–8), the submissiveness which yields to the 'merchant of jalaps' (14. 373) and invites him into the gates 'to wax fat and kick like Jeshurum' (14. 369–70).[52] Stephen will not serve—'With me all or not at all' (15. 4227–8)—and the chapter slyly supports him, exhibiting a servile Mulligan as court jester (15. 4166–80), for example.

But as Stephen's struggle deepens and intensifies, so the forces arrayed against him take or are represented in more powerful forms. This is vividly evident in the fox-hunt (15. 3951 ff.). The various fox references in *Ulysses* converge on this passage. In Ireland, fox-

[50] Psalms 43: 1–2. The words Stephen quotes are from the fourth verse.
[51] Note also his repeated use of 'gesture' to communicate in 'Circe', in conformity with his own reflections (15. 105–6).
[52] Stephen is re-experiencing the bitterness he expresses in the passage from 'Oxen' (14. 367–80) in a different mode in his confrontation with his Mother in 'Circe'. See e.g. 15. 4222–3.

hunting was largely an Anglo-Irish preserve.[53] It was a pastime of the
gentry and aristocracy.[54] In the 'Circe' passage, the fox is specifically
pursued by the Ward Union hunt, which Bloom has earlier connected
with Lady Mountcashel (8. 340–1).[55] The hunt is conflated with a
race between horses in large part owned by powerful members of the
English aristocracy (15. 3975–9).[56] Deasy the Ulster Unionist ultimately joins the field on his nag. However hilarious the details, here,
the political and cultural complexion of the combined pursuers is
clear enough. Lest we should mistake the point, Joyce includes 'ne-
groes waving torches' among the followers (15. 3960), thus momentarily turning Stephen into an escaped slave pursued by his owners
and their more submissive victims.

It is therefore appropriate enough that Carr and Compton
should be heard again immediately after Deasy has been pelted,
and that they should be singing 'My Girl's a Yorkshire Girl' (15.
4001–3), which is what the '[u]nseen brazen highland laddies' were
'blaring' and 'drumthumping' during the viceregal procession in
'Wandering Rocks' (10. 1249–57). It is likewise appropriate that
Stephen should soon be confronting the two soldiers. He is a green
rag to John Bull (15. 4497), and nothing else has prevailed against
him, so he is ultimately left facing simple, English force. He faces
it surrounded by evidence of the divisions, adulterations, incongruities, and grotesqueries inherent in colonial Irish culture, like
the bizarre wild goose figure who abuses the 'big grand porcos of

[53] On the influence of English on Irish hunts, see Commander W. B. 'Maintop' Forbes,
'The Foxhounds of Ireland', in Arthur W. Coaten (ed.), *British Hunting: A Complete History of the National Sport of Great Britain and Ireland from Earliest Records* (London:
Sampson Low, Marston and Co., 1909), 329–60. See also Gibson, 'Strangers in my House',
208–9 n. 46.

[54] If proof of this were needed, it can be had from histories of particular Irish hunts. See
e.g. Col. W. H. Wyndham–Quin, *The Fox Hound in County Limerick* (Dublin: Maunsel
and Co., 1919), 35 and *passim*; and the Earl of Mayo and W. B. Boulton, *A History of the
Kildare Hunt* (London: St. Catherine Press, 1913), 1–18, *passim*. See also Gibson,
'Strangers in my House', 209 n. 47.

[55] The Ward Union hounds were staghounds. Their eminence is clearly attested to in the
Irish Hunt Annual for 1908–9 (T. N. Foulis: Edinburgh, 1909).

[56] Cf. 2. 299–304, 8. 830. The conflation is not accidental. The owners of thoroughbreds
were likely to be keen huntsmen. Of the aristocratic owners Joyce mentions, both Hastings
and Beaufort belonged to English families traditionally associated with hunting in Ireland.
See e.g. Wyndham–Quin, *Fox Hound*, 7, and Forbes, 'Foxhounds', 359. Thoroughbreds in
hunting were another sign of Anglicization. They had become more and more important
in the Irish hunt. According to Wyndham-Quin, this was due to 'the ever increasing
communication with England' (*Fox Hound*, 16).

johnyellows' but whose name includes that of Sir John Pope
Hennessy, Irish conservative, anti-Parnellite, Catholic MP, and governor of several British colonies (15. 4506–9).[57] Edward VII
appears partly as a Catholic icon (15. 4450), and the bawd shouts
support for the soldiers, obviously for economic reasons (15.
4518–20). The allegiances of the crowd that witnesses the confrontation are similarly, chronically divided. So, too, in the chapter's pantomime version of a bloodboltered shambles (15.
4659–97), resistance and collusion coincide. Stephen is knowing
and sometimes satirical about the effects of Anglicization and the
hybridized culture it has produced.[58] But he is chiefly concerned
with his own exemplary inner struggle ('in here it is I must kill the
priest and the king', 15. 4436–7). He chooses 'sheet lightning
courage' (the kind that doesn't strike, 15. 3660). His is an attitude
of intellectual antagonism (15. 4513), and he treats English disin-
genuousness (15. 4432–6) and English claims to rationality, fairness, and justice (15. 4735) with sly irony. He repeats his '*Non
serviam*!' publicly, but courteously: 'I understand your point of
view though I have no king myself for the moment' (15. 4469–70).
He refuses to take Old Gummy Granny's knife whilst still maintaining that the soldiers are uninvited guests (15. 4370–1). As a
result, he is knocked down. The decisive, final fact is a triumph of
brute power.

'Circe' as Carnival

Irish Ireland and Irish cultural nationalists—Yeats, Pearse, Hyde,
Moran—conducted what Seamus Deane has called a 'crusade for
decontamination'. 'The Irish essence was to be freed of the infect-
ing Anglicizing virus', writes Deane, 'and thus restored to its pri-
mal purity and vigour'.[59] Stephen's effort to cleanse himself of
priest and king is an idiosyncratic version of this 'crusade', and is
fuelled by similar passions. But 'Circe' ends with Stephen subdued.
In 1904, this is hardly surprising. Joyce himself was completing
'Circe' in 1920, however, during the Anglo-Irish War and shortly

---

[57] See Gifford with Seidman, '*Ulysses*' *Annotated*, 485.
[58] See e.g. his perversion of the quotation from Swift's *Drapier's Letters* at 15. 4402, and
his reference to Samuel Lover's 'The Bowld Sojer Boy' at 15. 4407.
[59] *Joyce and Nationalism*, 94.

before independence. In that context, the chapter can be seen as recasting the hostility felt by Irish Ireland to English domination and English rule. The process involves an elaboration and transformation of Stephen's attitude of non-violent resistance. The art of 'Circe' recapitulates, develops, extends, and modifies Stephen's '*Non serviam!*'. Joyce responds to the political and cultural significance of Freemasonry, for example, with some familiar, derisive tactics: trivialization, corruption, and degradation. Where Freemasonry was likely to confer status, Joyce decries it and makes it look silly. The Masons in 'Circe' are partly real masons (15. 590–1). The Masonic '*passtouch*' is run together with the sexual lure (15. 2012) and the '*sign of past master*' with '*ventriloquial exorcism*' (15. 2721–6). The '*attitude of most excellent master*' is conflated with that of submissive animal and grovelling, ecstatic masochist (15. 2852–85). Edward VII may appear '*robed as a grand elect perfect and sublime mason*', but only with a parodic '*trowel and apron*' and '*a plasterer's bucket on which is printed* Défense d'uriner' (15. 4454–6). 'Circe' comically reverses most of the attributes with which the larger culture endows the Freemasons. In that respect, as in others, Joyce strikes back at an Anglicizing imposition.

In fact, the chapter is very much involved in retaliation. It showers a host of English and Anglo-Irish targets with ridicule, as Deasy is showered in '*a torrent of mutton broth*' (15. 3990–1). It mocks English nationalism in general (15. 4417–21). It also mocks individuals, from Carr and Compton's absurd English idiom (15. 615–18) to Beaufoy's parodic and bogus superciliousness (15. 818–55) to the antics of the respectable, Anglo-Irish, society ladies (15. 4550–2). In other words, 'Circe' is monstrously and deliberately 'bad-mannered', in very much the way that, as I noted in my introduction, early English reviewers suggested the novel was as a whole. It transgresses social and linguistic usage together. The humour is subtle as well as crude. The derisive representation of Edward VII, for example, manages to be hilariously and frankly offensive and shrewd, knowledgeable and acidly ironical at one and the same time (15. 4449–79). As much as anything else, we might think of 'Circe' as practising a 'retaliatory aesthetics'. As in 'Oxen' and elsewhere, this partly involves recontamination. Moran argued that Irish opposition to England 'must not only defend its own positions to its own followers', but also 'march abroad, invade the enemy's territory and attack every stronghold with all the horse, foot and artillery it can dispose of'.[60] In its own way, 'Circe' carries out exactly this kind of invasion.

Thus the residues of English high culture in 'Circe' are repeatedly burlesqued or traduced. Keats's *belle dame sans merci* becomes a common whore (15. 122). Dickens is demeaned through Beaufoy, who '*drawls*' like an upper-class Dickens character.[61] Wordsworthian epiphany is conflated with furtive masturbation (15. 3307–59). Tennyson himself features, ludicrously, as a '*gentleman poet in Union Jack blazer and cricket flannels, bareheaded, flowingbearded*' (15. 4396–7). His poetry is reduced to a few grandiose tags and clichés.[62] Arnold is represented by a music-hall double act, the '*Siamese twins, Philip Drunk and Philip Sober, two Oxford dons with lawnmowers*' (15. 2512–13). Keats's 'thing of beauty' becomes John Eglinton in '*mandarin's kimono of Nankeen yellow . . . and a high pagoda hat*' (15. 2249–54).[63] Kipling's 'The Absent-Minded Beggar' becomes a particular object of ridicule (15. 4417–20).[64] Quotations from Shakespeare are travestied (15. 3522, 3655), applied to quite incongruous situations (15. 3194, 4582), turned into nonsense or rendered half-recognizable (15. 3853), left oddly limp and pointless (15. 3922), or associated with pretences to respectability, with claims to being 'guiltless as the unsunned snow' (15. 1769). Shakespeare himself is 'brought on stage' to mouth childlike mock-archaisms (15. 3827), or set before us as a figure maniacally incoherent with sexual jealousy and rage, mangling quotations from his own plays (15. 3828–9, 3853). 'Circe' is full of blasphemous distortions of the imperial master's language and literature. Caliban casts out Ariel. The Yahoos overrun the Houyhnhnms.

Joyce very obviously took a gleeful, malevolent delight in twisting and perverting the forms of the imposed culture. The consequences are partly levelling or carnivalesque. Bakhtin certainly is relevant here. Like carnival in Bakhtin's description of it, 'Circe' has roots in popular laughter and parodies and travesties certain 'high genres'.

---

[60] *Philosophy*, 12.

[61] Cf. e.g. Lord Frederick Verisopht and Mrs Wititterly in *Nicholas Nickleby*, and the Hon. Bob Stables in *Bleak House*.

[62] See e.g. 15. 1600, 4397.

[63] The Nymph from *Photo Bits* is also 'a thing of beauty' (15. 3268).

[64] Though Joyce paid tribute to Kipling's imagination, his distaste for Kipling's sentimentally patriotic poem is obvious. He surely knew of Kipling's fiercely pro-Unionist stand both at the time of the Home Rule Bill and the First World War, and related it to Kipling's attitudes to the Boer War.

The chapter has a carnivalesque 'atmosphere of *joyful relativity*'. It launches a sustained assault on rationality, singular meaning, dogmatism, and 'one-sided rhetorical seriousness'.[65] It strikes at '*official* monologism' and its ready-made truths.[66] It works—as Bakhtin says carnival does—against those forces which are hostile to evolution and change and which threaten to make absolute 'a given social order'.[67] It subverts the prohibitions and restrictions that have made for inequalities and 'distance between people'.[68] It '[decrowns] all hierarchical positions people might hold',[69] spreads a 'free and familiar attitude' over 'all values, thoughts, phenomena, and things',[70] and produces the characteristically carnivalesque contacts between and combinations of the high and the low, noble and base, sacred and profane.

But such a procedure also has a very precise historical and political significance. In the first instance, it represents a kind of leavening of the cultural politics of Irish Ireland, a roguish dissent, not from that politics *tout court*, but from various aspects of it, including the solemnity with which it was adhered to. If Joyce partly shares the hostility of Irish Ireland to Anglicization, in responding to it carnivalistically rather than polemically, he also deliberately *trivializes* the issues. In this respect, he appears to have at least a little in common with the sort of fringe position within nationalist cultural politics that was occupied by the likes of the woman 'John Brennan', who argued for more light-heartedness and 'frivolity' in Irish Ireland entertainments.[71] Furthermore, in 'carnivalizing' 'Circe', Joyce was conducting his own 'revival'. He was awaking a particular Irish past to counter those to which others were turning.[72] For an element of carnival (in Bakhtin's sense) was evident in popular religiosity in Catholic Ireland until well into the nineteenth century. Orthodox Catholic beliefs still mingled with folk beliefs and practices only

[65] Mikhail Bakhtin, *Problems of Dostoevsky's Poetics*, ed. and trans. Caryl Emerson, with introd. Wayne C. Booth (Manchester: Manchester University Press, 1984), 107.
[66] Ibid. 110.　　[67] Ibid. 160.　　[68] Ibid. 132.
[69] Ibid. 158.　　[70] Ibid. 123.　　[71] Ward, *Unmanageable Revolutionaries*, 75.
[72] Richard Kearney has argued that, where Yeats 'moved back towards a pre–modern culture, Joyce moved forwards to a post–modern one'. See *Transitions: Narratives in Modern Irish Culture* (Manchester: Manchester University Press, 1988), 31. Cf. Deane on Joyce as 'a rebel against all that preceded him' ('Joyce and Nationalism', 100) who set himself against 'the closed world of limited and limiting historical fact' (ibid. 92). But the contemporary, Irish emphasis on an unrelentingly forward–looking Joyce, whilst very important, nonetheless tends to minimize his complex and obscure historical allegiances.

remotely connected with them.[73] Aspects of the semi-formal, rural celebration of the seasons still remained. So did rites and rituals associated with individual or communal change. There were the 'patterns', for example, assemblies which took place on fixed days at sites which were believed to be of a sacred character. They mixed 'Christian devotion and traditional magic' and often resembled 'a fair or carnival'.[74] Protestant clergy accused them of being the occasion of 'drunken quarrels and obscenities' and 'scenes of licentiousness'. They even suspected that the patterns were got up—as a rector of Co. Kilkenny suggested—' "to celebrate the orgies of the Prince of Darkness" '.[75] But, most of all, of course, there were the (often rather outrageous) wakes. Many of their most distinctive characteristics had much in common with some of the most striking features of 'Circe': drinking; singing and dancing; sexually suggestive and blasphemous games; mockery of priests and parodies of the Mass and the Passion; naked and sometimes transvestite actors; word games and extempore rhyming; practical jokes and torments inflicted on designated scapegoats; the performance of feats of strength, agility, and endurance; the parody of everyday activities; and—very importantly—the simple insistence on mirth in the house of mourning.[76] Wakes were a relic of pagan rites, and casually blended the sacred and profane, whilst also diluting and muddying 'the clear waters of ecclesiastical authority'.[77] Thus Irish Catholicism in the early and even the mid-nineteenth century was sometimes almost outrageously heterogeneous and accommodating. It exhibited a striking *catholicity*. Institutional religion and popular practices were not necessarily at odds with one another.

During the nineteenth century, however, the Church made increasing efforts to suppress such practices or reform them in the direction of respectability and modernity. Connolly makes it clear, for example, that, while there was certainly some opposition to the patterns amongst the Catholic clergy from the middle of the eighteenth cen-

---

[73] See Hoppen, *Ireland since 1800*, 64–9, 78–9, 144, 151–2. My discussion of 19th–cent. Irish Catholicism in this chapter is heavily indebted to his book.

[74] S. J. Connolly, *Priests and People in Pre–Famine Ireland 1780–1845* (Dublin: Gill and Macmillan, 1982), 136–7.   [75] Ibid. 140.

[76] See ibid. 149; and Hoppen, *Ireland since 1800*, 65–6. Interestingly, though, wakes were not always riotous affairs. There were times when riotousness was frowned upon. In particular, 'at the death of a young person . . . the wake was generally a quiet and mournful affair' (Connolly, *Priests and People*, 158). This may help to explain the mood established at the end of 'Circe' with the appearance of Rudy.

[77] Hoppen, *Ireland since 1800*, 66.

tury onwards, that opposition was neither 'unanimous' nor widely acted upon until the middle of the nineteenth century.[78] So too the wakes had always shocked and appalled some people. The Protestant antiquarian J. G. A. Prim (sic), for instance, attacked them for their 'gross obscenity' and explicit assertion of sexuality.[79] But the actual suppression of wakes by the priesthood was fuelled and intensified in the mid-nineteenth century by efforts to alter the character of popular leisure that were the result of English influence.[80] The scholar John O'Donovan lamented the disappearance of the older tolerance as a sign of Catholic priests increasingly inclining to Protestant notions and putting an end to venerable old customs.[81] Wilde's father lamented it, too, claiming that the tone of society was becoming 'more and more "Protestant" ' and respectable every year.[82] The irony was that, even as the Cullenite hierarchy increasingly denounced English influences, it was also steadily reforming the Church in the direction of Protestant, Anglo-Saxon puritanism and Victorian, English cleanliness. Thus Cullen condemned the older folk beliefs and practices as immoral, and saw to it that wakes, funerals, baptisms, and weddings were sanitized. In 'Circe', Joyce returns precisely to the 'carnivalesque' spirit and atmosphere of the earlier Catholic culture. He uses the earlier culture as a stick with which to beat the heavily puritanical, Cullenite Catholicism of which he had a more direct, personal experience. The older culture serves as a weapon against the more Anglicized culture Joyce knew. Ironically but crucially, it was a weapon which Irish Ireland was itself too puritanical—too Anglicized—to use. Here, again, Joyce did not so much set himself in opposition to Irish Ireland as take some of its attitudes far beyond the narrow limits they had for a movement itself not free of Anglicizing influences, and cast them into a radically ampler mould.

The same is true of his distortion and perversion of English forms in 'Circe', especially insofar as they are processes of retaliatory contamination and even appropriation. They constitute—again—an 'Irishisation' of things English. 'Circe' repeatedly gives an Irish inflection to English culture. Joyce insistently nudges English phrases and idioms in a more Irish-sounding direction. It is here that we

[78] Connolly, *Priests and People*, 140–6.   [79] See ibid. 152–3.
[80] See ibid. 171–2.   [81] See ibid. 113.
[82] W. R. Wilde, *Irish Popular Superstitions* (Dublin: McGlashan, 1852), 17.

encounter Joyce's 'Celtic revenge' at its haughtiest, most intransigent and superior. As I've mentioned before, 'Irishisation' was Hyde's term. He used it, not to designate a programme for the future or a call for a new aesthetics, but as a term for an earlier, prouder, more self-sufficient phase in Irish culture when the Irish actually 'Irishised' the invader.[83] For Hyde, however, such a project in the present could only seem impractical to the point of arrogance. For its part, Irish Ireland wanted merely to retreat into separateness and construct a provincial enclave. But Joyce was concerned to propel Ireland firmly into the mainstream of European culture. He also wanted to set it over and against the thitherto dominant English culture, even to *appropriate* English culture on its behalf. In this, perhaps, lies the most important of his various and complex differences with Irish Ireland. If 'Circe' is joyous in its unruliness, its joyousness stems from pride. Joyce knew how far Irish Ireland's call for decontamination spelt unresolved enslavement, bore witness to the invader's continuing power even whilst apparently resisting it. For a Stephen darkly brooding on the past, history was a nightmare: jousts, 'slush and uproar of battles, the frozen deathspew of the slain, a shout of spearspikes baited with men's bloodied guts' (2. 317–18). 'Circe' takes such images and transforms them, sardonically, rudely, facetiously, but, above all, gaily. We get Edward VII levitating '*over heaps of slain*' with his '*white jujube in his phosphorescent face*' (15. 4476–7), and Tweedy appearing '*moustached like Turko the terrible*', whilst casqued and armoured halberdiers '*thrust forward a pentice of gutted spearpoints*' (15. 4611–12). For Yeats, the nightmare rode upon sleep. For Joyce, it turns into pantomime. This is surely an important reason for there *being* so much pantomime in 'Circe': the concerns of the de-Anglicizers are treated in a form that acknowledges their importance, but also dramatically relativizes it.

'Circe' can therefore not be categorically separated from Irish Ireland. But nor is it to be read in the latter's terms. The many references back to earlier chapters, for example, put the novel through a mangle and squeeze out hitherto unremarked and seemingly innocent traces of Anglicization: English sentimentality, pomposity, respectability, moralism, and common sense. But 'Circe' does not only note and anatomize them. It mocks, desecrates, and 'Irishizes' them,

---

[83] Hyde, 'Necessity', 126.

too. The art of 'Circe' refuses the temporizations of the court jesters and gay betrayers. But Joyce is also relaxed enough to be aware of the possibility of common causes with certain forces at work in English culture. The key instance is Blake the radical poet. Blake partly colours the context around Stephen's climactic 'Non serviam!'[84] Joyce's cheerily patriotic Dolly Gray identifies herself with Blake's treacherous Rahab (15. 4419). On occasions, Stephen provides an Irish equivalent of Blake's prophetic voice (15. 4641–2). Even his desire to kill the mental priest and king sounds Blakean. Stephen's confrontation with Compton and Carr itself appears to have been partly modelled on Blake's confrontation with the soldiers Scholfield and Cock, in which Blake was alleged to have uttered 'seditious and treasonable expressions', expressed his attachment to the French cause and his desire to 'encourage and invite the Enemy to invade England', and told the soldiers they were slaves.[85] Joyce was drawn to Blake insofar as Blake was a poet not of England but of Albion, both an England buried and seemingly lost, and a future England, an England yet to be. He recognized the analogy between his project and Blake's, but also turned Blake's project to his own and Irish ends.

Joyce surely saw himself as a liberating spirit, partly in Blakean terms. But he could not afford a seriousness like Blake's. To adopt it, for Joyce, would have been to close the gap between the Citizen, young Stephen, and Irish Ireland on the one hand, and his own art on the other. Deane argues that Joyce categorically rejected Pearse and Moran's nationalism as 'too crude, too schoolboyish, too eager to demand a spirit of solidarity and service that has more in common with propaganda than it has with art'.[86] There was of course a 'schoolboyish' Joyce, and he leaves his traces in Ulysses. But the assertion that Joyce rejects political 'crudeness' is crucial. Once again, in 'Circe', Joyce's irony and subtlety allow him to steer between a Scylla and a Charybdis. They make him able comprehensively to advance beyond the aggressions of the citizen and the culture he represents without dismissing or belittling them. Joyce knew that Anglicization was not to be reversed. He determined instead to cast it into an art that would come to terms with, transcend, and master it;

---

[84] See esp. 15. 4244–5.
[85] See J. Bronowski, William Blake and the Age of Revolution (London: Routledge and Kegan Paul, 1972), 107–13.
[86] 'Joyce and Nationalism', 96.

reverse its 'mastery' in turn. Some of the laughter in 'Circe' is light. Some of it is scathing and savage. Some of it is robustly satirical, or wry, oblique, and muted. But the dominant laughter in the chapter is Nietzschean. It is a laughter that, at one and the same time, accepts and challenges historical circumstance, and triumphs over it, at least, in decisively transforming its proportions.

CHAPTER NINE

Mingle Mangle or Gallimaufry: 'Eumaeus'

The Language Properly So-Called

Eighteenth-century England saw an increasing concern with the state of the language. Many eminent figures shared it, grammarians not least. As John Barrell has amply shown, it was connected with the belief that the question of the English language was also a question of nationhood; in particular, that the language could be a powerful instrument for national unity. The language at issue was always the English of a few, the 'men of letters and education'.[1] In his *Philosophy of Rhetoric* (1776), George Campbell claimed that 'ninety-nine of a hundred' English speakers did not speak the language of 'custom' or 'the language properly so-called'.[2] Swift, Johnson, Burke, and many others asserted the need to protect the language against reform, innovation, and 'improper' usage. They insisted on 'national' standards of 'correctness'. At the same time, they also represented 'those who offended against the rules of good English' as 'excluding themselves from the national community'. The concept of 'the language properly so-called' offered an idea of unity and 'a notional cultural equality to men of all classes'. Ironically, however, it also confirmed 'the power of those who could speak it over those who could not'.[3]

The concept of a national, 'proper English', then, was supposedly inclusive but in fact exclusive. Whilst actually limited to an elite,

---

[1] William Kenrick, 'Advertisement', *A Rhetorical Grammar of the English Language* (London: R. Cadell and W. Longman, 1784); quoted in John Barrell, *English Literature in History 1730–1780: An Equal, Wide Survey* (London: Hutchinson, 1983), 127.

[2] *The Philosophy of Rhetoric* (2 vols., London: W. Strahan, T. Cadell, 1776), vol. i; quoted in Barrell, *English Literature*, 165.   [3] Barrell, *English Literature*, 175.

it was notionally binding on the British as a whole. An awareness of the concept and its history is important for Joyce's work in general and 'Eumaeus' in particular. For 'proper English' was not just an eighteenth-century concern. Quite the contrary: the nineteenth century saw it still more firmly established.[4] Benedict Anderson has shown that the work of linguists was central to the shaping of nineteenth-century nationalism in Europe, and Stefan Collini has argued a similar case with regard to England.[5] Most tellingly of all, Tony Crowley has demonstrated that nineteenth-century England saw a steady intensification of English linguistic nationalism that ran from De Quincey to Quiller-Couch and beyond. This took various forms, like the growth of the new academic discipline of 'the history of the language' in Victorian England.[6] What underpinned English linguistic nationalism was the conviction that what G. P. Marsh called the 'unity of speech' was essential to the unity of the people, and that the language was the site of national history.[7] Richard Chenevix Trench, for example, Archbishop of Dublin and grandfather of Dermot, the model for Haines, argued that language was 'the key to understanding the moral history of the group', in Crowley's phrase.[8] For Marsh, Trench, Furnivall, and other mid- to late nineteenth-century linguists, the English language—the imperial language, 'the great medium of civilization'—was a supposedly imperishable bond between all British subjects.[9] Many authorities (tendentiously) claimed that English was older than most

[4] Barrell argues that the power of those who can speak 'the language properly so-called' over those who do not continues to this day (ibid.).

[5] Anderson, *Imagined Communities: Reflections on the Origins and Spread of Nationalism* (London: Verso, 1991), 71; and Collini, *Public Moralists: Political Thought and Intellectual Life in Britain 1850–1930* (Oxford: Clarendon, 1991), 351.

[6] *The Politics of Discourse: The Standard Language Question in British Cultural Debates* (Basingstoke: Macmillan, 1989), 33. Crowley persuasively argues, against 'the commonplace view', that linguistic discourses did not shift from prescriptivism to descriptivism in the 19th cent. (ibid. 13). However, linguists more often sought scientific justifications for prescriptivism. See Crowley, *Language in History: Theories and Texts* (London: Routledge, 1996), 149.

[7] *Lectures on the English Language* (New York: C. Scribner, 1860), 221; quoted in Crowley, *Politics of Discourse*, 67.

[8] Crowley, *Language in History*, 154. On Joyce and Trench, see Gregory M. Downing, 'Richard Chenevix Trench and Joyce's Historical Study of Words', *Joyce Studies Annual* (1998), 37–68.

[9] The phrase is Edwin Guest's. See *A History of English Rhythm* (2 vols., 1838), ed. W. W. Skeat (London: G. Bell and Sons, 1882), 703; quoted in Crowley, *Politics of Discourse*, 72.

European tongues and had enjoyed an unbroken continuity in its development.[10] For Skeat and Davies, the language was a token of the superiority of the English race.[11] Watts looked forward to the time when the world was 'circled by the accents of Milton and Shakespeare'.[12]

The linguists were much concerned about the purity of English. They worried about its possible degeneration.[13] Not surprisingly, the later nineteenth century was much preoccupied with what was now called 'standard English'. 'Standard English' was a supposedly central, homogeneous, literary form of the language, round which could be grouped the sub-varieties, like dialects.[14] In principle, the concept of 'standard English' was objective and neutral. In practice, nineteenth-century linguists were as prescriptive as their eighteenth-century counterparts. 'Standard English' involved the construction of a monoglossia,[15] the imposition of 'a particular form of speech' as the one to which 'others had to rise'.[16] 'The Queen's English' was presented as 'a recognized and institutionalized form of the language', as distinct from local, 'peculiar' forms. It concealed the speaker's history and bore the stamp of a particular, well-bred, well-informed class.[17] Once again, rank and education were crucial. Only Arnold's cultured classes—the elegant, learned, and polite—could qualify as masters of the Queen's English.[18] The 'unpolished' were disqualified by error and impropriety. As W. Dwight Whitney put it, they were guilty of 'a host of inaccuracies, offences against the correctness of speech, as ungrammatical forms, mis-pronunciations, burdens of application, slang words, vulgarities'.[19] George Sampson referred to this uncultivated language as 'infected' English.[20] For G. F. Graham, it was an English

---

[10] See Collini, *Public Moralists*, 353.   [11] See Crowley, *Politics of Discourse*, 73.
[12] 'On the Probable Future Position of the English Language', *Proceedings of the Philological Society*, 4 (1850); repr. in Crowley, *Proper English?: Readings in Language, History and Cultural Identity* (London: Routledge, 1991), 125–35, at 132.
[13] See Crowley, *Politics of Discourse*, 75. For present-day versions of this anxiety, see Crowley, *Proper English?*, 9.   [14] See Crowley, *Politics of Discourse*, 104.
[15] See Crowley, *Language in History*, 166.
[16] See Crowley, *Politics of Discourse*, 129.   [17] See ibid. 131–2.
[18] See ibid. 145–51.
[19] *The Life and Growth of Language* (London: Henry S. King & Co., 1875), 155; quoted in Crowley, *Politics of Discourse*, 152.
[20] Sampson expressed the hope that education would progressively 'disinfect' the language of error. See 'The Problem of Grammar', *English Association Pamphlet*, 56 (1924), 28; quoted in Crowley, *Politics of Discourse*, 154.

corrupted by 'loose' and 'careless' ways and strewn with 'abortions' and 'deformations'.[21] If the common people had any linguistic pretensions or ambitions, these simply made matters worse. The vulgar 'admixture of foreign phrases', for instance, only succeeded in producing a 'Brummagem sparkle'.[22]

Collini has argued that, in the later nineteenth century, literature increasingly took over from language as 'the central symbolic expression' of imagined community in England.[23] But the late nineteenth and early twentieth centuries also witnessed a peculiar intensification of the drive for 'proper English'. The period saw the rise of the terms 'received English' and 'received standard English'.[24] According to Crowley, at this time, 'the articulate' were peculiarly concerned to distinguish themselves from 'the barbarians', and their language from an English full of 'errors and corruptions'. They were partly reacting against the alarming, new, democratic trends in British culture.[25] The 'murder' of the Queen's English was an increasingly significant issue. As Crowley shows, English cultural nationalism not only remained 'an important force' in linguistic debates between 1880 and 1920. It became a more hegemonic one.[26] In previous decades, different people had held diverse and conflicting views on the subject. Towards the end of the century, however, that diversity was disappearing. Henry Sweet wrote in 1890, for example, of the educated English person's 'terror' of sounding like a provincial or dialectal speaker of the language.[27]

By the early twentieth century, both linguists and the new professors of literature were arguing more insistently than ever that the language was an instrument for national unity. So, too, their anxieties about degeneration grew correspondingly more pronounced.[28] True, the emergence of English studies partly displaced the linguistic discourses. But it also gave them a formidable new boost. According to Crowley, Quiller-Couch feared that the deterioration of the language would 'bring about social, literary and personal

---

[21] Graham, *A Book about Words* (London: Longman and Green, 1869), excerpted in Crowley, *Proper English?*, 162–9, at 162, 169.

[22] Henry Alford, *The Queen's Idiom: A Manual of Idiom and Usage* (London: Longman and Green, 1884); excerpted in Crowley, *Proper English?*, 173–80, at 178.

[23] *Public Moralists*, 354.   [24] See Crowley, *Politics of Discourse*, 136.

[25] See ibid. 214–22.   [26] *Language in History*, 181.

[27] *A Primer of Spoken English* (Oxford: Clarendon Press, 1890), pp. vi–vii; quoted in Crowley, *Politics of Discourse*, 155.   [28] Cf. Crowley, *Language in History*, 184.

decay' in modern England.[29] H. C. O'Neill worried that a growing linguistic 'slackness' would finally corrupt 'our literature'.[30] Raleigh saw the First World War as a battle for the purity, even the supremacy, of the English language.[31] At the same time, linguistic nationalism was progressively institutionalized. When the English Association was founded in 1906, it expressly concerned itself 'with the development of a system of education centred upon a national consciousness' based upon 'the native language' as well as the literature.[32] Leading members of the Association wrestled with the question of how best to counter the degeneration of English or 'linguistic perversion'.[33] The Society for Pure English was founded in 1913 out of a sense that the language was under threat. Some suggested that the threat was a result of colonialism, of the global expansion of imperial, British power. As Robert Bridges put it:

no other language can ever have had its central force so dissipated. . . . wherever our countrymen are settled abroad there are alongside of them communities of other-speaking races, who, maintaining amongst themselves their native speech, learn yet enough of ours to mutilate it, and establishing among themselves *all kinds of blundering corruptions*, through habitual intercourse infect therewith the neighbouring English.[34]

The 'standard language' became the focus of the *New* (later *Oxford*) *English Dictionary* (1884–1928). Indeed, the concept of a 'standard' literary English was central to the whole project.[35] But,

[29] Crowley, *Politics of Discourse*, 253.

[30] *A Guide to the English Language* (London: T. C. Jack, 1915), 114; quoted in Crowley, *Politics of Discourse*, 252–3.

[31] In a letter of 6 July 1917 to John Sampson, Raleigh writes: 'The War is going to be All Right, my son. The English Language is safe to be the world language. The very Germans will treat their own tongue as a dialect.' Walter Raleigh, *Letters*, ed. Lady Raleigh (2 vols., London: Methuen & Co., 1926), ii. 468. On the mutation of literary and cultural nationalism during the war, see Chris Baldick, *The Social Mission of English Criticism 1848–1932* (Oxford: Clarendon, 1987), 86–92.

[32] Baldick, *Social Mission*, 95.

[33] Brian Doyle, *English and Englishness* (London: Routledge, 1989), 36. Cf. Charles Nowell Smith's account of the early years of the association in his chairman's address of 1942, *The Origins and History of the Association* (English Association; London: Sidgwick and Jackson, 1942), 3–5.

[34] 'The Society's Work', Society for Pure English, *Tract XXI* (1925), in W. F. Bolton and D. Crystal (eds.), *The English Language*, ii. *Essays by Linguists and Men of Letters* (Cambridge: Cambridge University Press, 1969), 86–99, at 88; italics mine.

[35] See Crowley, *Politics of Discourse*, 109. Crowley suggests that the linguistic concerns that led to the *New English Dictionary* also led to the modern conception of English literature and English literary history (ibid. 122).

once again, the culmination of this form of cultural nationalism can be found in the Newbolt Report. The Report argued for 'a national consciousness of pride' in English as a basis for 'a lasting national unity'.[36] It also urged the need for 'approved principles and methods' for the elimination of non-standard forms of English.[37] In sum, to many linguists, literature teachers, and educational theorists in the late nineteenth and early twentieth centuries, standard English was a 'last bastion' of Arnoldian sweetness and light.[38] Not surprisingly, the period saw a growing emphasis on it, and an increasing consolidation of its principles.[39]

The Usual Irish Blunders

The developing concept of 'proper English' tended to privilege a certain social and even racial group at the expense of others (colonials, cockneys, Celts, provincials). For Sweet, White, Wright, and other nineteenth-century linguists, 'standard English' was not only class- but region-specific. It was often effectively confined to southern England, or just the Home Counties.[40] But there was no reason why others should feel that correctness was beyond them. The 'more polished part of the inhabitants of England' might serve as an example to all.[41] The Irish, Scots, Welsh, Cornish, and other provincials should learn to speak as they did. If, from the eighteenth century onwards, the concept of 'the language properly so-called' was in principle binding on everyone, for that very reason, many argued that it must be diffused as widely as possible. As Crowley notes, figures like Thomas Sheridan and James Buchanan are thus especially significant. The Scot Buchanan wanted proper English 'imposed' on Scotland.[42] The Anglo-Irish Sheridan wished to see it spread in Ireland, as part of an 'ambitious project to set himself up in the colonial metropolis' as an expert in the colonizer's lan-

---

[36] Baldick, *Social Mission*, 95.   [37] See Doyle, *English and Englishness*, 51.

[38] Crowley, *Politics of Discourse*, 253.

[39] Crowley demonstrates this with reference to the work of Daniel Jones and Henry Wyld. See Crowley, *Politics of Discourse*, 164–206.

[40] See Crowley, *Language in History*, 164.

[41] John Walker, *A Critical Pronouncing Dictionary and Expositor of the English Language* (London, 1791); excerpted in Crowley, *Proper English?*, 94–110, at 105.

[42] Barrell, *English Literature*, 157.

guage.[43] Such figures effectively chose 'the smooth caress' (2. 46).
They asserted their 'prescriptions for "proper English"' from 'the
edges of the dominant culture', the very places where it seemed to
have least hold.[44] Indeed, it was often the Celtic margins that were
most likely to be singled out for improvement, notably by an elite
who had roots there. At the same time, 'standard English' was also
eminently exportable to the colonies as part of the civilizing mission.[45] For the tendency to linguistic 'impropriety' was particularly
obvious in the benighted 'natives of the British dominions'.[46]

The issue of 'proper English' had its longest and most profoundly
political history in Ireland. At times, indeed, Ireland virtually
became a metaphor for it. Writing in 1859, for example, Richard
Garnett referred to the region in England most notable for the use
of standard English as 'the English pale'.[47] The history of the question of 'good English' in Ireland can be traced at least as far back
as the man Joyce called 'the mocker' (CW, 169). When Giraldus
Cambrensis complained that the 'pest of treachery' in Ireland was
abetted by the 'evil communications' which corrupted 'good manners', he was referring to Irish perversions of the language.[48] Tudor
commentators were similarly dismissive. Richard Stanihurst
bemoaned the 'mingle mangle or gallimaufry' produced when the
Irish tried to speak English. They were capable only of the 'jangled
English' of 'country clowns'.[49] Similarly, the State Papers of Ireland
for 1609 express concern that the English language in Ireland
should 'be preserved, neat and pure, unto posterity'.[50] The
Cromwellian settlement saw a vigorous attempt to promote and
protect the English language through a massive onslaught on Irish.
The effects of this campaign were consolidated in the eighteenth
century. Above all, speaking and writing 'good English' became a

---

[43] Tony Crowley, *The Politics of Language in Ireland 1366–1922* (London: Routledge,
2000), 85. See also William Benzie, *Thomas Sheridan's Influence on Eighteenth-Century
Rhetoric and Belles Lettres* (Leeds: Leeds Texts and Monographs, 1972), 17–18, 110.

[44] Crowley, *Proper English?*, 73.   [45] Crowley, *Language in History,* 72.

[46] Thomas Sheridan, *A Course of Lectures on Elocution* (London, 1762), 1; quoted
in Crowley, *Language in History,* 79.

[47] *Philological Essays* (London, 1859); quoted in Crowley, *Language in History,* 163.

[48] *Topographia Hibernica* (London, 1863), 37–8; quoted in Crowley, *Politics of
Language in Ireland,* 13.

[49] *A Treatise Containing a Plain and Perfect Description of Ireland* (1577), in Raphael
Holinshed, *The Chronicles of England, Scotland and Ireland,* ed. John Hooker et al. (3
vols., London, 1587), excerpted in Crowley, *Politics of Language in Ireland,* 31–7, at 33.

[50] Excerpted in Crowley, *Politics of Language in Ireland,* 57–8, at 57.

crucial part of what elevated the Ascendancy above its barbarian other. For Swift and Sheridan, the use of 'good English' was a necessary badge of distinction from what Swift called Irishmen 'of the savage kind'.[51] Speaking poor English or Irish meant membership of a second-class, subjugated race. Some Anglo-Irishmen, like Francis Hutchinson, argued for the spread of English in Ireland in the interests of a 'real Union' of the two peoples.[52] Others kept up the old complaints about the 'maiming' and 'corruption' that English suffered once the Irish spoke it.[53] Certainly, from the eighteenth century onwards, in Britain, eminent Anglo-Irishmen and Unionists—Swift, Sheridan, Burke, Trench—were among those most concerned that English should be shielded from contamination. For them, the contamination in question was always principally Celtic. Sheridan insisted that 'some degree of disgrace' was invariably attached to the 'corrupt dialect' of the Irish.[54] He wanted his *Rhetorical Grammar and Pronouncing Dictionary* of 1780 to provide a uniform system of rules for English grammar and pronunciation that would be apppropriate to all peoples and classes.[55] It was effectively a Unionist text. In fact, questions of language were bound up with questions of national identity for the Anglo-Irish above all. Not surprisingly, they were therefore much concerned that the language should somehow be fixed, that it should be protected against history and mutability.

As Katie Wales has shown, in an important essay on 'Eumaeus', Joyce was keenly aware of and sensitive to the tradition I have described.[56] As a colonial Irishman, he had first-hand experience of the late nineteenth- and early twentieth-century intensification of the drive for the spread of 'proper English', not least at school and university. Contemporary, English, linguistic nationalism is clearly

---

[51] Swift, 'On Barbarous Denominations in Ireland', in *Prose Writings* (Oxford: Blackwell, 1973), vol. iii; excerpted in Crowley, *Politics of Language in Ireland*, 113–15, at 114.

[52] *The Church Catechism in Irish, With the English Placed Over It in the Same Karakter* (Belfast, 1722); excerpted in Crowley, *Politics of Language in Ireland*, 107–9, at 109.

[53] See Andrew Donlevy, *The Catechism, or Christian Doctrine by Way of Question and Answer* (Paris, 1742); excerpted in Crowley, *Politics of Language in Ireland*, 115.

[54] *Course of Lectures on Evolution*; excerpted in Crowley, *Proper English?*, 64–72, at 68.   [55] See Benzie, *Sheridan's Influence*, 29.

[56] '"With Apologies to Lindley Murray": The Narrative Method of the "Eumaeus" Episode in *Ulysses*', in Ingrid Tieken-Boon van Ostade (ed.), *Two Hundred Years of Lindley Murray* (Münster: Nodus, 1996), 207–16, esp. 208–9.

one determining condition of those epic moments in Joyce's work—like Stephen's exchange with the Dean of Studies in *Portrait*—which expressly articulate the question of the colonial subject's experience of the colonizer's language. The concept of what the editors of Joyce's selection of Tennyson's poetry called 'English undefiled' was amply apparent in his library in Trieste.[57] He was also acutely conscious of what 'proper English' defined as Irish solecism. He delighted in collecting examples of 'improper' uses of the language in the work of Irish writers (*CW*, 127). But he also understood exactly that laughter at 'these errors which exist amongst us' often indicated a 'pejorative conception of Ireland' (*CW*, 29, 171). For, as he told his irredentist audience at the Università Popolare in Trieste, the English had long seen the Irish as stereotypically error-prone, as 'the unbalanced, helpless idiots' portrayed 'in the lead articles of the *Standard* and the *Morning Post*' (*CW*, 171).

In 'The Mirage of the Fisherman of Aran', Joyce sardonically refers to what he calls 'the usual Irish blunders'. The context is important: he is recalling an Aran islander's observation that 'it has been a horrible summer, praise be to God' (*CW*, 236). The remark is a specimen of that most notorious form of Irish error, the bull. Joyce's ironical description of it as a 'blunder' is significant. For the English and Anglo-Irish repeatedly chose that word to characterize the bull. As the *OED* shows, bulls had been defined as such long before they were attributed to the Irish. In effect, they were English before they were Irish. Unsurprisingly again, the concept of the Irish bull seems to have appeared around the time of the Glorious Revolution. Thereafter, however, the belief that the Irish were disposed to a certain kind of linguistic and logical error grew commonplace. Swift wrote in 1740 that the Irish brogue 'makes the deliverer, in the last degree, ridiculous and despised; and, from such a mouth, an Englishman expects nothing but bulls, blunders and follies'.[58] By the time of the publication of the classic book on bulls, the Edgeworths' *Essay on Irish Bulls*, Irish bulls were a regular target for English mockery. The Edgeworths themselves are clear about this. From the beginning to the end of the nineteenth century—

---

[57] Introd. to Alfred, Lord Tennyson, *Selections*, ed. F. J. Rowe and W. T. Webb (London: Macmillan, 1889), p. xii.

[58] 'Barbarous Denominations', in Crowley, *Politics of Language in Ireland*, 114.

from the Edgeworths' *Essay* (1802) to G. R. Neilson's *The Book of Bulls* (1898)—bulls were referred to as blunders.[59]

The Irish bull offered the English and Anglo-Irish ample opportunity for a range of superior responses, from liberal patronage to derision.[60] However, as I suggested at the start of this book, the collection of bulls Joyce had in Trieste—H. P. Kelly's *Irish Bulls and Puns*—was *sui generis*. This emerges the more clearly if we contrast it with the Edgeworths' *Essay* and Neilson's book. For the Edgeworths, if bulls are blunders, as such, they are not confined to the Irish, but are widespread in English and European culture. Furthermore, if the Irish bull is a worldly blunder and indicates a lack of cunning or savoir-faire, it is never a blunder 'of the heart'.[61] It is inextricably linked to Irish ingenuousness, good humour, frankness, and generosity. It is 'justifiable by ancient precedents' or the result of the Irish habit 'of using figurative and witty language'.[62] Thus the English should cease to treat the Irish as a laughing-stock. They should realize instead that the joke may be on them.[63] Christopher Ricks describes the *Essay* as 'magnificent' in its magnanimity, wisdom, wit, and humanity.[64] In fact, again, it is strategically and precisely a Unionist text.[65] Published four years after the 1798 rebellion, to which it intermittently refers, it explicitly attempts 'to conciliate' England and Ireland in the wake of the Act of Union, chiefly by diffusing 'a more just and enlarged idea of the Irish than has been generally entertained'.[66] In this respect, it is

---

[59] According to Daniel Dewar, writing in 1812, such blunders occurred because the Irishman 'accommodates the acquired tongue to the idiomatic construction and phraseology of his own'. *Observations on the Character, Customs and Superstitions of the Irish* (London: Gale and Curtis, 1812); excerpted in Crowley, *Politics of Language in Ireland*, 141–4, esp. at 142.

[60] The English and Anglo-Irish responded to bulls in other ways, too. See Christopher Ricks's Anglocentric account of the Irish bull in *Beckett's Dying Words* (Oxford: Oxford University Press, 1993), ch. 4.

[61] Richard Lovell Edgeworth and Maria Edgeworth, *Essay on Irish Bulls* (5th edn., London: R. Hunter, 1823), 67.   [62] Ibid. 237.

[63] According to Marilyn Butler, the project of a pro-Irish satirical tract on bulls was Swiftian in origin. See 'General Introduction', in *The Novels and Selected Works of Maria Edgeworth*, i. *Castle Rackrent: Irish Bulls, Ennui*, ed. Jane Desmarais et al. (London: Chatto & Windus, 1999), pp. vii–lxxx, esp. p. xliv.

[64] *Becket's Dying Words*, 161, 191.

[65] Cf. Brian Hollingworth's account of the *Essay* in ch. 3 of *Maria Edgeworth's Irish Writing: Language, History, Politics* (London: Macmillan, 1997), esp. at 47.

[66] Edgeworths, *Essay*, 242–3. Cf. Tom Dunne, *Maria Edgeworth and the Colonial Mind* (Cork: Cork University Press, 1984), 4.

marked by its liberal condescension. Whilst critical of Samuel Johnson for treating Goldsmith (they thought) like an inspired idiot, the Edgeworths' patronage of the Irish is not altogether different in kind. In casting themselves as patrician defenders of the native people, they also carefully maintain their distance from them. They refer to themselves as English throughout the book, and give a list of 'Irish persons of genius' at the end that is exclusively Anglo-Irish.[67] In effect, for the Edgeworths, the bull is an engaging, endearing, even sophisticated feature of a culture whose naivety and impetuosity have nonetheless left it rightly subordinate to the colonial power.[68] Their hope is that a proper understanding of the culture in question will make that power behave less tyrannically and more benevolently.[69]

G. R. Neilson's book (which contains the Edgeworths' *Essay*) is more straightforward. Whilst granting the Irish bull its own logic and vitality as a form of expression, Neilson is clear: the bull is chiefly a feature of peasant culture. It is in large measure the consequence of Irish obtuseness (about the meaning of words, numbers, and so on). But it is also due to Irish 'emotionalism', which makes for 'very bad English'.[70] Bulls infringe the rules of 'proper English'. They are 'things which should have been otherwise expressed'.[71] Neilson suggests that the Edgeworths were mistaken in claiming that the Irish bull is not really specifically Irish (which presumably justifies his lapses into jokes about the 'Irish mob orator' and 'poor Pat').[72] Interestingly, Neilson (like Ricks) is prepared to grant that, in principle, the bull may be an expression of a recalcitrant and critical spirit.[73] But this notional concession has little effect on his book. By contrast, Kelly's collection reads as though it were written on behalf of the Irish. To return to the account of it I gave in my introduction: many of Kelly's bulls are expressions of political and cultural resistance. They often seem designed to get the better of an opponent, and are frequently notable for their cunning. Some of

---

[67] *Essay*, 242–3. On the Edgeworths' handling of their own national identity, see Hollingworth, *Maria Edgeworth's Irish Writing*, 65; Dunne, *Maria Edgeworth*, 12; and Marilyn Butler, *Maria Edgeworth: A Literary Biography* (Oxford: Clarendon Press, 1972), 364.
[68] Butler notes Maria Edgeworth's reliance on 'a stereotype of the Irish character', in the *Essay*. See *Maria Edgeworth*, 363.   [69] Cf. Dunne, *Maria Edgeworth*, 4–6.
[70] *The Book of Bulls* (London: Simpkin, Marshall, Hamilton, Kent & Co., 1898), 183.   [71] Ibid. 173.
[72] Ibid. 171.   [73] See ibid. 173; and Ricks, *Beckett's Dying Words*, 192–3.

them strike at religious orthodoxy (as when Paddy bests St Peter at heaven's gates).[74] Above all, however, a number of them score little victories over Englishmen of rank. Sometimes it is a matter of an Englishman committing a blunder which his Irish interlocutor then cleverly exploits.[75] Sometimes a bull actually corrects or improves on English usage.[76] The most important point is that many of Kelly's examples lack the feature most commonly associated with bulls: a comically Irish lapse from reason or failure in logical coherence. Kelly's collection effectively radically enlarges, even transforms the established conception of the bull. Certainly, it includes some of the 'usual Irish blunders'. It contains bulls that serve what Ricks takes to be the bull's main political purpose: a furtive display of insubordination by those resigned to their oppression.[77] But it also exhibits the bull as providing a little moment of victory, in which given structures of power and privilege are fleetingly reversed.

Errors of Genius

That Joyce owned Kelly's collection of bulls in particular is surely important, not least for 'Eumaeus'. For 'Eumaeus' converts blundering—that habit with which the English had long associated the Irish—into a bravura performance, and thus into a form of sustained, cultural triumph. The chapter proudly, even insolently steers clear of the Scylla of an elite, Anglo-Irish insistence on the central importance of good English to Irish culture. In this respect, it is significant that Joyce thought of 'Eumaeus' as composed in *prosa rilassata*, 'relaxed prose'.[78] But, at the same time, the fact that 'Eumaeus' is written in its own form of English, that Joyce takes such scrupulous pains over his imprecisions, that he labours so intensively on an art of linguistic defacement, shows how far, again, he also avoids the Charybdis of Irish Ireland. For, in Agnes

[74] See e.g. H. P. Kelly, *Irish Bulls and Puns* (London: Skeffington & Son, 1919), 11, 85–6.   [75] e.g. ibid. 36; cf. 76–7.
[76] e.g. ibid. 23.   [77] See Ricks, *Beckett's Dying Words*, 193.
[78] In the Linati schema. Quoted in Charles Peake, *James Joyce: The Citizen and the Artist* (London: Edward Arnold, 1977), 277. Fritz Senn feels rather that the words suggest 'less a mental attitude than a lax prose, one that has lost its tautness, with wobbling sinews' (note to the author).

O'Farrelly's phrase, Irish Ireland was increasingly inclined to identify 'the root of the cancer' of Anglicization in Ireland as the
English language itself, and accordingly promoted Gaelic.[79] Such
attitudes had a long history: if the English had often mocked Irish
'corruptions' of their language, Irish purists had long done the
same. In the seventeenth century, for example, the bards had repeatedly denounced or satirized 'the speaking of a half-acquired mon-
grel form of English'.[80] 'Eumaeus' does not accept the terms and
conditions the colonizer attaches to the use of his language. It is not
bound by his rules. But nor does it opt for the political narrowness
and unreality of categorical rejection. It is a glorious, wicked,
delighted perversion of a language (and a concept of 'propriety')
that Joyce nonetheless takes to be an unalterable, historical given.
It is thus that 'Eumaeus' forms part of his titanic struggle with
colonial, Irish history.

Joyce's practice in the chapter is in large measure a version of the
principle of the bull. But it raises that principle to a level of the
most extraordinary virtuosity and, in doing so, transforms it.
Whilst I would not want to argue that Joyce used (or needed to
'use') any of the collections, many of the features of the bull as
apparent in the Edgeworths', Neilson's, and Kelly's books are evident in Joyce's 'Eumaean' style. One way of thinking of the bull is
to conceive of it as Derridean deconstruction in a comically
grounded mode. In bulls, opposites repeatedly collapse into each
other; or, perhaps better, in the bull, the logic that places things in
opposition also turns out to join or unite them. One obvious example is the famous bull attributed to the 'prince of perpetrators' Sir
Boyle Roche: 'If the question is put to me, Mr. Speaker, I'll answer
at once boldly in the affirmative—No'.[81] Certain pairs of opposites
repeatedly come in for this kind of treatment or are handled 'clum-
sily' in bulls. Many of them appear in 'Eumaeus', too, and are handled in similar fashion: up and down (see for instance 'broken down
and fast breaking up', 16. 943);[82] in and out, which Joyce plays with
again and again (see for e.g. 'he takes great pride . . . out of you',
16. 261–2, and 'fumbled out . . . from his inside pocket', 16. 472; cf.

---

[79] *The Reign of Humbug* (Dublin: Gaelic League, 1901), excerpted in Crowley
Politics of Language in Ireland, 202–4. See esp. at 204.
[80] Crowley, *Politics of Language in Ireland*, 56.
[81] Neilson, *Book of Bulls*, 148, 150.   [82] Cf. Kelly, *Irish Bulls and Puns*, 53.

16. 105–6, 192–4, 250–1);[83] past and present or future (see e.g. 'today in fact, or to be strictly accurate, on yesterday', archly followed by Bloom's enquiry as to where Simon Dedalus lives 'at present', 16. 255–6);[84] life and death or youth and age (e.g. 'nipped in the bud of premature decay', 16. 1184);[85] presence and absence (e.g. 'conspicuous . . . by their total absence', 16. 1264–5);[86] existence and inexistence (e.g. 'the eyes that said or didn't say the words', 16. 1146–7);[87] sameness and difference (e.g. 'the cases' neither 'identical nor the reverse', 16. 1608);[88] and affirmation and negation (e.g. Bloom on being 'a Jew . . . though in reality I'm not', 16. 1084–5).[89] The more closely one looks at 'Eumaeus', the more clearly does it resemble the bull in depending on contradictions that manage to make a kind of sense, in spite of the fact that logic would condemn them.

But there are still more striking ways in which 'Eumaeus' shares the anti-rhetoric of the bull. The Edgeworths' book includes an invented exchange between an Irishman, an Englishman, and a Scot, in the middle of which the Scot draws from his pocket a book entitled *Deinology, or the Union of Reason and Elegance*:[90] '— "Look," said he, "look at this long list of tropes and figures, amongst them we could find apologies for every species of Irish bulls . . . ."'[91] Every 'trope and figure' in the Edgeworths' list can be found in 'Eumaeus'. The most obvious are *hyperbole* (e.g. 16. 356, 786), *ellipsis* (e.g. 16. 191, 681–2, 1421), *oxymoron* (16. 912), and *emphasis*. All four are evident in a precise, rhetorical sense.[92] Indeed, three distinct forms of emphasis are evident: ironical delicacy (e.g. 'Mr. Bloom, who was anything but a professional whistler', 16. 28–9; cf. 213, 302, 306–7, 835); the implication of more than is actually stated, either by the choice of an exceptionally strong word or phrase, or by saying less, but implying more (as in 'There would be a fall and the greatest fall

[83] Cf. Neilson, *Book of Bulls*, 173.   [84] Cf. ibid, 180.
[85] Cf. Kelly, *Irish Bulls and Puns*, 84.   [86] Cf. ibid, 73.
[87] Cf. Neilson, *Book of Bulls*, 180.
[88] Cf. Edgeworths', *Essay*, 18, 186; Neilson, *Book of Bulls*, 198.
[89] Cf. Kelly, *Irish Bulls and Puns*, 53; Neilson, *Book of Bulls*, 174.
[90] 'Hortensius', *Deinology, or the Union of Reason and Elegance: Being Instructions to a Young Barrister* (London: G. G. J. and J. Robinson, 1789). Neither this nor the 1801 edn. contains a list of terms. Both contain some but not all of those referred to by the Edgeworths.   [91] Edgeworths, *Essay*, 174.
[92] My definitions of the terms in question are derived from the Edgeworths' *Essay*, 174–5, the *OED*, and Richard A. Lanham's *A Handbook of Rhetorical Terms* (2nd edn., Berkeley and Los Angeles: University of California Press, 1991).

in history', 16. 1000; cf. 1308–10); and an omission or ambiguity that invites the complicity of the reader or auditor in completing it (as with the use of the single-word sentence 'Whereas.' at 16. 181; cf. 1043–7). There are also examples of *antimeria* (the use of one part of speech for another, as in the case of 'continental', 16. 1212). There are examples of the closely related *enallage* (the substitution of one case, person, gender, number, tense, or mood for another (as with 'people's mind', 16. 1586). Joyce uses *tautotes* (the repetition of the same idea in different words, as in 'the termination of his *finale*', 16. 1010; cf. 1396–7, 1428–31). He also uses *hysteron proteron* (syntax or sense out of normal or temporal order, as in the case of the man who 'starts a stained by coffee evening journal', 16. 602; cf. 1567, 1614–16). *Catachresis* is everywhere in 'Eumaeus' (the use of words wrenched from common usage; misuse or perversion of a word or term, especially a trope or metaphor: 'boarded', 16. 368; 'spew', 616; 'sublunary', 762; 'spoof', 828; 'unfurl a reef', 919). *Epizeuxis* occurs (emphatic repetition of words or phrases with no other words between them, as in the case of 'Ireland' at 16. 1008). There are examples of three forms of *antanaclasis* (play on the same word): the use of a word in two contrasting and usually comic senses (e.g. 'discharge', 16. 603; 'cape', 902; 'form', 984; 'climax', 1365); the homonymic play or pun ('sea' and 'see', 16. 380; 'caste' and 'cast', 525; 'be' and 'B.', 714); and the repetition of a word with a new signification ('point', 16. 219; 'by', 1501). Joyce also produces Eumaean variations on these figures: forms of repetition that are close but do not quite correspond to the definition of *epizeuxis*; plays on words that look like but are not exactly examples of *antanaclasis*; and so on.

Thus 'Eumaeus' is not merely composed of errors. If 'Ithaca'— as we'll see—is strewn with scientific blunders, 'Eumaeus' is given over to something like a science of blunder. Much of the 'science' in question derives from so-called habits of Irish error. In 'Eumaeus', it would seem, Joyce not only redeems the Irish bull, but transforms it into a cultural phenomenon quite beyond the compass of those who laugh at it; except of course for the fact that the chapter is not a collection of bulls and does not read like one. It would not be hard to extend the list of analogies between Joyce's chapter and the collections of bulls: Kelly's 'bulls' include tall tales, for example, that closely resemble D. B. Murphy's.[93] Nonetheless, however much

---

[93] See e.g. Kelly, *Irish Bulls and Puns*, 34.

of its substance 'Eumaeus' might seem to owe to a science of Irish error, reading it is not like reading Kelly's book. The errors in 'Eumaeus' seldom resemble Kelly's in either tone or texture. Joyce's comic sense is pervasive in the chapter. But it is not that of the court jester. As Joyce surely knew very well, and as theory of the bull from the Edgeworths to Ricks amply demonstrates, the problem with the bull is that, however shrewd or witty, it readily lends itself to being patronized. Still more pointedly, it may express resistance, but not a will to freedom. It outmanoeuvres power, but does not struggle to overcome it and its effects. Thus 'Eumaeus' has to move beyond a science of Irish error. For a more comprehensive and satisfying explanation of Joyce's practice, we need to look elsewhere.

Massacring of English

The reference to Lindley Murray (16. 1475) is important to an understanding of 'Eumaeus'. Murray was a key figure in the nineteenth- and early twentieth-century drive for 'proper English'. He was American, but spent the second half of his life in England, and it was during that time that he published his best-known texts, chiefly his hugely influential *English Grammar* (1795). During the nineteenth century, the book went through nearly fifty editions. Murray's abridgement of the 1816 edition went through 120 editions of 10,000 each. The nineteenth century styled him the father of English grammar. It thought of him as its most effective proponent of good English. Indeed, his name 'became a synonym' or a 'household word' for it (which is clearly what Joyce's reference is playing on).[94] Murray fits neatly into the tradition I have described. Sheridan was an important influence on the *Grammar*, especially the prosody section. Murray acknowledges the debt.[95] Benzie has even argued that parts of Sheridan's work find their widest circulation in Murray's, because Murray adopted them for the *Grammar*.[96] Throughout much of the nineteenth century, Murray's work enjoyed an extraordinary currency, notably in schools, and in some

[94] See *Dictionary of National Biography*, xxxix. 398; Stephen Allott, *Lindley Murray 1745–1826: Quaker Grammarian* (York: Sessions Book Trust, 1991), p. xiii; and Wales, 'Apologies to Lindley Murray', 209.   [95] See Benzie, *Sheridan's Influence*, 117.
[96] Ibid. 96.

of the colonies.[97] In other words, Murray was the principal point for the nineteenth-century dissemination and democratization of the tradition. According to Bernard Jones, 'until well into the second half of the twentieth century', English speakers were dogged by rules of correctness that can be traced back to eighteenth-century prescriptivism, but were disseminated by Murray above all.[98] Editions of Murray's work appeared in Dublin, Belfast, Madras, Calcutta, and Serampore.[99] It was through Murray above all that, during the nineteenth century and well beyond it, correct English grammar was hammered into innumerable young minds, both British and colonial.[100] Dickens connected him with Squeers and Dotheboys Hall. G. Washington Moon wrote of the 'terror' inspired in a schoolboy by Murray's name. For it summoned up the thought of the beatings that came if one failed to master Murray's rules.[101]

In concerning himself with the language, Murray also insistently concerned himself with questions of class. The *Grammar* amply demonstrates how far, for Murray, the best English was associated with the best people. Good usage was exemplified in sentences like 'The king, with his retinue, has just returned from Windsor'.[102] As Wales points out, Murray was also much concerned with questions of morality, 'purity', and 'propriety'.[103] He deliberately introduced examples of 'a moral and religious tendency'.[104] Murray's *Grammar* pervasively demonstrates how far doctrines of linguistic correctness coincided with and reinforced social, religious, and

---

[97] His popularity was at its peak in the 1840s, but he was still being published in the 1890s. See Ingrid Tieken-Boon van Ostade, 'Two Hundred Years of Lindley Murray: An Introduction', in van Ostade (ed.), *Lindley Murray*, 9–25, esp. 16.

[98] 'The Reception of Lindley Murray's English *Grammar*', in van Ostade (ed.), *Lindley Murray*, 63–80, at 78.   [99] See van Ostade, 'Introduction', 10.

[100] See T. S. Omond, *English Metrists in the Eighteenth and Nineteenth Centuries* (Oxford: Oxford University Press, 1907), 78.

[101] *The Bad English of Lindley Murray and Other Writers on the English Language* (London: Hatchards, 1869), 2.

[102] Murray, *English Grammar* (York: Wilson, Spence and Mawman, 1795), 93.

[103] See 'Apologies to Lindley Murray', 211.

[104] See Anon. 'Introduction', in Lindley Murray, *English Grammar, Adapted to the Different Classes of Learners* (Calcutta: School-Book Society's Press, 1831), p. viii. Murray's moralism was puritanical in its severity. He argued, for example, that the theatre gradually weakened 'our abhorrence of immoral indulgences'. See Lindley Murray, *Extracts from the Writing of Divers Eminent Authors of Different Religious Denominations, and at Various Periods of Time, Representing the Evils and Pernicious Effects of Stage Plays* (Philadelphia: Benjamin and Jacob Johnson, 1799), 21.

moral hierarchies and orthodoxies. 'Eumaeus' insistently subverts many of Murray's rules. Wales has shown this in detail.[105] If it is possible to add to her list of points, that merely underlines how comprehensive the subversion is, a point worth stressing in its own right. Murray warns against the use of 'expletives', for example (meaning words that serve as needless padding).[106] Joyce duly introduces them, as in the case of 'identically' (16. 642) or 'odd' (16. 902). Murray tells us that *a weaker assertion or proposition should never come after a stronger one*.[107] Joyce flouts that instruction (as at 16. 11–14, 1604–10). According to Murray, 'where [the] relative particles are out of their proper place', and especially when relative pronouns are separated from their antecedents, we find 'something awkward and disjointed in the structure of a sentence'.[108] Joyce relishes such separations or displacements of pronouns and the 'awkward' effects they produce (as in the case of 'the fact ... that [Parnell] had shared [Kitty O'Shea's] bedroom which came out in the witnessbox', 16. 1372–3, cf. 496–500, 1508–9). Murray writes of the lack of clarity that can result from poorly placed adverbs, specifically in the case of *only, more,* and *at least*.[109] In 'Eumaeus', all three are misplaced, making the sentences in question more awkward (16. 155, 167, 698, 842, 954, 1519, 1529, 1622–3). Joyce's resistance to Murray's rules is characterized by its sedulousness, care, and concentration. Where Murray emphasizes the supreme value of linguistic precision, Joyce both adopts and resists that value. He both precisely notes Murray's instructions and, in producing his own Eumaean imprecisions, precisely reverses them.

Thus the style of 'Eumaeus' hinges on its relation to a prescriptive voice. It ironically and mockingly complies with that voice, whilst also insistently defying it. Murray tells his readers that they should *attend particularly to the use of copulatives, relatives and all the particles employed for transition and connection*.[110] Joyce does this, but for reasons and to ends that are opposed to Murray's. Yet it is important not to overstate Murray's significance for the chapter. If Murray's is the only prescriptive voice that Joyce actually mentions, what is nonetheless at issue in 'Eumaeus' is the whole tradition of 'the language properly so-called' within a colonial politics

---

[105] See 'Apologies to Lindley Murray', 213–15.   [106] *English Grammar*, 201.
[107] Ibid. 207–8.   [108] Ibid. 195.   [109] Ibid. 191–2.
[110] Ibid. 202–3.

of discourse. If Joyce comprehensively resists Murray's rules, it is because 'Eumaeus' so comprehensively resists the tradition to which Murray's book belongs. In the very comprehensiveness of his resistance, like Kelly's jokers, but in a more sustained fashion, Joyce triumphs over power. He everywhere subjects the English language to the very process of corruption that the Victorian and Edwardian linguists so feared. 'Eumaeus' becomes a paradigm of the linguistic abortions and deformations, the loose and careless ways with English that the voices of authority repeatedly proscribed and associated with the provincial and under-educated. We can even find the 'Brummagem sparkle' of foreign phrases in 'Eumaeus' (which actually refers to 'Brummagem', 16. 1002). In a sense, Joyce produces the very linguistic degeneration about which there was so much anxiety in England. More importantly still, he turns corruption and degeneration into meditated practices and conscious skills. He infects 'the neighbouring English' with craft and by design. In 'Eumaeus', the fears of Giraldus Cambrensis are borne out: the pest of treachery spreads like a virus through the English language, sapping its strength. Joyce takes revenge on Swift's and Sheridan's culture in the name of those whom Swift and Sheridan had dubbed the savage Irish. He does so with a flair and invention that rivals and finally surpasses even Swift's.

If, as Joyce claimed, his 'revolt against the English conventions, literary and otherwise' was 'the main source' of his talent, self-evidently, this is nowhere more obvious than in his treatment of the English language.[111] Some of his early readers understood this very well, before the long work of deracinating him began. In England, the early reviewers of *Ulysses* attacked it as much for its violations of linguistic norms as for its obscurity. In this respect, their sense of the politics of Joyce's novel was exact and accurate. Holbrook Jackson exclaimed, for example, that in *Ulysses*, 'all the conventions of organised prose which have grown with our race and out of our racial consciousness ... have been cast aside as so much dross.'[112] Joyce's revolt against the 'conventions' that made for 'good English' is constantly evident in *Ulysses*. Like the end of 'Oxen', 'Eumaeus' is a peculiarly conspicuous instance of it. 'Good English' was associated with an English elite and its power and

---

[111] Arthur Power, *The Joyce We Knew*, ed. Ulick Connor (Cork: The Mercier Press, 1967), 107.   [112] 'Ulysses à la Joyce', *To-Day*, June 1922, in *CH* i. 47–9, at 48.

exclusivity, but also with its aspirations to cultural hegemony. 'Eumaeus' yokes genius to an altogether different form of English. It does so by 'massacring' the language in its 'proper' form. 'Massacring the language': both the phrase and the concept had long been present in English and in Irish life. In an Irish context, however, its overtones were sometimes bleak. In *A Political Anatomy of Ireland* (1691), for example, Sir William Petty expressed the wish to see more English spoken in Ireland. He felt that this might ensure that there was 'no massacring of *English*, as heretofore'.[113] Petty was reviewing the horrors of recent history. But the connection he establishes between questions of language and questions of power, resistance, and revenge in a colonized culture is extremely significant. In one respect, Joyce's position was close to Petty's, in another, remote from it. Violent antagonisms can and must be acted out, pursued and, if possible, resolved symbolically, in the cultural sphere. But this does not mean that there should be no 'massacring of English'. Like the Circean mob casting 'soft pantomime stones' (15. 1902), 'Eumaeus' conducts a form of aestheticized warfare.

[113] *The Political Anatomy of Ireland* (London: D. Brown and W. Rogers, 1691); excerpted in Crowley, *Politics of Language in Ireland*, 88–9, at 88.

CHAPTER TEN

An Aberration of the Light of Reason: 'Ithaca'[1]

Anglo-Irish Science

'Ithaca' is self-evidently concerned with contemporary, scientific discourses. In engaging with them, it also engages with the cultural politics of science in Ireland, and is partly to be understood as Joyce's intervention in that politics.[2] Frank A. J. L. James has asserted that, up to and including the period in question, there was no 'characteristically Irish' science. The scientific institutions existing in Ireland were not home-grown products, and must always be located within the context of a larger, i.e. British scientific activity.[3] The many scientists the British government employed in Ireland were mainly English and Anglo-Irish.[4] From its emergence with Molyneux and the Dublin Philosophical Society in 1684 through its consolidation with the foundation of the Royal Dublin Society and the Royal Irish Academy in the eighteenth century to the establishment of the Royal College of Science in Dublin in the 1860s, Irish science remained very largely an Ascendancy domain. Significant contributions to science were not confined to an elite.[5] There were exceptions: Richard Kirwan, Aeneas

---

[1] For an extended version of this chapter, see my ' "An Aberration of the Light of Reason": Science and Cultural Politics in "Ithaca" ', in Gibson (ed.), *Joyce's 'Ithaca'* (European Joyce Studies, 6; Amsterdam and Atlanta, Ga.: Rodopi, 1996), 133–74.

[2] Criticism has largely ignored this. For an account of the main features of 'Ithaca' criticism up to 1996, see my 'Introduction' to *Joyce's 'Ithaca'*, 3–27.

[3] 'George Gabriel Stokes and William Thomson: Biographical Attitudes towards their Irish Origins', in John R. Nudds et al. (eds.), *Science in Ireland 1800–1930* (Dublin: Trinity College, 1988), 75–96, at 75–6.

[4] See Nicholas Whyte, *Science, Colonialism and Ireland* (Cork: Cork University Press, 1999), 12.

[5] See John R. Nudds et al. 'Preface', in Nudds et al. (eds.), *Science in Ireland*, 4.

Coffey, Nicholas Callan. But a few exceptions do not make for heterogeneity. The notable figures in Irish science and technology up to 1920 were commonly Protestant, sometimes from landowning families, often with connections with the Church of Ireland, London, Trinity, or Belfast.[6] In the first major, book-length study of science and colonialism in Ireland, Whyte has recently asserted, not only that there was 'a comparative dearth of Catholics among Irish scientists',[7] but that there is 'a strong case' for thinking that the Protestant, scientific elite 'at least colluded' in the exclusion of Catholics.[8] Class was always in question. When there was a move to establish a Royal Irish Institute of Science and Art in Dublin in the late 1860s, for example, its proposers were 'leading noblemen and gentlemen, bankers, merchants &c. both in Dublin and the provinces', and the plan was to have the Institute 'placed under the management of noblemen and gentlemen interested in promoting the national weal'.[9]

In general, then, Irish science was dominated by the Protestant aristocracy and gentry. This is nowhere more the case than with astronomy, which undoubtedly helps to explain why it is so important for 'Ithaca'.[10] Along with medicine, astronomy was one of the two sciences to enjoy great success in Ireland in the nineteenth century.[11] This was the period that saw the foundation of the Irish observatories, beginning with Trinity College's Dunsink Observatory in the late eighteenth century. The class background and social provenance of the founders of the observatories were largely aristocratic or genteel.[12] Furthermore, up to the early decades of the twentieth century, like other forms of Anglo-Irish cultural activity, astronomy was very closely connected with England. The driving force behind the establishment of Dunsink was almost certainly not a Trinity figure at all, but Nevil Maskelyne, Astronomer Royal at Greenwich.[13] The most

[6] See e.g. Charles Mollan et al. (eds.), *Some People and Places in Irish Science and Technology* (Dublin: Royal Irish Academy, 1985).

[7] Whyte, *Science*, 6. See also 9–10, 59–62.   [8] Ibid. 7.

[9] *Some Suggestions for the Foundation of a Royal Irish Institute of Science and Art* (Dublin: Waller and Co., 1868), 5, 9.

[10] On 'the Irish astronomical tradition', see Whyte, *Science,* 26–41.

[11] See Susan M. P. McKenna-Lawlor, 'Astronomy in Ireland from the Late Eighteenth Century to the End of the Nineteenth Century', in Nudds et al. (eds.), *Science in Ireland*, 85–96.   [12] See Gibson, 'Aberration of the Light of Reason', 135.

[13] See P. A. Wayman, 'R.A. Brinkley: A New Start', in Nudds et al. (eds.), *Science in Ireland*, 99–104, at 97.

significant figure in the early development of Dunsink was the Revd John Brinkley, a Cambridge man who later became first Royal Astronomer of Ireland. What was true of Irish astronomy was equally true of other forms of Irish scientific activity. Some of the leading figures were actually of English origin. Many were distinguished members of the British Association for the Advancement of Science. Many frequently went to and fro between Ireland and London. In astronomy, at least, the Union seemed indissoluble.

This is strikingly evident in two instances: Robert Ball's *The Story of the Heavens*, and the history of the Armagh Observatory. Whilst hardly overtly political, *The Story of the Heavens* is very much an Ascendancy production and a Unionist text. Ball refers throughout to his work at Dunsink, and gives it as his chief example of 'the Astronomical Observatory'. The book is addressed to an imperial reader. Its main geographical points of reference are Greenwich and London, and it draws largely on English rather than Irish life for its metaphors.[14] It hymns the 'glories' of certain of the 'achievements' of English science.[15] It is aware, too, of the imperial extent of British astronomy, with 'the southern part of the heavens' being covered by various colonial observatories.[16] Irish Catholic culture has no place in it. Much of the political complexion of science in Ireland prior to independence can be gleaned from the history of Armagh Observatory. Begun in 1789, it expressed 'the cultural aspirations of the Anglo-Irish in the epoch of their greatest confidence and ambition'.[17] Grattan had cited literary figures and scientists in legitimation of the Irish nation. The *Transactions* concerning the new observatory accordingly echoed Grattan's concept of nationhood.[18] The driving force behind the establishment of the Observatory was Primate Richard Robinson, a Yorkshireman of wealthy gentry stock who had been educated at Westminster and Christ Church, Oxford. He was notably succeeded by Thomas Romney Robinson, who became president of the British Association for the Advancement of Science and

---

[14] Cf. *The Latest Achievement in Astronomy* (London: Daily Mail Publishing Office, 1904), where Ball asserts that 'we know time in the chalk cliffs of England' (p. 7). It would surely be difficult for most contemporary Irishmen and women to feel properly included in that 'we'.

[15] Sir Robert Ball, *The Story of the Heavens* (London: Cassell and Co., 1901), 325.

[16] Ibid. 27.

[17] See J. A. Bennett, *Church, State and Astronomy in Ireland: Two Hundred Years of Armagh Observatory* (Armagh and Belfast: Armagh Observatory and Institute of Irish Studies, 1990), 4.
[18] Ibid. 1.

the Royal Irish Academy, was unremittingly opposed to O'Connell and Catholic emancipation, and argued that it had been a mistake to admit Catholic students into Trinity. Thomas Robinson was immensely distinguished and influential, and the representative of the Observatory in its finest period. Indeed, as Bennett points out, the fortunes of the Observatory closely parallel, and can indeed be identified with, the fortunes of the Anglo-Irish, their party, and their church. In the late nineteenth century, the Observatory went into decline.[19] Indeed, most of the other Irish observatories closed between 1890 and 1920. Even Dunsink ceased to function for a while. Of course, the reversal in the fortunes of Irish science in the late nineteenth century cannot simply be seen as a consequence of the ebbing of Ascendancy power.[20] The transformation of scientific work and its cost, for example, were also important. But it is nonetheless the case that the growth of Catholic power in Ireland also sees the decline of science as an Anglo-Irish domain. 'Ithaca' itself might partly be thought of as a reflection of the shift in question.

Science and the 'Imperial Mission'

If there were forces making for a decline in Irish science in the late nineteenth and early twentieth centuries, however, other forces tended to resist them. One aspect of the English drive towards the regeneration of the national culture in the period 1880–1920 was a call for the promotion and advancement of British science. That call is audible in 'Ithaca', and the chapter responds to it. In 1902, for example, the Scot R. B. Haldane — a distinguished and powerful member of the 'national efficiency group' — was urging the need for more scientific knowledge. In particular, Haldane asserted that the 'captains of industry' must know more about science if Britain were to preserve its 'great commercial position', and with it the Empire.[21] Part of the problem was that Britain's competitors — the Germans,

[19] On the later history of the Observatory, see Bennett, *Church, State and Astronomy*.
[20] See Tom Hardiman, 'Science Policy', in Phyllis E. M. Clinch and R. Charles Mollan (eds.), *A Profit and Loss Account of Science in Ireland* (Dublin: Mount Salus Press, 1983), 1–21, esp. 3. Cf. Ian Inkster, 'Introduction: Aspects of the History of Science and Science Culture in Britain 1780–1850', in Ian Inkster and Jack Morrell (eds.), *Metropolis and Province: Science in British Culture 1780–1850* (London: Hutchinson, 1983), 11–54, esp. 16.
[21] *Education and Empire: Addresses on Certain Topics of the Day* (London: John Murray, 1902), pp. viii–x.

for example — were providing a superior education in science, and therefore industry. Haldane specified Ireland as one of the 'dark places' in which 'new light' was needed.[22] Indeed, Haldane's *Education and Empire* starts with Ireland, and Arnold on Ireland. So, too, addressing the Educational Science Section of the British Association for the Advancement of Science in Belfast in 1902, its then president, Henry Armstrong, argued that Britain would have to 'refit on scientific lines' if it were to weld the Empire into a coherent whole.[23] Armstrong quoted Arnold's claim that 'the want of the idea of science, of systematical knowledge' was the 'capital want' of 'English education and of English life'.[24] But Armstrong was concerned not simply with the spread of science but also with that of 'scientific method'.[25] He insisted 'that the endeavour [should] be made to inculcate the habits of observing accurately, of experimenting exactly, of observing and experimenting with a clearly defined and logical purpose and of logical reasoning from observation and the results of experimental inquiry'.[26] What mattered was a kind of steeling of the mind through the discipline of science.

Just a year earlier, Karl Pearson had made the same point. Pearson was professor of applied mathematics at University College, London. He was also interested in eugenics, an awareness of which is evident in 'Ithaca', as it is elsewhere in *Ulysses*. In England in the early years of the twentieth century, the drive for 'national efficiency' partly found expression in the eugenics movement.[27] Eugenics seemed especially attractive 'at a time of heightened nationalism, imperialistic competition and social Darwinism', and a social programme of racial improvement through selective breeding had gained currency in certain circles by the turn of the century.[28] Pearson was one of the ablest members of such circles. He thought science could tell people about both British nationhood and 'the best methods of fitting the nation for its task'.[29] For Pearson, 'the law of inheritance' was 'as inevitable as

[22] Ibid. 35.
[23] *The Teaching of Scientific Method and Other Papers on Education* (London: Macmillan, 1903), 71.   [24] Ibid. 11.
[25] Ibid. 1.   [26] Ibid. 8.
[27] See G. R. Searle, *Eugenics and Politics in Britain 1900–1914* (Leyden: Noordhoff International Publishing, 1976), 34.
[28] See Nancy Stepan, *The Idea of Race in Science: Great Britain 1800–1960* (London: Macmillan, 1982), 111–12 and *passim*.
[29] *National Life from the Standpoint of Science* (London: Adam and Charles Black, 1901), 14.

the law of gravity' and a source of progress.[30] It was thus that the superior races came to supplant or control the inferior ones.[31] But having taught us that, science could then equip us the better for the struggle of race against race and nation against nation. This was precisely where 'scientific method' and a training in 'reason', 'exactitude', and 'observation' were crucial. Science produced the man with the trained eye — the prospector, explorer, soldier, commercial adventurer, and even the spy — as required by colonial administrations and the diplomatic service. If the nation were to be 'kept up to a high pitch of external efficiency by contest, chiefly by way of war with the inferior races', then it had to be made '*intellectually* stronger' by the adoption of scientific habits of thought.[32]

Together with Haldane (also a eugenicist) and Armstrong, Pearson was representative in at least one respect: the late nineteenth and early twentieth centuries saw a massive proselytization on behalf of English science. It was inseparable from a specific stage in the politics of Empire. This was the period of 'imperial science', the kind of science with which 'Ithaca' is chiefly concerned. In the late nineteenth and early twentieth century, the British Association for the Advancement of Science (BAAS) became increasingly interested in reconstituting British society to meet new domestic and world conditions. It also argued for a 'reform' of British society involving and even determined by science and scientists. It gave itself an imperial role and exported its models abroad. One of the principal aims of the BAAS was the promotion of 'the intercourse of those who cultivate science in different parts of the British Empire'. This was its 'imperial mission'.[33] The link with Empire had long been true in certain particular cases, like astronomy. The Irish observatories fitted into a worldwide chain of such institutions that spanned the colonial territories. British astronomers claimed, for example, that, in Worboys's phrase, 'the "Southern Skies" ' had been 'annexed to the British Empire'.[34] For many of the members of the BAAS, science was a

---

[30] Ibid. 17.   [31] Ibid. 23.   [32] Ibid. 37, 40, 44.
[33] The term was actually coined later, by O. J. R. Howarth in 1930. See Howarth, 'The Work of the British Association in Relation to the Empire', *Journal of the Royal Society of Arts* 78 (1930), 845; quoted in Michael Worboys, 'The British Association and Empire: Science and Social Imperialism 1880–1940', in Roy Macleod and Peter Collins (eds.), *The Parliament of Science: The British Academy for the Advancement of Science 1831–1981* (Northwood: Science Reviews, 1981), 170–87, at 170.   [34] 'British Association', 171.

metaphor for what Empire might become. The BAAS dwelt on the supposed impartiality of science as something the Empire was bound to agree on, something that would unite it in a common sense of value and purpose. But not everyone saw British science as either neutral or universally valid: when the BAAS met in South Africa in 1905, for example, both Boer politicians and press immediately perceived it as a British and imperial organization.[35]

The BAAS became more and more concerned with encouraging scientific and technical education, largely because of unease at Britain's supposed industrial and economic decline. It also became increasingly involved in the popularization and diffusion of imperial science both at home and abroad.[36] The British Library Subject Index shows that a vast number of science primers, science textbooks, and popular introductions to science and the sciences in England were published during the last decade of the nineteenth and the first two decades of this century.[37] Huge numbers of astronomy primers appeared between 1900 and 1905. The primers frequently share the contemporary concern with utilitarian and commercial justifications for scientific activity and the usefulness of imperial science. Thus Chambers's *Pictorial Astronomy for General Readers*, for instance, assures its readers that astronomy has nothing to fear if 'tested' by commercial and utilitarian standards. For astronomy has made its contribution to accurate timekeeping, and therefore to national efficiency. Astronomers are indisputably important 'to our existence as a busy nation on land and a powerful nation at sea'.[38] Only occasionally is a book of this kind written in Ireland, let alone published there.[39] Insofar as science was circulating in Irish culture early in the century, it was in a London-centred form.[40] It is out of the world of English primers and textbooks that 'Ithaca' in large part emerges. W. M. Hooton's *Preliminary Course of Experimental Science* is a particularly interesting specimen of the literature in

[35] Ibid. 175.
[36] Bernard McGinley points out to me that the BAAS convened in Dublin in 1908.
[37] Cf. Hilary and Dik Evans, *Beyond the Gaslight: Science in Popular Fiction 1895–1905* (London: Frederick Muller Ltd., 1976), 27.
[38] *Pictorial Astronomy for General Readers* (London: Whittaker and Co., 1891), 234.
[39] See e.g. Charles T. Ovenden, *Popular Science for Parochial Evenings* (London: Elliot Stock, 1909). Ovenden was dean of Clogher, canon of St Patrick's Cathedral in Dublin, and rector of Enniskillen.
[40] See e.g. R. A. Gregory and A. T. Simmons, *Introductory Physics for Irish Intermediate Schools* (London: Macmillan & Co., 1901).

question. Hooton was a chemistry teacher at Repton. His book was 'specially written to meet the requirements of the Intermediate Education Board for Ireland'.[41] Hooton hoped that 'the order of presentation adopted, and the selection of questions' would make his book 'especially useful for pupils in Irish Secondary schools'.[42] Much in the 'presentation' is reminiscent of 'Ithaca', like the lists of questions mixed with occasional instructions that were typical of many such books. Above all, however, the book introduces its Irish readers, point by point, to the British Unit of Length, the Imperial Yard, the Imperial Pint, the English standard of area and the British unit of weight. The Irish reader is firmly reminded that the bar that measures the Imperial Yard and the platinum that is the exact measure of the pound avoirdupois are 'kept carefully by the government' in London.[43] He or she is therefore placed as alienated from the source of the relevant knowledge. England appears as the font and origin of exact measurement, Ireland as the place where, at one remove, a limited sense of it may be dutifully acquired.

Catholicism, Nationalism, and 'Technical' Culture

Given both the Anglo-Irish credentials of Irish science and the British proselytization on behalf of 'imperial science' around the turn of the century, one might expect to find an aggressively anti-scientific bent in the Irish cultural nationalism of the period, not least given the nationalists' hostility to what they took to be British pragmatism and materialism. From Thomas Davis onwards, nationalists had associated Anglicization with utilitarianism and industrialism.[44] Certainly, the Catholic Church's attitude to modern science was at best ambiguous. The Church had an acute sense of Irish Catholic civilization as under threat from British materialism and irreligion, and the scientific spirit was deemed to be part of that threat.[45] The Church had long been opposing any assertion of the right of men to exercise their intellectual faculties without restraint.[46] The fear was of

---

[41] See *A Preliminary Course of Experimental Science* (London: W. B. Clive, 1907). The phrase quoted is the subtitle to the book.   [42] Ibid. 1.

[43] Ibid.

[44] See Oliver MacDonagh, *States of Mind: A Study of Anglo-Irish Conflict 1780–1980* (London: Allen and Unwin, 1983), 111.   [45] See ibid. 103.

[46] For evidence, see E. R. Norman, *The Catholic Church and Ireland in the Age of Rebellion, 1859–1873* (London: Longmans, 1965), 195.

'indifferentism or infidelity'[47] (both of which, of course, are important in 'Ithaca'). Modern science seemed to be spreading the 'infection' of rationalism. In 1903 and 1904, the Catholic Parnellite F.
Hugh O'Donnell conducted a fierce polemic against this view,
which he took to be characteristic of the Catholic Ascendancy. The
modern world, said O'Donnell, was one in which science was increasingly important. By contrast, the Catholic Church had always
been intent on perpetuating mystery and obscurantism. This had
been nowhere more the case than with astronomy. For 'the Roman
Inquisition' had laid astronomy 'under anathema' when it
condemned Galileo.[48]

However, there were some signs that parts of the Church could
see the good that might come of scientific modernization. The more
progressive members of the clergy were cautiously sympathetic to
the Co-operative Movement. Initially, the Catholic hierarchy welcomed the establishment of the Department of Agriculture and
Technical Instruction (DATI) in Ireland (of which more in a moment). Nonetheless, there is little evidence of nationalist distrust of
science per se. John Hutchinson even argues that, in some ways,
Irish cultural nationalism took a rather progressive attitude towards
science. Whilst cultural nationalists certainly did look backwards to
what they took to be a traditional culture, they also looked forwards, to a regeneration of the nation through an assimilation of
scientific advance to tradition.[49] In fact, the leading figures in Irish
cultural nationalism in the first two decades of the century were not
exactly opposed to the idea of science or 'technical' instruction and
'technical' progress, to use their terms. Whyte points out that
prominent figures in nationalist politics 'regarded science and/or industry to a certain extent as important parts of their vision of state-
building'.[50] Patrick Pearse was critical of nationalists who prized
the spiritual at the expense of the material. Nationality was partly
material, and 'national freedom' therefore involved 'control of the

[47] Ibid. 253. Norman is quoting the Earl of Mayo.
[48] F. Hugh O'Donnell, *The Blackmailing of Education in Ireland* (London: C. J.
Thynne, 1904), 12. Cf. also O'Donnell, *The Ruin of Education in Ireland and the Irish
Fanar* (London: David Nutt, 1903). Galileo was a political issue for both Protestants and
Catholics. Cf. James J. Walsh, *The Popes and Science: The History of the Papal Relations
to Science during the Middle Ages and down to our Own Time* (London: Catholic Truth
Society, 1912), p. v. See also Gibson, 'Aberration of the Light of Reason', 137 and 147 n. 30.
[49] *The Dynamics of Cultural Nationalism: The Gaelic Revival and the Nation State*
(London: Allen and Unwin, 1987), 251, 253, and *passim*.   [50] *Science*, 15.

material things which are essential to the continued physical life and freedom of the nation'.[51] It was important to pay attention to the wealth-producing processes of the nation, its 'material resources', 'means of transport', and so on. Pearse's letters show he had a lay-man's enthusiasm for science and scientific education. Nationalists actually stressed technical advance as a means to industrial and eco-nomic progress. Early in the century, the Gaelic League committed itself to the principles of technical education and industrial re-vival.[52] So did Sinn Féin. Griffith argued for a major programme of industrialization, and wanted 'a strong middle class' with 'a techni-cal education'.[53] D. P. Moran complained that Irish science, scien-tists, and scientific inventions always seemed to be English inventions.[54] But he also argued the case for modernization, and did not include science in his catalogue of noxious English influences. Like Griffith, he identified 'technical education' with the emerging Catholic middle classes, whom he saw as the natural leaders of social progress.

But the nationalists' commitment to 'technical progress' was also charged with pathos. As *Ulysses* recognizes with amusement, the talk of Ireland's natural resources and the need for industrial renewal was commonly vague. In reality, in terms of scientific and technical cul-ture, Catholic Ireland was chronically deprived.[55] British funding of scientific activity and scientific education in Ireland had steadily de-creased in the late nineteenth century. Between 1871 and 1900, for in-stance, funds for science in Irish schools fell by nearly two-thirds, and the number of boys presenting in science in the Intermediate Exami-nations by more than three-quarters between 1891 and 1899. In 1901 there were only six laboratories in the secondary schools of Ireland. As far as science was concerned, the Irish at the turn of the century were almost wholly unschooled. In 1903, there was 'a dearth of [Irish] science teachers' with 'practical knowledge of experimental work'. Any acquaintance Irish men and women made with science

---

[51] *The Sovereign People* (Dublin: Whelan and Son, 1916), 3, 5. Cf. *The Separatist Idea* (Dublin: Whelan and Son, 1916), at 19.

[52] For a relevant historical context, see Hutchinson, *Dynamics of Cultural Nationalism*, 180.

[53] Ibid. 172. Cf. Tom Garvin, *Nationalist Revolutionaries in Ireland* (Oxford: Clarendon Press, 1987), 113.

[54] See *The Philosophy of Irish Ireland* (Dublin: James Duffy and Co., 1905), 17–18.

[55] Bernard McGinley has reminded me of the industrialization of Ulster. In this as in other respects, the North was a different case.

was likely to be 'theoretical'.[56] Nationalist enthusiasm for science was therefore likely to be abstract and even mystical in tenor. The same cannot be said about Ithacan science, however, and that tells us something important about the chapter.

Plunkett and the DATI

Throughout the 1890s, however, there were calls for better scientific and technical education in Ireland. In 1899, these finally led to the formation of the DATI. Sir Horace Plunkett — well known for his work with the Co-operative Movement and the Irish Agricultural Organization Society (IAOS) — was appointed its vice-president. His progress is informative. Plunkett administered all the grants for science and controlled the scientific institutions in Ireland, including the Royal College of Science. He was in charge of scientific education everywhere but in the universities.[57] The British government established the DATI in response to the perceived lack of adequate provision for science education in Ireland. This was partly to help 'kill Home Rule by kindness': to a large extent, Plunkett made headway because his activities 'fitted in extremely well both with the Irish policy of the British government and with its attitude to the state's role in science'.[58] But Plunkett was dedicated to the work of the DATI. He saw himself as putting the benefits of modern science at the disposal of the Irish. He argued for 'a practical programme of national development' and for 'more advanced economic and scientific methods' in Irish business and industry.[59] He effectively embodied scientific progress in Ireland in the first few years of the century. He was strikingly successful, too. By the end of 1902, 101 permanent and 49 provisional science laboratories had been established in Irish schools. Plunkett's efforts were initially supported by much of the Catholic clergy. The Gaelic League allied itself with him and committed itself to technical education and industrial revival. In his turn, Plunkett wrote of the League as likely to give the Irish the strength of character which would move them 'to industrial or commercial

[56] Graham Balfour, *The Educational Systems of Great Britain and Ireland* (Oxford: Clarendon Press, 1903), 203.

[57] See Trevor West, *Horace Plunkett, Cooperation and Politics: An Irish Biography* (Gerrards Cross: Colin Smythe Ltd., 1986), 63. [58] Whyte, *Science*, 91.

[59] *Ireland in the New Century* (2nd edn., London: John Murray, 1905), 296, 177.

activity'.[60] For a few years, Plunkett seemed to bridge the gap between classes and cultures.

Then, in 1904, he published *Ireland in the New Century*. His intention was to lay out his plans for national development. But he also wanted to argue that the Irish had 'certain defects of character' which were 'economically paralysing' and needed remedying.[61] The trouble lay partly with Catholicism. Plunkett thought that, while Protestantism was closely connected with and sympathetic to the spirit of scientific and industrial progress, Catholicism was not. This was evident from the marked lack of industrial progress in Catholic countries. But the problems in Ireland were also the result of the 'weaknesses' in Irish 'moral fibre'.[62] The Irish had not preserved the qualities 'a modern people must possess if it is to succeed, or even to survive, in the industrial fight'.[63] For all its eminence, Trinity College had had 'but little influence upon the minds or the lives of the people'.[64] The Irish mind was 'warped and diseased, deprived of good nutrition and fed on fancies and fiction'.[65] It was too inclined to whimsy, inconsequence, 'inactivity, or random-thinking'.[66] 'In practical life', wrote Plunkett, 'what is Celtic in us "reacts against the despotism of fact"'.[67] That was why the Irish temperament needed 'a training in science'. For the latter would cultivate the habits of ' "education, observation and reasoning" '.[68] Plunkett was an ingenuous, good-hearted, enterprising man. But he was nonetheless capable of lapsing into a discourse that made him sound close to the scientific and educational reformers and even the eugenicists who were his English contemporaries.

Ireland in the New Century appalled the Catholics and nationalists because it insistently produced this sort of judgement. It was widely seen as 'one prolonged libel on the Irish people'.[69] Nationalism turned against Plunkett and 'technical instruction'. His critics attacked his department and determined to drive him from office. By 1908, he had been forced to retire from the DATI, and nationalism was heading back in the direction of neo-traditionalism and anti-materialism.[70] The progress of the situation, however, was surely inevitable. Plunkett was a Unionist and an aristocrat. His ties were with

[60] *Ireland in the New Century*, 155.   [61] Ibid. 304.   [62] Ibid. 58.
[63] Ibid. 305.   [64] Ibid. 138.   [65] Ibid. 123.
[66] Ibid. 139.   [67] Ibid. 304.   [68] Ibid. 125. Plunkett is quoting Thomas Wyse.
[69] *FJ* (5 Mar. 1904); quoted in West, *Horace Plunkett*, 74.
[70] See Hutchinson, *Dynamics of Cultural Nationalism*, 183–4.

England and the Anglo-Irish establishment. He enthusiastically arranged part of Edward VII's itinerary around the West of Ireland. He was closely connected with the leading figures of the Anglo-Irish Literary Revival: Yeats, Lady Gregory, O'Grady, Eglinton, and Sigerson were all friends. Russell worked with Plunkett at the IAOS, becoming assistant secretary there.[71] Plunkett deplored the effects on Irish national life of what he called 'the exclusion of the landlord and the industrial classes from positions of leadership and trust'.[72] His fate is an exact indication of the political connotations of science and 'technical' progress in early twentieth-century Ireland. In the end, nationalism was bound to have an ambiguous view of science. There was always likely to be a fundamental alienation or *distance* from science within the Catholic community. The interest remained 'theoretical'. This is clearly an important factor in Joyce's practice in 'Ithaca'.

'Ithaca' in Contexts

To some extent, 'Ithaca' shares a vocabulary with many of the texts I have been discussing: terms like 'method' and 'observation' recur in the chapter, as they do in the work of turn-of-the-century scientific thinkers and writers. Joyce was clearly well aware of the contemporary emphasis on imperial science as a training for the mind. He was also aware of selections or collections of 'model pedagogic themes . . . for the use of preparatory and junior grade students' (17. 647–9). 'Ithaca' reflects various concerns evident in early twentieth-century, scientific discourses: the 'utility' of science, for example, and scientific progress as a means to increased efficiency, as when Bloom muses on 'the translation in terms of human or social regulation of the various positions of clockwise moveable indicators' (17. 914–15). That the theme of race or the 'ethnically irreducible' (17. 762) should also

---

[71] Russell's own relationship to the 'technical' world was ambivalent. He was much involved in promoting technical progress and technical education. See e.g. Henry Summerfield, *That Myriad-Minded Man: A Biography of George William Russell 'A.E.' 1867–1935* (Gerrards Cross: Colin Smythe Ltd., 1975), 125. But the very peasant Russell wished to transform he also valued because of his alleged dreaminess and impracticality. Cf. similar incongruities in Russell's interest in 'astro-mysticism' and 'the astro-mystic school of megalithic research'. See Martin Brennan, *The Stars and the Stones: Ancient Art and Astronomy in Ireland* (London: Thames and Hudson, 1983), 30. See also Gibson, 'Aberration of the Light of Reason', 153 n. 42. [72] *Ireland*, 63.

loom large is unsurprising. As we have seen, scientific and racial discourses were sometimes closely related in contemporary English culture. The phrase 'instinct of tradition' (17. 894) calls the eugenicists
to mind, particularly Pearson's theory of the inherited nature of the
social instinct or tribal belonging.[73] Bloom also sounds close to
Pearson when he advocates 'colonial . . . expansion' and 'the evolutionary theories of Charles Darwin' together (17. 1763–4). The alienation of the Irish in English modes of measurement, too, is evident in
the reference to the 'naggin and a quarter' that helps make 'one imperial pint' (17. 312–15). Plunkett's world is in the chapter, too, in the
mention for example of the Irish Model Dairy, which was run by the
DATI (17. 311). Indeed, the very eclecticism or variability of what
purports to be 'scientific' discourse in 'Ithaca' is a reflection of a similar diversity in contemporary culture.[74]

Joyce's awareness of the different aspects of science in Ireland is
crystallized in two passages. The first is the description of Bloom's
fantasy home, his 'country residence' with 'stepped-up' lifestyle
(17. 1497–1615). The passage is a fantasy involving elevation to
'social status among the county families and landed gentry'
(17. 1606–7). It assumes 'ascending powers of hierarchical order' and
ends in the appropriate apotheosis (17. 1608–15). It is only such a
lifestyle, after all — the lifestyle of a gentry with English connections
that is therefore caught in the Robert Ball divide — that could ever
provide one with a 'botanical conservatory' or a glass summer-
house 'equipped in the best botanical manner' (i.e. from the colonies,
17. 1553, 1568), or the luxury and freedom for proper 'contemplation
of the celestial constellations' (17. 1590–1). Joyce indicates the
Anglo-Irishness of a certain kind of science very clearly, here. Significantly, the second passage — the account of resources and industrial
opportunities in Ireland (17. 1698–1743) — comes soon after the
first. Comically, the resources in question turn out to be 'waste paper,
fells of sewer rodents, human excrement possessing chemical properties' (17. 1702–3). Joyce sardonically reminds his reader of the
actual poverty belying the claims of the nationalist 'modernizers'.
He also indicates how far British economic might hugely overshad-
ows any small Irish endeavour (17. 1731–8). On the one hand, then,

[73] See Pearson, National Life, 46–7.
[74] In 1900, science covered a much wider field than it does today. See Evans, Beyond the
Gaslight, 28.

there is a fullness or plenty that belongs elsewhere, with the English and Anglo-Irish. On the other hand, there is a deprivation only poorly masked by rhetoric, whether the latter is belligerent or progressive.

Joyce, of course, has already subjected such rhetoric to ironical treatment, notably in 'Cyclops' (12. 1300–10). In 'Ithaca', he does not so much ironize or parody as *skew* it. He sows it with discrete incongruities or non-sequiturs. Ireland gets muddled with Agendath Netaim (17. 1699–1700), for instance, and the familiar nationalist project of reafforestation with the 'cultivation of orange plantations and melonfields' (17. 1701). The plan for the 'esplanade' begins well, with 'casinos', but loses energy as it progresses to 'readingrooms' and 'establishments for mixed bathing' (17. 1717–18). The 'scheme for the use of dogvans and goatvans for the delivery of early morning milk' hardly seems to hold out the prospect of 'vast wealth' (17. 1719–20). Joyce subjects the nationalist enthusiasm for an Irish revival through 'technical' progress to some affectionate mockery, combined with a feeling for its 'ingenuous insularity' (*Letters*, ii. 164). The scientific or 'technological' aspects of the Bloom Cottage fantasy are likewise skewed. It is hard to imagine, for example, how a 'shaded and sheltered' sundial could possibly do its job (17. 1569). But the dominant emphasis in the passage is on a 'sterile landscape' which combines ludicrous superfluity and 'tepid security' (17. 1598–9). The absurd over-inflation of the fantasy is typified by the 'timekeeper with cathedral chime' (17. 1529), and its unreality and political nullity by the 'agreeable cottagers' fires' nearby (17. 1598).

Testimonial Supermanence

Both these passages bubble with laughter. Yet again, Joyce slyly steers a course between Scylla and Charybdis. 'Ithaca' conducts a sustained assault on science as an English and Anglo-Irish preserve. But it also massively fleshes out the 'theoretical' nature of the nationalist commitment to science, whilst combating the Anglo-Irish conception of Gaelic culture as impractical and dreamy. 'Ithaca' exhibits precisely the 'despotism of fact' to which Englishmen and Anglo-Irishmen like Plunkett thought the Celtic spirit was essentially resistant. Indeed, it comprehensively outbids the likes of Plunkett, demonstrating a range of scientific reference that goes far beyond theirs. The chapter is self-consciously the product of an artist of Irish Catholic stock who knows what copperas is (17. 684), knows that 'psychophysi-cotherapeutics' actually exists and what the term signifies (17. 295), knows that 'equidifferent' means 'having equal differences' or 'arith-metically proportional', and uses it accordingly (17. 71). He knows that the moon was approaching perigee on 16 June 1904 (17. 1043) and that a 'precession of equinoxes' (17. 1048–9) is the earlier occur-rence of the equinoxes in each successive sidereal year. He can bur-lesque the prose style of the psychoanalytic case study (17. 850–63) and the medical report form (871–4). He knows about parallactic drift (17. 1052), contemporary spectroscopy (17. 1104–5), and molecular physics (17. 1061–3). There is often a kind of scientific wit at work in 'Ithaca', as at 17. 317, where the reference to the 'battery of jamjars' is clearly made in the knowledge that the first battery actually connected up a set of Leyden jars.

Joyce contests the assumption that the Irish mind and the scientific spirit are antithetical to one another. But 'Ithaca' also provides a gar-gantuan supplement to the slightness of the nationalist conception of science. This is why the precise use of terms and fine discrimina-tions in meaning are so important, in the chapter. Joyce knows, for example, that 'vertical' is not the same as 'perpendicular', and that the 'fume' from Bloom's 'diminutive volcano' can therefore be both 'vertical and serpentine' (17. 1331–2). He knows that Bloom can suffer from 'concussion' without being knocked out (17. 100). The emphasis is on *technical* correctness. The narrator in 'Ithaca' can be trusted to get the difference between reflection and refraction right, as Bloom could not (17. 267). Indeed, he gives us a host of facts that have so far been missing from the novel. In 'Hades', Bloom notices a bird 'sat tamely perched on a poplar branch'. 'Like stuffed', he thinks to himself. 'Like the wedding present alderman Hooper gave us. Hoo! Not a budge out of him' (6. 949–50). 'Ithaca' explains the 'Hoo!' exactly by telling us what the present was (an owl, 17. 1338–9). The chapter often clarifies matters. It ostentatiously displays its precisions in space and time and its mastery of classifica-tory discourses. It lays strenuous claim to powers of empirical and systematic method — clarity, reason, deliberation, exactitude, obser-vation — whose lack amongst the Irish the Anglo-Irish frequently deplored, and nationalist rhetoric seemed only to confirm. Joyce appears determined to wrest a mode of thought, a set of instruments, and a collection of discourses from the possession of the English and Anglo-Irish and claim them on behalf of his own culture, whilst rebuking that culture for its lack of Joycean pride and Joycean self-assertion.

An Inherited Tenacity of Heterodox Resistance

But if Joyce is concerned to demonstrate a serious command of science, scientific terminology, and scientific discourses, he also travesties and burlesques them, insistently and often hilariously. Some of the scientific-sounding terms in 'Ithaca' are coinages, fake or parodic: 'paraheliotropic' (17. 14), for example; 'aquacities' (17. 240); 'diambulist' (17. 929); 'imprevidibility' (17. 980); 'paraphenomena' (17. 1264); and 'rutilance' (17. 1327). 'Annular cinctures' (17. 1107) is not only unscientific but apparently tautological. Some of the terminology in 'Ithaca' is obsolete: the last recorded use of 'imbalsamation' (17. 913) was in 1803, and 'seminators' (17. 2223) had not been in use since the seventeenth century. The scientific vocabulary in 'Ithaca' is partly comically ersatz, conveying the impression of a narrator whose reach exceeds his grasp, and who therefore has occasionally to make things up as he goes along. Joyce also repeatedly employs scientific terms in more or less unscientific ways. At the turn of the century, the most precise and common sense of 'fluxion' was the one it had in the Newtonian form of the infinitesimal calculus: the rate or proportion at which a flowing or varying quantity increases in magnitude. Joyce merely uses the word to designate the action of flowing (17. 1626). 'Ithaca' also revitalizes the strict, etymological meaning of technical words, as in the case of 'hirsute comets' (17. 1112), which reawakens the derivation of the word from the Greek *kometes*, having long hair. Even more strikingly, Joyce continually calls to mind the unscientific or everyday meaning of scientific terms, 'rescuing' them from the clutches of science, as in the case of 'tangent' (17. 1224) or 'increased and multiplied' (17. 1963). He also thickens and blurs scientific discourse, mixing it with what it usually (and in principle) excludes: the sensory, affective, perspectival, and connotative dimensions to language.

Furthermore, Ithacan science is sometimes plain wrong. 'Facts' like the depth of the Sundam trench turn out to be wilful inventions (17. 186–8). The narrator appears to believe that semen is produced by 'distillation' (17. 2224), no doubt remembering the male genitals as pictured in biological and medical textbooks of the period, which often made them look like stills. The science may also be obsolete, as in the case of Mercator's projection (17. 186). Descriptions may seem casual and prone to error: Bloom's body at 17. 88, for example, is clearly not exactly moving 'freely in space'. Terms are sometimes slightly incorrect: the *OED* says that 'effracted' means 'broken off', for instance (as in 'effracted boughs'), but gives no indication that something (like a nail) might effract *through* something else (like a sock, 17. 1486). Calculations repeatedly go astray, as at 17. 270–1, 17. 447–61, or 17. 2282–3. Does the narrator believe that the earth rotates 'westward' through space, rather than eastward (17. 2308)? Ithacan science is erratic, untrustworthy, delusive. If the rigour of scientific discourse is sedulously maintained, it is also gleefully corrupted.

So, too, the chapter repeatedly introduces a principle of excess into scientific or technical discourse, as with the descriptions of the naming of the parts of the key and the unlocking of the back gate at 17. 1215–19. Scientific discourse becomes a parody of itself, or collapses under its own weight. Measurements abruptly go haywire. The narrator's science is adulterated with quite alien material: superstition, folklore, false belief. Hermetic numerology gets mixed in with astronomy, molecular physics, mathematics, and biology (17. 1058–82). Whilst capable of elaborate mathematical calculations (e.g. 17. 447–61), the narrator also appears to believe that Methuselah lived for 969 years. But science in 'Ithaca' is also supplemented: by metaphor (17. 1331–2), rhythm, alliteration, and rhyme (17. 2–10); by lyricism, as in the case of 'the heaventree of stars hung with humid nightblue fruit' (17. 1039); and by Gothic (17. 1132–6). Scientific discourse is seen or made to fail, to prove less than adequate to its task. We are constantly alerted, for example, to the distance between it and the delicate personal concerns and questions of feeling that flicker through the chapter. Alternatively, little personal quirks and preoccupations get oddly refracted through the technical discourse, as when the advantages to Bloom of 'shaving by night' are made to include 'softer skin if unexpectedly encountering female acquaintances in remote places at incustomary hours' (17. 277–80). Absurd incongruities open up between scientific terms and ordinary concerns, as in the notion of suffering 'with arithmetical progression of intensity' (17. 1089). The tone and manner of 'Ithaca' repeatedly suggest knowledge and clarity where, on close inspection, there is only uncertainty, obscurity, vagueness, and muddle. What on earth is going on, for example, when Stephen and Bloom advance, accept, modify, decline, restate in other terms, reaccept, ratify, and reconfirm their counterproposals (17. 960–1)? As the discourse in 'Ithaca' seeks to establish categories and classifications, so the subject matter resists it, slides out of its formulations, blurs its dividing lines. The scientific discourses likewise frequently give an appearance of reason to what is actually oneiric, speculative, or whimsical logic, disconnected discourse, as in the comparison of Milly and the cat (17. 896–908). 'Ithaca' takes its revenge on imperial science partly in the name of immediate, local life, particular historicity, as when the narrator calculates Bloom's fall, but according to his weight 'as certified by the graduated machine for periodical selfweighing in the premises of Francis Froedman, pharmaceutical chemist' (17. 92–3). But above all, the scientific principle is contained within and transgressed by what, for Joyce, is the larger principle of profound and complex play. Such play may be evident in the minutest detail: the reference to the 'uncondensed milky way' at 17. 1044, or the appearance of an 'angle of inclination' — in the fraction 5 5⁄11 — immediately after Joyce uses the phrase (17. 917–18). One of the best examples of such play is the word 'osculation' (17. 2243), which turns out to be a mathematical and zoological term that not only means 'kiss', but also contains words for mouth (os) and bottom (cul).

If 'Ithaca' tears science from the strangers' grasp, then, it is also another instance of Joyce's 'Celtic revenge', sending science back to the strangers in a twisted or perverted form. Joyce 'masters science' as one of the strangers' preserves, then goes beyond or 'overcomes' it, interrogating its premises and displacing its emphases. He 'taints' scientific discourse with the qualities that Englishmen and Anglo-Irishmen repeatedly associated with the Irish: fancy, inconsequence, random thinking, whimsy, 'darkness of soul'. ('You find my words dark', said Stephen to himself, in 'Proteus', perhaps imagining another exchange with Haines. 'Darkness is in our souls, do you not think?', 3. 420–1.) Yet Joyce's practice goes far beyond Haldane's and Plunkett's — and Haines's — stereotypes. Joyce knew that any adequate resistance to the stranger had to encounter him on his terms. It had to work from within, from a position of expertise, rather than from outside, rhetorically and despairingly. In that respect, again, he ups the stakes for nationalism. He does not seek a feeble separation from the invader's culture. He seeks to register its full force, withstand, match, and ultimately rise superior to it.

An Actuality of the Possible as Possible

The aesthetics of 'Ithaca' are therefore intransigent. But the chapter is concerned, not just with a set of discourses, but with a methodology and ideology underlying them. Both methodology and ideology are amply evident in a host of British science primers and textbooks published between 1880 and 1920. But they are handily summed up in a book in a series highly praised in the *Irish Educational Journal*, A. E. Ikin's *Methods of Science: A Thesis in Logic and Methodology* (1903).[75] Ikin's book is a little compendium of the principles of turn-of-the-century, imperial science. Ikin describes the fundamental principles of scientific research and scientific knowledge, largely by surveying developments (above all, British ones) in a range of scientific fields. For Ikin, science vitally depends on 'exactitude of measurements' and 'accuracy of knowledge'.[76] Quantitative measurements are not yet always possible in all sciences. But they are currently being established 'in various branches of science which at first sight might appear to a non-scientific man as incapable of quantitative measurement, such as for instance Experimental Psychology'.[77] The aim in science must therefore be to make measurability universal; to obtain a unit for every kind of measurable quantity; and to apply the relevant units as and where appropriate. Quantitative exactitude, however, is only the first of three prerequisites in the sciences: the second is knowledge of the degree of certainty of the measurements taken, the limits within which they are true. The third is completeness of knowledge.

Along with these prerequisites go various methodological imperatives. Definition is one of them. Without 'definite questions', the scientific enquirer can hardly so much as start.[78] Terms must be definite, too. It is only on the basis of definite terms that we can 'reason step by step with rigid logicality'.[79] Units must also be exactly defined. Vagueness is unacceptable. The second imperative is what Ikin calls

[75] *Methods of Science: A Thesis in Logic and Methodology* (London: Normal Correspondence College Press, 1903). The puff is on p. 90.   [76] Ibid. 6–7.
[77] Ibid. 7.   [78] Ibid. 85.   [79] Ibid. 31.

'*consistency with fact*', the very criterion 'of the truth or validity of knowledge'.[80] Reason in science must proceed from 'facts of Nature', not from authority or 'the products of the imagination'.[81] Thirdly, there must be accuracy in observation. The scientist works by experiment, and must guard against any errors made 'through some bias of mind'.[82] Fourthly, science always *makes decisions*. It decides between more and less probable, convincing, and valid hypotheses.[83] Finally, on the basis of experiment and observation, the scientist formulates general laws. These laws represent the 'completeness of knowledge' at which science aims. For it constantly advances towards the ideal of a full and accurate knowledge 'of all the relationships of the inter-related elements of the Unity of Nature'.[84]

Ikin's conception of science is paradoxical: scientific method moves inductively, from analysis to synthesis. But it does so in order to formulate general laws whose existence it has taken for granted from the start. The paradox is unsurprising: imperial science assumed it was increasingly 'stating' the 'universal laws of nature'.[85] Explanation 'is only possible or intelligible on the assumption that Nature is a systematic unity'.[86] 'Something unknown', writes Ikin, 'wants expressing in terms of things known'.[87] He cannot imagine that the unknown might require expression in terms that are incommensurable with the known and specific to itself. The politics of such blindness — evident everywhere in the discourses of imperial science — must have been self-evident to Joyce. Accordingly, 'Ithaca' travesties the very methodology to which Ikin is so committed. For instance: because Nature is a systematic unity, says Ikin, science must be systematic. Hence the importance of the practice of classification to 'complete knowledge'. The divisions into classes must be on one basis only. No object can belong to two classes at once. But the point about the 'catalogue' of Bloom's books (17. 1362–1407), for example, is that it does not proceed on a single basis. Joyce plays the system of the catalogue off against the unsystematic nature of his list, which provides heterogeneous kinds of detail. Here there is no singular foundation for knowledge at all.

Like Pearson, Ikin is obsessed with measurement: more and more precise measurements of more and more kinds, spreading into an

---

[80] Ibid. 11.   [81] Ibid. 12.   [82] Ibid. 45.
[83] Ibid. 55.   [84] Ibid. 60.   [85] Ibid. 69.
[86] Ibid. 73.   [87] Ibid. 72.

increasing number of fields. Measurement spreads everywhere in 'Ithaca', too. It spreads into fields, like psychology and the emotions, to which it seems alien, but where Ikin hoped to see it flourish. In 'Ithaca', the lunacy of such a project is made laughably self-evident. There is likewise a comedy of numbers in the chapter, as at 17. 1777–8. The deadpan precisions to measurements are often farcical (as in the case of the 'chart of the measurements of Leopold Bloom compiled before, during and after 2 months' consecutive use of Sandow-Whiteley's pulley exerciser', 17. 1815–19). Ikin articulates a turn-of-the-century dream of life made reducible to quantitative description. 'Ithaca' functions partly as a ludicrous realization of that dream. Exactitude becomes outrageously comic. In giving the longitude and latitude of Bloom's and Molly's positions in the bed (17. 2303–5), the narrator also describes what Ikin calls 'the *exact* relationship' between two of 'the various elements in the system of nature'.[88] But far from aiding our understanding, such exactitude tells us nothing about the charged relationship in the bed in question.

What is missing at such moments in 'Ithaca' is a principle of thought that was intrinsic to imperial science. Ikin dwells on the importance of analogy or 'apparent resemblance' for scientific hypothesis. Joyce establishes analogies only to let them comically collapse, or founder into ambiguity or confusion, as at 17. 896–908. The 'common ground' necessary for the analogy to work is lacking. 'Ithaca' likewise both acknowledges and comically betrays the aspiration to complete knowledge or what Ikin calls 'exhaustiveness'.[89] The account of 'the alterations effected in the disposition of the articles of furniture' in Bloom's house produces an impression of exhaustiveness (17. 1279–90). In fact, however, the reader cannot reconstruct the scene with any precision. The passage gives us no ground or fixed point of reference which would make that possible. Where Ikin insists on precise definitions, too, Joyce subverts them. The scientific 'definition' to the questions in the chapter is often incongruous or comically redundant, as when the questioner asks whether Bloom and Stephen's 'views' were 'on some points divergent' (17. 27). In any case, the precise definition of units frequently serves only as the basis for inappropriate and erroneous calculations. Ikin wants to eliminate error and abhors vagueness. 'Ithaca' revels in both. Ikin

---

[88] *Methods of Science: A Thesis in Logic and Methodology* (London: Normal Correspondence College Press, 1903), 69.   [89] Ibid. 76.

dwells on the importance of consistency between scientific reason and natural fact. Joyce leaves us uncertain about the 'natural facts' alluded to by his 'scientific' discourse, and opens up inconsistencies between scientific mode and mundane content. Ikin argues for observation cleansed of any 'bias of the mind'.[90] Joyce introduces bias into or draws attention to bias in observation, as at 17. 1003–4. Where Ikin sets a premium on decidability in scientific method, Joyce stresses undecidability or the double or multiple aspects of objects. It is impossible to know exactly what the departure of the cat at 17. 886–8 is actually 'contemporaneous' with. For Ikin, science can have no truck with imagination. Joyce continually infects the first with the second, with conceits or witty, bizarre, and comic speculations, as at 17. 1086–1100. 'General laws' count for little in 'Ithaca': here the 'law of the conservation of energy' is hardly scientific at all (17. 842). Ikin seeks the expression of the unknown in terms of the known. 'Ithaca' proceeds 'from the known to the unknown' (17. 1013). It opens *Ulysses* itself up to (yet) more incertitude. The 'sham crown Derby' in 'Calypso' (4. 283–4) would seem to be real in 'Ithaca' (17. 300). Real or sham, we shall never know the truth.

Joyce therefore mocks the triumphalism of imperial science, its confident certainties, the assurance with which it claims to be proceeding to a final conquest of the world. He resists its efforts to present what is particular to it as universal. He fiercely rejects the premiss without which imperial science cannot function: the conviction that there is or can be a singular foundation for knowledge. In this respect, at least, he has something in common with the Lyotard of *The Differend*. The answers imperial science finds are already implicit in the questions that it asks. 'Ithaca' repeatedly produces parodic versions of this circular logic, as at 17. 569–70. It is much concerned with exposing imperial science as both a rhetoric and a limited, historically contingent form of knowledge. Joyce was acutely conscious of the historical and cultural specificity of the discourses of imperial science. As Avrom Fleishman has remarked, the science of 'Ithaca' is that of the period and culture in which the novel is *set*.[91] Yet Joyce, of

---

[90] Ibid. 46.
[91] 'Science in "Ithaca" ', *Wisconsin Studies in Contemporary Literature* 7 (1967), 377–91. Alan J. Friedman points out that the astronomical terms in 'Ithaca' are 19th-cent. ones. See '*Ulysses* and Modern Science', in Bernard Benstock (ed.), *The Seventh of Joyce* (Brighton: Harvester, 1982), 198–206, at 201. Cf. S. B. Purdy on the science in *Finnegans Wake* in 'Let's Hear what Science has to Say: *Finnegans Wake* and the Gnosis of Science',

course, was also aware of the new developments in modern European science at the time he was writing *Ulysses*. His own intellectual world was more that of Einstein, Heisenberg, and Planck than Sir Robert Ball.[92] If the new science makes little or no explicit appearance in 'Ithaca', it also pervades it.[93] The chapter repeatedly emphasizes 'fluctuating incertitude' and split or 'distinct different' views of things (17. 503, 557). Joyce draws our attention to the relativity of measurements in time, as at 17. 91–9. But in 'Ithaca', the new science is chiefly evident in a practice, as a mode of consciousness, a relativizing habit of thought which is what makes Joyce so alert to the historical contingency of imperial science. In other words, Joyce surely saw that contemporary relativity theory raised important questions for any conception of the fixity of the actual. To think relativistically is to keep potentiality always in mind and to preserve its power. Such thought imagines what might have come into being, but did not. But it also imagines what has not yet come into being. It conceives of the latter as distinct and *sui generis*, as still to be created and irreducible to the terms of present actuality. According to such thought, any given system of knowledge like imperial science is only 'an actuality of the possible as possible' (2. 67). As 'the masters of the Mediterranean are fellaheen today' (7. 911), so imperial science is doomed to decay. Indeed, it was already effectively decaying by the time Joyce was writing 'Ithaca'. The chapter, again, is a vandal's scrawl over a crumbling ruin.

The theme of actuality and possibility is everywhere in 'Ithaca'. The narrator frequently dwells on what did not come to pass, like the 'topical song' Bloom did not complete (17. 417–23; cf. the various possible 'advantages' mooted at 17. 935–9). It is potentiality that interrupts the account of the relation between Stephen's and Bloom's ages. The purity of hypothesis increasingly prevails over real calculations, and twists them out of true (17. 447–65). The 'imaginary' constantly threatens to assume the same status as the 'real' (17. 387, 433). The possible weakens the actual, makes it ambivalent, spectral. Joyce opens up a given, limited historical 'knowledge' to the pressure

in Benstock (ed.), *Seventh of Joyce*, 207–17; esp. 207–8; and Alan David Perlis on 'Ithaca' and the Newtonian world-view in 'The Newtonian Nightmare of *Ulysses*', in Benstock (ed.), *Seventh of Joyce*, 191–7. See also Gibson, 'Aberration of the Light of Reason', 172 n. 46.

[92] But see also Friedman, '*Ulysses* and Modern Science', 198–201.
[93] See also ibid. 202.

exerted by 'the incertitude of the void' (17. 1014–15). That pressure is a principal article of political faith. If Joyce both embraces and resists the 'despotism of fact', he also both embraces and resists the despotism that, at a given time and in a given culture, decrees the very nature of factuality itself. To contemporary scientists, imperial science must have seemed securely lodged in the room of the infinite possibilities it had ousted. Joyce takes his revenge on it in the name of potentiality. 'Ithaca' refuses to be 'fettered' and 'branded' (2. 50). It is in this refusal that the politics of the chapter is at its most powerful and assumes its largest dimensions.

CHAPTER ELEVEN

The End of All Resistance: 'Penelope'

Guns Guns Guns

Why does Joyce give Molly Bloom a childhood and youth specifically in Gibraltar? The Rock had apparently no personal significance for Joyce, and he never visited it. So why does Gibraltar figure so significantly in the closing pages of *Ulysses*? With one or two notable exceptions, like Susan Bazargan,[1] critics have seldom addressed this question. As Bazargan indicates, however, one principal issue is clearly Gibraltar's status as a British colony; a colony, moreover, where, because of the relative smallness of the place and the concentration of its armed forces, the British presence was uniquely conspicuous. However, the generality of 'colonial status' tells us too little. In fact, it was only from 1830 that Gibraltar was officially dubbed a colony, as opposed to a garrison, or simply a fortress.[2] In the late nineteenth and early twentieth centuries, it was probably best described as a 'military colony' or a colony 'grafted on' to a fortress.[3] Gibraltar was (and still is) a colonial possession with a very particular history and very particular political, military, and symbolic functions. It has attracted a highly specific set of discourses. These were not lost on the Irish. Indeed, Gibraltar has a history of relations with Ireland, and Joyce was clearly aware of some of them, and the inflections they were acquiring in the period 1880–1920.

Britain first became interested in possessing a base in or around the Straits of Gibraltar in the early seventeenth century. To start with, the

---

[1] 'Mapping Gibraltar', in Richard Pearce (ed.), *Molly Blooms: A Polylogue on 'Penelope' and Cultural Studies* (Madison: University of Wisconsin Press, 1994), 119–38.

[2] See Tito Benady, *The Gibraltar Police* (Gibraltar: Mediterranean Sun Publishing Co., 1980), 10.

[3] Capt. Fred. P. Warren, *Gibraltar: Is It Worth Holding? and Morocco* (London: Edward Stanford, 1882), 4–5.

principal concern was probably the protection of trading interests. But so, too, was power in the Mediterranean, the possibility of a Protestant stronghold in Catholic territory.[4] According to one of Joyce's sources, Cromwell saw the advantage of taking Gibraltar as early as 1656.[5] But its military significance dates from the War of the Spanish Succession. The area surrounding the Straits was an important factor in the struggle between Protestant William of Orange and Catholic Louis XIV, supporter of James II and the Old Pretender.[6] The British presence in Gibraltar dates from 1704. This was the very year that saw what one of Joyce's sources calls that great English 'triumph', Marlborough's 'dissipation', at Blenheim, of Louis XIV's dream of 'universal empire'.[7] When Spain formally ceded Gibraltar to Britain in the Treaty of Utrecht (1713), it was as an explicit concession to the legitimacy of Protestant power and the Protestant succession in England.[8] In effect, by the late 1720s, Gibraltar had become identified with the cause of the Protestant nation.[9] George I repeatedly linked them.[10]

In England, Gibraltar therefore assumed an almost sacred status. In spite of this, throughout the eighteenth century and after, ministries and ministers (Stanhope, Pitt the elder, Townshend, Shelbourne) kept on trying to give it back to Spain.[11] Such efforts, however, were always fiercely resisted by both the Commons and 'the multitude', to whom it remained 'an object of political importance'.[12] This importance was magnified by the various sieges of Gibraltar, notably the Great Siege (July 1779–March 1783), in which the Rock was very obviously still a Protestant garrison, a fact made clear by the presence of Hanoverian Regiments alongside British

[4] See Sir William G. F. Jackson, *The Rock of the Gibraltarians: A History of Gibraltar* (Grendon: Gibraltar Books Ltd., 1987), 76–81.
[5] Frederic J. Stephens, *A History of Gibraltar and its Sieges*, with photographs by J. H. Mann (London: Provost & Co., 1870), 221–2.
[6] See George Hills, *Rock of Contention: A History of Gibraltar* (London: Robert Hale & Co., 1974), 159; and cf. Stephens, *History of Gibraltar*, 224.
[7] Anon., *Gibraltar and its Sieges* (London: Thomas Nelson & Sons, 1879), 9. For Joyce's use of this source, see Phillip F. Herring (ed.), *Joyce's 'Ulysses' Notesheets in the British Museum* (Charlottesville, Va.: University Press of Virginia, 1972), 69–71.
[8] See Article X of the Treaty of Utrecht, in Jackson, *Rock of the Gibraltarians*, 333–4.
[9] Hills, *Rock of Contention*, 280.
[10] See Capt. Sayer, *The History of Gibraltar and of its Political Relation to Events in Europe* (London: Saunders, Otley & Co., 1862), 177.   [11] See ibid. 151.
[12] John Drinkwater, *A History of the Late Siege of Gibraltar* (London: T. Spilsbury and Son, 1790), 45. Cf. Jackson, *Rock of the Gibraltarians*, 120. Joyce would have known this from Stephens, *History of Gibraltar*, 278–9.

ones.[13] Gibraltar was subsequently important in the Peninsular War and the Napoleonic Wars: HMS *Victory* was towed to Gibraltar after Trafalgar. Otherwise, however, throughout the nineteenth century, the Rock enjoyed a period of uninterrupted peace. Yet its military significance also steadily grew: it became a key point in the administration, expansion, and patrolling of the Empire, a starting point for forays into Africa, India, the Near and Far East, and the Mediterranean itself.[14] It was a major link in a 'chain of fortresses' that spanned much of the globe.[15] Above all, however, historians and commentators — including those Joyce read — almost invariably emphasize the sheer awesomeness of the fortifications in nineteenth-century Gibraltar, the sheer number and sophistication of its gun emplacements.[16] This armed might was strengthened throughout the century.[17] Joyce was well aware of it. 'Guns guns guns', he wrote, in the 'Penelope' notesheets.[18] He noted the phrase in Field,[19] where he no doubt also noted the rousing quotation from 'The Charge of the Light Brigade' that followed it.

At the turn of the century, nearly a quarter of the population of Gibraltar was military. Joyce's copy of the *Gibraltar Directory* would have told him of this.[20] He would also have known that the Rock was notable for its military memorials and graveyards, especially for the Trafalgar dead. To some extent, the government of Gibraltar was characterized by its military strictness. From the Treaty of Utrecht onwards, however, British rule in Gibraltar was unusually tolerant in religious matters.[21] The authorities also frequently seemed indulgent

[13] See Anon., *Gibraltar and its Sieges*, 45. See also Capt. John Spilsbury, *A Journal of the Siege of Gibraltar 1779–1783* (Gibraltar: Gibraltar Garrison Library, 1908), 117, 138; and Jackson, *Rock of the Gibraltarians*, 153. The sense of the Protestant heritage was preserved in names like 'Prince Orange's Battery'. See S. Ancell, *A Circumstantial Journal of the Long and Tedious Blockade and Siege of Gibraltar* (Liverpool: Charles Wosencroft, 1784), 198, 226.
[14] This is brought out, e.g., in Henry M. Field's *Gibraltar* (London: Chapman and Hall, 1889), 35.
[15] See e.g. Richard Ford, *A Handbook for Travellers in Spain* (2 vols., 4th edn., London: John Murray, 1869), ii. 127–8. The 'chain' included Malta, Aden, and Bombay.
[16] See esp. Anon., *Gibraltar and its Sieges*, 25–30. Cf. e.g. Dorothy Ellicott, *Our Gibraltar* (Gibraltar: Gibraltar Museum Committee, 1975), 110.   [17] Ford, *Handbook*, i. 127.
[18] Herring (ed.), *Joyce's 'Ulysses'*, 512.   [19] *Gibraltar*, 23.
[20] Cavendish Boyle and R. Bandury, *Gibraltar Directory and Guidebook* (Gibraltar: Garrison Library Printing Establishment, 1902), 29.
[21] See Article X, in Jackson, *Rock of the Gibraltarians*, 333–34; and R. Montgomery Martin, *Possessions in Europe: Gibraltar*, introd. Anthony A. D. Seymour (Gibraltar: Gibraltar Books Ltd., 1998), 7.

towards smuggling and petty crime.[22] But at the same time, from the
Treaty, which excluded Jews and Moors from Gibraltar, through the
Alien Act of 1873 to the Aliens Order and Strangers' Ordinance of
1900, policy regarding 'aliens' and immigration was draconian.[23]
The period 1880–1920 saw a marked expansion of Gibraltar as a
military base. The naval dockyard and port were built, transforming
both the Rock and its economy. At the same time, Gibraltar also
experienced its first outbreaks of industrial unrest, and even occasional riots.[24] For the first time, the power of the 'masters of the
Mediterranean' (7. 911) over the Rock was challenged from within.
The fact is more than incidentally relevant to 'Penelope'.

I have dwelt at some length on the history of Gibraltar because it
looms large in everything Joyce read about the place. But the history
of Gibraltar was itself a discursive phenomenon. It was reflected in a
historiographical tradition. It existed as a quite unusually coherent
and homogeneous set of discourses. The mainstream consisted of
the major historical accounts of the Rock and its sieges: James,
Spilsbury, Ancell, Drinkwater, Congreve, Gardiner. Joyce would have
known about most of these, though probably only at second-hand.
Then came the descriptions of Gibraltar in popular, nineteenth-
century guides to Spain, like Ford's and O'Shea's. Joyce would have
known of the first of these. He read and used the second.[25] From
these guides, the tradition continued into twentieth-century volumes
like those Joyce consulted: Henry M. Field's *Gibraltar*, Frederic G.
Stephens's *A History of Gibraltar and its Sieges*, the 1902 *Gibraltar
Directory*, and the anonymous *Gibraltar and its Sieges*.[26] The discourse in question has two conspicuous features. First, of course, it is
preoccupied with military themes. From James and Spilsbury to the

[22] See Field, *Gibraltar*, 117–18. For criminal activities involving the mail in particular, see Richard J. M. Garcia and Edward B. Proud, *The Postal History of Gibraltar 1704–1971* (Heathfield: Postal History Publications 1998), *passim*. Cf. Bloom's reference to crooked dealings in Gibraltar at 4. 64–5, 68.

[23] See Philip Dennis, *Gibraltar and its People* (London and Newton Abbot: David and Charles, 1990), 25; Warren, *Gibraltar*, 4; and Boyle and Bandury, *Gibraltar Directory*, 65–6.   [24] See Benady, *Gibraltar Police*, 17–20.

[25] According to Herring (ed.), *Joyce's 'Ulysses'*, 72.

[26] On Joyce's use of these sources, see ibid. 69–72; and James Van Dyck Card, *An Anatomy of 'Penelope'* (London and Toronto: Associated University Presses, 1984), 22–30. Field was American, but his book is nonetheless a fulsome tribute to imperial, British power. It makes substantial use of the earlier histories and clearly belongs to the his-toriographical tradition I have described. Field's book is 'for the most part loyal, and where it is not, it describes [Gibraltarian] scenery' (CW, 97).

present day, most of the substantial histories of Gibraltar have been written by military men and are packed with military detail. Thus the literature of Gibraltar reflects its history. Any reader is made constantly aware of a British military presence: soldiers, armaments, military exercises, parades, drills, and, above all, guns. Secondly, the discourse has an ideological content evident in the accounts not only of Gibraltar's recent but also of its pre-colonial and even ancient history. For the anonymous author of *Gibraltar and its Sieges*, for example, the Pillars of Hercules are 'the proud memorials' of Hercules's 'westward conquest'.[27] The historians repeatedly construct Gibraltar as portentously central to matters of great historical moment.[28] More specifically, they make it the site of titanic, imperial struggles for power and domination, with the conflict between the Spanish and the Moors anticipating that of the modern European nations. Gibraltar thus becomes a symbol of 'the victory of the Christians over the infidel'.[29] It is the symbolic point at which civilized, Protestant Europe holds Barbary at a distance, 'in constant awe of us'.[30]

The principal emphases of this historical discourse were patriotic, triumphalist, and, from the early nineteenth century, imperial. The Rock was a very important symbol of national pride.[31] It was a focal point for 'heroic memories',[32] the proverbial paradigm of political and military strength.[33] It was the very image of the proud, indomitable, unflappable, tenacious character of the British which so suited them for Empire. 'The spirit of Britons is unparalleled [*sic*]', proclaimed Ancell, 'no superiority of power will make them yield'.[34] 'British officers maintain that Gibraltar cannot be taken by all the powers of Europe combined', wrote Field, enthusiastically.[35] Gibraltar, he claimed, was the place where 'the British lion roars loudest'.[36] He was merely repeating a well-established refrain. The

---

[27] *Gibraltar and its Sieges*, 118.

[28] For a representative example, see H. W. Howes, *The Story of Gibraltar* (London: Philip & Tracey Ltd., 1946), 14.

[29] Henry O'Shea, *Guide to Spain and Portugal* (Edinburgh: Adam and Charles Black, 1848), 150.

[30] Lt.-Col. Thomas James, *The History of the Herculean Straits, Now Called the Straits of Gibraltar* (2 vols., London: Charles Rivington, 1771), ii. 112.

[31] For an 18th-cent. example of the investment of 'national vanity' in Gibraltar, see Sayer, *History of Gibraltar*, 319.   [32] Field, *Gibraltar*, 109.

[33] This was the case not only in English but, as the English ironically noted, also in French.   [34] *Circumstantial Journal*, 146.

[35] *Gibraltar*, 124.   [36] Ibid. 26.

Great Siege was central to the mythology in question. It had been one of the foremost 'among the brilliant episodes of [British] military history'.[37] It had also been a struggle between Protestants and 'bigoted' Catholics,[38] with the Rock emerging as a triumphant symbol of continuing Protestant power.[39] If Gibraltar was a symbol of resolution, as such, it stood opposed to all the doubters and the faint-hearted, especially those who wanted to give it back.[40] It was a popular symbol. After all, it had been kept in British hands by the sheer power of the people's will.[41] Even the sceptics had to grant this: 'Woe be to the man who denies the public gods', wrote Warren, ruefully, having tried to argue for the Rock's return.[42]

But as Joyce would have known, it was an Anglo-Irishman who, in the late eighteenth century, provided a much-quoted, patriotic (and indeed Unionist) expression of the symbolic value of Gibraltar. For Burke, Gibraltar was 'a post of power, a post of superiority — one which makes us invaluable to our friends and dreadful to our enemies'. Field gives the phrase, and then comments:

Not an Englishman passes through the Straits whose heart does not swell within him to see the flag of his country floating from the top of the Rock, from which, as he believes, the whole world cannot tear it down. Every true Briton would look upon the lowering of that flag as the abdication of Imperial power.[43]

In the nineteenth century, the Rock also became a symbol of 'the superiority of the British at sea'.[44] The very name of the Bay of Gibraltar had become resonant. For it was 'associated with the names of Rodney, and Howe, and Nelson, and Collingwood'.[45] Gibraltar was now closely linked to Trafalgar. The two place names were sometimes even hyphenated. By the late nineteenth century, too, the

---

[37] Anon., *Gibraltar and its Sieges*, 25.   [38] Ibid. 62.

[39] For a long time, the enemy of British interests on Gibraltar was deemed to be Catholicism at least as much as Spain. The Great Siege was cast as a struggle between 'their Catholic and Britannic majesties'. See e.g. Field, *Gibraltar*, 8. Stephens notes the significance of Gibraltar in conflicts between Protestant and Catholic nations. See *History of Gibraltar*, 218–23.

[40] See e.g. Drinkwater, *Late Siege*, 9.45; Hills, *Rock of Contention*, 280; Sayer, *History of Gibraltar*, 151; Stephens, *History of Gibraltar*, 240, 278; and General Sir William J. Codrington, *Gibraltar and Ceuta* (London: Edward Stanford, 1882), 14–15.

[41] See e.g. Boyle and Bandury, *Gibraltar Directory*, 'Historical Notes', 9.

[42] *Gibraltar: Worth Holding?*, 7.   [43] *Gibraltar*, 120.

[44] Anon., *Gibraltar and its Sieges*, 15. Foreigners, particularly French and Spanish, were quoted in support of this view. See e.g. ibid. 48.   [45] Ibid. 38.

emphasis on Gibraltar as a symbol of undaunted tenacity had a new urgency, a prospective as well as a retrospective value. It was now linked symbolically to boundless ambition, the thought of 'commerce illimitable' and 'the gate-pillars of all knowledge'.[46] At the same time, around the turn of the century, in a period of anxiety over the long-term future of the Empire, the Rock was also 'a symbol of power which we cannot relinquish without disgrace',[47] a figure for an imperial grip which the British could not afford to loosen.

This change in emphasis is also reflected in the literary significance of Gibraltar. In the earlier nineteenth century, there was some relaxation in the discourse I have just described. The Rock became a subject for fiction. Colonel E. B. Hamley wrote tales of comic romance for *Blackwood's*, like 'A Legend of Gibraltar' and 'The Jew's Legacy'.[48] A Major Hort published a whimsical, sub-Landorian collection of 'legends, narratives and songs' of Gibraltar, complete with music.[49] Later in the century, the literary concern with Gibraltar expanded in scope, but also hardened back into older forms. Arnold wrote of 'Gibraltar's cannoned steep' in terms which made it central to the business of Empire.[50] Tennyson linked the Straits of Gibraltar to stubborn persistence, heroic endeavour, the insatiable will to push out further into the world.[51] Browning fulsomely celebrated the great, historic sites of southern Spain (' "Here and here did England help me, — how can I help England? — say" ').[52] At the end of the century, with the emergence of the new cultural nationalism, Browning's kind of emphasis grew still more pronounced. Mary Anderson provided a generalized, diffuse confirmation of colonial ideology in *Tales of the Rock*.[53] G. A. Henty vigorously beat the patriotic drum

---

[46] Stephens, *History of Gibraltar*, 12.   [47] Anon., *Gibraltar and its Sieges*, 112.

[48] See 'A Legend of Gibraltar', *Blackwood's Magazine*, vol. 70/5 (Nov. 1851), 522–43; and 'The Jew's Legacy: A Tale of the Siege of Gibraltar', vol. 70/6 (Dec. 1851), 648–69.

[49] *The Rock* (London: Saunders and Otley, 1839), p. xi.

[50] In 'A Southern Night', first published in *Victoria Regia* (1861). See *The Poems of Matthew Arnold*, ed. Kenneth Allott, 2nd edn. by Miriam Allott (London: Longman, 1979), 496–500, at 496 (l. 23). The poem is about Arnold's brother, who had died in Gibraltar on his way back from service in India. The line provides the epigraph to Anon., *Gibraltar and its Sieges*.

[51] *The Poems of Tennyson*, ed. Christopher Ricks (London: Longman, 1989), 560–4, esp. l. 63 and Rick's note.

[52] 'Home Thoughts from the Sea'. See *The Poems of Browning*, ed. John Woolford and Daniel Karlin, ii. *1841–1846* (London: Longman, 1991), 247 (l. 5).

[53] *Tales of the Rock* (London: Downey & Co., 1897).

in *Held Fast for England: A Tale of the Siege of Gibraltar*.[54] J. Edwin Barton's Newdigate Poem of 1897, 'Gibraltar', presented Gibraltar as bidding the English 'look forward' to still greater imperial triumphs.[55] In the late nineteenth century, discourses on Gibraltar were also likely to be explicitly racist: 'We do not seek to denationalize the aborigines [of Gibraltar]', wrote Gilbard in 1888, 'whether men or monkeys'.[56] Of course, the 'natives' had long been demeaningly known as the 'scorpions' or 'rock-scorpions'.[57]

The symbolism of Gibraltar as imperial British and Protestant stronghold was clear enough to Irish minds. It was also vividly present in Irish memories, often for depressing reasons. The British seized Gibraltar at the time when, following the defeat of James II, the wild geese were flocking to France and Spain. The forces that James's natural son the Duke of Berwick led against Marlborough and others contained many Irish soldiers.[58] But the Irish presence was also conspicuous on the British side. The first governor of Gibraltar was actually an Irish Catholic wild goose (though he represented the Habsburgs, not the British).[59] Irish troops were present in the area as part of the English army from the 1660s, and the regiments serving in Gibraltar during the eighteenth century were often 'recruited' in Ireland.[60] This was true even of regiments that did not sound Irish at all (the Dorsets, the Scottish Borderers).[61] Gibraltar had its own Irishtown from the 1720s, and its own Irish Catholic community by the mid-eighteenth century.[62] Needless to say, the story running just below the surface, here, is often one of casual brutality and gross injustice, notably in the case of the Irishwomen who were shipped to Gibraltar along with 'other necessaries'.[63] But from time to time, there were also signs of Irish defiance and covert treachery: a soldier expelled from the garrison for drinking the Pretender's health;

---

[54] *Held Fast for England: A Tale of the Siege of Gibraltar* (London: Blackie and Son, 1892). [55] *Gibraltar* (Oxford: Blackwell, 1897).

[56] *A Popular History of Gibraltar, its Institutions and its Neighbourhood on Both Sides of the Straits* (Gibraltar: Garrison Library Printing Establishment, 1888), 33. Gilbard claims to be quoting Ford, but I have not been able to trace the 'quotation' and it does not sound like its alleged source.

[57] See Sayer, *History of Gibraltar*, 481.

[58] See Anon., *Gibraltar and its Siege*, 10; Hills, *Rocks of Gibraltar*, 207.

[59] He was Henry Nugent, Count de Valdesoto. See Jackson, *Rock of the Gibraltarians*, 104. [60] See Hills, *Rock of Contention*, 149, 271.

[61] Ibid. 359. [62] See Jackson, *Rock of the Gibraltarians*, 143.

[63] See 'S.H's' ms., *Journal of the Siege* (Gibraltar Museum); quoted in Hills, *Rock of Contention*, 272.

unruly and disruptive Irish soldiery causing trouble in 1783; a Cork sloop provocatively flying the Irish colours, which the Commodore threatened to have burnt by the hangman.[64] The British, of course, had worried about a Spanish-Irish alliance since the time of the Armada, and secret efforts to establish one seem to have been made even in the late eighteenth century.[65] Maud Gonne and John MacBride plotted to assassinate Edward VII on Gibraltar.[66] Most notoriously, in 1988, three members of the IRA planned to set off a bomb during the Changing of the Guard. They were killed by the SAS.

How much of the history of the Irish in Gibraltar Joyce knew must of course be open to doubt, though, according to Hills, it was 'an aspect of British colonialism' which lingered long 'in the memories of "John Bull's Other Island" '.[67] Joyce would surely have been aware of the larger historical context. He would have read about it (if he really needed to) in the historians he had in his collection: Hume, Lingard, Freeman.[68] He would certainly have been well aware of the discursive construction of Gibraltar. He would have come across most of the emphases, much of the detail, and even most of the literary quotations I have discussed in his sources for 'Penelope'. He would also have been well aware of the historiographical tradition: the historians (including those Joyce read) cite their predecessors with remarkable frequency. The tradition looms in the background of Joyce's chapter, which is partly a response to it. In 'Penelope', through Molly, Joyce lays siege to the great, British, Protestant, im-

[64] See Boyle and Bandury, *Gibraltar Directory*, 'Historical Notes', 86; Spilsbury, *Journal*, 103; and Hills, *Rock of Contention*, 359. Cf. the Irish chaplain to the Spanish king who brokered the Anglo-Spanish negotiations on the return of the Rock in 1779–80, Sayer, *History of Gibraltar*, 315–27.

[65] The plan was apparently to recover Gibraltar and create an Irish State under Spanish suzerainty. Its prime mover was Manuel Godoy, Chief Minister, Admiral, and Generalissimo to Charles IV of Spain, at least, according to his biographer, Hans Roger Madol, who claims that the project was wrecked 'by the excessive claims of the Irish for subsidies in advance'. See Howes, *Story of Gibraltar*, 72–3.

[66] See A. Norman Jeffares, 'Introduction', *The Gonne-Yeats Letters 1893–1938*, ed. with introds. Anna MacBride White and A. Norman Jeffares (London: Pimlico, 1993), 17–48 at 31, and 168n. See also Margaret Ward, *Maud Gonne: A Life* (London: Pandora, 1993), 38. I am grateful to Deirdre Toomey for drawing my attention to this.

[67] *Rock of Contention*, 272.

[68] See David Hume, *The History of England from the Invasion of Julius Caesar to the Revolution in 1688* (8 vols; London: Cadell & Davies, 1818), vols. vii and viii; John Lingard, *Abridgement of the History of England* (Dublin: James Duffy, n.d.), esp. at 579–88; and Edward A. Freeman, *General Sketch of European History* (London: Macmillan & Co., 1874), 281–301. See esp. his account of the War of the Spanish Succession at 285–6 and 288–9.

perial stronghold of the Rock. He repudiates the colonizer's definition of it and understanding of its meaning and value. The predomi-
nant concerns of the bluff, masculine, often rather formal-sounding
discursive tradition were military and political. Molly focuses on aspects of Gibraltarian life that were marginal to it. She emphasizes
Gibraltar's Catholic culture, for instance (e.g. 18. 760–2). Where
Field lauds the 'stamp' the English have left on the place,[69] Molly
emphasizes its Spanishness. In this respect, it is clearly significant
that she has so vivid a memory of 'stepping over' the wire at la Linea,
the remains of the old, fortified Spanish border (18. 625–6).[70] There
are more Spanish words and even Spanish names in Joyce's short
chapter than there are in almost any of the historical books. The
emphases on Catholicism and Spanishness are linked but not identical. At certain historical junctures, Gibraltar had been predominantly
Catholic but not predominantly Spanish. Joyce indicates other
Catholic presences on the Rock: Genoan, for instance (18. 975–6). He
notes the Irish strain in Gibraltar culture. He also makes the Rock
'more Irish'. Obviously enough, Molly's account of it has a distinctively Irish flavour, partly because of its associations with Mulvey and
Tweedy, partly, of course, because she is remembering it from Dublin.
Above all, however, Joyce emphasizes Gibraltar's racial mix. Historically, it was striking how far, for all the restrictive, colonial legislation, Gibraltar was a melting-pot. The historians occasionally
acknowledged this, but largely with the stiff self-consciousness of
superior power. By contrast, Joyce and Molly celebrate the Gibraltarian conflux of peoples (18. 1586–94). In Molly's monologue, the culture of the Rock emerges as richly and beguilingly hybrid. In this
respect, 'Penelope' stands in stark contrast to English discourses on
Gibraltar, particularly in the period 1880–1920.

Indeed, the point about Molly's Rock is how un-Rocklike it
turns out to be. Militarism is perhaps the feature of the Gibraltar
histories to which 'Penelope' runs most radically counter. Whilst
composing his chapter, Joyce asked Budgen to send him what he
referred to as 'Conan Doyle's *History of the South African War*'
(*Letters*, i. 169–70). As Herring suggests, he clearly meant Doyle's

---

[69] *Gibraltar*, 50.
[70] The fortifications were erected in 1727 and destroyed in 1810. La Linea subsequently
fell into a state of dereliction, but was developed again in the 1880s. The bull-ring dates
from this time (cf. 16. 626). See Gilbard, *Popular History*, 83–5.

The Great Boer War.[71] This was an imperialist and triumphalist classic of popular history. It was also an instance of contemporary, English, cultural nationalism. For though himself a Scot, Conan Doyle was concerned with national regeneration. The 'unity' and 'cohesion', the prosperity, the very future of the Empire had been 'at stake' in the war.[72] Victory had produced 'a national resuscitation of spirit and a closer union with our great Colonies which could in no other way have been attained'.[73] British military superiority had been crucially important to the morale of both nation and Empire: 'Who has seen [the British] Army and can forget it — its spirit, its picturesqueness — above all, what it stands for in the future history of the world?'[74] 'Penelope' resists both this kind of strenuously upbeat evocation of British imperial prospects and the system of value underlying it. Thus Molly's reference to the Moors 'like kings' (18. 1593) calls our attention to former 'masters of the Mediterranean' who 'are fellaheen today' (7. 911). Above all, however, Joyce's resists Conan Doyle's kind of imperial militarism. Molly's reflections on Gardner's fate are markedly opposed to it ('they could have made their peace in the beginning', 18. 394). More generally, Joyce plays Molly's attitudes to arms off against his sources and the tradition to which they belonged. Molly likes the look of soldiers and is inclined to sympathize with the 'unfortunate poor devils' stationed at Gibraltar (18. 686), like 'the sentry in front of the governors house' (18. 1585). But she has little time for militarism or the British army in itself. She is irritated by its 'damn guns bursting and booming all over the shop' (18. 679–80). They have been responsible for the deaths of far too many 'finelooking men' (18. 396). When she calls the Army to mind, Molly often adopts a tone of amused condescension, and this tone is a large part of the point. It indicates how far Joyce is working to invert the perspectives which made imperial militarism loom so large on the Rock. So, too, 'Penelope' closes with a lyrical evocation of kinds of experience quite beyond both the imperial and military purview and the historical discourses promoting it. Molly's monologue is full of references to aspects of life which seemed to have little or no place in Gibraltar and its literature: young love and budding sexuality (18. 769–72, 777–8,

---

[71] Herring (ed.), *Joyce's 'Ulysses'*, 69.

[72] Sir Arthur Conan Doyle, *The Great Boer War* (London: Smith, Elder & Co., 1902), 72, 742.   [73] Ibid. 739–40.

[74] Ibid. 742.

787–825, 850–3); lewdness (18. 440); sensuousness, colour, and warmth (18. 605–11, 973, 1598–1603); literature (18. 652–7), music (18. 644), games (18. 1583–4); splendid scenery (18. 399–400, 790–2), exotic flora and fauna (18. 665, 784–7, 871, 973–5).[75] To the historians, Gibraltar was almost unimaginable in such terms. They were incompatible with both its military discipline and its symbolic functions. Gibraltar was 'essentially a garrison town, a fortified post, in which art and beauty [are] subordinated to the useful'.[76] But in this way as in others, 'Penelope' refuses to be 'subordinated'. Similarly, where the literature of Gibraltar was increasingly emphasizing its alleged global importance, Molly takes a sceptical, pitying view of 'the voyages those men have to make to the ends of the world and back' (18. 853–4). She is much more interested in ordinary and little things, street life and domestic life (18. 748–51, 1586–96). Here as in other respects, the Irishwoman's discourse is strikingly resistant to imperial pomp and pretension.

In fact, 'Penelope' effectively functions as a continuation of the fitful tradition of Irish dissidence relative to Gibraltar. It is worth emphasizing, here, just how radically heterodox Molly's monologue is. The most frequently cited account of the impact military Gibraltar had on its visitor was Thackeray's. The Victorian novelist had listened wakefully to 'marching and countermarching, challenging and relieved guard all night through all over the huge rock in the darkness'.[77] In details like Molly's account of 'the fun [she and Mulvey] had running along Williss road to Europa point' (18. 848–9), Joyce seems pointedly to make her evoke a wholly different world to Thackeray's. The passage serves its own small purpose within a concerted transformation of an austere and joyless colonial geography. The transformation in question is seditious, but in a distinctively Joycean way: the meaning of sedition is itself transformed. For if an imperial discourse associated Gibraltar, above all, with a proud refusal to surrender, supremely in the case of the Great Siege, Molly associates it with yielding and giving in. Throughout the history of colonial Gibraltar, the authorities had been concerned about the

---

[75] Molly's curious but essentially mundane interest in the local flora and fauna should of course be distinguished from the zoological and botanical concerns that were intermittently a feature of Gibraltar literature.   [76] Anon., *Gibraltar and its Sieges*, 122.

[77] For Thackeray on Gibraltar, see *Notes on a Journey from Cornhill to Grand Cairo* (London: Smith, Elder & Co., 1851), 28–9, 42–53. Joyce would have known of Thackeray's account from Field, *Gibraltar*; see esp. 128.

possibility of a collapse in military discipline. They worried that the soldiery might incline to sloth, and even debauchery.[78] Once again, Molly reverses the emphasis: she turns the great fortress into Lotus-Eater-land ('you could do what you liked lie there for ever', 18. 795–6). She softens the hard heart of the Rock and saps its defences. She serves as a traitor to its cause.

That Joyce saw 'Penelope' as partly an act of betrayal is beyond doubt. It is clear, above all, in the name he gave to Molly's best friend. For as he would have known from his sources, Stanhope was the surname historically most closely associated with the idea of surrendering Gibraltar to the Spanish.[79] In the early twentieth century, however, the name of Hester Stanhope would more readily have called a more notorious character to mind. The Hester in question was a famously eccentric, aristocratic Englishwoman. She was niece to William Pitt and sought after by some of the most eminent Europeans of her time, including Lamartine. In 1810, she famously left England for the Levant, where she settled, adopted Eastern manners and customs, and vowed never to return. She was in fact a paradigm for the cultural 'treachery' involved in 'going native'. In other words, she surrendered her cultural identity, rather than stoutly defending it. Throughout this book, I have insisted that, both as theme and practice, the adulteration of Englishness is central to *Ulysses*. Hester Stanhope was a particularly well-known figure for it. That her name should resonate in the novel's closing chapter is obviously significant.

All the Big Stupoes

But any adequate discussion of 'Penelope' must also finally account for one seeming contradiction: its treatment of Gibraltar hardly seems to square with its treatment of Dublin. Molly's version of the Rock amounts to a provocative subversion of imperial British power.

---

[78] This was notably the case in the early 19th cent. See Dorothy Ellicott, *From Rooke to Nelson: 101 Eventful Years in Gibraltar* (Gibraltar: Garrison Library, 1965), 48. Edward, Duke of Kent served as troubleshooter, and became Gibraltar's only royal governor. The debauchery in question was drunkenness, above all. Joyce would have known about this from Boyle and Bandury, *Gibraltar Directory*, 'Historical Notes', 14–15.

[79] See e.g. Stephens, *History of Gibraltar*, 240–1. Between 1716 and 1721, General James (later Earl) Stanhope tried to negotiate the return of Gibraltar no less than six times, mainly in an attempt to lure Spain into the Quadruple Alliance and secure peace. See Hills, *Rock of Contention*, 116–21.

As such, however, it is not presented as emerging from any solidarity
with the cause of Dublin's Catholic community. If anything, the reverse is true: Molly's attitudes to many of the dominant figures in
that community — most notably those whom the novel has made
into dominant figures — are quite as disrespectful as Joyce's treatment of the discourses on Gibraltar. In the 'Telemachiad' and, above
all, in 'Aeolus', Joyce and Stephen displayed a great deal of tenderness for members of the Catholic community, its life and culture.[80] As
I argued in my second chapter, Bloom may partly be alienated from
that culture, but he also substantially identifies with it. Molly,
however, is entertainingly but comprehensively devastating about
the Dubliners around her. This is obvious enough in the cases of
Bloom and Boylan. But the list also includes Lenehan ('that sponger',
18. 426); Ben Dollard ('balmy ballocks', 18. 1288); M'Coy ('white
head of cabbage', 18. 1267); Power ('keeping that barmaid', 18. 1272);
Val Dillon ('that big heathen', 18. 429); Larry O'Rourke ('the old
mangy parcel', 18. 452); Paddy Dignam ('comical little teetotum',
18. 1281); Menton ('that big babbyface', 18. 39, 'and thats called a
solicitor', 18. 43–4); Tom Kernan ('that drunken little barrelly man'
(18. 1264–5); Breen ('a thing like that might murder you any moment', 18. 224); Goodwin ('old frostyface' 18. 335–6, 'a potent professor of John Jameson', 18. 1333); Dlugacz ('queerlooking man . . .
a great rogue' (18. 911–12); Burke ('that other beauty . . . always
where he wasnt wanted . . . youd vomit a better face', 18. 964–7); and
Simon Dedalus ('turning up half screwed singing the second verse
first', 18. 1291; 'such a criticiser with his glasses up with his tall hat up
at the cricket match and a great big hole in his sock', 18. 1088–9). As
a group, Molly finally dismisses them with affectionate contempt
('theyre a nice lot all of them', 18. 1275). Though the list extends
beyond its members, the whole post-Parnellite male coterie that has
featured so prominently in *Ulysses* becomes an object of ridicule.
Joyce appears to have deliberately set out to belittle the male-
dominated ethos and masculine assumptions of a particular, Irish
political culture. Yet the culture in question has otherwise dominated
the novel, and even underpinned its aesthetic strategies and linguistic
and stylistic practices.

---

[80] For a brilliant account of 'Aeolus' that discusses many of the most important aspects
of the chapter and is relevant to my point, see Len Platt, *Joyce and the Anglo-Irish: A Study
of Joyce and the Literary Revival* (Amsterdam and Atlanta, Ga.: Rodopi, 1998), 60–73.

Them Sinner Fein

What is true of Molly's attitudes to the Catholic community is also true of her attitudes to its republican and nationalist elements and traditions. Here, again, her monologue is repeatedly scathing. Whilst she was once apparently an enthusiast for 'home rule and the land league', she now believes she was merely taken in by Bloom's 'blather' ('O wasnt I the born fool', 18. 1187–8). She has no time for 'them Sinner Fein . . . or whatever they call themselves'. They will only make Bloom talk his 'usual trash and nonsense' (18. 383–4). Molly is especially sceptical in her attitude towards Bloom's enthusiasm for 'the coming man' Griffith ('well he doesnt look it thats all I can say', 18. 385–6). She recalls him chiefly as 'the little man [Bloom] showed me dribbling along in the wet'. She is willing to acknowledge that Griffith is 'capable and sincerely Irish' only if he is judged 'by the sincerity of the trousers I saw on him' (18. 1228–31). Of course, in the summer of 1921, when Joyce was writing 'Penelope', Griffith was indeed 'the coming man'.[81] He had been acting president of the Dáil in 1919 but was arrested in 1920. Shortly after his release in July 1921, he headed the Irish delegation in the Treaty negotiations. In 1922, he was elected first president of the Irish Free State.[82] Joyce obviously referred to Griffith in 'Penelope' because he was aware of Griffith's progress and current status. The mockery in Molly's account of Griffith — her deflation of president-in-waiting to abject, Beckettian clown — seems aimed not only at the man, but at the political prospects he represents.

Thus if Joyce's treatment of Gibraltar is provocatively anticolonial, his construction of Molly might have almost been designed to annoy his nationalist contemporaries. Molly shows a marked distaste for nationalist responses to the Boer War, for example ('I hate the mention of their politics after the war that Pretoria and Ladysmith and Bloemfontein', 18. 387–8). Griffith actually fought for the Boers. Molly implies that, if she had to choose a side, she would choose the British (18. 866–8). True, Molly's attitude stems largely from her affection for Gardner ('a lovely fellow in khaki', 18.390). But for early twentieth-century Irish nationalists, an

---

[81] The chapter was with the printers by 7 Oct. See Card, 'Penelope', 19; and Richard Ellmann, *James Joyce* (rev. edn., Oxford: Oxford University Press, 1982), 519.

[82] R. F. Foster, *Modern Ireland 1600–1972* (London: Penguin, 1989), 456–7.

expression of affection for an English soldier who had fought in South Africa was immediately political. As we saw earlier, the Irish girl who consorted with an 'enemy soldier' was an almost allegorical figure whose significance was treachery to the Irish cause. Molly responds warmly to British soldiers, if not the British Army ('I love to see a regiment pass in review', 18. 397–8; 'the lancers theyre grand', 18. 402). Indeed, on the whole, British men, and Irishmen who have taken the British side, appear to come out of 'Penelope' better than nationalists, republicans, and Dublin Catholics.

In fact, Molly flouts a range of nationalist pieties, seemingly on Joyce's behalf. She fantasizes about being of royal English birth (18. 502–3). She is wilfully provocative in nationalist company, 'singing the absentminded beggar and wearing a brooch for Lord Roberts'. Not surprisingly, she has been partly ostracized for 'not [being] Irish enough' (18. 377–9). As the daughter of an officer in the British Army, she is snobbishly dismissive of 'Irish homemade beauties' ('theyd die down dead off their feet if ever they got a chance of walking down the Alameda on an officers arm like me on the bandnight', 18. 883–5). Her attitude to colonization is indulgent: she is caustically dismissive of a resentful Mrs Rubio ('she never could get over the Atlantic fleet coming in . . . and the Union Jack flying with all her carabineros because 4 drunken English sailors took all the rock', 18. 754–6). So, too, Joyce responds to nationalist allegories of Irish womanhood by giving Molly fond memories of sleeping all night in the arms of an Englishwoman (18. 641–2) and making her surrender Irish Mulvey's Claddagh ring to English Gardner on the eve of the latter's departure to fight the Boers (18. 866–7). Molly recalls being embarrassed about her Irishness in front of a young Englishman (18.889–90). This, too, is significant. In this respect, Molly's recollections invert the symbolic structure of the relationship between Stephen and Haines in 'Telemachus'. Coming at the end of the novel, the reversal seems to encapsulate Joyce's point.

Flora Calpensis

I have suggested that two starkly contradictory practices or strands of thought are present in 'Penelope', one powerfully anti-imperial, the other, apparently, wickedly anti-nationalist. My description of the second of these may even sound suspiciously as though I am reverting to a concept of a hibernophobic Joyce that was dear to an older critical tradition but has been rightly called in question, most admirably by Emer Nolan.[83] It may seem as though, in this respect, I have resisted the tradition only finally to smuggle its emphases back into my book. However, it is the relationship between the two practices I have just mentioned that is chiefly significant: if we think it through as carefully as possible, it tells us something very important about both 'Penelope' and *Ulysses*.

There is nothing new in the idea that 'Penelope' is full of contradictions. The critical tradition quickly fastened on it.[84] Contradiction offered what seemed to be a useful key to Molly's psychology and even her 'femininity'. For Card, for example, Molly's contradictions showed how right Joyce was to call her 'untrustworthy'.[85] Feminist critics comprehensively and rightly trounced such readings.[86] Recently, however, the theme of contradiction has resurfaced and been placed in new contexts, notably colonial ones. Thus for Bazargan, for example, Molly's monologue is an illustration of how far 'at the core of the colonial psyche lie ambivalence and contradiction since colonialism, in essence, operates on opposing principles'.[87] Such a case may seem close to my own. In fact, it raises a problem: though clearly post-feminist, the critics in question actually return to a pre-feminist assumption about the way 'Penelope' works. For like the earlier moralists in Joyce studies, they understand Joyce as having constructed Molly as an object of analysis and critique. This places author and reader together in the position of what Michel Serres has described as the

[83] See *James Joyce and Nationalism* (London: Routledge, 1995), 1–22.

[84] See e.g. David Hayman, 'The Empirical Molly', in Thomas F. Staley and Bernard Benstock (eds.), *Approaches to 'Ulysses'* (Pittsburgh: University of Pittsburgh Press, 1970), 103–35, esp. 120. For an account of the contradictions that aims to be comprehensive, see Card, '*Penelope*', 38–55.   [85] Card, '*Penelope*', 39.

[86] For the feminist revision of the male-dominated (and frequently rather negative) tradition of accounts of Molly, see e.g. Bonnie Kime Scott, *Joyce and Feminism* (Brighton: Harvester, 1984), 156–83; Frances L. Restuccia, *Joyce and the Law of the Father* (New Haven and London: Yale University Press, 1989), 165–75; and Suzette Henke, *James Joyce and the Politics of Desire* (London: Routledge, 1990), 126–63.

[87] Bazargan, 'Mapping Gibraltar', 121. Similar emphases are perceptible in the two other essays in Pearce's *Molly Blooms* that deal substantially with colonialism: see Carol Shloss, 'Molly's Resistance to the Union: Marriage and Colonialism in Dublin, 1904', 105–18; and Brian W. Shaffer, 'Negotiating Self and Culture: Competing Discourses and Ideological Becoming in "Penelope" ', 139–51.

Kantian tribunal.[88] But nothing in 'Penelope' or anywhere else — except, perhaps, for the vestiges of a Leavisite habit founded in a preference for English novelists like George Eliot — indicates that we should judge Molly from a superior point of view, even as an example of a false consciousness induced by colonialism. Why should we suppose that Joyce did not simply 'mean' Molly herself, *in toto*? After all, 'Penelope' evidently revels in her modernity, her sexuality, her scorn, her humour, her caustic wit, and, above all, the vitality of her language.

But if Joyce 'meant Molly', then what is the point to the contradiction I referred to earlier? Not, I would suggest, the critical exposure of conflicting drives that have been 'smoothed over' by ideology,[89] but an effort to promote their coexistence. I take this to be the crucial significance of a Molly Bloom offered to the world and, above all, Ireland in 1922 and, even more significantly, composed in 1921. For 1921 was the year of accommodation in Ireland. It saw the Anglo-Irish Treaty and truce between the IRA and the British Army. The latter was agreed on 7 July, at more or less exactly the time when Joyce was planning 'Penelope'. Joyce told Louis Gillet that the word 'yes' as used in 'Penelope' '*se prononce à peine, signifie l'acquiescement, l'abandon, la détente, la fin de toute résistance*'.[90] *Abandon* implies concession. *Détente* already had political connotations that later became more familiar during the Cold War. But *détente* — a relaxation of hostilities, saying yes to the enemy — is achieved only painfully (*à peine*), with difficulty. 'Penelope' is about 'the end of all resistance' in at least two senses: the end of all resistance is to challenge, subvert, overthrow, maybe even transform the power resisted. But it is also to cede, to be reconciled to the effects of

---

[88] *L'Hermaphrodite: Sarrasine sculpteur* (Paris: Flammarion, 1986), 64. See also my *Towards a Postmodern Theory of Narrative* (Edinburgh: Edinburgh University Press, 1996), 112.

[89] Brian W. Shaffer borrows the phrase quoted from Catherine Belsey, 'Constructing the Subject: Deconstructing the Text', in Judith Newton and Deborah Rosenfelt (eds.), *Feminist Criticism and Social Change: Sex, Class and Race in Literature and Culture* (New York: Methuen, 1985), 45–64, at 46. See 'Negotiating Self', 140.

[90] 'I had found the word "yes," which is barely pronounced, which denotes acquiescence, renunciation, relaxation, the end of all resistance'. See Ellmann, *James Joyce*, 712. He is quoting from Louis Gillet, *Stèle pour James Joyce* (Marseilles: Sagittaire, 1941), 164–5. As the dictionaries show, in Proust as in Molière, *à peine* can mean 'painfully', as well as 'barely' or 'hardly'. Joyce was surely aware of the ambiguity. He must also have used the word 'abandon' in awareness of its connotations both of giving way and giving up on something.

that power. Lodged in the room of the infinite possibilities it has
ousted, the colonial history of Ireland is not to be thought away. So,
too, the long history of the British presence in Ireland cannot simply
to be erased. For it has left its traces everywhere, sometimes most
markedly on its antagonists. Indeed, paradoxically enough, opposition to it may serve only to reinforce it, in more or less obvious and direct ways. This is a point that Joyce emphasizes in 'Penelope'. For
Molly, the culture of Irish Catholic masculinity is partly one of fatal
violence ('and they call that friendship killing and then burying one
another', 18. 1270–1). As such, it is to some extent a mirror image of
the culture of imperial, British militarism paraded on the Rock. So,
too, throughout both 'Penelope' and *Ulysses* as a whole, in a host of
little details often drawn from the more obscure corners of domestic
and private life, Joyce underlines an ineradicable, Irish involvement
in the systems of value and structures of thought and feeling intrinsic
to the colonizer's culture.

   In my introduction, I referred to Foster's account of what he calls
the 'Anglophobia' of Irish political and cultural nationalism from the
late nineteenth century through to the Free State.[91] As I have said,
Joyce partly shared the profound hostility to England that was common in the culture in which he grew up. But he did not share the de-
Anglicizers' belief in the possibility, desirability, or necessity of
'cleansing' Ireland of the effects of English culture.[92] At the same
time, his differences with Irish cultural nationalism have little or
nothing to do with a commitment to those values whose alleged absence from 'Anglophobic', nationalist discourses Foster deplores:
justice, fairness, tolerance, reasonability. More precisely, Joyce is profoundly sceptical of those values *in their English definition*. He
rather recognizes the point at which resistance may be more damaging than acceptance for the resisters themselves. Again, Joyce's view
of Rooney's poetry seems pertinent, here: it has been written by 'one
in whom the spirit is in a manner dead . . . a weary and foolish spirit,
speaking of redemption and revenge, blaspheming against tyrants'

[91] See Foster, *Modern Ireland*, chs. 18–23, *passim*, esp. pp. 447–50, 453–4, 471–2, 506, 508, 516–19.
   [92] This point cannot have been wholly clear in my 'Circe' essay, at least, if David Pierce's rather disastrous misreading of it is anything to go by. See ' "Strangers in my House, Bad Manners to Them!": England in "Circe" ', in Andrew Gibson (ed.), *Reading Joyce's 'Circe'* (European Joyce Studies, 3; Amsterdam and Atlanta, Ga.: Rodopi, 1994), 179–221; and Pierce's review of the volume, 'Asymmetrical Circe', *James Joyce Literary Supplement* (Fall 1994), 16, 18. Pierce specifically misrepresents my argument e.g., at 186–7.

(CW, 86). As a result, it lacks proper independence. So, too, *Ulysses* repeatedly insists that, ultimately, the posture of anatagonism or continued belligerence and indeed the historical obsession are chronically disempowering. They weaken, because they keep wounds open and even allow them to fester, rather than letting them heal. Ironically, they therefore inhibit the growth of autonomy, of cultural pride and self-assertion.

In that respect, the chapter Joyce gives wholly to a woman is also the one that finally makes explicit a complex paradigm of cultural sanity and health that has been progressively emerging throughout the novel. It indicates a very different direction to the one taken by the Irish Free State. Part of the point about Molly and 'Penelope' is that they are cheerfully *at ease* with contradiction. Or, to put matters differently: 'Penelope' decisively relaxes the structure of the titanic cultural struggle evident in *Ulysses* since Stephen first alluded to his imperial masters. If the novel relaxes from struggle, however, it neither abandons it nor sets it at naught. On the one hand, 'Penelope' produces a powerfully corrosive treatment of an imperial, British symbol. On the other, it is more or less affectionately dismissive of an Irish culture rootedly opposed to the British imperium. In that respect, Joyce's chapter is a specimen of that 'brilliant' Irish literature of 'national self-criticism' which D. P. Moran took to be so important to cultural self-assertion.[93] Thus at the end of *Ulysses*, like a conscientious Derridean, Joyce both sustains and relinquishes the terms of a ferocious, polar opposition. He insists on the importance of an anti-imperial practice that is not automatically and in principle based on unwavering allegiance to Irish Catholic and nationalist culture. Indeed, it is the very intensity of Joyce's hostility to the stranger that finally provokes him to change its proportions.

From time to time, the literature of Gibraltar refers to a botanical specimen, the *flora calpensis* ('flower of Calpe', the ancient name for Gibraltar). Joyce would have known of it.[94] 'Flora Calpensis' was also the pen-name of the authoress of *Reminiscences of Gibraltar* (1880) and *The Life of a Rock Scorpion* (1881).[95] These two little books are quite distinct from the others I have mentioned. 'Flora' was a patriotic, colonial spirit. But her curiosity and the warmth and

[93] *The Philosophy of Irish Ireland* (Dublin: James Duffy & Co., 1905), 79.

[94] It is referred to, e.g., in Boyle and Bandury, *Gibraltar Directory*, 'Historical Notes', 22.

[95] 'Flora Calpensis', *Reminiscences of Gibraltar* (London: Samuel Tinsley & Co., 1880); and *The Life of a Rock Scorpion* (London: Charing Cross Publishing Co., 1881).

intelligence of her responses to the climate of Gibraltar, its people and culture, its animal and plant life, the bustle of its streets, its nooks and byways, set the tone and concerns of the historians and military men in grim relief. This is the more remarkable in that, like Molly's, 'Flora's' father was an army officer. The 'flower of Calpe' blooms in unpropitious circumstances, even against the odds. So, too, with Molly: the phrase 'flower of the mountain' recurs insistently at the end of 'Penelope' (18. 1576, 1602, 1606). The point seems clear: Gibraltar was a British colony with a Catholic majority and a conspicuous British, military presence. It had a history of military conflict, discriminatory legislation, the imposition of alien, administrative, educational and legal systems, and devastating onsets of disease. In these and other respects, it closely resembled Ireland. Molly Bloom has grown up in such a world. Yet she has emerged from it averagely happy, averagely sane. It is an image of the possibility of ordinary sanity and happiness that Joyce finally presented to Ireland in the year of its independence.

Bibliography

Works by Joyce

'Daniel Defoe', ed. and trans. Joseph Prescott, *Buffalo Studies*, 1/1 (Dec. 1964), 3–27.

The Critical Writings of James Joyce, ed. Ellsworth Mason and Richard Ellmann (New York: Viking Press, 1959).

Dubliners: An Annotated Edition, ed. John Wyse Jackson and Bernard McGinley (London: Sinclair-Stevenson, 1993).

A Portrait of the Artist as a Young Man, the definitive text corrected from the Dublin holograph by Chester G. Anderson and ed. Richard Ellmann (London: Jonathan Cape, 1968).

Stephen Hero, ed. Theodore Spencer, rev. edn. with additional foreword by John J. Slocum and Herbert Cahoon (London: Jonathan Cape, 1956).

Ulysses, ed. Hans Walter Gabler with Wolfhard Steppe and Claus Melchior, afterword by Michael Groden (New York and London: Garland Publishing, 1984, 1986).

Finnegans Wake (3rd edn., London: Faber & Faber, 1964).

Letters of James Joyce, vol. i, ed. Stuart Gilbert (London: Faber and Faber, 1957); vols. ii and iii, ed. Richard Ellmann (London: Faber and Faber, 1966).

Periodicals, Journals, and Magazines 1880–1920

The Countess Novelette
The Daily Express (Dublin)
Fortnightly Review
Freeman's Journal
Irish Homestead
Irish Hunt Annual
Irish Times
The Lady's Own Novelette
Lady's Pictorial
The Leader
The Obstetrical Journal
Pearson's Weekly
The Princess's Novelettes
Publications of the Irish Unionist Alliance

Publications of the English Association
The Times
United Irishman
The Workers' Republic

Joyce Biography and Criticism

Adams, R. M., *Surface and Symbol: The Consistency of James Joyce's 'Ulysses'* (New York: Oxford University Press, 1962).

Atherton, J. S., 'The Oxen of the Sun', in Hart and Hayman (eds.), *James Joyce's 'Ulysses'*, 313–39.

Attridge, Derek, *Joyce Effects: On Language, Theory and History* (Cambridge: Cambridge University Press, 2000).

—— and Howes, Marjorie (eds.), *Semicolonial Joyce* (Cambridge: Cambridge University Press, 2000).

Bazargan, Susan, 'Mapping Gibraltar', in Pearce (ed.), *Molly Blooms*, 119–38.

Beja, Morris, Herring, Phillip, Harmon, Maurice, and Norris, David (eds.), *James Joyce: The Centennial Symposium* (Urbana, Ill.: University of Illinois Press, 1986).

Benstock, Bernard (ed.), *The Seventh of Joyce* (Brighton: Harvester, 1982).

—— *Narrative Con/Texts in 'Ulysses'* (London: Macmillan, 1991).

—— 'Telemachus', in Hart and Hayman (eds.), *James Joyce's 'Ulysses'*, 1–16.

Brooker, Joseph, 'Reading in Transit: A Study of Joyce's Anglophone Reception' (Ph.D. thesis, University of London, 1999).

Brown, Richard, *James Joyce and Sexuality* (Cambridge: Cambridge University Press, 1985).

Budgen, Frank, *James Joyce and the Making of 'Ulysses'*, introd. Clive Hart (Oxford: Oxford University Press, 1972).

Bush, Ron, Review of Len Platt, *Joyce and the Anglo-Irish* and Marilyn Reizbaum, *Joyce's Judaic Other*, *Textual Practice*, 14/2 (Summer 2000), 396–400.

Bushrui, Suheil Badi, and Benstock, Bernard (eds.), *James Joyce, An International Perspective: Centenary Essays in Honour of the Late Sir Desmond Cochrane,* foreword by Richard Ellmann (Gerrards Cross: Colin Smythe, 1982).

Card, James Van Dyck, *An Anatomy of 'Penelope'* (London and Toronto: Associated University Presses, 1984).

Castle, Gregory, ' "I Am Almosting It": History, Nature and the Will to Power in "Proteus" ', *James Joyce Quarterly*, 29/2 (Winter 1992), 281–96.

—— 'Ousted Possibilities: Critical Histories in James Joyce's *Ulysses*', *Twentieth-Century Literature*, 39/3 (Fall 1993), 306–28.

Cheng, Vincent J., *Joyce, Race and Empire* (Cambridge: Cambridge University Press, 1995).

—— and Martin, Timothy (eds.), *Joyce in Context* (Cambridge: Cambridge University Press, 1992).

Colum, Padraic and Mary, *Our Friend James Joyce* (London: Gollancz, 1959).

Costello, Peter, *James Joyce: The Years of Growth 1882–1915* (London: Kyle Cathie, 1992).

—— 'James Joyce, *Ulysses* and the National Maternity Hospital', in Farmar, *Holles Street*, 208–16.

Davison, Neil R., *James Joyce, 'Ulysses' and the Construction of Jewish Identity: Culture, Biography and 'the Jew' in Modernist Europe* (Cambridge: Cambridge University Press, 1996).

Deane, Seamus, 'Joyce and Stephen: The Provincial Intellectual', in *Celtic Revivals: Essay in Modern Irish Literature 1880–1980* (London: Faber, 1985), 75–91.

—— 'Joyce and Nationalism', in *Celtic Revivals*, 92–107.

—— ' "Masked with Matthew Arnold's Face": Joyce and Liberalism', in Beja et al. (eds.), *James Joyce*, 9–21.

Deming, Robert H. (ed.), *James Joyce: The Critical Heritage* (2 vols., London: Routledge & Kegan Paul, 1970).

Downing, Gregory M., 'Skeat and Joyce: A Garner of Words', *Dictionaries*, 18 (1997), 33–65.

—— 'Richard Chenevix Trench and Joyce's Historical Study of Words', *Joyce Studies Annual* (1998), 37–68.

Duffy, Enda, *The Subaltern 'Ulysses'* (Minneapolis: University of Minnesota Press, 1994).

Duggan, Francis, ' "Phrases of the Platform": Irish Political Oratory 1782–1922 in the Work of James Joyce' (Ph.D. thesis, University of London, in preparation).

Dunleavy, Janet E., Friedman, Melvyn J., and Gillespie, Michael Patrick (eds.), *Joycean Occasions: Essays from the Milwaukee James Joyce Conference* (Newark, Del.: University of Delaware Press, 1991).

Ellmann, Richard, *'Ulysses' on the Liffey* (London: Faber & Faber, 1972).

—— *The Consciousness of Joyce* (London: Faber & Faber, 1977).

—— *James Joyce* (rev. edn., Oxford: Oxford University Press, 1982).

Empson, William, 'Joyce's Intentions', *Using Biography* (1970; London: Chatto & Windus, 1984), 203–16.

Fairhall, James, *James Joyce and the Question of History* (Cambridge: Cambridge University Press, 1993).

Fleishman, Avrom, 'Science in "Ithaca" ', *Wisconsin Studies in Contemporary Literature*, 7 (1967), 377–91.

French, Marilyn, *The Book as World: James Joyce's 'Ulysses'* (London: Abacus, 1982).

Friedman, Alan J., 'Ulysses and Modern Science', in Benstock (ed.), Seventh of Joyce, 198–206.

Friedman, Susan Stanford (ed.), Joyce: The Return of the Repressed (Ithaca, NY: Cornell University Press, 1993).

Gibson, Andrew (ed.), Reading Joyce's 'Circe' (European Joyce Studies, 3; Amsterdam and Atlanta, Ga.: Rodopi, 1994).

—— ' "Strangers in my House, Bad Manners to Them!": England in "Circe" ', in Gibson (ed.), Reading Joyce's 'Circe', 179–221.

—— (ed.), Joyce's 'Ithaca' (European Joyce Studies, 6; Amsterdam and Atlanta, Ga.: Rodopi, 1996).

—— ' "An Aberration of the Light of Reason": Science and Cultural Politics in "Ithaca" ', in Gibson (ed.), Joyce's 'Ithaca', 133–74.

—— ' "Let All Malthusiasts Go Hang": Joyce's "Oxen of the Sun" and the Economists', Literature and History, 10/2 (Autumn 2001), 62–78.

Gifford, Don, with Seidman, Robert J., 'Ulysses' Annotated: Notes for James Joyce's 'Ulysses' (rev. edn., Berkeley and Los Angeles: University of California Press, 1988).

Gilbert, Stuart, James Joyce's 'Ulysses': A Study (London: Faber & Faber, 1930).

Gillespie, Michael, 'Sources and the Independent Artist', James Joyce Quarterly, 20/3 (Spring 1983), 325–36.

—— Inverted Volumes Improperly Arranged: James Joyce and his Trieste Library (Ann Arbor: UMI Research Press, 1983).

—— James Joyce's Trieste Library: A Catalogue of Materials at the Harry Ransom Humanities Research Center, University of Texas at Austin, ed. with the assistance of Erik Bradford Stocker (Austin: The Centre, 1986).

Goldberg, S. L., The Classical Temper: A Study of James Joyce's 'Ulysses' (London: Chatto and Windus, 1961).

Groden, Michael, 'Ulysses' in Progress (Princeton: Princeton University Press, 1977).

Hart, Clive, 'Wandering Rocks', in Hart and Hayman (eds.), James Joyce's 'Ulysses', 181–216.

—— and Hayman, David (eds.), James Joyce's 'Ulysses': Critical Essays (Berkeley and Los Angeles: University of California Press, 1974).

Hayman, David, 'The Empirical Molly', in Staley and Benstock (eds.), Approaches to 'Ulysses', 103–35.

—— 'Ulysses': The Mechanics of Meaning (new edn., rev. and expanded, Madison: University of Wisconsin Press, 1982).

Henke, Suzette, James Joyce and the Politics of Desire (London: Routledge, 1990).

Herr, Cheryl, Joyce's Anatomy of Culture (Urbana, Ill.: University of Illinois Press, 1986).

Herring, Phillip F. (ed.), Joyce's 'Ulysses' Notesheets in the British Museum (Charlottesville, Va.: University Press of Virginia, 1972).

—— (ed.), *Joyce's Notes and Early Drafts for 'Ulysses': Selections from the Buffalo Collection* (Charlottesville, Va.: University Press of Virginia, 1977).

—— *Joyce's Uncertainty Principle* (Princeton: Princeton University Press, 1987).

Hodgart, Matthew, *James Joyce: A Student's Guide* (London: Routledge & Kegan Paul, 1978).

Jackson, John Wyse, with Costello, Peter, *John Stanislaus Joyce: The Voluminous Life and Genius of James Joyce's Father* (London: Fourth Estate, 1997).

Janusko, Robert, *The Sources and Structures of James Joyce's 'Oxen'* (Ann Arbor: UMI Research Press, 1983).

—— 'Another Anthology for "Oxen": Barnett and Dale', *James Joyce Quarterly*, 27/2 (Winter, 1990), 257–81.

—— 'Yet Another Anthology for "Oxen": Murison's *Selections*', *Joyce Studies Annual*, 1 (1990), 117–31.

Kain, Richard, *Fabulous Voyager: James Joyce's 'Ulysses'* (Chicago: University of Chicago Press, 1947).

Kenner, Hugh, *Dublin's Joyce* (London: Chatto and Windus, 1955).

—— *Joyce's Voices* (London: Faber & Faber, 1978).

—— *Ulysses* (London: George Allen and Unwin, 1980).

Kiberd, Declan, 'The Vulgarity of Heroics: Joyce's *Ulysses*', in Bushrui and Benstock (eds.), *James Joyce*, 156–69.

—— 'Introduction', *Ulysses* (London: Penguin, 1992), pp. ix–lxxx.

Knowles, Sebastian D. G., *The Dublin Helix: The Life of Language in Joyce's 'Ulysses'* (Gainesville, Fla.: University Press of Florida, 2001).

Kumar, Udaya, *The Joycean Labyrinth: Repetition, Time and Tradition in 'Ulysses'* (Oxford: Clarendon Press, 1991).

Lawrence, Karen, *The Odyssey of Style in 'Ulysses'* (Princeton: Princeton University Press, 1981).

Litz, A. Walton, 'Ithaca', in Hart and Hayman (eds.), *James Joyce's 'Ulysses'*, 385–405.

Lowe-Evans, Mary, *Crimes against Fecundity: Joyce and Population Control* (Syracuse, Kan.: Syracuse University Press, 1989).

Lyons, J. B., *James Joyce and Medicine* (Dublin: Dolmen Press, 1973).

MacCabe, Colin, *James Joyce and the Revolution of the Word* (London: Macmillan, 1978).

McGee, Patrick, *Paperspace: Style as Ideology in Joyce's 'Ulysses'* (Lincoln, Nebr.: University of Nebraska Press, 1988).

—— *Joyce beyond Marx: History and Desire in 'Ulysses' and 'Finnegans Wake'* (Gainesville, Fla.: University Press of Florida, 2001).

McGinley, Bernard, *Joyce's Lives: Uses and Abuses of the Biografiend* (London: University of North London Press, 1996).

Magalaner, Marvin, 'The Anti-Semitic Limerick Incidents in Joyce's Bloomsday', *PMLA* 68 (1953), 1219–23.

Mahaffey, Vicky, *Reauthorizing Joyce* (Cambridge: Cambridge University Press, 1988).

Manganiello, Dominic, *Joyce's Politics* (London: Routledge & Kegan Paul, 1980).

Mason, Michael, *James Joyce: 'Ulysses'* (London: Edward Arnold, 1972).

Mercanton, Jacques, 'The Hours of James Joyce', in Potts (ed.), *Portraits of the Artist in Exile*, 206–52.

Morrison, Mark, 'Stephen Dedalus and the Ghost of the Mother', *Modern Fiction Studies*, 39/2 (Summer 1993), 345–68.

Morrison, Steven, 'Heresy, Heretics and Heresiarchs in the Works of James Joyce' (Ph.D. thesis, University of London, 1999).

Nadel, Ira B., *Joyce and the Jews: Culture and Texts* (Iowa City: University of Iowa Press, 1989).

Newman, Robert D., and Thornton, Weldon (eds.), *Joyce's 'Ulysses': The Larger Perspective* (Newark, Del.: University of Delaware Press, 1987).

Nolan, Emer, *James Joyce and Nationalism* (London: Routledge, 1995).

Norris, Margot, *Joyce's Web: The Social Unravelling of Modernism* (Austin: University of Texas Press, 1992).

O'Neill, Christine, *Too Fine a Point: A Stylistic Analysis of the 'Eumaeus' Episode in James Joyce's 'Ulysses'* (Trier: Wissenschaftlicher Verlag Trier, 1996).

Osteen, Mark, *The Economy of 'Ulysses': Making Both Ends Meet* (New York: Syracuse University Press, 1995).

Owens, Coílín, 'The Mystique of the West in Joyce's "The Dead" ', *Irish University Review*, 22/1 (Spring–Summer 1992), 80–92.

Parrinder, Patrick, *James Joyce* (Cambridge: Cambridge University Press, 1984).

Peake, Charles, *James Joyce: The Citizen and the Artist* (London: Edward Arnold, 1977).

Pearce, Richard (ed.), *Molly Blooms: A Polylogue on 'Penelope' and Cultural Studies* (Madison: University of Wisconsin Press, 1994).

Perlis, Alan David, 'The Newtonian Nightmare of *Ulysses*', in Benstock (ed.), *Seventh of Joyce*, 191–7.

Platt, Len, *Joyce and the Anglo-Irish: A Study of Joyce and the Literary Revival* (Amsterdam and Atlanta, Ga.: Rodopi, 1998).

Potts, Willard (ed.), *Portraits of the Artist in Exile: Recollections of James Joyce by Europeans* (Dublin: Wolfhound, 1979).

Power, Arthur, *The Joyce We Knew*, ed. Ulick Connor (Cork: The Mercier Press, 1967).

Purdy, S. B., 'Let's Hear what Science has to Say: *Finnegans Wake* and the Gnosis of Science', in Benstock (ed.), *Seventh of Joyce*, 207–17.

Quillian, William H., 'Shakespeare in Trieste: Joyce's 1912 *Hamlet* Lectures', *James Joyce Quarterly*, 12/1–2 (Fall 1974–Winter 1975), 7–63.

Radford, F. L., 'King, Pope and Hero-Martyr: *Ulysses* and the Nightmare of Irish History', *James Joyce Quarterly*, 15/4 (Summer 1978), 275–323.

Reizbaum, Marilyn, *James Joyce's Judaic Other* (Stanford: Stanford University Press, 1999).

Restuccia, Frances L., *Joyce and the Law of the Father* (New Haven and London: Yale University Press, 1989).

Reynolds, Mary T., *Joyce and Dante: The Shaping Imagination* (Princeton: Princeton University Press, 1981).

Riquelme, Jean Paul, *Teller and Tale in Joyce's Fiction: Oscillating Perspectives* (Baltimore: Johns Hopkins University Press, 1983).

Schwarz, Daniel R., *Reading Joyce's 'Ulysses'* (Basingstoke: Macmillan, 1987).

Scott, Bonnie Kime, *Joyce and Feminism* (Brighton: Harvester, 1984).

—— *James Joyce* (Brighton: Harvester, 1987).

Senn, Fritz, *Joyce's Dislocutions: Essays on Reading as Translation*, ed. John Paul Riquelme (Baltimore and London: Johns Hopkins University Press, 1984).

—— 'Joycean Provections', in Dunleavy et al. (eds.), *Joycean Occasions*, 171–94.

—— ' "Circe" as Harking Back in Provective Arrangement', in Gibson (ed.), *Joyce's 'Circe'*, 63–92.

—— ' "Ithaca": Portrait of the Chapter as a Long List', in Gibson (ed.), *Joyce's 'Ithaca'*, 31–76.

—— *Inductive Scrutinies: Focus on Joyce*, ed. Christine O'Neill (Dublin: Lilliput, 1997).

Shaffer, Brian W., 'Negotiating Self and Culture: Competing Discourses and Ideological Becoming in "Penelope" ', in Pearce (ed.), *Molly Blooms*, 139–51.

Sherry, Vincent, *James Joyce: 'Ulysses'* (Cambridge: Cambridge University Press, 1994).

Shloss, Carol, 'Molly's Resistance to the Union: Marriage and Colonialism in Dublin, 1904', in Pearce (ed.), *Molly Blooms*, 105–18.

Spoo, Robert, *James Joyce and the Language of History: Dedalus's Nightmare* (Oxford: Oxford University Press, 1994).

Staley, Thomas F., and Benstock, Bernard (eds.), *Approaches to 'Ulysses'* (Pittsburgh: University of Pittsburgh Press, 1970).

Sultan, Stanley, *The Argument of 'Ulysses'* (Columbus, Oh.: Ohio State University Press, 1964).

Sutton, Mark, ' "All Livia's Daughtersons": Death and the Dead in the Prose Fiction of James Joyce' (Ph.D. thesis, University of London, 1997).

Tymoczko, Maria, *The Irish 'Ulysses'* (Berkeley and Los Angeles: University of California Press, 1994).

Valente, Joseph, *James Joyce and the Problem of Justice: Negotiating Sexual and Colonial Difference* (Cambridge: Cambridge University Press, 1995).

Wales, Katie, *The Language of James Joyce* (London: Macmillan, 1987).
——— ' "With Apologies to Lindley Murray": The Narrative Method of the "Eumaeus" Episode in *Ulysses*', in van Ostade (ed.), *Lindley Murray*, 207–16.
Watson, G. J., 'The Politics of *Ulysses*', in Newman and Thornton (eds.), *Joyce's 'Ulysses'*, 39–59.
Williams, Trevor L., *Reading Joyce Politically* (Gainesville, Fla.: University Press of Florida, 1997).

Historical and Other

Aberdeen, Countess of (ed.), *Women in Politics: The Transactions of the International Congress of Women, 1899*, vol. v (London: T. Fisher Unwin, 1900).
——— *Women in Industrial Life: The Transactions of the International Congress of Women, 1899*, vol. vi (London: T. Fisher Unwin, 1900).
Ainger, Alfred, *Crabbe* (London: Macmillan, 1903).
Allen, Kieran, *The Politics of James Connolly* (London: Pluto, 1990).
Allott, Stephen, *Lindley Murray 1745–1826: Quaker Grammarian* (York: Sessions Book Trust, 1991).
Altick, Richard D., *The English Common Reader: A Social History of the Mass Reading Public 1800–1900*, foreword by Jonathan Rose (2nd edn., Columbus, Oh.: Ohio State University Press, 1998).
Ancell, S., *A Circumstantial Journal of the Long and Tedious Blockade and Siege of Gibraltar* (Liverpool: Charles Wosencroft, 1784).
Anderson, Benedict, *Imagined Communities: Reflections on the Origins and Spread of Nationalism* (London: Verso, 1991).
Anderson, Mary, *Tales of the Rock* (London: Downey & Co., 1897).
Anderson, W. K., *James Connolly and the Irish Left* (Blackrock: Irish Academic Press, 1994).
Annals of the Kingdom of Ireland, by the Four Masters, from the Earliest Period to the Year 1616, ed. and trans. John O'Donovan (7 vols., Dublin: Hodges and Smith, 1848).
Anon., *Some Suggestions for the Foundation of a Royal Irish Institute of Science and Art* (Dublin: Waller and Co., 1868).
Anon., *Gibraltar and its Sieges* (London: Thomas Nelson & Sons, 1879).
Anstie, James, *Colloquies of Common People* (London: Smith, Elder and Co., 1902).
Armstrong, Henry, *The Teaching of Scientific Method and Other Papers on Education* (London: Macmillan, 1903).
Arnold, Matthew, *Culture and Anarchy* (1869; New Haven and London: Yale University Press, 1994).
——— 'Copyright', *Fortnightly Review*, 27 (1880), 19–34.

—— *The Poems*, ed. Kenneth Allott, 2nd edn. by Miriam Allott (London: Longman, 1979).

Bakhtin, Mikhail, *Problems of Dostoevsky's Poetics*, ed. and trans. Caryl Emerson, introd. Wayne C. Booth (Manchester: Manchester University Press, 1984).

Baldick, Chris, *The Social Mission of English Criticism 1848–1932* (Oxford: Clarendon Press, 1987).

—— *Criticism and Literary Theory: 1890 to the Present* (London and New York: Longman, 1996).

Balfour, Graham, *The Educational Systems of Great Britain and Ireland* (Oxford: Clarendon Press, 1903).

Ball, Sir Robert, *The Story of the Heavens* (London: Cassell and Co., 1901).

—— *The Latest Achievement in Astronomy* (London: Daily Mail Publishing Office, 1904).

Bannerman, John, *The Beatons: A Medical Kindred in the Classical Gaelic Tradition* (Edinburgh: John Donald, 1986).

Barker, Charles Albro, *Henry George* (New York: Oxford University Press, 1955).

Barnard, T. C., *Cromwellian Ireland: English Government and Reform in Ireland 1649–1660*, Oxford Historical Monographs (Oxford: Oxford University Press, 2000).

Barnett, Annie, and Dale, Lucy (eds.), *An Anthology of English Prose (1332 to 1740)*, pref. by Andrew Lang (London: Longmans, Green and Co., 1912).

Barrell, John, *English Literature in History 1730–1780: An Equal, Wide Survey* (London: Hutchinson, 1983).

Barrington, Ruth, *Health, Medicine and Politics in Ireland 1900–1970* (Dublin: Criterion Press, 1987).

Barton, J. Edwin, *Gibraltar* (Oxford: Blackwell, 1897).

Bate, Jonathan, *Shakespearean Constitutions* (Oxford: Clarendon Press, 1989).

Beach, Sylvia, *Shakespeare and Company* (New York: Harcourt and Brace, 1959).

Beale, Jenny, *Women in Ireland: Voices of Change* (London: Macmillan, 1986).

Benady, Tito, *The Gibraltar Police* (Gibraltar: Mediterranean Sun Publishing Co., 1980).

Bennett, J. A., *Church, State and Astronomy in Ireland: Two Hundred Years of Armagh Observatory* (Armagh and Belfast: Armagh Observatory and Institute of Irish Studies, 1990).

Benzie, William, *Thomas Sheridan's Influence on Eighteenth-Century Rhetoric and Belles Lettres* (Leeds: Leeds Texts and Monographs, 1972).

Blanshard, Paul, *The Irish and Catholic Power* (London: Derek Verschoyle, 1954).

Bolton, W. F., and Crystal, D. (eds.), *The English Language*, ii. *Essays by Linguists and Men of Letters* (Cambridge: Cambridge University Press, 1969).

Boner, Harold A., *Hungry Generations: The Nineteenth-Century Case against Malthusianism* (New York: King's Crown Press, 1955).

Bourke, Joanna, *Husbandry to Housewifery: Women, Economic Change and Housework in Ireland 1890–1914* (Oxford: Clarendon Press, 1993).

Boyce, D. George, *Nineteenth-Century Ireland: The Search for Stability* (London: Gill & Macmillan, 1990).

—— 'Ulster Unionism: Great Britain and Ireland, 1885–1921', in Patrick J. Roche and Brian Barton (eds.), *The Northern Ireland Question: Nationalism, Unionism and Partition* (Aldershot: Ashgate, 1999), 30–46.

Boylan, Thomas A., and Foley, Timothy P., 'A Nation Perishing of Political Economy?', in Morash and Hayes (eds.), *Fearful Realities*, 138–50.

Boyle, Cavendish, and Bandury, R., *Gibraltar Directory and Guidebook* (Gibraltar: Garrison Library Printing Establishment, 1902).

Boyle, John F., *The Irish Rebellion of 1916: A Brief History of the Revolt and its Suppression* (London: Constable & Co., 1916).

Breathnach, Séamus, *The Irish Police from Earliest Times to the Present Day* (Dublin: Anvil, 1974).

Brennan, Martin, *The Stars and the Stones: Ancient Art and Astronomy in Ireland* (London: Thames and Hudson, 1983).

Bronowski, J., *William Blake and the Age of Revolution* (London: Routledge and Kegan Paul, 1972).

Brooker, Peter, and Widdowson, Peter, 'A Literature for England', in Colls and Dodd (eds.), *Englishness*, 116–63.

Browne, Alan (ed.), *Masters, Midwives and Ladies-in-Waiting* (Dublin: A. & A. Farmar, 1995).

Browning, Robert, *The Poems*, ed. John Woolford and Daniel Karlin (2 vols., London: Longman, 1991).

Buckley, David N., *James Fintan Lalor: Radical* (Cork: Cork University Press, 1990).

Butler, Marilyn, *Maria Edgeworth: A Literary Biography* (Oxford: Clarendon Press, 1972).

Butt, Isaac, *Land Tenure in Ireland: A Plea for the Celtic Race* (Dublin: John Falconer, 1866).

—— *The Irish People and the Irish Land* (Dublin: John Falconer, 1867).

Cadogan, Mary, and Craig, Patricia, *You're a Brick, Angela!* (London: Gollancz, 1986).

Cameron, Sir Charles A., *Report upon the State of Health in the City of Dublin for the Year 1902* (Dublin: Cahill & Co., 1903).

—— *Report upon the State of Health in the City of Dublin for the Year 1903* (Dublin: John Falconer, 1904).

—— *Report upon the State of Public Health in the City of Dublin for the Year 1904* (Dublin: John Falconer, 1905).

Canning, A. S., *Shakespeare Studied in Eight Plays* (London: T. Fisher Unwin, 1903).

Cecil, Mirabel, *Heroines in Love 1750–1974* (London: Michael Joseph, 1974).

Chambers, George F., *Pictorial Astronomy for General Readers* (London: Whittaker and Co., 1891).

Chambers, R. W., *The Teaching of English in the Universities of England*, *English Association Pamphlet*, 53 (July 1922).

Cheyette, Bryan, *Constructions of 'the Jew' in English Literature and Society: Racial Representations 1875–1945* (Cambridge: Cambridge University Press, 1993).

Clare, Maurice, *A Day with William Shakespeare* (London: Hodder & Stoughton, 1913).

Clarkson, L. A., 'Famine and Irish History', in Crawford (ed.), *Famine*, 220–36.

Clear, Catríona, 'The Limits of Female Autonomy', in Luddy and Murphy (eds.), *Women Surviving*, 15–50.

Clinch, Phyllis E. M., and Mollan, R. Charles (eds.), *A Profit and Loss Account of Science in Ireland* (Dublin: Mount Salus Press, 1983).

Coakley, Davis, *The Irish School of Medicine* (Dublin: Town House, 1988).

Coaten, Arthur W. (ed.), *British Hunting: A Complete History of the National Sport of Great Britain and Ireland from Earliest Records* (London: Sampson Low, Marston and Co., 1909).

Codrington, General Sir William J., *Gibraltar and Ceuta* (London: Edward Stanford, 1882).

Collier, William Francis, *History of Ireland for Schools* (London: Marcus Ward & Co., 1884).

Collini, Stefan, *Public Moralists: Political Thought and Intellectual Life in Britain 1850–1930* (Oxford: Clarendon Press, 1991).

Collison Black, R. D., *Economic Thought and the Irish Question*, foreword by Jacob Viner (Cambridge: Cambridge University Press, 1960).

Colls, Robert, and Dodd, Philip (eds.), *Englishness: Politics and Culture 1880–1920* (London: Croom Helm, 1986).

Colum, Mary, *Life and the Dream* (Dublin: Dolmen Press, 1966).

Colum, Padraic, *Arthur Griffith* (Dublin: Browne & Nolan, 1959).

Conan Doyle, Sir Arthur, *The Great Boer War* (London: Smith, Elder & Co., 1902).

Connell, K. H., *The Population of Ireland 1750–1845* (Oxford: Clarendon Press, 1950).

Connolly, James, *Selected Writings*, ed. P. Berresford Ellis (Harmondsworth: Penguin, 1973).

Connolly, S. J., *Priests and People in Pre-Famine Ireland 1780–1845* (Dublin: Gill and Macmillan, 1982).

—— 'Marriage in Pre-Famine Ireland', in Cosgrove (ed.), *Marriage in Ireland*, 78–98.

—— Houston, R. A., and Morris, R. J. (eds.), *Conflict, Identity and Economic Development: Ireland and Scotland 1600–1939* (Preston: Carnegie Publishing, 1995).

Connor, Steven, *Theory and Cultural Value* (Oxford: Blackwell, 1992).

Cooke-Trench, Thomas Richard Frederick, *A Memoir of the Trench Family* (London: Spottiswoode and Co, 1897).

Cord, Steven B., *Henry George: Dreamer or Realist?* (Philadelphia: University of Pennsylvania Press, 1965).

Corish, Patrick J., 'Catholic Marriage under the Penal Code', in Cosgrove (ed.), *Marriage in Ireland*, 67–77.

Corkery, Daniel, *The Hidden Ireland* (Dublin: M. H. Gill and Son, 1926).

Corrigan, D. J., *On Famine and Fever as Cause and Effect in Ireland* (Dublin: J. Fannin & Co., 1846).

—— *Lectures on the Nature and Treatment of Fever* (Dublin: J. Fannin and Co., 1853).

Cosgrave, Dillon, *North Dublin: City and Environs* (Dublin: Catholic Truth Society of Ireland, 1909).

Cosgrave, E. MacDowel, and Strangways, Leonard R., *The Dictionary of Dublin* (Dublin: Sealy, Bryers and Walker, 1895).

Cosgrove, Art (ed.), *Marriage in Ireland* (Dublin: College Press, 1985).

Costello, Con, *Botany Bay: The Story of the Convicts Transported from Ireland to Australia 1791–1852* (Cork and Dublin: Mercier, 1987).

Coulter, Carol, *The Hidden Tradition: Women and Nationalism in Ireland* (Cork: Cork University Press, 1993).

Crawford, E. Margaret (ed.), *Famine: The Irish Experience 900–1900, Subsistence Crises and Famines in Ireland* (Edinburgh: John Donald 1989).

Crawley, W. J. Chetwode, *Caementaria Hibernica* (Dublin: M'Gee, 1895).

Crowe, W. Fred. J. W., *The Irish Master Mason's Handbook* (London: Kenning, 1909).

Crowley, Tony, *The Politics of Discourse: The Standard Language Question in British Cultural Debates* (Basingstoke: Macmillan, 1989).

—— *Proper English?: Readings in Language, History and Cultural Identity* (London: Routledge, 1991).

—— *Language in History: Theories and Texts* (London: Routledge, 1996).

—— *The Politics of Language in Ireland 1366–1922* (London: Routledge, 2000).

Daly, Mary, *Dublin, the Deposed Capital: A Social and Economic History 1860–1914* (Cork: Cork University Press, 1984).

—— *The Famine in Ireland* (Dublin: Dundalgan Press, 1986).

Dalziel, Margaret, *Popular Fiction A Hundred Years Ago* (London: Cohen & West, 1957).

Dancyger, Irene, *A World of Women: An Illustrated History of Women's Magazines* (Dublin: Gill and Macmillan, 1978).

Darwin, Charles, *On the Origin of Species (1859)*, in *The Works of Charles Darwin*, ed. Paul H. Barrett and R. B. Freeman, vol. xv (London: William Pickering, 1988).

—— *On the Origin of Species (1876)*, in *The Works of Charles Darwin*, ed. Paul H. Barrett and R.B. Freeman, vol. xvi (London: William Pickering, 1988).

—— *The Descent of Man, and Selection in Relation to Sex, Part One*, with essay by T. H. Huxley, in *The Works of Charles Darwin*, ed. Paul H. Barrett and R. B. Freeman, vol. xxi (London: William Pickering, 1989).

Davis, Richard, *Arthur Griffith* (Dundalk: Dundalgan Press, 1976).

Davitt, Michael, *The Fall of Feudalism in Ireland* (London and New York: Harper & Bros., 1904).

Deane, Seamus, with Carpenter, Andrew, and Williams, Jonathan, *Field Day Anthology of Irish Writing* (3 vols., Derry: Field Day Publications, 1991).

—— *Strange Country: Modernity and Nationhood in Irish Writing since 1790* (Oxford: Clarendon Press, 1997).

de Grazia, Margreta, *Shakespeare Verbatim* (Oxford: Clarendon Press, 1991).

Delamont, Sara, 'The Contradictions in Ladies' Education', in Delamont and Duffin, *Nineteenth-Century Woman*, 134–63.

—— 'The Domestic Ideology and Women's Education', in Delamont and Duffin, *Nineteenth-Century Woman*, 164–87.

—— and Duffin, Lorna, *The Nineteenth-Century Woman: Her Cultural and Physical World* (London: Croom Helm, 1978).

Dennis, Philip, *Gibraltar and its People* (London and Newton Abbot: David and Charles, 1990).

Dobson, Michael, *The Making of the National Poet: Shakespeare, Adaptation and Authorship 1660–1769* (Oxford: Oxford University Press, 1992).

Dockrell, Mrs Maurice, 'Irishwomen in Local Government', in Countess of Aberdeen (ed.), *Women in Politics*, 87–9.

Dodd, Philip, 'Englishness and the National Culture', in Colls and Dodd (eds.), *Englishness*, 1–28.

Donnelly, James S., *The Land and the People of Nineteenth-Century Cork: Studies in Irish History*, 2nd ser., vol. ix (London: Routledge & Kegan Paul, 1975).

Dowden, Edward, *Shakspere* (1877; London: Macmillan, 1930).

—— 'Hopes and Fears for Literature', *Fortnightly Review*, 45 (1889), 166–83.

Dowden, Edward, *Introduction to Shakespeare* (London: Blackie & Son, 1893).
—— *Transcripts and Studies* (London: Kegan Paul, Trench, Trübner & Co., Ltd., 1896).
—— *Shakspere: A Critical Study of his Mind and Art* (1875; London: Kegan Paul, Trench, Trübner & Co., 1901).
—— *Letters* (London: J. M. Dent & Sons Ltd., 1914).
Doyle, Brian, *English and Englishness* (London: Routledge, 1989).
Drinkwater, John, *A History of the Late Siege of Gibraltar* (London: T. Spilsbury and Son, 1790).
Duffy, Sir Charles Gavan, Sigerson, George, and Hyde, Douglas, *The Revival of Irish Literature* (London: T. Fisher Unwin, 1894).
Dunne, Tom, *Maria Edgeworth and the Colonial Mind* (Cork: Cork University Press, 1984).
Dyhouse, Carol, 'Good Wives and Little Mothers: Social Anxieties and the Schoolgirl's Curriculum, 1890–1920', *Oxford Review of Education*, 3/1 (1977), 21–35.
—— *Girls Growing Up in Late Victorian and Edwardian England* (London: Routledge & Kegan Paul, 1981).
Edge, J. H., *A Short Sketch of the Rise and Progress of Irish Freemasonry* (Dublin: Ponsonby and Gibbs, 1913).
Edgeworth, Maria, *The Novels and Selected Works of Maria Edgeworth*, i. *Castle Rackrent: Irish Bulls, Ennui*, ed. Jane Desmarais, Tim McLoughlin, and Marilyn Butler, with a general introd. by Marilyn Butler (London: Chatto & Windus, 1999).
Edgeworth, Richard Lovell, and Edgeworth, Maria, *Essay on Irish Bulls* (5th edn.; London: R. Hunter, 1823).
Eglinton, John, *Irish Literary Portraits* (London: Macmillan, 1935).
—— Yeats, W. B., Larminie, A. E. and William, *Literary Ideals in Ireland* (London: T. Fisher Unwin, 1899).
Ellicott, Dorothy, *From Rooke to Nelson: 101 Eventful Years in Gibraltar* (Gibraltar: Garrison Library, 1965).
—— *Our Gibraltar* (Gibraltar: Gibraltar Museum Committee, 1975).
Elze, Karl, *William Shakespeare: A Biography* (London: George Bell & Sons, 1901).
Evans, Hilary and Dik, *Beyond the Gaslight: Science in Popular Fiction 1895–1905* (London: Frederick Muller Ltd., 1976).
Eversley, D. E. C., *Social Theories of Fertility and the Malthusian Debate* (Oxford: Clarendon Press, 1959).
Ewatt, G. J. H., *British Medical Journal: A Report on the Poor-Law Medical System of Ireland* (London: British Medical Association, 1904).
Farmar, Tony (ed.), *Holles Street 1894–1994: The National Maternity Hospital—A Centenary History* (Dublin: A. & A. Farmar, 1994).
Felperin, Howard, 'Bardolatry Then and Now', in Marsden (ed.), *Appropriation of Shakespeare*, 129–44.

Fennell, Desmond, 'Irish Socialist Thought', in Kearney (ed.), *Irish Mind*, 188–208.

Ferguson, Marjorie, *Forever Feminine: Women's Magazines and the Cult of Femininity* (Aldershot: Gower, 1985).

Ferguson, Sir Samuel, *Lays of the Red Branch*, introd. Lady Ferguson (London: T. Fisher Unwin, 1897).

Field, Henry M., *Gibraltar* (London: Chapman and Hall, 1889).

Finnane, Mark, *Insanity and the Insane in Post-Famine Ireland* (London: Croom Helm, 1981).

Fitzgerald, Brian, *The Geraldines: An Experiment in Irish Government 1169–1601* (London: Staples Press, 1951).

Fitzpatrick, David, 'Marriage in Post-Famine Ireland', in Cosgrove (ed.), *Marriage in Ireland*, 116–31.

—— 'The Modernization of the Irish Female', in O'Flanagan et al. (eds.), *Rural Ireland*, 162–80.

Fitzpatrick, Samuel A. Ossory, *Dublin: A Historical and Topographical Account of the City* (London: Methuen, 1907).

'Flora Calpensis', *Reminiscences of Gibraltar* (London: Samuel Tinsley & Co., 1880).

—— *The Life of a Rock Scorpion* (London: Charing Cross Publishing Co., 1881).

Forbes, Commander W. B. 'Maintop', 'The Foxhounds of Ireland', in Arthur W. Coaten (ed.), *British Hunting: A Complete History of the National Sport of Great Britain and Ireland from Earliest Records* (London: Sampson Low, Marston and Co., 1909), 329–60.

Ford, Richard, *A Handbook for Travellers in Spain* (2 vols., 4th edn., London: John Murray, 1869).

Foster, R. F., *Modern Ireland 1600–1972* (London: Penguin, 1989).

Foucault, Michel, *The History of Sexuality* i. *Introduction*, trans. R. Hurley (Harmondsworth: Penguin, 1990).

Fowler, J. H., 'De Quincey as Literary Critic', *English Association Pamphlet*, 52 (July 1922).

France, John, 'Salisbury and the Unionist Alliance', in Lord Blake and Hugh Cecil (eds.), *Salisbury: The Man and his Policies* (London: Macmillan, 1987), 219–51.

Freeman, Edward A., *General Sketch of European History* (London: Macmillan & Co., 1874).

Gailey, Andrew, *Ireland and the Death of Kindness: The Experience of Constructive Unionism 1890–1905*, Studies in Irish History (Cork: Cork University Press, 1987).

Garcia, Richard J. M., and Proud, Edward B., *The Postal History of Gibraltar 1704–1971* (Heathfield: Postal History Publications 1998).

Garvin, Tom, *Nationalist Revolutionaries in Ireland* (Oxford: Clarendon Press, 1987).

Geary, Laurence M., ' "The Late Disastrous Epidemic": Medical Relief and the Great Famine', in Morash and Hayes (eds.), *Fearful Realities*, 49–59.

George, Henry, *Progress and Poverty* (New York: D. Appleton & Co., 1880).

—— *The Irish Land Question* (New York: D. Appleton & Co., 1881).

Gibbon, Peter, *The Origins of Ulster Unionism: Popular Protestant Politics and Ideology in Nineteenth-Century Ireland* (Manchester: Manchester University Press, 1975).

Gibbons, Luke, 'Identity without a Centre: Allegory, History and Irish Nationalism', *Cultural Studies*, 6/3 (Oct. 1992), 358–75.

—— *Transformations in Irish Culture* (Cork: Cork University Press, 1996).

Gilbard, Lt.-Col., *A Popular History of Gibraltar, its Institutions and its Neighbourhood on Both Sides of the Straits* (Gibraltar: Garrison Library Printing Establishment, 1888).

Gilbert, John J., *A History of the City of Dublin* (Dublin, 1854–9); introd. F. E. Dixon (3 vols., Shannon: Irish University Press, 1972).

Ginnell, Lawrence, *The Brehon Laws: A Legal Handbook* (London: T. Fisher Unwin, 1894).

Glandon, Virginia, *Arthur Griffith and the Advanced-Nationalist Press in Ireland, 1900–1922* (New York: P. Lang, 1985).

Gogarty, Oliver St John, *Tumbling in the Hay* (London: Constable & Co., 1939).

Gonne, Maud, 'The Rights to Life and the Rights of Property', *The Workers' Republic* (Aug. 1898).

—— and Yeats, W. B., *The Gonne–Yeats Letters 1893–1938*, ed. with introds. Anna MacBride White and A. Norman Jeffares (London: Pimlico, 1993).

Grady, Hugh, *The Modernist Shakespeare* (Oxford: Clarendon Press, 1991), 47–56.

—— 'Disintegration and its Reverberations', in Marsden (ed.), *Appropriation of Shakespeare*, 111–24.

Gregory, Lady Augusta, *Poets and Dreamers: Studies and Translations from the Irish* (London: Hodges, Figgis & Co. Ltd., 1903).

—— *The Kiltartan History Book* (Dublin: Maunsel & Co., 1909).

—— *The Kiltartan Poetry Book: Prose Translations from the Irish* (Dundrum: Cuala Press, 1918).

Gregory, R. A., and Simmons, A. T., *Introductory Physics for Irish Intermediate Schools* (London: Macmillan & Co., 1901).

Griffith, Arthur, *The Resurrection of Hungary: A Parallel for Ireland* (Dublin: James Duffy & Co., 1904).

Gross, John, *The Rise and Fall of the Man of Letters* (Harmondsworth: Penguin, 1973).

Hachey, Thomas E., *Britain and Irish Separatism: From the Fenians to the Irish Free State, 1867–1922* (Chicago: Rand McNally, 1977).

Haldane, R. B., *Education and Empire: Addresses on Certain Topics of the Day* (London: John Murray, 1902).

Hamley, Col. E. B., 'A Legend of Gibraltar', *Blackwood's Magazine*, 70/5 (Nov. 1851), 522–43.

—— 'The Jew's Legacy: A Tale of the Siege of Gibraltar', *Blackwood's Magazine*, 70/6 (Dec. 1851), 648–69.

Hardiman, Tom, 'Science Policy', in Clinch and Mollan (eds.), *Profit and Loss Account*, 1–21.

Harris, Frank, *The Man Shakespeare and his Tragic Life Story* (London: Frank Palmer, 1909).

Harrison, Robert F., 'Medical Education at the Rotunda Hospital 1745–1995', in Browne (ed.), *Masters*, 66–76.

Hawkes, Terence, *That Shakespeherian Rag* (London: Methuen, 1986).

Hay, Mary Cecil, *Nora's Love Test* (London: John Maxwell and Co., 1878).

Hearn, Mona, 'Life for Domestic Servants in Dublin, 1880–1920', in Luddy and Murphy (eds.), *Women Surviving*, 148–70.

Henty, G. A., *Held Fast for England: A Tale of the Siege of Gibraltar* (London: Blackie and Son, 1892).

Hills, George, *Rock of Contention: A History of Gibraltar* (London: Robert Hale & Co., 1974).

Holderness, Graham (ed.), *The Shakespeare Myth* (Manchester: Manchester University Press, 1988).

Hollingworth, Brian, *Maria Edgeworth's Irish Writing: Language, History, Politics* (London: Macmillan, 1997).

Homer, *The Odyssey*, done into English Prose by S. H. Butcher and A. Lang (London: Macmillan & Co., 1879).

Hooton, W. M., *A Preliminary Course of Experimental Science* (London: W. B. Clive, 1907).

Hoppen, K. Theodore, *Ireland since 1800: Conflict and Conformity* (London: Longman, 1989).

Hort, Major, *The Rock* (London: Saunders and Otley, 1839).

'Hortensius', *Deinology, or the Union of Reason and Elegance: Being Instructions to a Young Barrister* (London: G. G. J. and J. Robinson, 1789).

Howes, H. W., *The Story of Gibraltar* (London: Philip & Tracey Ltd., 1946).

Hume, David, *The History of England from the Invasion of Julius Caesar to the Revolution in 1688* (8 vols., London: Cadell & Davies, 1818).

Hutchinson, John, *The Dynamics of Cultural Nationalism: The Gaelic Revival and the Nation State* (London: Allen and Unwin, 1987).

Hyde, Douglas (ed., trans., and annot.), *Beside the Fire: A Collection of Irish Gaelic Folk Stories* (London: D. Nutt, 1890).

—— (ed., trans., and annot.), *Love Songs of Connacht* (London: T. Fisher Unwin, 1893).

Hyde, Douglas, 'The Necessity for De-Anglicizing Ireland', in Duffy et al., *Revival of Irish Literature*, 115–61.

—— *A Literary History of Ireland from Earliest Times to the Present Day* (London: T. Fisher Unwin, 1899).

—— (ed., trans., and annot.), *Songs Ascribed to Raftery* (Dublin: Gill agus a Mhac, 1903).

Ikin, A. E., *Methods of Science: A Thesis in Logic and Methodology* (London: Normal Correspondence College Press, 1903).

Inkster, Ian, 'Introduction: Aspects of the History of Science and Science Culture in Britain 1780–1850', in Inkster and Morrell (eds.), *Metropolis and Province*, 11–54.

—— and Morrell, Jack (eds.), *Metropolis and Province: Science in British Culture 1780–1850* (London: Hutchinson, 1983).

Innes, C. L., *Woman and Nation in Irish Literature and Society 1880–1935* (London: Harvester Wheatsheaf, 1993).

The Irish Catholic Directory and Almanac (Dublin: J. Duffy and Co., 1904).

Jackson, Sir William G. F., *The Rock of the Gibraltarians: A History of Gibraltar* (Grendon: Gibraltar Books Ltd., 1987).

James, Frank A. J. L., 'George Gabriel Stokes and William Thomson: Biographical Attitudes towards their Irish Origins', in Nudds et al. (eds.), *Science in Ireland*, 75–96.

James, Lt.-Col. Thomas, *The History of the Herculean Straits, Now Called the Straits of Gibraltar* (2 vols., London: Charles Rivington, 1771).

Jameson, Mrs [Anna], *Shakespeare's Heroines: Characteristics of Women Moral, Poetical, and Historical* (London: J. M. Dent, 1910).

Jones, Bernard, 'The Reception of Lindley Murray's *English Grammar*', in van Ostade (ed.), *Lindley Murray*, 63–80.

Jones, Edgar R., *Selected English Speeches* (London: Oxford University Press, 1913).

Junius, *Letters*, ed. John Cannon (Oxford: Clarendon Press, 1978).

Kabdebo, Thomas, *The Hungarian-Irish 'Parallel' and Arthur Griffith's Use of his Sources* (Maynooth: St Patrick's College, 1988).

Kaplan, Fred, *Thomas Carlyle: A Biography* (Cambridge: Cambridge University Press, 1983).

Kearney, Richard (ed.), *The Irish Mind: Exploring Intellectual Traditions* (Dublin: Wolfhound Press, 1985).

—— *Transitions: Narratives in Modern Irish Culture* (Manchester: Manchester University Press, 1988).

—— 'Towards a Postnationalist Archipelago', *Edinburgh Review*, 103 (2000), 21–34.

Kelly, Fergus, *A Guide to Early Irish Law*, Early Irish Law Series, vol. iii (Dublin: Dublin Institute for Advanced Studies, 1988).

Kelly, H. P., *Irish Bulls and Puns* (London: Skeffington & Son, 1919).

Keogh, Dermot, *Jews in Twentieth-Century Ireland* (Cork: Cork University Press, 1998).

Kiberd, Declan, *Inventing Ireland: The Literature of the Modern Nation* (London: Vintage, 1996).

—— 'Oscar Wilde: The Resurgence of Lying', in Peter Raby (ed.), *The Cambridge Companion to Oscar Wilde* (Cambridge: Cambridge University Press, 1997), 276–94.

Lalor, James Fintan, *Collected Writings* (Poole, Washington DC: Woodstock Books, 1997).

Lanham, Richard A., *A Handbook of Rhetorical Terms* (2nd edn., Berkeley and Los Angeles: University of California Press, 1991).

Law, Ernest, *Shakespeare as a Groom of the Chamber* (London: G. Bell & Sons Ltd., 1910).

Lee, J. J., 'Women and the Church since the Famine', in MacCurtain and Ó'Corrain (eds.), *Women in Irish History*, 37–45.

Lee, Sidney, *Great Englishmen of the Sixteenth Century* (London: Constable, 1907).

Lepper, John Herron, and Crossle, Philip, *History of the Grand Lodge of Free and Accepted Masons of Ireland*, vol i (Dublin: Lodge of Research C.C., 1925).

Levenson, Samuel, *Maud Gonne* (London: Cassell, 1976).

Lingard, John, *Abridgement of the History of England* (Dublin: James Duffy, n.d.).

Lloyd, David, *Anomalous States: Irish Writing and the Post-Colonial Moment* (Dublin: Lilliput, 1993).

Loughlin, James, *Ulster Unionism and British National Identity since 1885* (London and New York: Pinter, 1995).

Luddy, Maria (ed.), *Women in Ireland 1800–1918: A Documentary History* (Cork: Cork University Press, 1995).

—— and Murphy, Cliona (eds.), *Women Surviving: Studies in Irish Women's History in the Nineteenth and Twentieth Centuries* (Dublin: Poolbeg, 1990).

Ludwigson, Kathryn R., *Edward Dowden* (New York: Twayne, 1973).

Lyons, F. S. L., *Culture and Anarchy in Ireland 1890–1939* (Oxford: Clarendon Press, 1979).

Lyons, J. B., *Brief Lives of Irish Doctors* (Dublin: Blackwater, 1978).

McArthur, Sir William, 'Famine Fevers in England and Ireland', *Journal of the British Archaeological Association*, 3rd ser., 9 (1944), 66–71.

Macaulay, Thomas Babington, *Critical and Historical Essays* (London: Longmans, Green, Reader and Dyer, 1874).

MacBride, Maud Gonne, *A Servant of the Queen: Reminiscences* (Bury St Edmunds: Boydell and Brewer, 1983).

McCarthy, Michael J. F., *The Irish Revolution*, i. *The Murdering Time, from the Land League to the Present* (London and Edinburgh: William Blackwood & Sons, 1912).

McClintock, Anne, *Imperial Leather: Race, Gender and Sexuality in the Colonial Contest* (New York: Routledge, 1995).

MacCurtain, Margaret, and Ó'Corrain, Donncha (eds.), *Women in Irish Society: The Historical Dimension* (Dublin: Arlen House, 1979).

MacDonagh, Oliver, *Ireland: The Union and its Aftermath* (London: Allen and Unwin, 1977).

—— *States of Mind: A Study of Anglo-Irish Conflict 1780–1980* (London: Allen and Unwin, 1983).

Mackay, Jane, and Thane, Pat, 'The Englishwoman', in Colls and Dodd (eds.), *Englishness*, 191–229.

McKenna-Lawlor, Susan M. P., 'Astronomy in Ireland from the Late Eighteenth Century to the End of the Nineteenth Century', in Nudds et al. (eds.), *Science in Ireland*, 85–96.

Macleod, Roy, and Collins, Peter (eds.), *The Parliament of Science: The British Academy for the Advancement of Science 1831–1981* (Northwood: Science Reviews, 1981).

Madden, Samuel, *Reflections and Resolutions Proper for the Gentlemen of Ireland* (Dublin: G. Ewing, 1738).

Malthus, T. R., *An Essay on the Principle of Population* (London: Ward, Lock & Co., 1890).

—— *Occasional Papers on Ireland, Population and Political Economy*, ed. and introd. Bernard Semmel (New York: Franklin, 1963).

Marcus, Phillip L., *Yeats and the Beginning of the Irish Renaissance* (Ithaca, NY and London: Cornell University Press, 1970).

Marsden, Jean I. (ed.), *The Appropriation of Shakespeare: Post-Renaissance Reconstructions of the Works and the Myth* (London: Harvester Wheatsheaf, 1991).

Martin, Peter, *Edmond Malone, Shakespeare Scholar: A Literary Biography* (Cambridge: Cambridge University Press, 1996).

Martin, R. Montgomery, *Possessions in Europe: Gibraltar*, introd. Anthony A. D. Seymour (Gibraltar: Gibraltar Books Ltd., 1998).

Martindale, C. C., SJ, *Bernard Vaughan, S.J.* (London: Longmans, Green & Co., 1923).

Mayhew, Henry, *London Labour and the London Poor*, selected and introd. Victor Neuburg (Harmondsworth: Penguin, 1985).

Mayo, the Earl of, and Boulton, W. B., *A History of the Kildare Hunt* (London: St Catherine Press, 1913).

Meredith, George, *The Ordeal of Richard Feverel: A History of Father and Son* (2 vols., Leipzig: Bernhard Tauchnitz, 1875).

—— *The Ordeal of Richard Feverel: A History of Father and Son*, ed. with introd. and notes by Edward Mendelson (London: Penguin, 1998).

Merriman, Brian, *The Midnight Court and the Adventures of a Luckless Fellow*, trans. Percy Arland Ussher, pref. by W. B. Yeats (London: Cape, 1926).

—— *The Midnight Court*, trans. D. Marcus (Dublin: Dolmen Press, 1953).

Mill, John Stuart, *Collected Works*, vi. *Essays on England, Ireland and the Empire*, ed. John M. Robson, introd. Joseph Hamburger (Toronto: University of Toronto Press and Routledge & Kegan Paul, 1982).

Mitchel, John, Preface, *Irish Political Economy, by Jonathan Swift, Dean of St. Patrick's, and George Berkeley, Bishop of Cloyne* (Dublin: William Holden, 1847), pp. iii–vi.

—— *The History of Ireland from the Treaty of Limerick to the Present Time* (New York: D. and J. Sadlier & Co., 1868).

Mollan, Charles, Davis, William, and Finucane, Brendan (eds.), *Some People and Places in Irish Science and Technology* (Dublin: Royal Irish Academy, 1985).

Montague, Lily H., 'The Girl in the Background', in E. J. Urwick (ed.), *Studies of Boy Life in Our Cities, Written by Various Authors for the Toynbee Trust* (London: J. M. Dent & Co., 1904), 233–54.

Moon, G. Washington, *The Bad English of Lindley Murray and Other Writers on the English Language* (London: Hatchards, 1869).

Moran, D. P., *The Philosophy of Irish Ireland* (Dublin: James Duffy & Co., 1905).

Morash, Chris, and Hayes, Richard (eds.), *Fearful Realities: New Perspectives on the Famine* (Dublin: Irish Academic Press, 1996).

Morley, Edith J. (ed.), *The Teaching of Literature in Schools*, English Association Pamphlet, 43 (May 1919).

Murison, A. F. (ed.), *Selections from the Best English Authors (Beowulf to the Present Time)* (London: W. & R. Chambers, 1907).

Murphy, Cliona, *The Women's Suffrage Movement and Irish Society in the Early Twentieth Century* (London: Harvester, 1989).

Murray, Lindley, *English Grammar* (York: Wilson, Spence and Mawman, 1795).

—— *Extracts from the Writing of Divers Eminent Authors of Different Religious Denominations, and at Various Periods of Time, Representing the Evils and Pernicious Effects of Stage Plays* (Philadelphia: Benjamin and Jacob Johnson, 1799).

—— *English Grammar, Adapted to the Different Classes of Learners* (Calcutta: School-Book Society's Press, 1831).

National Union of Public Employees, Women's Committee, Northern Ireland, *An Oral History of Women's Health in Northern Ireland, 1900–1990* (Dublin: Attic Press, 1992).

Neilson, G. R., *The Book of Bulls* (London: Simpkin, Marshall, Hamilton, Kent & Co., 1898).

Newenham, Thomas, *A Statistical Inquiry into the Progress and Magnitude of the Population of Ireland* (London: C. & R. Baldwin, 1805).

Nolan, Janet A., *Ourselves Alone: Women's Emigration from Ireland 1885–1920* (Lexington, Ky.: University of Kentucky Press, 1989).

Norman, E. R., *The Catholic Church and Ireland in the Age of Rebellion, 1859–1873* (London: Longmans, 1965).

Nowell-Smith, Simon (ed.), *Letters to Macmillan* (London: Macmillan, 1967).

Nudds, John R., McMillan, Norman D., Weaire, Denis L., and McKenna-Lawlor, Susan M. P. (eds.), *Science in Ireland 1800–1930* (Dublin: Trinity College, 1988).

O'Brien, Conor Cruise, *States of Ireland* (St Albans: Panther, 1974).

O'Brien, Gerard, 'Scotland, Ireland and the Antithesis of Enlightenment', in Connolly et al. (eds.), *Ireland and Scotland 1600–1939*, 125–34.

O'Brien, R. Barry, *The Life of Charles Stewart Parnell*, pref. by John E. Redmond MP (London: Thomas Nelson & Sons, 1910).

—— *Dublin Castle and the Irish People* (2nd edn., London: Kegan Paul, Trench, Trübner & Co., 1912).

O'Donnell, F. Hugh, *The Ruin of Education in Ireland and the Irish Fanar* (London: David Nutt, 1903).

—— *The Blackmailing of Education in Ireland* (London: C. J. Thynne, 1904).

O'Flaherty, Roderic, *A Chorographical Description of West or H'Iar Connacht*, with notes and illustrations by James Hardiman (Dublin: Irish Archaeological Society, 1846).

O'Flanagan, Patrick, Ferguson, Paul, and Whelan, Kevin (eds.), *Rural Ireland 1600–1900: Modernization and Change* (Cork: Cork University Press, 1987).

Ó Gráda, Cormac, *Ireland Before and After the Famine: Explorations in Economic History 1800–1925* (2nd edn., Manchester: Manchester University Press, 1993).

—— and Duffy, Niall, *Fertility Control Early in Marriage in Ireland c.1900: Some Local Contrasts* (Dublin: University College, 1983).

O'Grady, Standish, *History of Ireland: The Heroic Period* (2 vols., London: Sampson Low & Co., 1878–80).

—— *History of Ireland: Critical and Philosophical*, vol. i (London: Sampson Low & Co., 1881).

O'Leary, John, *Recollections of Fenians and Fenianism* (2 vols., London: Downey and Co., 1897).

O'Mahony, Charles, *The Viceroys of Ireland* (London: John Long, 1912).

Omond, T. S., *English Metrists in the Eighteenth and Nineteenth Centuries* (Oxford: Oxford University Press, 1907).

O'Neill, T. P., 'The Food Crisis of the 1890s', in Crawford (ed.), *Famine*, 176–97.

Ordish, Thomas Fairman, *Shakespeare's London: A Commentary on Shakespeare's Life and Work in London* (London: J. M. Dent & Co., 1904).

O'Riordan, Revd M., *Catholicity and Progress in Ireland* (London: Kegan Paul, Trench, Trübner & Co., 1905).

O'Shea, Henry, *Guide to Spain and Portugal* (Edinburgh: Adam and Charles Black, 1848).

O'Shea, Katharine, *Charles Stewart Parnell: His Love Story and Political Life* (2 vols., London: Cassell & Co., 1914).

Ovenden, Charles T., *Popular Science for Parochial Evenings* (London: Elliot Stock, 1909).

Owens, Rosemary Cullen, *Smashing Times: A History of the Irish Women's Suffrage Movement 1889–1922* (Dublin: Attic Press, 1984).

Parnell, John Howard, *Charles Stewart Parnell: A Memoir* (London: Constable & Co. Ltd., 1916).

Paulin, Tom, *Ireland and the English Crisis* (Newcastle: Bloodaxe, 1984).

Peacock, W. (ed.), *English Prose from Mandeville to Ruskin* (London: Grant Richards, 1903; 4th imp., London: Oxford University Press, 1912).

Pearse, Patrick, *The Sovereign People* (Dublin: Whelan and Son, 1916).

—— *The Separatist Idea* (Dublin: Whelan and Son, 1916).

Pearson, Karl, *National Life from the Standpoint of Science* (London: Adam and Charles Black, 1901).

Phillipps-Wolley, Clive, *Songs of an English Esau* (London: Smith, Elder and Co., 1902).

Pittock, Murray G. H., *Poetry and Jacobite Politics in Eighteenth-Century Britain and Ireland* (Cambridge: Cambridge University Press, 1994).

Plunkett, Sir Horace, *Ireland in the New Century* (London: John Murray, 1905).

Prior, Sir James, *Life of Edmond Malone* (London: Smith & Elder, 1860).

Programmes, Feis Ceoil (Irish Music Festival), Dublin, 1897–1904.

Quantrill, Esther Maeve, 'Anthological Politics: Poetry and British Culture 1860–1914' (Ph.D. thesis, University of Texas at Austin, 1995).

Raleigh, Walter, *Shakespeare* (London: Macmillan, 1909).

—— *Letters*, ed. Lady Raleigh (2 vols., London: Methuen & Co., 1926).

Redmond, Brigid, *The Story of Dublin: City and County* (Dublin: Browne and Nolan, 1921).

Rhodes, Rita M., *Women and the Family in Post-Famine Ireland: Status and Opportunity in a Patriarchal Society* (New York and London: Garland, 1992).

Rhys, John, *Lectures on the Origin and Growth of Religion as Illustrated by Celtic Heathendom* (London: Williams & Norgate, 1888).

Richards, Thomas, *The Commodity Culture of Victorian England: Advertising and Spectacle 1851–1914* (London: Verso, 1991).

Ricks, Christopher, *Beckett's Dying Words* (Oxford: Oxford University Press, 1993).

Saintsbury, George, *A History of English Prose Rhythm* (London: Macmillan & Co., 1912).

Sarbu, Aladar, 'Literary Nationalism: Ireland and Hungary', in Wolfgang Zach and Heinz Kosok (eds.), *Literary Interrelations: Ireland, England and the World* (3 vols., Tubingen: Gunter Narr Verlag, 1987), iii. *National Images and Stereotypes*, 19–26.

Sawyer, Roger, *We are but Women: Women in Ireland's History* (London: Routledge, 1993).

Sayer, Captain, *The History of Gibraltar and of its Political Relation to Events in Europe* (London: Saunders, Otley & Co., 1862).

Searle, G. R., *The Quest for National Efficiency: A Study in British Politics and Political Thought 1899–1914* (London: Ashfield, 1990).

—— *Eugenics and Politics in Britain 1900–1914* (Leyden: Noordhoff International Publishing, 1976).

Serres, Michel, *L'Hermaphrodite: Sarrasine sculpteur* (Paris: Flammarion, 1986).

Shakespeare, William, *Collected Works* (the 'Universal' edn., London: Frederick Warne and Co., 1890).

Shaw, George Bernard, *Shaw on Shakespeare*, ed. and introd. Edwin Wilson (Harmondsworth: Penguin, 1969).

Sheehy-Skeffington, Francis and Hanna, *Democracy in Ireland since 1913* (n.p.: n.pub., 1917).

Sheehy-Skeffington, Hanna, 'Sinn Féin and Irishwomen', *Bean na hÉireann* (Dec. 1909), repr. in Luddy (ed.), *Women in Ireland*, 301–4.

Sigerson, George, *Bards of the Gael and Gall: Examples of the Poetic Language of Errin* (London: T. Fisher Unwin, 1897).

. Smith, Charles Nowell, *The Origins and History of the Association* (English Association; London: Sidgwick and Jackson, 1942).

Smith, Sydney, *Works* (4 vols., London: Longman, 1839).

Some Suggestions for the Foundation of a Royal Irish Institute of Science and Art (Dublin: Waller and Co., 1868).

Spilsbury, Capt. John, *A Journal of the Siege of Gibraltar 1779–1783* (Gibraltar: Gibraltar Garrison Library, 1908).

Stepan, Nancy, *The Idea of Race in Science: Great Britain 1800–1960* (London: Macmillan, 1982).

Stephens, Frederic J., *A History of Gibraltar and its Sieges*, with photographs by J. H. Mann (London: Provost & Co., 1870).

Stone, J. S., *George Meredith's Politics, as seen in his Life, Friendships and Works* (Port Credit: P. F. Meany, 1986).

Styan, J. L., *The Shakespeare Revolution: Criticism and Performance in the Twentieth Century* (Cambridge: Cambridge University Press, 1977).

Summerfield, Henry, *That Myriad-Minded Man: A Biography of George William Russell 'A.E.' 1867–1935* (Gerrards Cross: Colin Smythe Ltd., 1975).

—— (ed.), *Selections from the Contributions to the Irish Homestead* (2 vols., Gerrards Cross, Colin Smythe, 1978).

Swift, Jonathan, *Polite Conversation*, introd. with notes and commentary by Eric Partridge (London: Andre Deutsch, 1963).

Syllabi of Prize Competitions, Feis Ceoil (Irish Music Festival), Dublin, 1897–1904.

Taylor, Gary, *Reinventing Shakespeare: A Cultural History from the Restoration to the Present* (London: Vintage, 1990).

Tennyson, Alfred, Lord, *Selections*, ed. F. J. Rowe and W. T. Webb, with introd. and notes (London: Macmillan and Co., 1889).

—— *The Poems of Tennyson*, ed. Christopher Ricks (London: Longman, 1989).

Thackeray, William Makepeace, *Notes on a Journey from Cornhill to Grand Cairo* (London: Smith, Elder & Co., 1851).

Tomes, Jason, *Balfour and Foreign Policy: The International Thought of a Conservative Statesman* (Cambridge: Cambridge University Press, 1997).

Toomey, Deirdre, 'Moran's Collar: Yeats and Irish Ireland', *Yeats Annual*, 12 (1996), 45–86.

Treble, H. A. (ed.), *English Prose: Narrative, Descriptive and Dramatic* (London: Oxford University Press, 1917).

van Ostade, Ingrid Tieken-Boon (ed.), *Two Hundred Years of Lindley Murray* (Münster: Nodus, 1996).

—— 'Two Hundred Years of Lindley Murray: An Introduction', in van Ostade (ed.), *Lindley Murray*, 9–25.

Vaughan, Bernard, *Her Golden Reign: A Sermon* (London: Burns & Oates, 1887).

—— *The Sins of Society* (London: Kegan Paul, Trench, Trübner & Co., 1905).

Visnawathan, Gauri, *Masks of Conquest: Literary Study and British Rule in India* (London: Faber, 1990).

Walker, John, *Walker's Critical Pronouncing Dictionary and Expositor of the English Language, to which are Prefixed Principles of English Pronounciation; Likewise, Rules to be Observed by the Natives of Scotland, Ireland, and London, for avoiding their Respective Peculiarities, and Directions to Foreigners, for Acquiring a Knowledge of the Use of This Dictionary*, corrected and enlarged with upwards of three thousand words by Revd. John Davis (Belfast: Simms and McIntyre, 1830).

Walsh, James J., *The Popes and Science: The History of the Papal Relations to Science during the Middle Ages and down to our Own Time* (London: Catholic Truth Society, 1912).

Ward, A. W., *Chaucer* (London: Macmillan, 1893).

Ward, Revd. Mgr. Bernard, *Cardinal Vaughan* (London: Catholic Truth Soc., 1903).

Ward, Margaret, *Unmanageable Revolutionaries: Women and Irish Nationalism* (London: Pluto, 1983).

—— *Maud Gonne: A Life* (London: Pandora, 1993).

Ward, W. Peter, *Birth Weight and Economic Growth: Women's Living Standards in the Industrializing West* (Chicago and London: University of Chicago Press, 1993).

Warren, Capt. Fred. P., *Gibraltar: Is It Worth Holding? and Morocco* (London: Edward Stanford, 1882).

Wayman, P. A., 'R. A. Brinkley: A New Start', in Nudds et al. (eds.), *Science in Ireland*, pp. 99–104.

West, Trevor, *Horace Plunkett, Cooperation and Politics: An Irish Biography* (Gerrards Cross: Colin Smythe Ltd., 1986).

White, Cynthia, *Women's Magazines 1693–1968* (London: Michael Joseph, 1970).

White, Harry, 'Music and the Irish Literary Imagination', in Gerard Gillen and Harry White (eds.), *Irish Musical Studies*, iii. *Music and Irish Cultural History* (Blackrock: Irish Academic Press, 1995), 212–27.

Whyte, Nicholas, *Science, Colonialism and Ireland* (Cork: Cork University Press, 1999).

Wilde, W. R., *Irish Popular Superstitions* (Dublin: McGlashan, 1852).

Wilson, J. Dover, *Life in Shakespeare's England: A Book of Elizabethan Prose* (Cambridge: Cambridge University Press, 1911).

Worboys, Michael, 'The British Association and Empire: Science and Social Imperialism 1880–1940', in Macleod and Collins (eds.), *Parliament of Science*, 170–87.

Wyndham-Quin, Col. W. H., *The Fox Hound in County Limerick* (Dublin: Maunsel and Co., 1919).

Yeats, W. B., *Ideas of Good and Evil* (Dublin: Maunsel and Co., 1905).

—— *Collected Letters*, i. *1865–1895*, ed. John Kelly and Eric Domville (Oxford: Clarendon Press, 1986); ii. *1896–1900*, ed. Warwick Gould, John Kelly, and Deirdre Toomey (1997); iii. *1901–1904*, ed. John Kelly and Ronald Schuchard (1994).

Younger, Calton, *Arthur Griffith* (Dublin: Gill and Macmillan, 1981).

Index

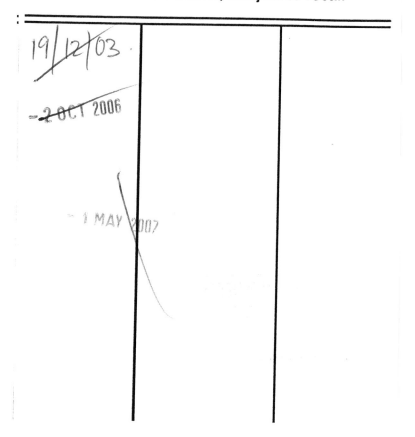